CRIMINOLOGY

A CROSS-CULTURAL PERSPECTIVE

CRIMINOLOGY

A CROSS-CULTURAL PERSPECTIVE

Robert Heiner, EDITOR

Plymouth State College

WEST PUBLISHING COMPANY

MINNEAPOLIS/ST. PAUL   NEW YORK   LOS ANGELES   SAN FRANCISCO

PRODUCTION CREDITS

Text Design: Roslyn Stendahl, Dapper Design

Composition: Parkwood Composition Services, Inc.

Copyediting: Cindi Gerber

WEST'S COMMITMENT TO THE ENVIRONMENT

In 1906, West Publishing Company began recycling materials left over from the production
of books. This began a tradition of efficient and responsible use of resources. Today, up to
95 percent of our legal books and 70 percent of our college and school texts are printed on
recycled, acid-free stock. West also recycles nearly 22 million pounds of scrap paper annually—the equivalent of 181,717 trees. Since the 1960s, West has devised ways to capture
and recycle waste inks, solvents, oils, and vapors created in the printing process. We also
recycle plastics of all kinds, wood, glass, corrugated cardboard, and batteries, and have
eliminated the use of Styrofoam book packaging. We at West are proud of the longevity
and the scope of our commitment to the environment.

Production, Prepress, Printing, and Binding by West Publishing Company

British Library Cataloguing-in-Publication Data. A catalogue record for this book is
available from the British Library.

Library of Congress Cataloging-in-Publication Data

Criminology : a cross-cultural perspective / [edited by] Robert Heiner
     p. cm.
  Includes bibliographical references and index.
  ISBN 0-314-06364-1 (soft)
  1. Criminology—Cross-cultural studies.   2. Law enforcement—Cross-cultural studies.
3. Criminal justice, Administration of—Cross-cultural studies.   I. Heiner, Robert.
HV6025.C745   1996
364—dc20   95-23124
                                                                CIP

to my mother

Contents

PART THREE

CONCEPTIONS OF JUSTICE
AND SOCIETAL RESPONSES

PART FOUR

CORRECTIONAL SYSTEMS

Introduction

It has been said that unless sociologists take into account societies other than their own, they are not engaging in a truly sociological inquiry. Though perhaps it is a little less self-evident, the same can also be said of criminological inquiry. An understanding of crime and criminal justice in the United States cannot help but be facilitated by an understanding of crime and criminal justice in other countries. By examining other countries, we become aware of possible explanations for crime as well as possible responses to crime that might otherwise be obscured if we were to isolate our inquiry to our own country. Further, as the global community becomes increasingly interconnected, opportunities for the exchange of data and ideas have become increasingly available, and cross-cultural studies in all of the social sciences have taken on greater importance.

There are at least four fundamental reasons for the study of cross-cultural or "comparative" criminology. First of all, an examination of crime and reactions to crime may provide us with some insights into how we can improve the crime situation in our own country. Not many people in this country are pleased with the way we deal with our crime problem. (I cannot remember too many politicians running for public office saying that the criminal justice system is fine just the way it is.) But what can we do about it? More specifically, the comparative criminologist wants to know: What can we learn to improve our public policy from the ways other societies deal with their crime problems?

The second reason for the study of cross-cultural criminology is that it is essential in evaluating current criminological theories. In testing these theories, other countries can serve as our laboratories. The social sciences, as all other sciences, are engaged in the search for *universal laws,* and if a relationship between two or more variables is asserted in a theory, then it should be observable in other countries as well as our own. If the relationship is not observable, then the reason for this inconsistency needs to be identified or the theory needs to be reworked. For example, if we make the simple theoretical statement "Poverty causes crime," then we should be able to observe a correlation between poverty and crime in all countries. It may well be that such a correlation does not exist in some countries because in these countries almost all of the people are poor, they accept poverty as their lot in life, and they are not motivated to improve their conditions through crime. Therefore, it becomes apparent that our theory needs to be modified to include variables such as inequality and material expectations. Cross-cultural comparisons often reveal strengths and deficiencies in social scientific theories.

The third reason for comparative criminology is that it can be a useful tool in the understanding of other cultures. Crime and reactions to crime are fundamental and integral components of a social structure. Societies are held together by their norms. To put it another way, what makes a society "a society" is its norms. One cannot understand a society without understanding its norms; and sociologists specializing in the area of deviance have long known that the best way to study norms is to study the *violation* of norms. Norms are omnipresent and likely to be taken for granted and overlooked; they often do not become apparent until they are broken; then they come sharply into focus. (You, for example, have probably not thought much about the norms for eating spaghetti, but you would if the person sitting across the table from you was eating it with his fingers.) So, by studying violations of norms (in this case, crime) and the way people and societies react to these violations, we are able to gain valuable insights into other cultures.

A fourth and perhaps more important reason for studying crime in other countries is the fact that it gives us a different vantage point for the understanding of the phenomenon. While the problems of ethnocentrism and objectivity will be discussed at some length below, it should be noted here that, in some ways, we can be more objective about crime in countries other than our own. People tend to become emotionally involved with their country. It is a phenomenon everybody knows as "nationalism" or "patriotism," and we tend to see crime as a threat to that which we hold dear. It is difficult, therefore, to view crime objectively in our own country. On the other hand, in that we are less emotionally involved in the affairs of other countries, we can be more objective about crime in those countries. So the study of crime in other countries allows us a certain understanding of crime in our own country that we could not otherwise get.

In addition to the above reasons for the study of cross-cultural criminology, we might also add that this subject lends itself to the examination of international crime issues that have traditionally been given scant consideration by American criminology textbooks. Hence, selections have been included in this book that cover such topics as terrorism, hate crime, and war crime.

To further elaborate the value and potential pitfalls of cross-cultural criminology, let us return now to the issue of public policy. Over the last fifteen years or so, the principle way in which our society has tried to "fix" the criminal justice system has been to "get tougher" on criminals. If the goal of this measure was to reduce crime, it seems to have been a failure. The U. S. has the highest *known* rate of incarceration in the world; we dispense more sentences and longer sentences than most countries; we are among only a few industrialized countries to make use of the death penalty; and yet we have one of the highest crime rates in the world. Furthermore, the crime rate in the U.S. has not gone down substantially *since* the implementation of get-tough policies. (According to the FBI's *Uniform Crime Reports,* the crime rate has generally gone up. According to nationwide victimization surveys, the crime rate has remained relatively stable.)

Note that we just concluded that our get-tough policies have been ineffective, basing our conclusion on *comparisons*. First we compared our incarceration rates and sentencing policies to those of other countries, then we compared our crime rates. We proceeded to compare crime rates in the U.S. before and after the implementation of get-tough policies. Virtually all scientific evidence is based upon comparisons (e.g., comparisons of fossils over time, comparisons of chemicals that have been exposed to another and those that have not, comparisons of mice whose behavior has been reinforced versus those whose have not). This is the method of comparative criminology, and it would seem to indicate that we are doing something wrong in the U.S. when it comes to crime control.

However, we must be very cautious when we are comparing cultures. If we look to other cultures for answers to our own problems we must be certain that the measures we use and the cultures we study are indeed comparable—and this is rarely the case. If we use crime rates as the measure of success or failure of a policy, we are treading on very shaky ground. Different countries have different ways of defining, categorizing, detecting, and reporting crime. For example, differing robbery rates between two countries may simply mean that robberies are more likely to come to the attention of the authorities in one country than in the other, not that more robbery (or what we call "robbery") actually occurs there.

Aside from the problem of measuring crime, cross-cultural comparisons are precarious because cultures are extremely complex; therefore, the extent to which they can be compared is quite likely unknowable. Indeed, factors operating independently of the criminal justice system affect crime (e.g., economic systems, family systems, political systems, the media). Differing criminal justice policies are likely to have far less influence on crime than these other factors. We cannot conclude, therefore, that one country has less crime than we have simply because that country employs different policies in its criminal justice system.

Another issue with regard to cross-cultural comparisons is the likely insurmountable problem of ethnocentrism. It is difficult, if not impossible, to characterize another culture without the biases of our own culture. The problems most often engendered by ethnocentrism are the tendencies to stereotype and to focus on the differences between cultures rather than their similarities. For example, the Japanese are often stereotyped as being group-oriented and the Germans as being authoritarian. Whatever truth there may or may not be to these stereotypes, they serve to highlight *alleged* differences between their cultures and our own, while obscuring similarities. In comparative studies there is great temptation to focus on contrasts rather than similarities. Contrasts are intrinsically more captivating; in that they "stand out," they are more easily noticed. (There is nothing like a good anecdote from someone who has just traveled to a foreign land about how "strange" the customs are there.) Similarities, on the other hand, are easily overlooked. Though contrasts may be intrinsically more interesting than similarities, they are not scientifically or objectively more relevant; and it is very difficult to achieve a balance between the two.

Due to these methodological problems, we really cannot look toward comparative criminology for *answers* to our problems. However, we can derive *insights* from an examination of other cultures and their responses to crime. Despite the imperfectability of comparative criminology, it would be the heighth of provincialism to assert that the U.S. and American criminologists have nothing to learn from other countries in regard to crime and criminal justice.

It is my belief that the get-tough approach to crime that the U.S. has employed over the past fifteen years or so has been, if not an abject failure, then certainly not a success. We resort to knee-jerk get-tough policies in large part because politicians are able to make political capital from alarmist law and order rhetoric, while at the same time the media have found it profitable to give us as much blood and gore crime coverage as possible. The result has been a very narrowly conceived response to crime that can only benefit by examining how other societies deal with their crime problems.

The reader will find that, as a whole, this book leans in the direction of conflict theory, more so than functionalist theory. Conflict theory is generally associated with liberal politics, and functionalism with conservative politics. Functionalism does have something to offer in terms of our understanding of other cultures and their responses to crime; and the functionalist orientation is not entirely excluded from the following selections. However, this book is designed to stimulate discussion about changes that can be made in our society and our criminal justice system, given knowledge of other societies and their criminal justice systems. Conflict theory is generally oriented toward change, while functionalism is oriented toward "more of the

Though the readings contained in this volume were all first published relatively recently, this book, to an extent, is historical. The states of crime and criminal justice in a given part of the world were not frozen with the publication of a book or article; they are in constant flux. Considerable social, political, and economic changes have been taking place throughout the world in the last decade, and continue to do so. An article about West Germany that predates the reincorporation of East Germany, though it was written relatively recently, is not contemporary. By the same token, because of rapid social change, an article written within the last year about criminal justice in Russia may not be contemporary by the time it gets published. As soon as an article or book is published, it describes a historical situation. That such an article may describe the recent past better than the present certainly does not make it irrelevant to the student of criminology. This book is about possiblities—possible crime problems, and possible ways to respond to crime. Thus, in terms of the future, historical possibilities are no less relevant than present realities.

This book is divided into four parts. Each part contains a selection of readings; and each reading is preceded by a brief discussion of each of the articles, highlighting their significance with regard to issues of concern to American criminologists. Part I, "Crime," is designed simply to provide the reader with an idea of the varieties, as well as similarities, of the crime problems facing countries other than our own. Some prominent themes in this section include the relationships between crime and culture (selections #1, #3, #5, and #8), between crime and gender (#4, #6, and #7), and between crime and social change (#2, #9, and #10). Part II on "Police" focuses on two important issues: abuses of power (#11, #12, and #13) and the current trend toward community policing (#14 and #15). Part III, "Conceptions of Justice and Societal Responses," addresses a variety of issues, including: the treatment of minorities (#16), criminal justice in "repressive" societies (#17 and #18), problems with defining and prosecuting "war crimes" (#19), an innovative response to the problem of drugs (#20), and capital punishment (#21). Part IV, "Correctional Systems," begins with an introduction to the conservative model of crime control (#22), followed by an overview of correctional problems around the world (#23), a descriptions of different prison systems (#24, #25 and #26), and finally, a discussion of some problems facing community-based corrections (#27).

It is the intent of this book to provide the reader with a sampling of criminological phenomena around the world. Of course, all criminological phenomena and the whole world are not covered. A number of considerations went into the selection of articles in this reader. First of all, I was looking for readings that served one or more of the the four purposes outlined earlier in terms of their contributions to public policy, criminological theory, the understanding of other cultures, and/or the understanding of crime and crime control in our own country. I was also looking for articles that pertained to current criminological trends that are international in scope and often not discussed in standard criminology texts. Finally, I was seeking *readable* articles from the social science literature. Much of the literature written in the social sciences is highly quantitative, laden with jargon, and not very accessible to anybody other than social scientists. The few exceptions that did not come from the social science literature, I chose because of their topicality and readability.

Again, this book does not cover all criminological issues and countries; such exhaustive coverage simply is not possible. My apologies to those who would like to see other issues and countries which are not covered in the following selections.

Acknowledgments

First, I would like to thank those who reviewed earlier drafts of this manuscript. They include:

Thomas Carroll
University of Missouri

Thomas Courtless
University of Missouri

Marjorie Donovan
Pittsburg State University

Leroy Gould
Florida State University

Joseph Jacoby
Bowling Green State University

Richard Lundman
Ohio State University

Barbara May
Montgomery County Community College

Terry Reuther
Anoka Ramsey Community College

James Standley
Stephen F. Austin State University

George Stine
Millersville University

Prabha Unnithan
Colorado State University

Craig Winston
Savannah State College

Their comments, praise, and criticism are greatly appreciated.

Many thanks go to Peter Marshall, the executive editor of this project, who recognized a need for such a book, and who deftly guided me through its preparation. I am very grateful to Sandy Gangelhoff, the production editor, who made this whole process surprisingly painless. Also, at West Publishing, I'd like to thank Angela Musey, Jane Bass, and the others who have assisted me on this project. It has been a real pleasure working with all of them.

A book such as this, requiring materials from all over the globe, would not have been possible without inter-library loans. I would like to thank those who helped me acquire these materials. They include David Bunnell, Deborah Harrington, and Bret Heim at the Thomas Byrne Memorial Library at Spring Hill College, and Debbie Cobb at The University of South Alabama Library.

For their advice, assistance, and support, I wish to thank Maria Battaglia, Mike Behrend, Glen Bell, Larry Hall, Neil Hamilton, Sue Hodges, Gloria Palileo, and Floria Salazar.

Finally, I would like to thank Gresham Sykes. His knowledge, wit, and humanity have long been a source of inspiration.

PART ONE

Crime

Lessons in Order

■ *DAVID H. BAYLEY*

INTRODUCTORY NOTES

This first selection provides a good illustration of the linkages between crime and culture. It is well known that Japan has a much lower crime rate than the U.S. even though its criminal justice system is not nearly as punitive. The author, David Bayley, cites a number of possible causes for this disparity, including the certainty of punishment in Japan and its very strict gun control laws. But, not surprisingly, it seems that Japan's lower crime rate has more to do with elements of their culture other than the criminal justice system.

The famous French sociologist, Emile Durkheim, argued that since crime has been and always will be present in all societies, it cannot be viewed as a pathology (*The Rules of Sociological Method,* 1966). In fact, it can be a sign of a healthy society. It is only because we are free enough to consider violating the laws that crime occurs.

Bayley asserts that one of the reasons the Japanese have so little crime is because their society, by American standards, is so constrictive. While Americans may envy Japan's crime rate, it is not likely that many Americans would be willing to opt for the Japanese way of life in order to achieve it.

While Durkheim may have argued that crime is the price we pay for a free society, he did not mean the more crime, the better; and if he were alive today, he probably would be quite critical of a society, such as ours, that generates such high levels of crime. The American concept of freedom is tied in with the value we place on individuality. When individuality runs rampant, said Durkheim, people feel less allegiance to their community and a myriad of social problems will result, including soaring crime rates.

The gangster office was located in a modern two-story detached structure in an open space at the end of a passageway between two tall brick buildings. On the first floor was a large office containing desks and filing cabinets, along with an alcove furnished with leatherette couches and easy chairs providing a view through glass panels of a well-tended Japanese-style garden. The name of the gangster organization was etched onto a large, lacquered cross-section of tree trunk displayed prominently just inside the door. The boss was a tough-looking man of forty-five, dressed in dark slacks and a maroon turtleneck under a buttoned cardigan. As the two patrol officers and I sat drinking green tea prepared by one of the casually dressed male underlings, the boss explained that this was a headquarters supervising forty or fifty branch offices. The two patrol officers took their hats off and enjoyed a relaxed smoke while

SOURCE: David H. Bayley, *Forces of Order: Policing Modern Japan* (Berkeley: University of California Press, 1991), 168–182. Reprinted by permission from the publisher and the author.

prompting the boss with questions that they thought would interest me. After fifteen minutes, we were bowed out the door, past conical piles of salt arranged for good luck on the doorstep.

Police estimate that there are at least 80,000 *yakuza* in Japan—that is, full-fledged members of 1,500 organized criminal groups, loosely federated into several larger competing syndicates.[1] They commit 6 percent of all Penal Code crimes—3 percent of murders, 16 percent of robberies, 15 percent of rapes—and are instrumental in drug and gun smuggling.[2] Frequently fighting among themselves for turf and position, they commit most of the crimes involving firearms, as well as most of the offenses against the gun laws. Their illegal activities include gambling, prostitution, selling protection, strikebreaking, blackmail, and loan-sharking, although increasingly they are investing their illegal proceeds in legitimate businesses, especially in the entertainment industry. Uniformed patrol officers routinely visit their offices to show the flag, and also to note the names of gang members displayed on wall-mounted rosters and the schedule of monthly events written on large chalkboards, as in any Japanese office.

The visibility of organized criminal gangs and their close surveillance by the police does not mean that Japan's reputation for being the safest country among the developed democracies is false. Japan's rate of serious crime is indeed less than one-third of the American, and there is no reason to doubt the figures.[3] But it certainly raises questions about how this orderliness has been achieved and what the role of the police is in it. To understand what is going on in Japan, I shall compare factors that are commonly expected to affect crime and its control in order to see if they can account for the remarkable difference in orderliness between Japan and the United States. I shall begin by examining criminalogenic conditions.

REASONS FOR PUBLIC ORDER

In searching for an explanation of Japan's dramatically lower crime rates, several factors can immediately be set aside. Japan is fully as modern as the United States, transformed equally during the last century by processes of urbanization, industrialization, and technological development. Japan is not a Third World backwater. Especially confounding is the fact that its population congestion, sometimes suspected of being associated with social disorganization and high crime, is much greater than that of the United States. To appreciate what it would be like if the United States were as densely populated as Japan, imagine California if half the U.S. population moved there. If they did, can one believe that our crime rate would fall?

Japan is also not politically repressive; its people are not subjected to the iron hand of government regimentation. It is as democratic as the United States, with the rights of speech, expression, association, and electoral competition protected by law and an independent judiciary. This has not always been the case. Democracy is less than fifty years old in Japan, dating from the Allied Occupation in 1945. For centuries government had exercised very tight control. While it seems doubtful that many Japanese are inhibited by fear of governmental abuses of power, one might argue that the habits of subservience to authority learned in earlier times remain a part of Japan's political culture and might inhibit expressive behavior. The sole serious contemporary exception to its fine human rights record is the practice of extended precharge detention.[4] Because it is used so seldomly and the cultural promptings of confession are so powerful, I doubt that this practice has any important effect on either crime—or clearance—rates.

Turning to economic conditions, informative differences between Japan and the United States begin to emerge. Although per capita wealth is about the same, the distribution of income is significantly more egalitarian in Japan than in the United States. That is, rich people earn a larger proportion of the country's income in the United States than they do in Japan.[5] Furthermore, unemployment is generally much lower in Japan than in the United States by a factor of two or three.[6] And a much smaller proportion of the working population is involved in strikes in Japan.[7] Although there is poverty in Japan and homelessness, there are few slums—that is, areas of chronic poverty, unemployment, family pathology, and high crime.[8] There are probably only two in all of Japan that qualify—the Airin area of Osaka, home to 20,000 day laborers, and the Sanya section of Tokyo, which has 7,000.[9] These areas are notorious throughout Japan.

More important, Japan does not have ghettoes, meaning areas inhabited by chronically impoverished people who are members of groups that are subjected to discrimination by the general population. Only about one-half of 1 percent of the population is ethnically not Japanese, mostly Koreans and Chinese.[10] By contrast, about 13 percent of the American population is African-American and 8 percent is Hispanic.[11] As Japanese often point out, Japan probably has the largest homogeneous population of any country in the world. This is not to suggest that crime is mostly interracial or interethnic. It is not. Rather, Japan lacks the kind of racial and cultural diversity that so frequently reinforces economic inequality to produce successive generations of the misery, hopelessness, rage, and family disintegration that are so strongly associated with crime.

Americans expect the operations of the criminal justice system to inhibit crime. Comparing its operation in Japan and in the United States, however, the few differences would seem to work to give Japan higher rather than lower crime rates. The two systems are very similar in form, which is hardly surprising, since the Japanese system is the product of American reform after World War II, overlaying earlier borrowings from Germany and France. The Japanese actually invest less of their gross national product in police, courts, and corrections (0.88 percent) than does the United States (1.26 percent).[12] Japan spends a smaller proportion of government revenues on criminal justice (2.5 percent) than does the United States (3.2 percent).[13] Japan does spend proportionately more of its gross national product on police—0.76 percent versus 0.50 percent—but per capita expenditures on police are higher in the United States.[14] Altogether, criminal justice investments would hardly seem to account for Japan's lower crime rates.

Contrary to what Americans would expect in a country with low crime rates, sentences for similar crimes are invariably more lenient in Japan than in the United States, which is reflected in the fact that five times as many Americans as Japanese, proportionate to population, are in prison.[15] Japan did keep the death penalty while the United States experimented briefly from 1972 to 1976 with its abolition, but that single difference in deterrent severity was short-lived. Since World War II about 550 people have been executed in Japan, about 5 a year during the last fifteen years. In the United States, from 1945 to 1987, 1,640 were executed, about 20 a year in the mid-1980s.[16] If the Japanese criminal justice system is having an impact on crime, it is not, therefore, through the greater rigor of its punishments. It may, however, be doing so through its sureness. A suspect is charged and officially dealt with in some manner in more than one-third of all crimes reported to the Japanese police. In the United States, the comparable figure is a meager 5 percent. Crime is much more risky in Japan than in the United States. The sureness of punishment in Japan, even if it is mild, may have a more deterrent effect than the more severe but uncertain punishments in the United States.

There is only one difference in legal context that might help to account for the disparity in crime rates. Japan has the toughest laws on the ownership of firearms, especially handguns, of any democratic country in the world. Registration is required for all firearms, knives, and swords.[17] No handguns are permitted in private hands, even registered, with the exception of people who participate in international shooting competitions.[18] There were forty-five such persons in 1989.[19] Even they cannot take their guns home, but must deposit them at a police station or with registered administrators of shooting ranges. Shotguns and small-caliber rifles are permitted for hunting. There were 29,000 registered rifles and about 450,000 registered shotguns in 1989. Permits for owning weapons are issued by prefectural public safety commissions.[20] No one knows how many handguns are privately held in the United States, although estimates run into the hundreds of millions. Surveys have shown that 23 percent of American homes have handguns.[21]

As a result, the use of firearms in Japanese crime is negligible. Out of approximately 51,000 felonious or violent offenses committed in Japan in 1988, less than 250 involved handguns.[22] Ninety-four percent of these were committed by yakuza. In the United States, about 59 percent of all murders (17,859 instances) in 1987 were committed with firearms, 21 percent of all aggravated assaults (792,457 instances), and 33 percent of all robberies (498,632 instances).[23] The uncertainty, wariness, and honest fear that American police officers feel in making street contacts and responding to summonses for assistance are totally unfamiliar to the Japanese police. Less than twenty officers are killed feloniously each year, hardly ever by firearms. In the United States eighty-four officers on average were killed each year during the last decade, three-quarters of them by handguns.[24]

The National Rifle Association, the major source of opposition to efforts to restrict gun ownership in the United States, developed a slogan that many believe makes the case convincingly against legislation restricting gun ownership. "When guns are outlawed, only outlaws will have guns." This is exactly what has occurred in Japan. And the Japanese think this is a very good thing.[25]

A final factor that is often considered influential in explaining crime, especially violent crime, is popular culture. Japan's is hardly less violent than that of the United States. Its history is certainly as blood-soaked. For centuries justice was meted out on the basis of class; until a little over a hundred years ago a samurai had the right to cut down with a sword any peasant who insulted him. Executions for crime were quick and brutal. There was and still is a cult of the sword in Japan similar to the cult of the gun in the United States. Martial values and regimen, which Americans tend to deprecate, have been extolled in Japan for generations. Political assassination has been far more common in Japanese history than in American. Since 1945 eight political leaders have been killed or injured in attacks.[26] Several assassination plans are discovered in their early stages each year. Both countries fought civil wars at approximately the same time. Although the bloodletting was less extensive in Japan, the parochial loyalties overcome were probably as intense. Furthermore, two generations ago Japan launched a fanatical imperial war whose excesses are still remembered throughout Asia as well as in the United States.

Contemporary popular culture, too, is replete with violence. Theater, films, television, and the ubiquitous "manga"—adult comic books—are saturated with violence, much of it with strong erotic overtones that feature women as victims.[27] Violence on television, on which many American ills are blamed, appears to be as prevalent in Japan as in the United States.[28] Samurai dramas are a staple of television, as Westerns used to be and police detective shows now are in the United States. The sword-wielding warrior, especially if he has turned outlaw, fascinates the Japanese. However, there may be some important differences in the portrayal of violence in both countries. Violence in Japan is more ritualized, more easily recognized as theater, distanced more from the settings of contemporary life. Furthermore, violence is usually portrayed tragically; people who use it die, often with their problems unresolved.[29]

Looking generally then at the circumstances within which Japanese and Americans live, there are some differences that would explain the lower crime rates in Japan. On the one hand, income distribution is more equitable in Japan, unemployment is less, and poverty is less concentrated in particular localities, especially neighborhoods defined by race or ethnicity. Japan also regulates gun ownership much more stringently than does the United States. On the other hand, its popular culture is as violent as that of the United States, and its criminal justice system, while more efficient, is less rigorous in its punishments. Criminal prosecution is hampered by civil rights, very much as in the United States except for the extended precharge detention period.

It is impossible to determine scientifically, given limitations on data in both countries, whether these differences in social circumstances can account entirely for Japan's enviable crime record. At the same time, it is clear that there are other processes at work in Japan that help to produce its remarkable orderliness. These are processes of social interaction, part of general culture, that bear directly on the behavior of the Japanese. Crime, more generally the impulse to deviance, is inhibited by mechanisms that are peculiar to Japan in their strength and extensiveness. Although these mechanisms can be found in American society too, they are much weaker and more attenuated. Control of deviant behavior in Japan, I shall argue, is obtained through a unique combination of propriety, presumption, and pride.

First: propriety. Japanese are bound by an infinite number of rules about what is proper. To an American, Japan is supremely uptight. There is nothing casual or relaxed about it. In order to avoid giving offense, modes of speech shift as one addresses a man or a woman, a child or an adult, an older or a younger sibling, an elderly person, one's peer, a first-time acquaintance or a long-time friend, a workmate or an outsider, and so forth. Informal dress codes are strict, and people dress exactingly so as to conform to what is expected on particular occasions as well as in particular roles. All schoolchildren wear the uniform distinctive of the school they attend, identical down to purses, backpacks, width of trousers, and length of skirts. Businessmen and government bureaucrats invariably wear dark suits, dark ties, white shirts, and black shoes. Construction workers can be recognized by knickers, soft two-toed boots, and woolen belly-warmers. Female street sweepers wear long scarves; truck and taxi drivers often wear white gloves. Revealingly, a customer in a Western-style dress shop will be asked, "What size are you?" in a kimono store,

"How old are you?"[30] People in Japan are what they look like, which means they must conform in order to be what they want to be.

Decorum is all-encompassing: not sitting on desks and surfaces people use for work; not putting shod feet on chairs, so that mothers carefully take off the tiny tennis shoes of their children when they pull them onto subway seats; encasing wet umbrellas in disposable plastic sacks when entering department stores; tying a *ukata* (bathrobe) one way for a man, another for a woman; and not looking directly into the eyes of another person in public. Japanese calculate the depth as well as the number of bows so that proper deference is shown. Department stores have mechanical calibrators that help personnel learn the appropriate bowing angle for different sorts of people.[31] Late one morning in a popular Tokyo restaurant I heard chanting from the kitchen. Peering surreptitiously through an open door, I saw the manager rehearsing the staff in saying, "What can I do for you?" "How can I help you?" and "Thank you, come back," in the proper bright and cheery way.

Japanese are surrounded by rules in all they do, from the serious to the trivial. In relation to Americans, they are compulsively watchful about decorum. Etiquette, civility, morality, and law blend together. Japanese learn early that someone is paying attention to everything they do, and that departures from propriety will be met with visible expressions of disapproval. A sense of constraining order is always present in Japanese life. A person is never offstage.

The pervading sense of propriety produces startling demonstrations of orderliness. An English businessman was so astonished at the absence of litter that he personally inspected 1,200 yards of subway corridors in the Yurakicho-Ginza subway station during an evening rush hour to count discarded trash. Although this complex is ten times larger than London's Picadilly Circus Underground Station, he found only nineteen cigarette ends, twenty-eight matchsticks, eleven candy wrappers, and four pieces of paper.[32] Japanese pedestrians rarely jaywalk, dutifully waiting for the crossing-lights to turn green even if there is no car in sight and it is late at night.

The instinctive obedience to shared rules of order is wonderfully captured in a story about a burglar who was caught fleeing an apartment in the daytime. It is important to understand that Japanese remove their shoes on entering a private home, especially if its floor is the traditional raised floor made of thick woven-straw (tatami). The burglar had crossed such a room to ransack a bureau, but was apprehended by the police because, when he heard them, he had stopped to put his shoes back on.[33]

Japanese orderliness in large matters, such as crime, seems to be related to orderliness in small things. If this is true, then the lack of regimentation that Americans value in personal life may affect the amount of criminal disorder in public life. Would Americans, one wonders, be willing to obtain a greater measure of safety if they were required to tie their bathrobes in a prescribed way?[34]

Second: presumption. Japanese are enmeshed in closely knit groups that inhibit behavior through informal social controls. Japanese are not raised to stand alone, develop their individual potential, or "do their own thing." They are taught to fit into groups and to subordinate themselves to the purposes of those groups. The most important and enduring groups are family, school, and workplace. Becoming an organic part of them—belonging—is the source of the deepest emotional satisfaction Japanese feel. Thus, fitting in becomes the ultimate discipline in Japan. Japanese are encapsulated in small groups of well-known people who have the presumptive right to tell them how to behave.

Accepting the obligations of belonging is not like being directed to conform, though that is the result. Japanese tolerate the presumptions of membership because in exchange they are nurtured, supported, and cared for. This may take the form of lifetime employment, or the covering up of errors, or assistance in carrying out tasks, or simply an understanding of personal problems. Americans are more calculating about the costs and benefits of membership. Groups are instruments of individual purpose, rather than being ends in themselves. Americans are therefore less bound by the obligations of membership in any particular group, whether it be family, marriage, job, sports team, or social club. Because Japanese depend so entirely on a much smaller number of affiliations, they lose the ability to discriminate between the claims of the individual and those of the group, the obligations of the personal as opposed to those of the public.

The difference between Japanese and Americans is not in valuing the favorable regard of others or in the need to conform; it lies in the range of significant external references. Americans are "outer directed," to use David Reisman's famous phrase, in a generalized way; Japanese are "outer directed" in a focused way.[35] Studies have in fact shown that among strangers Americans conform more quickly than Japanese.[36] Japanese do not accept the presumptions of any group, but only of a small number of groups. The universal desire for fellowship and community provides enormous leverage in Japan because it is not counterbalanced by the obligations of other affiliations.

The presumptive control that immediate social groups can exercise can be seen in the importance placed on unspoken communication in Japan. People who properly belong do not have to be told; they understand instinctively what the wishes of the group are. For example, a husband in a properly attuned marriage does not need to apologize to his wife if he spills hot tea-water on her hand, because she understands without being told that he did not intend to hurt her and also that he is sorry. The most cutting remark a man can make about his wife is that she has to be told what he needs.[37] Businessmen complain that they do not like to be sent abroad for long periods because they lose instinctive knowledge of their group. When they return they feel like strangers, having to be told what everyone else understands. As the Japanese say, the expectation in most of life is that when you talk "others can finish the sentence." It is not an acceptable excuse in Japan to say, "I wasn't told."[38]

Japanese learn the value of belonging early in life. In schools children advance automatically, as a group, helping one another as they go. Individual achievements are deemphasized in favor of group accomplishments. Children learn not to embarrass schoolmates by showing them to be wrong. Instead, they correct others by saying, "I want to help Yakuda-kun" or "I agree with Kato-san but I also think this way."[39] Individual test scores are not known among classmates. Separation according to ability occurs impersonally, usually as the result of formal examinations allowing students to move from one level of schooling to another. Young children compete athletically by classes, not as individuals. Students also perform together many of the custodial chores at schools, like sweeping floors, washing dishes after lunch, picking up trash, putting away equipment, and rearranging chairs. Teachers and students explain constantly to laggards what is expected, reiterating that unless something or other is done the class will be disappointed, the student will be letting down the side, or everyone will be ashamed if the student does not try. Emotional blackmail, Americans would call this, and would resent it.

Even before schooling, Japanese children learn that fitting in brings warmth and love. Observers of early child-raising practices have noted that Japanese mothers carry their children with them everywhere, both inside and outside the house. Children sleep with their parents until the age of four or five. American mothers put down happy children, encouraging them to play by themselves. American children are left with baby-sitters, a practice still uncommon in Japan. They learn early to attract attention by crying and demanding; Japanese mothers anticipate the needs of their children so they do not have to cry or demand.[40]

When Japanese preschool children misbehave, parents threaten them with being locked out of the home. They tearfully bang on the front doors, pleading to be allowed back in. In the United States parents threaten badly behaving children with exactly the reverse—being kept in. The children are "grounded." The effect is that American children are taught that it is punishment to be locked up with one's family; Japanese children are taught that punishment is being excluded from one's family.[41] Small wonder, then, that Japanese schools and work groups have leverage over individual behavior later in life—and that adult affiliations in the United States have less.

The power of informal social control is what the Japanese criminal justice system relies on when it accepts apologies for minor infractions, does not insist on arresting suspects, allows people to be free without bail pending trial, and suspends prosecution or the execution of sentences. The vitality of group supervision is what allows police, prosecutors, and judges to act on the philosophy that they "hate the crime but not the criminal." The Japanese criminal justice system is founded not on deterrence but rather on "reintegrative shaming."[42] The purpose of the system is to shame individuals into accepting the obligations of their social setting and to shame groups into accepting responsibility for the errant member. Individuation makes sense in Japan, as it often does in the United States as well, when people are situated in specific, binding social networks.

Learning to accept the presumptions of groups does not mean that groups are without conflict and disagreement. Japanese often feel frustrated and inhibited. Unlike Americans, however, they are more willing to manage the conflict, deflecting or repressing it.[43] They make an explicit distinction linguistically between what is apparent and what is real in social situations. *Tatemae* refers to the appearance that must be maintained; *honne* is the inside story, what is truly felt. Americans too understand the tension between gut-feeling and propriety, but are more likely to be led by the former. Conversely, they value sincerity, being uncomfortable with hollow conformity. Japanese stifle nonconformity for the sake of maintaining the *tatemae* of group harmony, even though they know it is a pretense.

Social order in an individualistic society like the United States requires the discipline of conscience; social order in a communitarian society like Japan requires the discipline of presumption. Both societies learn to accommodate some of the other perspective. Japanese society does not wholly trample individual identity; American society does not forfeit entirely the capacity for cooperative endeavor. But the balance is different. As two observers of both countries have said, "One may even venture to suggest that while Americans learn to live with an illusion of complete self-reliance, self-sufficiency and autonomy, many Japanese tend to live with an illusion of total harmony, mutual understanding and consensus among them."[44]

Third: pride. Discipline is maintained in Japan because people take enormous pride in performing well the roles demanded of them. Distinctive occupational dress is one indication of the prideful identification people have with their work. Japanese society is hierarchical in terms of authority, but it is egalitarian in its evaluation of the worth of work. What is important is the dedication brought to the job, not its status. Interestingly, anyone who teaches in Japan, from university professors to instructors in cutting up raw fish, are called *sensei*. One reason Japanese women have accepted differentiated sex roles more readily than American women may be that the emotional rewards are greater. Being a wife and mother is regarded as a demanding and responsible job in Japan. It is not denigrated as being "just housework."[45]

The essential ingredient in achieving success at anything is *seishin*, literally "spirit." But the word has strong overtones of effort, discipline, self-control, and even suffering. Inner fulfillment comes from developing the *seishin* necessary to accept demanding obligations willingly, whether artistic and craft skills, work routines, athletic feats, or social responsibilities. Japanese respect the *seishin* shown by the daughter-in-law who uncomplainingly performs her duties in the house of an overbearing mother-in-law for the sake of the family, or the student who practices tea-ceremony for years in order to achieve a higher ranking, or the baseball player who trains despite personal injury without asking for time off.[46] In arts, crafts, and social relations, Japanese learn by rote, by endlessly copying approved behavior. High achievement is obtained by fanatical application, not by gifted innovation. Great effort earns great respect. Indeed, Japanese tend to excuse marginal performance as long as exemplary *seishin* was shown. By being perfectionist in effort, Japanese protect themselves against censure. Americans, on the other hand, are more ends-oriented, excusing slipshod preparation if the results are good.

Pride given to work helps Japanese accept conformity. As Edwin O. Reischauer, former ambassador to Japan, has said, "social conformity to the Japanese is no sign of weakness but rather the proud, tempered product of inner strength."[47] A symbol of this is the bonzai tree, a unique expression of aesthetic taste with which Japanese identify. Bonzai is a dwarf tree that has been restricted by binding and pruning so that it grows into strange, artificial shapes. A bonzai tree achieves beauty by being constricted, some might say deformed. Japanese orderliness is achieved in the same way.

In conclusion, propriety, presumption, and pride can be analytically and anecdotally separated, but they are part of a single dynamic. The enwrapping web of propriety is held in place by the myriad presumptive corrections of primary social groups. Careful attention to the forms of human interaction allows tightly knit groups to hold together despite the vagaries of circumstance and personality. Pride allows for the internalization of the discipline necessary for subordination to small groups. Presumption becomes bearable when society rewards those who accept it.

Americans can understand, perhaps even empathize with, this dynamic. But they reverse the values. Propriety in the United States is limited, individuals being free to live their lives bound only by the commodious limits of the law. Behavior is bound more exclusively by law, or a very general morality, because the texture of American society is too loosely knit to rely on the presumptive enforcement of small groups. Norms of decorum and civility are not shared across the spectrum of American life. American pride is rooted in individual accomplishment, not in the acceptance of the disciplines of primary social groups. Americans kick against the restrictions of propriety, having been taught to question conventions of dress, language, taste, and morality.

If crime is caused to an important extent by customary patterns of social interaction, then Japan and the United States may both be getting what they have contrived.

➤ DISCUSSION QUESTIONS

Durkheim said that crime is the price we pay for a free society. What freedoms does this article suggest we have in the U.S. that might contribute to our crime rates? Which of these freedoms do you think most Americans would be willing to give up in order to effect lower crime rates?

NOTES

1. *Yakuza* is a slang word for gangster. More politely, gangsters are known as *boryokudan*.

2. M. Tamura, "Yakuza and Stimulants: Drug Problems in Japan" (Paper for the International Conference on Crime, Drugs, and Social Control, Hong Kong, December 14–16, 1988), p. 3; S. Miyazawa, "Learning Lessons from Japanese Experience: Challenge for Japanese Criminologists" (Paper prepared for the U.S./Japan Bilateral Session, Tokyo, 1988), Appendix 25. See also the *White Paper on Police, 1987*.

3. See chapter 1. *Forces of Order,* David H. Bayley, 1991.

4. See chapter 7, the issue of "substitute prisons." *Forces of Order,* Bayley, 1991.

5. Income inequality as measured by the gini-coefficient was 0.278 in Japan, 0.366 in the United States. *Japan Times,* 24 February 1989, p. 24, from data provided by the European Economic Community and the Japanese Economic Planning Agency. Values for the gini-coefficient run from 0 to 1, with higher values indicating greater inequality. Elliott Currie, *Confronting Crime: An American Challenge* (New York: Pantheon, 1985), p. 161, says that Japan's equality of income was exceeded among OECD countries only by Holland, Sweden, and Norway.

6. In 1987, for example, unemployment rates were 2.8 percent in Japan and 6.2 percent in the United States; in 1989, 2.5 percent in Japan, 5.5 percent in the United States. *Japan Times,* 24 February 1989.

7. In 1987, 256,000 person-days were lost to strikes in Japan, 4,481,000 in the U.S. *Ibid.*

8. H. Wagatsuma, "Social Control of Juvenile Delinquency in Arakawa Ward of Tokyo" (Paper prepared for the Social Science Research Council Workshop on the Japanese City, April 1976), pp. 34–39.

9. Figures supplied by the respective police forces.

10. See chapter 5, *Forces of Order,* Bayley, 1991.

11. *Statistical Abstract of the United States,* 1989, pp. 14,16.

12. Japan spent Y2,900 billion in 1988 on police, prosecution, courts, and corrections; the United States, $53.5 billion in 1986. Information from the Ministry of Justice and National Police Agency, 1989, and the *Sourcebook of Criminal Justice Statistics,* 1988, p.2. The GNP of Japan was Y330,116 billion in 1987; of the United States, $4,235 billion in 1986. Keizai Koho Center, Tokyo, Japan, 1989, p. 14.

13. Same sources as n. 12.

14. See chapter 8, *Forces of Order,* Bayley, 1991.

15. See chapter 7, *Forces of Order,* Bayley.

16. Ministry of Justice, 1989, and *Sourcebook of Criminal Justice Statistics, 1988,* p. 671.

17. This includes rivet guns, rope-discharging guns, and signal guns for athletic games. "Law Controlling Possession, Etc., of Fire-arms and Swords," Article 3(1), clause 8 (Law No. 6, March 1958). Swords and knives over six inches long or with blades that automatically extend by mechanical action are prohibited except under permit.

18. Article 4.

19. National Police Agency, 1989.

20. Article 4.

21. *Sourcebook of Criminal Justice Statistics,* 1988, pp. 231–232.

22. *White Paper on Police,* 1988, p.78.

23. *Sourcebook of Criminal Justice Statistics,* 1988, pp. 446, 454, 453.

24. Federal Bureau of Investigation, *Uniform Crime Reports: Law Enforcement Officers Killed and Assaulted 1988* (Washington, D.C.: U.S. Department of Justice, 1989).

25. The place of firearms in Japan is even more interesting because they were once fairly widely used and manufactured in Japan. Japan is disarmed today as a result of deliberate government policy. This experience, and the reasons for the government decision, is described in a short illustrated book by Noel Perrin, *Giving Up the Gun: Japan's Reversion to the Sword* (Boston: Godine, 1979).

26. National Police Agency, 1989.

27. Ian Baruma, *Behind the Mask* (New York: Pantheon, 1984), chap. 10.

28. Albert Axelbank, *Black Star over Japan* (London: Allen and Unwin, 1972), and George Comstock, Syracuse University, speech, May 12, 1982.

29. Baruma and Comstock.

30. W. Caudill and H. Weinstein, "Maternal Care and Infant Behavior in Japan and America," in *Japanese Culture and Behavior,* T. S. and W. Lebra, eds. (Honolulu: University of Hawaii Press, 1974), pp. 225–76.

31. Peter Hazelhurst, formerly Tokyo correspondent for the *Sunday Times* and the *Straits Times.*

32. Peter Hazelhurst.

33. Robert Trumbull, formerly Tokyo correspondent for the *New York Times.* I once saw a squad of plainclothes detectives break into a yakuza apartment on a drug-bust and stop inside the front door to remove their shoes before undertaking their search.

34. James Q. Wilson and George L. Kelling have argued that police should concentrate on maintaining decorum on the streets in order to discourage more serious criminal behavior. "Broken Windows," *Atlantic Monthly* (March 1982), pp. 29–38. Experimental evidence for a connection between visible signs of disorder and criminal actions was found by Professor Philip Zimbardo, Stanford University, in 1969.

35. David Reisman, *The Lonely Crowd* (Garden City, N.Y.: Doubleday, 1953).

36. H. Wagatsuma and Arthur Rosett, "Cultural Attitudes toward Contract Law: Japan and the U.S. Compared" (Draft article, 1982), p. 22.

37. Robert J. Smith, *Japanese Society: Tradition, Self, and the Social Order* (Cambridge: Cambridge University Press, 1983), pp. 57–58.

38. In *Hidden Differences: Doing Business with the Japanese* (New York: Anchor Press/Doubleday, 1987), Part I, Edward T. and Mildred R. Hall describe Japan as a "high context" society, meaning that people need a great deal of information about the people they work with in order to work together successfully. Americans, on the other hand, need much less, preferring to limit the dimensions of interaction with the people they work with. The same distinction is made by Howard Gardner, *Frames of Mind* (New York: Basic Books, 1985), in distinguishing "particle" societies, where autonomous individuals interact, from "field" societies, where individuals are subordinated to groups.

39. Takie S. Lebra, *Japanese Women: Constraint and Fulfillment* (Honolulu: University of Hawaii Press, 1984), chap. 5.

40. See Caudill and Weinstein (n. 30 above).

41. *Mura hachibu* is the term for being excluded. It was a very serious punishment in villages. This is similar to the practice in the British labor movement of sending colleagues "to Coventry," not talking to them, when they defied group norms.

42. John Braithwaite, *Crime, Shame, and Reintegration* (Cambridge: Cambridge University Press, 1989).

43. Takie S. Lebra, "Nonconfrontational Strategies for Management of Interpersonal Conflicts," in Ellis S. Krauss et al., *Conflict in Japan* (Honolulu: University of Hawaii Press, 1984), chap. 3.

44. Wagatsuma and Rosett, "Cultural Attitudes."

45. Suzanne H. Vogel, "Professional Housewife: The Career of Urban Middle Class Japanese Women," *Japan Interpreter* 12, no. 1 (Winter 1978): 16–43.

46. Robert Whiting, *You Gotta Have Wa* (New York: Macmillan, 1989), p. 317.

47. *The Japanese Today* (Cambridge: Harvard University Press, 1988), p. 166.

Works Cited in Editor's Notes

Durkheim, Emile

1966 *The Rules of Sociological Method*. S.A. Solvey and J.H. Mueller, trans., G.E.G. Catlin, ed., New York: The Free Press, originally published 1938, copyright renewed 1966.

Rising Crime Rates in the Czech Republic

■ *L. CRAIG PARKER*

INTRODUCTORY NOTES

This article concerns the trend toward increasing crime in the former Soviet territories, the Czech Republic in particular. In much the same way as the previous article implies a relationship between freedom and crime, it appears that as the Czechs gained more freedom with the fall of the Soviet Union, they also acquired a more serious crime problem. A number of reasons help to explain this increase in crime. For one thing, the old Soviet regime was able to keep close tabs on the whereabouts of its citizens; this provided a significant deterrent as potential offenders knew their chances of being apprehended were quite high.

Another factor has to do with the transition from a totalitarian socialist system to a democratic capitalist system. This represents an enormous upheaval, both politically and economically. Such transitions are rarely made without serious negative consequences. In the course of such momentous change, old norms and values lose their meaning before they are replaced by new ones. Durkheim called this condition — when the norms lose their meaning— *anomie;* and Merton related this concept to the problem of crime. In that people are tied to their society by the norms, when these norms lose their meaning, the people become less tied to the community, more individualistic, and more prone to commit crime. In this regard the transition from "communism" to capitalism is likely to be especially problematic because capitalist ideology promotes the individual pursuit of profit—that is, individualism.

Such massive social, economic, and ideological upheavals are not going on in just the former Soviet territories; as Third World countries rapidly industrialize and adapt their economies to the world market, they too will undergo similar changes. Furthermore, the development of global communications technology (i.e., the satellite, and the videotape), introducing Western values to the Third World, also threatens to produce rapid changes in values and norms in these countries. Increased crime rates could well be a by-product of these changes.

SOURCE: L. Craig Parker, "Rising Crime Rates and the Role of Police in the Czech Republic" *Police Studies*, vol. 16, no. 2 (1993): 39–42. Reprinted with permission from Anderson Publishing Company and the author.

While Czech citizens now enjoy political freedom, and although the economy is beginning to stir in the wake of the Velvet Revolution of 1989, rising crime rates have spread alarm throughout the country. Information gathered during a two month visit, including interviews with legal scholars, criminologists, police officers and private citizens, provides a picture of rampant crime. As a visiting researcher at the Czech Republic's Ministry of Justice, I wanted to obtain a fuller picture of the crime problem and the role of police beyond the sparse reports that I had read in the American press.

Being based in Prague, my research focused on the Czech Republic as opposed to the Slovakian republic. The two republics became separate countries on January 1, 1993. Nonetheless, the information that I gathered seems in many respects to mirror the pattern of crime being reported in the general region and in the nearby former Communist countries of Poland, Hungary, and East Germany.

Now, with communism dead, criminals have begun to seize opportunities on many different fronts. Borders have opened up in both countries and security controls have weakened since 1989. From drugs to prostitution and organized crime thefts of valuable art objects, the justice system has more than it can handle. In addition to soaring crime rates, the public is overly fearful of the new predatory criminal activity. For a moment I thought I was back in the United States as one private citizen employed in downtown Prague stated that she feared going into the center of the city during the evening.

As is common in many parts of the world where crime rates have risen, the fear of crime has become even greater than the actual incidence, according to survey and conversations with private citizens. The new Czech nation has a high degree of literacy, and the public has been inundated with sensationalized reporting of crime and in turn has become overly fearful. A recent survey of citizens in the Czech Republic indicated that, despite the current economic uncertainties, the crime problem was ranked number one ahead of economic concerns.

Even Edward Urbanek (1992), the highly respected senior sociologist of Charles University, became visibly distressed when he discussed the escalating crime rates that have gripped Czechoslovakia. He noted that "yes, in the past we had criminality here, but like Durkheim noted many years ago when he discussed anomie, a kind of normlessness exists now in Czechoslovakia. We currently have citizens who believe that we no longer have moral and psychological boundaries. The situation is viewed as wide open, and if you commit a crime you can get away with it." Zbynek Cerovsky (1992), the head of Prague Prison, echoes this view: "As a result of forty years of totalitarianism, along with the failures of the educational system, we have increasing numbers of younger offenders who are not fearful of the consequences of committing crime."

Several Czech criminologists expressed the idea that the increased time needed to process offenders from arrest to sentencing, which now takes nine months rather than three, contributed by weakening the deterrent effect. Criminologist Jana Valkova (1992) offered her view that the atmosphere of the "open society" provided a false sense of security to young offenders that they would not be apprehended.

In discussing the background for the present surge in crime, Professor Urbanek (1992) noted that previously there was a rigid state security apparatus that was very oppressive and that crime was well controlled. Movement across national borders was severely restricted, and citizens were required to report all contacts with foreigners. In this context, the state was readily able to arrest, try, and convict offenders.

The Czech Republic, at least, is moving toward rejoining the Western European mainstream. Specifically, this appears to include the desire to seek membership in the European Economic Community. These broad social and economic aspirations have meant major changes in the criminal justice system that have in turn had a significant impact on the crime problem. This liberalization process, combined with the rapid transformation of society, has compounded the major weaknesses and gaps in the legal system. The entire system of constitutional and penal law is undergoing reform. Much of that work has yet to be completed. Furthermore, as Deputy Director Zelenicky Frant (1992) of the Czech Republic police force stated in my interview with him, "Huge numbers of prosecutors and judges have fled the justice system to make money in the private sector." By his accounting, some jurisdictions have courts and prosecutors' offices that are 85% understaffed. He noted that these lawyers are now making six to eight times as much money in the private sector since the Czech Republic has moved to create a market economy. For example, while previously most property was state-owned, lawyers now make large sums in transactions involving private property.

Loopholes exist in the tax laws, and criminologist Valkova (1992) noted that during the transition from communism to the new democratic state many taxes were no longer being collected. Enforcement of tax violations was very minimal, she stated, and although the tax law is scheduled to be revised in January 1993, which will include provisions for tougher enforcement, the state is presently losing large sums of money. She added, "Many people just ignore the government's request that people pay what they owe."

Interior Minister Jan Ruml, in an interview with *The Prague Post* (Auster, 1992), stated that in 1989 in the rush "to correct excesses of the old regime" new laws and regulations weakened police powers. He pointed out that police are allowed only 24 hours to detain suspects before bringing charges and that proposed legislation would give them 48 hours. Police have argued that the longer time frame is needed to establish a suspect's identity and to do the necessary paperwork in filing charges.

CRIME STATISTICS

Top police officials of both the Czech republic and Prague police agencies stated that overall crime rates have roughly tripled since the 1989 revolution *(Yearbook of Ministry of Interior and Czech Republic Police, 1992)*. This high rate has slackened a bit since the shift to a democratic society but is still climbing. During the most recent period for which statistics were available, overall reported crime in the Czech Republic rose from 216,852 offenses in 1990 to 282,998 offenses in 1991, showing a 30.5% increase. Most offenses have been robberies, burglaries, and thefts, but property crimes generally have increased dramatically. From 1990 to 1991 they increased from 166,638 to 231,372, a 38.3% jump. Robberies have escalated from 3,855 in 1990 to 4,142 in 1991 in the Czech Republic, and increasingly involve the use of firearms.

Deputy Chief Charvat (1992) of the Prague Police Department commented that guns are now generally more available and the "regulations have softened." Furthermore he stated that while people such as taxi drivers and hunters still sought proper permits, criminals were readily obtaining illegal firearms on the black market and that the available supply was continuing to increase. In mid-1992, as Russian soldiers started to leave Czechoslovakia, even more weapons were dumped into Czech society. Earlier, before guns were easily available, criminals resorted to a paralytic gas and knives. Female gypsies often lured foreigners with an offer of sex and subsequently drugged their victims in hotel rooms — with some eventually dying from overdoses.

Homicides may or may not be leveling off over the past three years, but are up significantly from the 1989 prerevolutionary period. In 1990, 212 murders were recorded in the Czech Republic, while the number dropped slightly to 194 in 1991 *(Yearbook of Ministry of Justice and Czech Republic Police, 1992)*. While I was riding with police officers on patrol in Prague one evening, the shift commander stated that while there used to be one or two murders per month in the city, that number had doubled over the past two years.

As previously mentioned, the criminal justice system has been weakened by losses of manpower among judges, prosecutors, and, to a lesser extent, among police. The overburdened police, who were unprepared for the increased crime, have experienced a further erosion in crimes "cleared" — a common measure of police effectiveness (Frant, 1992). Clearance rates dropped from 38.4% in 1990 to just 33.3% in 1991. Not only are police resources stretched to the limit, but as Deputy Chief Charvat (1992) noted, as early as 1964 there had been a plan to increase the Prague police force by 700 personnel. That goal, to reach a total of 3,200 uniformed police, had never been attained despite the fact that the city's population has since increased by 350,000. He added that "currently Prague 4 (district 4) has just one small station serving 80,000 inhabitants." One private citizen I later encountered told me that during the three years he had lived in that section of Prague he had only once seen a police officer in the district and that was because of a murder in a nearby dwelling.

Efforts to form better relationships between police and citizens appear to have succeeded since 1989, according to conversations with private citizens, police officers, and criminologists. Charvat (1992) stated that prior to the revolution citizens were apprehensive about any involvement with the police, but that the "hotline" was now working effectively. Earlier, citizens rarely called to report on crime against fellow citizens but currently it is common to do so. He stated that on a typical day during the pre-1989 period about 199 calls would be received, but that now the number has grown to approximately 700 calls per day. Some of the calls involved requests for crime prevention information, and the tone of calls revealed more trust in the police. In response to a question about whether the department had any interest in implementing a philosophy of community policing (including the extensive use of foot patrols, which has become popular in the United States), Charvat (1992) observed that there was already an extensive use of walking patrols and that ideally they would be increased, but that the lack of police personnel had forced the department to maintain a large number of motorized patrols to respond to crises. Police agencies are struggling to maintain even their present low numbers as officers are poorly paid. Comparable to many government workers, a police officer's starting salary is just 4,200 Czech korunas per month ($162 U.S.), and with inflation there is a lot of anxiety among government salaried workers generally.

In addition to the political and psychological sense of freedom that prevailed after the revolution of 1989, prison administrators and criminologists point to the "amnesty" offered to imprisoned offenders by former Czech President Vaclav Havel (Valkova, 1992). All offenders, not just those incarcerated for political offenses, who were serving two years or less, were suddenly released onto the streets of Prague and other communities. While several criminologists applauded Havel's good intentions, they claimed that Czech society was totally unprepared for the vast numbers who were released without funds, jobs, housing, or community ties. Director-General Karabec (1992) of the Czech Republic prison administration noted that the prison population was abruptly reduced from 28,000 in 1989 to just 13,000 by September 1992. Not surprisingly, some offenders have already been rearrested, as significant numbers of them returned to a life of crime.

ORGANIZED CRIME

In interviews with Czech Republic police administrators, they emphasized the role of "organized crime" as one of the major problems facing law enforcement. They noted that other than illegal money-changing schemes, the "East Bloc" countries had not experienced this type of criminal activity before. However, criminal gangs that had formed "cells" to exchange money on the black market have shifted gears and expanded into other areas. Art objects and antiques are now favorite targets, including castles and religious shrines in the countryside. Even tombstones have been fair game according to Barrett (1992). Prostitution has become more rampant, and criminal gangs have gotten their share of the profits. Government officials and police are now moving to regulate prostitution and to limit it to certain municipal districts, much like the way it has been controlled in cities such as Amsterdam, the Netherlands. Czech Republic Deputy Police Chief Frant (1992) also noted that foreigners from Russia, Bulgaria, Greece, and other countries are part of this new form of crime and that he expected matters would get worse before they get better. Rings of car thieves have begun to operate, and recently "luxury" cars have begun turning up in Poland.

Finally, interviews with police officials as well as doctors at Prague's "Drop-In" clinic, which treats drug abusers, revealed that drug abuse has yet to reach the epidemic proportions that it has in places like the United States (Griffin, 1992). Police claim that while organized crime elements are using Czech territory as a transit point for illicit substances, many Czech citizens are not affluent enough to purchase cocaine and heroin. Among the most commonly abused substances are amphetamines and anti-asthmatic drugs, according to psychologist Ivan Dovda (1992). He noted that it is possible to buy marijuana in Czechoslovakia and that some citizens have grown their own. While not happy with the current law enforcement practice of ignoring users while arresting sellers of illegal drugs, the Drop-In clinic staff have acquiesced with the new policy.

In summary, the new Czech Republic, like the other former communist nations of Eastern Europe that are moving toward democracy, will undoubtedly continue to experience increased crime rates unless some of these major problems can be addressed.

➤ DISCUSSION QUESTIONS

Periods of rapid change can produce negative consequences, among them crime. What political, economic, or social changes are taking place throughout the world that may help to explain current crime trends? What changes are taking place in the U.S. that may help to explain some of our crime problems?

REFERENCES

Auster, A. 1992 "Police Probe Abuse Charges," *The Prague Post,* October 27, Volume 2, No. 42, p. 1.

Barrett, A. 1992 "From Thefts of Art to Toilet Paper, Czechoslovakia Crime Wave Spreads," *The Wall Street Journal,* November 6, p. A10A.

Cerovsky, Z. 1992 Personal Communication to the Author, September 9.

Charvat, R. 1992 Personal Communication to the Author, September 25.

Dovda, I. 1992 Personal Communication to the Author, October 1.

Frant, Z. 1992 Personal Communication to the Author, September 22.

Griffin, M. 1992 "Charges Against Doctor Reflect Disagreement Over Czech Drug Policy," *The Prague Post,* September 8, p. 3.

Karabee, Z. 1992 Personal Communication to the Author, September 15.

Urbanek, E. 1992 Personal Communication to the Author, September 17.

Valkova, J. 1992 Personal Communication to the Author, September 24.

Yearbook of Ministry of Interior and Czech Republic Police 1992 "Development of Crime on the Territory of the Czech Republic," Government Publication of the Czech Republic.

The Sociocultural Approach in Controlling Violent Crime: A Case Study of *Siri* in Buginese-Makassarese Community

SOUTH SULAWESI, INDONESIA

■ *MUHAMMED MUSTOFA*

INTRODUCTORY NOTES

The following brief article examines the effects of the Buginese-Makassarese honor code on the incidence of violent crime in their society. In defense of a cultural standard of honor, natives are expected to carry out acts of violence (e.g., homicide) under certain circumstances in order to maintain their reputation and dignity. This standard may seem alien to the American reader, but one should keep in mind that the defense of honor may be the cause of many, if not most, homicides in the U.S. Luckenbill has noted that homicidal transactions almost always involve "face games" (David F. Luckenbill, "Criminal Homicide as a Situated Transaction," Social Problems, 25:1, 1977). These transactions begin when one participant interprets the other as having issued an insult. Ultimately, lethal violence is administered as a means of *saving face*. Likewise, Katz (1988) has argued that homicides are very typically preceded by an interaction in which one participant loses face, then becomes humiliated, and then flies into a rage (Jack Katz, *Seductions of Crime*, 1988).

Such responses, according to the "subculture of violence" thesis, are much more likely to occur in some communities than in others. Accordingly, members of certain socio-economic, racial, regional, or ethnic groups are more likely to accept violence as an appropriate response in certain situations than members of other groups. This has been one of the theories explaining why the predominance of homicides in the U.S. occurs in lower class communities.

SOURCE: Muhammad Mustofa, "The Sociocultural Approach in Controlling Crime: A Case Study of 'Siri' Phenomenon in Buginese-Makassarese Community, South Sulawesi, Indonesia," from *International Trends in Crime: East Meets West*, H. Strang and J. Vernon, eds. pp. 25–30. Reprinted with permission from the Australian Institute of Criminology, Canberra, Australia.

Why does crime occur? The explanation may be biological, psychological, juridical, anthropological, or sociological. Whatever approach is applied in explaining crime, criminological studies should always aim to be relevant and useful to the society in which such studies are carried out.

It ought then to follow that the result of criminological inquiries should provide bases for policies leading to the reduction of crime. In this regard Sellin has mentioned that "the result of such a study may afford a basis for social action or public policy which is in harmony with dominant attitudes" (Sellin, 1970, p. 6).

This paper will take a sociocultural approach, which seems the most appropriate in discussing strategies for controlling violent crime in Buginese-Makassarese society in Sulawesi. According to some studies (Nur, 1982, Ishak, 1985; Thontowi, 1986; Ariyanny, 1987), a considerable proportion of violent crime in that society flows from a particular sociocultural feature of the society, namely the phenomenon of *siri*.

Siri is best interpreted as the concept of honor, dignity, or reputation of a person and his family. If one's *siri* is perceived to have been downgraded by another in public, then according to customary law (*adat*), that person and his family are obliged to restore their *siri* through the execution of violent conduct (usually homicide) against those who have caused the loss of *siri*. If such action is not taken, then those who have lost their *siri* will be considered worthless by society.

The knowledge of crime causation in the case of *siri* is very valuable for controlling crime. Sutherland and Cressey mentioned that such a knowledge: "would be useful in control of crime, provided it could be 'applied' in much the same way as an engineer 'applies' the scientific theories of the physicist" (Sutherland & Cressey, 1977, p. 522).

In line with the assertion of Sutherland & Cressey, violent crime in the Buginese-Makassarese society, which is attributable to *siri*, may be controlled through social planning to alter the orientation of the society from the use of violence in resolving conflict, into more acceptable behavior in accordance with dominant attitudes in the society, which are anti-violent.

To explain how the sociocultural approach might work in controlling violent crime in Buginese-Makassarese society, the discussion will be divided into two parts: the sociocultural circumstances in which *siri* is used as a rationale to execute violent behavior; and the requirements for an effective and successful sociocultural approach in controlling *siri*.

THE SOCIOCULTURAL CIRCUMSTANCES IN WHICH *SIRI* IS USED AS A RATIONALE TO EXECUTE VIOLENT BEHAVIOR

Literally, *siri* means dignity or honor or reputation, but as a sociocultural concept it has two meanings which seem contradictory. Firstly, *siri ripakasiri* is the deep feeling of shame that one's dignity has been degraded by others in public. Secondly, *siri masiri* is a way of life which directs one's spirit to gain success.

This paper deals only with the *ripakasiri* issue. In the case of *ripakasiri*, if a person perceives that his dignity has been degraded by others, he is socially expected to restore his dignity by killing the offenders. The reason is that, according to the Buginese-Makassarese value system, a person who has lost his *siri (mate siri)* is no longer valuable as a human being. His status is the same as an animal, so it is better to die than to live without dignity. To die as a consequence of fighting for *siri* is a worthy way of dying (Abidin, 1983, p. 7).

Ripakasiri is felt not only by the direct victim himself but also by all of his family. Thus, the duty to restore *siri* is not only the duty of the victim but the duty of every member of the family. The duty to restore *siri* will be executed any time or anywhere whenever possible, even though the incident may have occurred in the past. In Buginese-Makassarese society this solidarity strengthens the *siri* value.

As violence in *ripakasiri* is socially or culturally accepted or even expected, Abidin (1983, p. 3) comments that it is not a revenge but a customary moral obligation that must be observed. Errington (1977, p. 43) further reports that for the Buginese-Makassarese, there is no more important goal in their life than to maintain *siri*.

Situations in which *ripakasiri* might occur originally related to marriage affairs — for instance, elopement as a result of a young man and his girlfriend not obtaining approval for their marriage from the girl's parents. Elopement might also occur if no agreement could be reached between the parties concerning the number or the value of the bridegroom's gifts to the bride. Beside marriage affairs, homicide, rape and sexual harassment are the most common situations resulting in *ripakasiri*.

Nowadays, *ripakasiri* may also include any incident which is perceived to be humiliating even though such incidents may be regarded as trivial elsewhere. For instance, in the Mandarese community (another ethnic group in South Sulawesi which has the *siri* concept), to touch somebody's head is considered to cause loss of *siri*. Such an act would cause one to feel *ripakasiri* which could lead to violent conduct in order to restore *siri*.

Even though *ripakasiri* is expected to be restored through violent conduct, conciliation between conflicting parties is available. In Buginese society, if the case has been brought before the customary leader, the person who feels *ripakasiri* is not allowed to take any action against the offenders until the dispute is heard. However, in the Makassarese community the dispute is discontinued only if the offenders have sought asylum and have been granted protection by the customary leader, and are on the premises of the protector. If the offender is outside the yard of the customary leader's house, the protection is no longer in force.

Intervention from the customary leader to the disputing parties is possible because both parties respect the *siri* of the leader. However, if the intervention fails, or the disputing parties do not respect the leader's decision, it will be perceived by the leader as degrading his *siri* and will cause *ripakasiri*.

The customary leaders in Buginese-Makassarese society are known as *Pabicara*. Their tasks are to mediate between their followers and officials of the government, to arrange marriages, to conduct customary ceremonies, and to settle disputes. Unfortunately, the role of *Pabicara* in settling disputes is not acknowledged in the Indonesian legal system. Moreover, at present there remain only a small number of *Pabicara* who have the authority of the custom. Their role and position will not be replaced in the future because the influence of the custom has declined (see, for example, Mattulada, 1980, p. 106).

Even so, the value of *siri* still exists in Buginese-Makassarese society because the value is transferred to the young generation through the socialization process. However, observers of the culture believe that the *siri* value which is now observed is distorted, because now the Buginese-Makassarese are only acquainted with the *siri ripakasiri* rather than *siri masiri*, and disputes which now result in the use of violent conduct to restore siri are not like previous disputes.

In comparing the Buginese-Makassarese with other subcultures where violence flows from the value system (see Wolfgang & Ferracuti, 1970), there are similarities because of the readiness to use a weapon. In this regard, there is a traditional curved dagger which is almost always carried by the Buginese-Makassarese male—the *badik*. Because violent crimes in South Sulawesi almost always involved the use of the *badik*, between 1985 and 1987 the police in that area conducted operations to seize *badiks* from owners, sellers and producers. It was expected that the operation would result in the reduction of violent crimes. In fact it did not. The failure of the police operation was blamed on defects in the operation itself, which did not consider the sociocultural circumstances which predisposed violent crime, that is the existence of the *siri* value.

A SOCIOCULTURAL APPROACH IN CONTROLLING *SIRI*

To run an effective sociocultural approach in dealing with *siri*, it should be based on knowledge of how Buginese-Makassarese society operates. In this respect, a carefully planned program of research is the answer.

The research program should be staffed by anthropologists, communication experts, psychologists, legal specialists and criminologist-sociologists. The main goal of the research would be to reformulate the *siri* value into an acceptable value in accordance with the dominant, non-violent, attitudes. The program could be executed through the promotion of non-violent values.

The first task of the researchers would be to identify sociocultural resources which can be utilized in the promotion activities. For instance, they need to identify:

1. who has the capacity to act as agents of change, if the customary leaders no longer exist;

2. what kind of folklore exists which could be utilized for the transformation of new ideas;

3. what, how, and by whom should the reformulation of the *siri* value be carried out.

In these tasks, the anthropologists might take the dominant role.

After the sociocultural resources which can be utilized have been identified, the next stage is to plan what kind of communication can be used in transforming new ideas effectively in the community. It is important to investigate what circumstances exist in the community which might be helpful in this process. This stage is the responsibility of the communication experts and psychologists.

Finally, it should be determined in which area the program would be executed, how long it should take and when the local community would be involved. Since the results of the program would not be visible in the short term, they need to be determined by monitoring and evaluating instruments in the program's design. A control area also needs to be identified, which would be used later in the measurement of the program's effectiveness.

It is vital that the researchers in the program act simply as facilitators who provide ideas to the local communities. Thus, it is necessary to consider how we can ensure that the local community perceives that the program is based on their own activities, in their own interest.

Based on the empirical experience gained through the program, the legal experts could plan how the sociocultural values and customs of local community could be adopted by the formal legal system in the conciliation process of dispute settlements.

Finally, criminologists might learn the advantages and disadvantages of the sociocultural approach in dealing with crime which might lead to some useful proposals in criminal policies.

➤ DISCUSSION QUESTIONS

It could be said that the Buginese-Makassarese constitute a "subculture" within the larger Indonesian population. The norms and values of this subculture prescribe violence in particular situations. Is this "subculture of violence" thesis relevant to crime in the U.S.? Why do you think such a thesis might be a very controversial one?

REFERENCES

Abidin, A. Z. 1983 *Persepsi Orang Bugis, Makasar Tentang Hukum Negara Dan Dunia Luar,* Bandung, Alumni.

Ariyanny, R. 1987. "Tinjauan Kriminologis Atas Masalah *Siri*," Unpublished Sarjana Thesis, University of Indonesia.

Errington, S. 1986 Meaning and Power in a Southeast Asian Realm, Book Manuscript, February.

Ishak 1985 "Pembunuhan Yang Disebabkan Oleh *Siri*," Unpublished Sarjana Thesis, Hasanuddin University.

Mattulada 1980 "Manusia dan Kebudayaan Bugis-Makasar," in *Berita Antropologi*, vol. XI, no. 38, July-September.

Nur, M. N. 1982 "Delik Pembunuhan Dalam Hubungannya Dengan *Siri*," Unpublished Sarjana Thesis, Hasanuddin University.

Sellin, T. 1970 "A Sociological Approach," in *The Sociology of Crime and Delinquency*, M.E. Wolfgang, L. Savits & N. Johnston, eds., New York: John Wiley & Sons Inc., p. 6.

Sutherland, E. H. & Cressey, D 1977 "Learning and Transmitting Criminal Behavior", in *Crime and Justice*, L. Radzinovics & M.E. Wolfgang, eds., vol. 1., New York: Basic Books Inc., p.522.

Thontowi, J. 1986 *Siri* dan Konflik Sosial di Sulawesi Selatan," in *Keadilan*, no. 4, p. XIII.

Wolfgang, M.E. & Ferracuti, F. 1979 "The Subculture of Violence," *The Sociology of Crime and Delinquency*, pp. 380–91.

Imaginary Constructions and Forensic Reconstructions of Fatal Violence Against Women: Implications for Community Violence Prevention

SOUTH AFRICA

- ■ *ALEXANDER BUTCHART*
- ■ *LEONARD B. LERER*
- ■ *MARTIN TERRE BLANCHE*

INTRODUCTORY NOTES

The following is an article originally published in the journal *Forensic Science International*. A forensic scientist (also called a criminalist) is the expert who examines the crime scene and the criminal evidence, and is often called upon to testify as to the evidence in court. However, this article follows very much in the tradition of social psychology and is relevant to the study, not so much of crime, but of the public perceptions of crime. Our perceptions of criminal victimization often bear little correlation to the reality of criminal victimization.

A principle tenet of social psychology is called the *Thomas Theorem* (coined by sociologist W.I. Thomas); it states that "If people define situations as real, they are real in their consequences." If people perceive that the crime rate is soaring they will react accordingly, irrespective of whether or not the crime rate is actually increasing. The fear of crime is as real as crime itself. In the U.S. it is likely that the fear of crime is as much (or more) the result of media coverage of crime as it is of crime itself. Fear of crime is very important to the criminologist because it affects both people's quality of life and society's response to crime. Inasmuch as the media distorts the actual picture of crime—by exaggerating the likelihood of

SOURCE: A. Butchart, L.B. Lerer, and M.T. Blanche, "Imaginary Constructions and Forensic Reconstructions of Fatal Violence Against Women: Implications for Community Violence Prevention", from *Forensic Science International*, vol. 64, (1994) pp. 21–34 (edited). Reprinted with permission from Elsevier Science Ireland Ltd.

violent victimization, especially stranger-to-stranger violence —it impedes our ability to recognize the most likely dangers of crime and respond appropriately.

Perhaps one of the most important points made in this article is that patterns of homicide are gender-specific. That is, the situations in which men and women are killed are often quite different. This pattern holds true not just in South Africa, but in the U.S. and probably throughout most of the world.

Another important point relevant to the American reader is the authors' use of the phrases "entrapment in the endemic violence of poverty" and "the violence of everyday life amongst the poor." In the inner cities of the U.S., as well as in Cape Town, South Africa, people lose their lives by stepping in the line of fire, or knowing a criminal, or being mistaken for knowing a criminal. These events, while not frequent in lower class neighborhoods, are so rare in middle or upper class neighborhoods that they might be considered absolutely freakish.

INTRODUCTION

Increasing attention is being paid to interpersonal violence as a public health priority in the developing world [1]. In South Africa, seemingly interminable political and factional violence [2] should be viewed against the backdrop of unacceptable levels of premature death due to injury [3] and endemic interpersonal violence [4,5]. As this interpersonal violence is rooted in poverty and deprivation [6,7], the key to its attenuation may therefore lie in massive socioeconomic and political transformation. These, however, are long term objectives and public health professionals are faced in the short term with the need to provide appropriate interventions in particular at-risk populations [8]. These interventions should be designed for specific groups, such as women [9,10], where multiple burdens of racial, social and sexual oppression [5,11–13] trap victims, potential victims and perpetrators in a complex mix of structural and psychological dynamics that render such violence resistant to social and political change.

To design appropriate and acceptable interventions it may be important to take into account not only the existing body of descriptive epidemiological data [4,5,11–13] or population perspective on violence against women, but also individual perspectives. This has been described by Jeffery as providing "a way to translate epidemiologic findings into terms that are salient to individuals" and is based on the public health utility of exploring the difference between population perspectives (based on epidemiological data) and individual perspectives (based on personal estimates of risk) of risk factors and "unhealthy" behavior [14]. A particular problem such as violence against women may from the population perspective be regarded as an urgent public health priority, whereas the individual woman may see the odds of her avoiding this problem as stacked in her favor—with or without behavior change. The disjunctions between the two perspectives may cause information, which from the population perspective appears salient to prevention, to appear irrelevant from the individual perspective. It is this tension that requires articulation in the case of particular populations and this paper aims to contrast imaginary constructions of fatal violence against women (individual perspectives) with forensic data on actual homicides (population perspectives) in Cape Town, South Africa, and to explore the implications of this juxtaposition for violence prevention.

SUBJECTS AND METHODS

Imaginary Constructions of Female Homicide
(the Individual Perspective)

Fifty African[1] women (median age 27.7 years) were interviewed during February, 1992, at a major railway station in Cape Town. [There] were two female African medical students who had spent a period training in reflexive interviewing techniques. They were instructed to approach all African women waiting on the platform and request an interview with the statement that they were doing research into what women thought about violence and that all responses would be totally anonymous. Interviewees who assented were then asked: "Imagine you were to die violently at the hands of another person, can you tell me how it will happen?" The response, in the home language of the interviewee, was tape recorded and thereafter transcribed and translated into English. The interviews were conducted in the late afternoon with almost all the respondents being on their way home from work. Of 62 women approached, 50 agreed to be interviewed, with the majority of those refusing claiming that they did not have sufficient time for the interview. Five interviews were not included in the analysis due to technical problems relating to the quality of the tape recording.

The type of story elicited from respondents is illustrated by the following example:

> My boyfriend and I were coming from a New Year's Eve festival in the morning. In the street three guys came and started quarrelling with my boyfriend. They stabbed him and took his money. Then they raped me on the side of the road before killing me too (Respondent 40).

To analyze and compare both the content and structure of the 45 narratives, the following procedure was adopted. Each individual narrative was read as a story composed of discreet but related elements through which the plot unfolds to construct a scenario of violent death. The example presented above commences by setting the scene through a description of the context in which the attack will occur—it is New Year's Eve and the victim is with her boyfriend. This is the first element of the plot. Then, the narrator introduces an element of potential threat as "three guys" approach—this is the second element. The third element consists of provocative verbal and physical actions—quarrelling followed by stabbing, robbery and rape—that confirm that this will be a violent episode and transform the "three guys" from neutral strangers into aggressors. Finally, the fourth element consists of the homicide itself, in this case referred to simply as "killing" by the narrator.

By analyzing each story in this way, all these elements were extracted from the stories, grouped according to their positioning within the stories, and these groups were labelled with headings and subheadings that capture the essence of their contribution to the plot. This structured collection of narrative elements used by the respondents to construct their stories of imaginary death is known as a "discursive repertoire", and is used in discourse analysis to identify the "building blocks" available to individuals speaking or writing in particular domains about particular topics [15].

Forensic Data from Actual Female Homicides
(the Population Perspective)

A sample of 73 African homicide victims (median age 29.5 years) was extracted from a detailed study of female homicide in metropolitan Cape Town between January

1990 and July 1991 [5]. The information obtained from the postmortem records was supplemented with a study of the police reports. This sample represented over 95% of the African female homicides that were investigated in metropolitan Cape Town during these 18 months and reflects the intensity of violence in specific residential areas. Blood alcohol concentrations (BAC) were available for 60 (82%) of the homicides and these are illustrated together with type of death in Table 1.

RESULTS AND DISCUSSION

It was as if a female death could be entrusted only to words; that only words could see it through.   (Nicole Loraux) [16]

Imaginary Constructions of Female Homicide

The repertoire of events produced through the extraction and labelling of the elements present in the 45 stories is presented in Table 2. Inspection of this table shows that it was possible to classify the elements under four main headings, each representing a distinct phase in the homicidal process.

The first phase was labelled "Incipient Context" and consisted of scene-setting elements that suggest the type of incident which was to follow. Within the phase, elements suggesting that they would be "mugged" (in particular while commuting to a legitimate destination such as work, the shops, or home) were just over twice as common as those suggesting that they would be killed in the course of domestic conflict, political or criminal violence, or "mayhem".

The second phase was labelled "Becoming Conspicuous" as it consisted of elements whereby respondents portrayed processes through which the woman was singled out for attack or came to attention as a potential victim. Two subcategories of elements were particularly prominent, being those where the victim is approached by a group, and those where she met an individual (usually a stranger). Scenarios where the victim came to prominence while witnessing a fight or robbery in progress were also quite common.

The third phase, labelled "Provocation and Pacification", consisted of a clearly defined collection of verbal and non-verbal actions that impelled the encounter between victim and aggressor into a physically violent confrontation. Here, non-verbal and verbal provocation by the aggressor appeared most frequently. On the part of

TABLE 1: African female homicides by recorded blood alcohol concentration and type of death, January 1, 1990–June 30, 1991 [5]

BAC (g/100 ml)	SHARP HOMICIDE	BLUNT HOMICIDE	FIREARM HOMICIDE
0.00	15	5	10
0.01–0.09	2	0	0
0.10–0.19	2	5	1
0.20–0.29	11	4	0
>0.30	4	1	0

TABLE 2: The homicide repertoire, with frequency of element occurrence (in parentheses)

1. INCIPIENT CONTEXT[a]

Mugging (22)
Aa. Robbery (4)
Ab. Narrator journeying to legit. destin. (18)

Mayhem (10)
Ac. Tranquil at home (5)
Ad. At club/shebeen (4)
Ae. At school

Domestic Tension (13)
Af. Sibling rivalry (3)
Ag. Lovers'/spouses' tiff (3)
Ah. Sexual jealousy (6)
Ai. Family feud (1)

Criminal/Political (9)
Aj. Gangland (4)
Ak. Taxi war (2)
Al. Assassination (1)
Am. Racial/political intolerance (2)

2. BECOMING CONSPICUOUS

Approached by group (12)
Ba. On street (11)
Bb. Enter house (1)

Meet individual (13)
Bc. Meet stranger (8)
Bd. Meet ex-lover/rival (5)

Group loyalty/membership (3)
Bf. Ethnic affiliation questioned (1)
Bg. Group loyalty challenged (1)
Bh. Suspected informant (1)

Avoidance (1)
Bi. Avoid conflict (1)

Killer sees money (2)

Narrator approaches (2)

Bj. Looks at victim's purse (2)

Bk. Offers charity (1)

Narrator witnesses (8)

Bl. Drunkenly greets (1)

Bm. Quarrel/fight (7)
Bn. Break-in (1)

3. PROVOCATION AND PACIFICATION

Aggressor provocation (79)
Verbal (3)
Ca. Interrogatory questioning (4)
Cb. Lewd proposition (5)
Cc. Demand (5)
Cd. Threaten to kill unless... (3)
Ce. Accuse (9)
Cf. Abuse/demean (3)
Cg. Lure out (1)

Non-verbal (49)
Da. Rob victim (3)
Db. Reveal weapon (4)
Dc. Beat up (10)
Dd. Circle/follow (6)
De. Manhandle (8)
Df. Rape (9)
Dg. Forcibly enter victim's dwelling (5)
Dh. Abduct (4)

Narrator provocation (14)
Verbal (6)
Ga. Refuse to talk (3)
Gb. Fail to understand (1)
Gc. Intervene (2)

Non-Verbal (8)
Ha. Identify attacker (3)
Hb. Struggle against
Hc. Ignore (2)

Narrator pacification (18)
Verbal (12)
Ia. Answer (4)
Ib. Explain (3)
Ic. Cry for help (5)

Non-Verbal (7)
Ja. Attempt escape (5)
Jb. Keep still (1)
Jc. Comply (1)

4. KILLING

Narrator (45)
La. Stabbed (16)
Lb. Blunt force (5)
Lc. Shot (8)
Ld. "Killed" (13)
Le. Petrol bombed (1)
Lf. Thrown from train (1)
Lg. Strangled (1)

Aggressor
—— Empty ——

[a] Elements in this category total 54, as nine of the stories began with phrases suggesting more than one incipient context.

victims, the most commonly imagined actions in this phase were verbal attempts to pacify the aggressor, although a number of provocative actions by the victim were also depicted.

The final phase, "Killing", described the homicide itself, and in it stabbing was the most frequently imagined type of force resulting in death, followed by unspecified "killing", shooting and blunt force.

To summarize these findings, the most commonly imagined scenario was one in which a woman on her way to or from a legitimate destination was either approached by a group or met an individual. Following this, the stories converge around clusters of provocatory and pacificatory actions, with verbal provocation by the attacker and verbal attempts at pacification on the victim's part preceding non-verbal aggressor and victim actions such as physical abuse and attempts to fight back that were immediate precursors to the killing.

Contrasting Imaginary and Real Female Homicide

In the absence of comprehensive information including the testimony of witnesses and suspected perpetrators, forensic data of actual homicide victims cannot reconstruct the homicidal process with anything approaching the rich detail produced through the analysis of imaginary accounts. However, in the present study, examination of 73 actual female homicide victims coupled with scrutiny of the largely impoverished police records available for each victim did yield some idea of the events preceding death. These data are now reported in tandem with a comparison between them and the imaginary accounts, which revealed the following divergencies and convergencies.

In contrast to the dominant image in the imaginary accounts of a woman being raped and then killed while commuting, police data records the homicidal incidents in 86% of the actual cases as occurring at or in close proximity to the victims' homes. For over 50% of actual cases, the perpetrator was recorded as being someone intimately acquainted with or well known to the victim, while only 13 out of 45 (29%) of the imagined incidents depicted the aggressor as a spouse, lover or acquaintance.

A major disjunction was also seen with respect to the role of alcohol as a proximal cause of the events culminating in death. Of the 60 cases in the mortuary sample where BACs were obtained, over 50% were elevated [5]. While this would lead one to expect alcohol being accorded a prominent role in imaginary accounts, this was not the case. Only a single respondent depicted her own consumption of alcohol as contributing to the generation of a homicidal context:

> It was the festive season and I was in a very happy mood, so I had gone down to the local shebeen (tavern) to enjoy myself and I had quite a lot to drink. I was sitting with this other guy who was my friend from another place. Then my boyfriend with whom I have a child came there and didn't ask any questions. He assumed that it was my boyfriend that I was sitting with, so he grabbed me from there, he started hitting me with the handle of a pick axe, and then he damaged my brain and I died in hospital. (Respondent 19)

A further two stories refer to the attacker's alcoholism, although in both cases he is depicted as sober at the time of the killing, while two more imaginary homicides occur after parties or visits to shebeens—contexts in which it must be assumed drinking takes place.

While the divergence between imagined and forensically reconstructed scenarios of female homicide outweighed points of agreement, there were three areas of convergence. The first concerned the violent interaction between aggressor and victim immediately preceding death, with the manhandling and physical abuse which was prominent in the imaginary accounts being mirrored in the forensic evidence, with 53% of the mortuary sample having multiple wounds on their bodies. The second concerned the rape of victims prior to death, with police data referring to this possibility in 18% of the mortuary sample, while rape and attempted rape was depicted in 20% of the imaginary accounts. The third relates to the type of force resulting in death, with both imaginary accounts and forensic records (Table 1) agreeing on the predominance of sharp force.

When these points of divergence and convergence are considered together, it is evident that the divergencies cluster around the circumstance and personal actions that put a woman at risk for entering a violent situation—place of injury, relationship with attacker and the role of alcohol. In contrast, the convergencies concern the physical abuse, possible rape, and use of sharp force that precede a killing—all concrete actions that unfold once a violent situation has been entered.

Limitations of This Study

Interviewees were mostly employed commuters who may not represent the same sample base from which the actual homicides were drawn. Sampling bias of the actual interviewees was limited due to the high response rate, although it must be noted that the venue (a railway station) may have influenced the responses. However, commuter attack scenarios were equally prominent in a sample of imaginary accounts of non-fatal violence drawn from male and female residents of Soweto who were interviewed at home (Butchart and Terre Blanche, unpublished data). This suggests it is unlikely that the site of interview exerted a significant influence upon narrative content. Another limitation is that the attempt to contrast imaginary and actual incidents may be problematic in that it poses a question concerning a fatal attack to interviewees for whom non-fatal violence against women would be a more relevant issue.

It may, therefore, be appropriate in similar studies to vary the way in which the interviews are conducted. For instance, women who are first asked to talk about non-fatal violence may be more willing to countenance husbands and boyfriends in the role of perpetrators than those who are asked at the outset to imagine deadly violence. Further, asking respondents to imagine a violent incident involving "a woman" as opposed to the respondent herself could reduce the level of psychological threat and defensiveness associated with talking about such dangers in the first person ("I"). However, this latter strategy is problematic, insofar as it invites the tendency to attribute risks to others but not to oneself, identified by Taylor and Brown [27] as one of the mechanisms by which people maintain a positive sense of psychological well-being.

The forensic data are based on police accounts which are often impoverished and possibly biased reflections of the circumstances surrounding a homicidal attack, and, as in the case of the imaginary narratives, concentrate exclusively on fatal violence. It is unlikely that many non-fatal attacks on women even come to the attention of the police in South Africa, and all law enforcement activities in this country should be viewed in the broader context of a "culture of violence" [2].

Images and Themes of Fatal Violence

Incidents of violence against women occur largely "behind closed doors" [17] and this invisibility is further increased by the complex psychological dynamics that trap battered women in a vicious circle of abuse and reconciliation [18]. This inaccessibility may force non-victims to base their beliefs and attitudes on indirect, vicarious experiences of interpersonal violence obtained through sources such as rumor, gossip and the media. If this is the source of the "factual" aspects of the narratives, then it is likely that the backdrop would reflect the texture of township life, and the following section highlights some of the common themes relating to both imagined and real fatal violence against women.

Perpetrators and Victims

Thirty-six of the 45 interview respondents (80%) imagined themselves being killed by men. Most of these imaginary accounts did not reflect the reality that attacks against women are often carried out by members of family or intimate acquaintances, a victim-aggressor relationship closely paralleled in the developed world [9,19,20]. Of the seven who imagined that another woman might be the killer, five nevertheless accorded pivotal roles to men (boyfriends or husbands), who were presented as catalysts of sexual rivalry that culminated in killing. Respondent 31 succinctly captures the tenor of references to power and gender relationships characteristic of almost all the stories:

> If I had to think of being violently attacked, I would think of being violated by men. Maybe a situation of being physically violated, being raped and then killed afterwards.

Rape

The large number of stories involving rape suggests that female homicide is experienced as an element in a wider theme of gender related violence [10, 11]. A rape-kill sequence concluded the story of seven respondents, as in the following examples:

> they raped me—after that they killed me (Respondent 14)

> He just came in, raped me and killed me (Respondent 24)

> then he raped me and afterwards he killed me (Respondent 38).

In other instances the rape and killing were described in greater detail but still occurred in quick succession, as in the following story:

> They took me to their house and tied me on the bed and raped me, exchanging me amongst themselves. When they were finished they shot me to death (Respondent 47).

The immediate precursor to the homicide is not, of course, always presented as rape, but the weak position of women relative to men is emphasized in a variety of other ways. Sexual jealousy on the part of husbands or boyfriends accounted for four of the killings, while in other cases women imagined being killed simply as a consequence of being associated with husbands or lovers.

Victim Precipitation

Another group of stories depicted scenarios where a man's temper was ignited by the victim saying the wrong thing, or by her refusal to respond to his verbal advances. These male attackers were presented as forcing themselves on women, or as bearing grudges for being rejected, and simultaneously believing, as did Respondent 44's imaginary father, "that he will never be told what to do by a woman". The term "victim precipitation" was created to describe a situation in which the victim was the first to use physical force during the fatal confrontation [21]. Large variations exist between the proportion of homicides in which victim precipitation is thought to play a role [21, 22] and little information is available on the role of verbal provocation by the victim.

Types of Violence

The method of fatal attack may reflect the types of violence that predominate in a particular society [5,19]. In the case of Cape Town, knives are the most commonly used weapons in violent attacks [5], although the increasing availability and use of firearms may result in higher mortality associated with family and intimate assault [23].

Alcohol

A clear association exists between alcohol consumption and interpersonal violence [24]. It can be hypothesized that the relative exclusion of alcohol consumption from the imaginary accounts expresses a reluctance to present oneself as given to drinking. This may be due to "flawed" personal constructions of violence that blame the intoxicated victim [25], and the sociocultural complexities of alcohol use [26], which include the tendency of entertainment and advertising to romanticize the effects of alcohol and mask its negative associations [14].

Disempowerment and Social Enmeshment

Pervasive female disempowerment would appear to be modulated in its expression by regional and socioeconomic specifics. In this study these included entrapment in the endemic violence of poverty [11, 12] as articulated by the expectation of eight women that they would be killed as a consequence of being able to identify criminals. For example:

> The thing which caused them to kill me was because they saw that I could recognize one of them because I called his name (Respondent 16)

> When they saw that I had seen them, they just shot me (Respondent 31)

> When they came back they heard rumors that I was the one who told the police about them. (Respondent 41)

A further three women imagined that homicide might follow from being identified (albeit mistakenly in one instance) as criminals or associates of criminals:

This person had been sent to kill someone, and when they are going on an assassination they killed the wrong person—me (Respondent 11)

and they said it was me who sold her children out with the tsotsies (gangsters) (Respondent 37)

In the township there are rumors that my brothers are the ones who are killing people. (Respondent 42)

Other stories problematized identity by constructing scenarios where the attacker made a point of dragging personal information (such as name and destination) out of his victim, and overall the identity issue appears related to the ethos of revenge that pervaded many stories. Attackers, although perhaps nominally strangers, suddenly reveal themselves as bearing a grudge from some past incident or, alternatively, metamorphose from friends into killers when a past grudge is revealed.

IMPLICATIONS FOR PREVENTION

Regulatory Strategies

Regulatory strategies are most effective "when the risk behaviors of many individuals have a common pathway through publicly controllable institutions" [14]. Violence against women occurs, for the most part, in domestic settings beyond the public eye and at the hands of known assailants [5,17], making it singularly unamenable to prevention through regulatory means.

There is no common pathway through the "publicly controllable institutions" referred to by Jeffery [14]—except through post-hoc action, possibly of limited utility, such as the prosecution of perpetrators [9]. If killings were actually most likely to occur while women were commuting to or from work, as the majority of our sample imagined, improved security measures on trains and taxis, and in township streets, could have a major impact on female homicide (as it may well have for male homicide), but the privacy of the domestic setting renders it very difficult to regulate the behavior of perpetrators.

Alcohol use can to a certain extent be regulated. The large number of informal taverns or "shebeens" operating in South Africa's townships have increasingly joined into larger networks and, for the most part, obtain their liquor from central merchants, thus facilitating regulation through price control [28]. Further, control could be exerted over the commercial promotion of alcohol in an attempt to reduce the unrealistically positive light in which advertising portrays its use [14].

Educational Strategies

Educational strategies work best when individuals expect substantial benefits at little personal cost from behavior change [14]. From the point of view of an individual woman, the risk of homicidal death is small, while the personal cost of behavior change to avoid the identified "risk factors" (being at or near one's home, in the company of male friends or relatives, drinking) is impossibly high. There may, however, be some utility in alerting women to the fact that the real threat comes from men who are "near and dear", rather than from faceless strangers in public places, and to point out that they may be at greater risk when drinking. Although avoiding these risks is, for the most part, impossible, greater vigilance in such situations could increase a woman's safety, an assumption that underlies educational programs aimed at alerting female adolescents to the dangers of "date rape" [29]. The tendency to generalize on the assumption that "if it hasn't happened to me yet, it probably will not (happen to me) in the future" [30], could be highlighted in the area of abusive relationships which have not yet resulted in physical violence, and an educational program dealing with the precursors of violence such as the combination between alcohol and verbally provocative behavior [might be useful].

Whatever form educational interventions take, fine-grained information could alert women about how women think about the possibility of being killed and can provide invaluable clues on how to structure preventive messages. Besides the factual information provided, this study indicated that violence, whether imaginary or real, has an element of "process, narrative or choreography" as the fatal attack unfolds. This aspect is especially highlighted by the difference between perceptions and realities concerning the circumstances surrounding a fatal attack. The tensions between the imaginary and factual aspects, such as violence in intimate relationships, the role of alcohol and provocatory behavior combined with the idea that violence is not an isolated event but a "process", yielded a hypothetical foundation for an experimental violence prevention program. A community-based dance-theatre company, Jazzart, was approached with the research material and asked to incorporate the salient features of both the imaginary and actual homicide data in a program designed for presentation at various venues including factories, community centers and public areas [31,32]. The dance sequences depict both fictitious commuter scenarios commonly found in stories about female death and the interpersonal violence suggested by forensic evidence, embedding these within the wider context of poverty and oppression. The success of the intervention in broadening audiences' repertoires for thinking about violence against women is currently being evaluated using both questionnaires and a methodology similar to that described in this paper.

CONCLUSION

Imaginary narratives of violent death produce an evocative portrait of a population at risk and expose the violence of everyday life amongst the poor. The present study is limited by its use of only one method to collect and analyze individual women's perspectives and this exclusive focus on women, furthermore, provides a partial view of the problem, and risks blaming the victim, a situation distant from the true determinants of violence against women [5,33]. It is also important to acknowledge that a different reading of the fictional accounts (such as from an explicitly feminist perspective) may well have revealed different and equally important common factors. The perceptions of men—both perpetrators and non-perpetrators —need to be articulated too. Only once a comprehensive picture is produced that merges population and individual perspectives drawn from potential victims and aggressors will it be possible to design fully comprehensive prevention strategies. Despite these limitations, the present study not only revealed some remarkable similarities and important disjunctions between perceptions and realities of female homicide, but also emphasized the preventive utility of interpreting epidemiological data in the light of the psychosocial milieu reflected in ordinary peoples' talk about violent death.

NOTE

1. Disparities in socioeconomic and health status in South Africa are strongly linked to legally defined racial categories. As (until recently) official terminology made use of the terms white, Asian, and colored, we have used the term African in place of black for the purposes of clarity.

➤ DISCUSSION QUESTIONS

How do you think the imaginary constructions of one's own violent death compare between South African black women and American black women? What about between American black women and American white women? What about between American women and American men? What do these comparisons say about our respective societies, and about the gender-specific nature of criminal victimization?

NOTES

1. S.K. Stansfield and G.S. Smith, McGreevey, Injury. Forthcoming in D.T. Jamison, W.H. Mosely, J.L. Bobadilla and A.R. Measham (eds.), *Disease Control Priorities in Developing Countries*, Oxford University Press for the World Bank, New York, 1993.

2. S. Marks and N. Andersson, The epidemiology and culture of violence. In N.C. Manganyi and A. du Toit (eds.), *Political Violence and the Struggle in South Africa*, Southern Books, Halfway House, 1990, pp. 29–70.

3. D. Bradshaw, R.E. Dorrington and F. Sitas, The level of mortality in South Africa in 1985—what does it tell us about health? *S. Afr. Med. J.*, 82 (1992) 237–240.

4. A. Butchart and D.S.O. Brown, Non-fatal injuries due to interpersonal violence in Johannesburg, Soweto: Incidence, determinants and consequences. *Forensic Sci. Int.*, 52 (1991) 35–51.

5. L.B. Lerer, Women, homicide and alcohol in Cape Town, South Africa. *Forensic Sci. Int.*, 53 (1992) 93–99.

6. J.R. Blau and P.M. Blau, The cost of inequality: Metropolitan structure and violent crime. *Am. Sociol. Rev.*, 47 (1982) 114–129.

7. H.A. Bulhan, *Frantz Fanon and the Psychology of Oppression*, Plenum Press, New York, 1985.

8. D. Yach and J. Seager, *Urbanisation and Health in South Africa: The Medical Research Council's Experience* (Medical Research Council report to the President's Council), Medical Research Council, Cape Town, 1991.

9. A. Goetting, Female victims of homicide: A portrait of their killers and the circumstances of their deaths. *Violence Victims*, 6 (1991) 159–168.

10. Council on Scientific Affairs, Violence against women. *J. Am. Med. Assoc.*, 267 (1992) 3184–3189.

11. J.A. Grisso, A.R. Wishner, D.F. Schwarz, B.A. Weene, J.H. Holmes and R.L. Sutton, A population based study of injuries in inner city women. *Am. J. Epidemiol.*, 134 (1991) 59–68.

12. A.R. Wishner, D.F. Schwarz, J.A. Grisso, J.H. Holmes and R.L. Sutton, Interpersonal violence related injuries in an African-American community in Philadelphia. *Am. J. Public Health*, 81 (1991) 1474–1476.

13. L.E. Saltzman, J.A. Mercy, M.L. Rosenberg, W.R. Elsea, G. Napper, N.K. Sikes, R.J. Waxweiler and the Collaborative Working Group for the Study of Family and Intimate

Assaults in Atlanta. Magnitude and pattern of family and intimate assault in Atlanta, Georgia, 1984. *Violence Victims*, 5 (1990) 3–17.

14. R.W. Jeffery, Risk behaviors and health: Contrasting individual and population perspectives. *Am. Psychol.*, 44 (1989) 1194–1202.

15. J. Potter and M. Wetherell, *Discourse and Social Psychology: Beyond Attitudes and Behavior*, Sage, London, 1987.

16. N. Loraux, *Tragic Ways of Killing a Woman*, Harvard University Press, Cambridge, MA, 1987, p. 9.

17. N. Avni, Battered wives: The home as a total institution. *Violence Victims*, 6 (1991) 137–149.

18. Z. Dangor, Women and violence in our time. *Azanian Labour J.*, 4 (1992) 19–24.

19. A.L. Kellerman and J.A. Mercy, Men, women and murder: gender specific differences in rates of fatal violence and victimisation. *J. Trauma* 33 (1992) 1–5.

20. J.L. Thomsen, S.B. Albrektsen, O. Aalund, V.B. Beiting, L. Danielsen, K. Helwig-Larsen, J. Jacobsen, H. Kjaerluff, and H. Staugaard, Injuries due to deliberate violence in areas of Denmark. II. Victims of homicide in Copenhagen areas. *Forensic Sci. Int.*, 40 (1989) 291–297.

21. M.E. Wolgang, *Patterns in Criminal Homicide*, University of Pennsylvania, Philadelphia, 1958, pp. 252–254.

22. L.A. Curtis, *Criminal Violence*, Lexington Books, Lexington, MA, 1964.

23. L.E. Saltzman, J.A. Mercy, P.W. O'Carroll, M.Z. Rosenberg and P.H. Rhodes, Weapon involvement and injury outcomes in family and intimate assault. *J. Am. Med. Assoc.*, 267 (1992) 3043–3047.

24. J.J. Collins, *Drinking and Crime: Perspectives on the Relationship between Alcohol and Criminal Behavior*, Guilford Press, New York, 1981.

25. B. Aramburu and B. Critchlow Leigh, For better or worse: Attributions about drunken aggression towards male and female victims. *Violence Victims*, 6 (1991) 31–41.

26. Alcohol and Violence (Editorial). *Lancet*, 336 (1990) 1223–1224.

27. S.E. Taylor and J.D. Brown, Illusion and well-being: A social psychological perspective on mental health. *Psychol. Bull.*, 103 (1988) 193–210.

28. D. Levy and N. Sheflin, New evidence on controlling alcohol use through price. *J. Stud. Alcohol*, 44 (1983) 929–937.

29. G. Marie, Breaking the silence, destroying the lies: An educational program on violence against women. *Stud. Contin. Educ.*, 7 (1989) 337–355.

30. N.D. Weinstein, Unrealistic optimism about illness susceptibility: Conclusions from a community-wide sample. *J. Behav. Med.*, 10 (1987) 481–500.

31. G. Davis, "Unclenching the fist": Jazzart Dance Theatre. *Speak*, 46 (1992) 5–7.

32. C. Terre Blanche, Intervening with dance. *Vrye Weekblad*, 178 (1992) 35.

33. L. Walker, *The Battered Woman*, Harper and Row, San Francisco, 1979.

Physical Punishment of Children and Wifebeating in Cross-Cultural Perspective

■ *DAVID LEVINSON*

INTRODUCTORY NOTES

There has been a good deal of research on family violence over the past two decades. Before that, family violence was almost completely ignored by the social sciences. Now we have come to realize that the family is one of the most dangerous environments of all. One norm that helps explain this—and that is only gradually changing—is the one that gives parents virtual property rights over their children. When this is combined with the normative use of physical discipline in the U.S., it is inevitable that some parents will cross the line between socially acceptable levels of physical discipline and unacceptable levels—abuse.

Just as parents "rear" their children, it seems also that many husbands rear their wives. The expression "rule of thumb," in fact, comes from a centuries old law that allowed a husband to hit his wife with a rod—as long as it was no thicker than his thumb. Men's superior physical strength combined with a patriarchal heritage that allowed them to treat their wives as property has led to a great deal of physical abuse in this and other patriarchal societies.

The theory examined in this selection posits a direct correlation between child abuse and wife abuse. It holds that children who are beaten will learn that violence is a means of solving problems of personal relationships and will transfer this problem-solving technique into their marriages. This study finds the relationship between the physical punishment of children and wifebeating a little more complex than that. It also finds—perhaps to the surprise of many Americans—that there are many societies in which parents rarely, if ever, hit their children.

This paper reports the results of a worldwide cross-cultural study of the relationship between wifebeating and the physical punishment of children. The notion that wifebeating and physical punishment of children may be linked is derived from the Straus [6,8] feedback model of wifebeating. Straus argues that "family socialization

SOURCE: David Levinson, "Physical Punishment of Children and Wifebeating in Cross-Cultural Perspective" from *Child Abuse and Neglect,* vol. 5, no. 4 (1981). Reprinted with permission from Elsevier Science Ltd., Pergamon Imprint, Oxford, England.

through violence" is one of a number of sociocultural factors leading to frequent wifebeating. Family socialization through violence involves children observing parental violence, violence among siblings, the encouragement of violent behavior in boys, and physical punishment of children. Straus suggests a snowball effect, with family socialization through violence leading to high rates of wifebeating, and high rates of wifebeating maintaining other forms of violence within the family.

In this paper we report a test of the hypothesized linkage between wifebeating and physical punishment of children with a sample composed of 60 small-scale and folk societies. A small-scale society is a distinct cultural unit with no indigenous written language. A folk society is a society whose members share a common cultural tradition, produce at least 50% of their own food, and are under the political control of a larger nation-state.

This paper is divided into three sections. In the first section we discuss the methods used to test the wifebeating–physical punishment hypothesis. In section two we present the results of the test. And in the final section we discuss the implications of the test results.

METHODOLOGY

The sample for this study is the Human Relations Area Files Probability Sample Files (PSF) composed of 60 well-described small-scale and folk societies representing all major cultural regions of the world. [2,5] All of the data used in this study were collected from ethnographic reports included in the Human Relations Area Files data archive. The HRAF data archive is a cross-referenced, cross-indexed collection of ethnographic reports describing the ways of life of some 315 different ethnic, national, and subcultural groups from all geographical regions of the world. Because of missing data for either the wifebeating or physical punishment variable, the sample size is reduced to 46 societies.

Wifebeating is defined as the physical assault of a woman by her husband and is measured on a four-point scale:

4. Common—wifebeating occurs in all or nearly all households in the society.
3. Frequent—wifebeating occurs in a majority but not nearly all households in the society.
2. Infrequent—wifebeating occurs in a minority of households in the society.
1. Rare—wifebeating does not occur or occurs in only a small minority of households in the society.

Physical punishment is defined as the use of physical force by caretakers to discipline, motivate, or punish a child or infant and is also measured on a four-point scale:

4. Common—physical punishment is used more often than other socialization techniques such as scolding or withholding of privileges.
3. Frequent—physical punishment is used as often as other socialization techniques.
2. Infrequent—physical punishment is used less often than other socialization techniques.
1. Rare—physical punishment is either not used at all or it is used rarely in comparison to other techniques.

TABLE 1: Relationship between Physical Punishment and Wifebeating

WIFEBEATING	PHYSICAL PUNISHMENT			
	Rare	Infrequent	Frequent	Common
Rare	Andamans	Rural Irish		
	Copper Eskimo	Hopi		
	Ifugao	Trobrianders		
	Iroquois			
	Ona			
	Thailand			
Infrequent	Kanuri	Klamath	Ashanti	
	Lapps	Masai	Cagaba	
	Lau	Ojibwa	Garo	
	Mataco	Pygmies	Pawnee	
	Tucano	Santal	Wolof	
		Taiwan		
		Tikopia		
		Tzeltal		
Frequent	Bororo	Kapauku	Azande	Amhara
	Iban	Korea	Dogon	
	Tarahumara	Kurd	Somali	
		Toradja		
Common	Chukchee	Aymara	Ganda	Serbs
	Tlingit	Hausa	Truk	
	Yanoama			

Gamma = .34, *p* < .05

RESULTS

The descriptive results of this study indicate that wifebeating occurs more often than the physical punishment of children and infants. In the 46 societies sampled, wifebeating is common in 17%, frequent in 24%, infrequent in 39%, and rare in 19%. Physical punishment is common in only 4%, frequent in 22%, infrequent in 37%, and rare in 37% of the societies sampled. This finding supports Barry and Paxon [1] who report also that harsh disciplinary techniques tend to be absent in small-scale societies.

As regards the hypothesized relationship between wifebeating and physical punishment, statistical analysis supports such a relationship. The *gamma* coefficient of .34 (*p* < .05) displayed in Table 1 indicates that the use of physical punishment as a socialization technique with children is associated with frequent wifebeating. However, if we examine the distribution of the societies listed in Table 1, we find that the relationship is more complex than is suggested by this one correlation coefficient alone. The distribution of the societies in the top half of the table (columns 1–4, rows 1–2) shows a strong relationship between rare or infrequent physical punishment of children and rare or infrequent wifebeating. Of the 27 societies listed in the top half of Table 1, 22 follow the low punishment–low wifebeating pattern. However, the distribution of the societies in the lower half of the table (columns 1–4, rows 3–4) shows a muddled relationship between frequent physical punishment and wifebeating. In fact, the distribution in the lower half runs opposite Straus' prediction, with 12 societies showing a low punishment–high wifebeating pattern and only 7 showing the predicted high punishment–high wifebeating pattern. Straus, of course, suggests that frequent wifebeating will be associated with frequent physical punishment.

While this analysis supports Straus' hypothesis in general terms, it shows, more specifically, at a societal level that rare or infrequent physical punishment of children is associated with rare or infrequent wifebeating,[9] while frequent or common wifebeating is unrelated to the frequency with which physical punishment is used as a socialization technique.[5]

IMPLICATIONS

This brief study has two important implications. First, it shows that there are many cultures in the world where caretakers rely on physical punishment of children as a socialization technique far less often than in the United States, where 90% of parents use physical punishment.[6] This finding may be the result of two factors. First, the large number of societies included in the sample with extended family households.[3,4,7] In accord with this general pattern, 21 of the 34 societies in this study which report rare or infrequent physical punishment are societies with extended or polygynous family households. The extended or polygynous family household–low physical punishment linkage most likely reflects the presence of alternative caretakers in the household who share child rearing responsibilities. Second, the inclusion in the sample of a number of hunting and gathering societies with nuclear family households such as the Copper Eskimo or Ona. In these types of societies, too, children are rarely treated harshly.[7]

Third, while this paper provides only partial support for Straus' wifebeating–physical punishment hypothesis,[8] it more strongly supports his claim that one way to control wifebeating is to control the physical punishment of children.[8] This analysis shows that in societies where physical punishment is relatively unimportant as a socialization technique, wifebeating is far more likely to be absent than present. Thus, while wifebeating and physical punishment of children are not linked in a causal sense, they do seem to be linked in terms of prevention or control of violence in the family.

➤ DISCUSSION QUESTION

In some societies parents rarely, if ever, physically punish their children; whereas in the U.S. physical punishment is quite common. Some argue that physical punishment is necessary as a deterrent; yet the prisons today are filled with people who were physically punished as children. Do you think physical punishment deters more crime than it creates?

NOTES

1. Barry, H. III and Paxon, L.M. "Infancy and early childhood: Crosscultural codes, 2." *Ethnology* 10 (October, 1971):466–509.

2. Lagace, R.O. "The HRAF probability sample: Retrospective and prospect." *Behavior Science Research* 14 (July, 1979):211–229.

3. Levinson, D. "Population density in cross-cultural perspective." *American Ethnologist* 6 (November, 1979):742–751.

4. Minturn, L. and Lambert, W. *Mothers of Six Cultures: Antecedents of Child Rearing.* New York: John Wiley, 1964.

5. Naroll, R. "The proposed HRAF probability sample." *Behavior Science Notes* 2 (April, 1967):70–80.

6. Owens, D.M. and Straus, M.A. "The social structure of violence in childhood and approval of violence as an adult." *Aggressive Behavior* 1(3, 1975):193–211.

7. Rohner, R.P. *They Love Me, They Love Me Not.* New Haven: HRAF Press, 1975.

8. Straus, M.A. "A sociological perspective on the prevention and treatment of wifebeating," in *Battered Women: A Psychological Study of Domestic Violence*, pp. 194–238. Edited by Maria Roy. New York: Van Nostrand, 1977.

9. Straus, M.A. "Wife beating: How common and why?" *Victimology: An International Journal* 2(3/4, 1977-78):433–458.

Prostitution and the Status of Women in South Korea

■ *ROBERT HEINER*

INTRODUCTORY NOTES

As mentioned in the introduction to this book, an unavoidable problem in comparative criminology is that of ethnocentrism. This article illustrates the bias of an "outsider looking in." The tendency of an outsider looking in is to emphasize differences between the subject culture and the researcher's own culture. But, as you are reading this article keep in mind that some of the same forces that perpetuate prostitution in South Korea are at work doing the same in many other cultures, including our own. Given that we are equally or more biased when viewing our own culture, it may, in fact, be easier to see these forces in operation in another culture such as South Korea's.

Frequently, social scientists are also ethnocentric in their egalitarianism. While often claiming in one breath that they are value-neutral and that there is no universal standard, in the next breath they are condemning practices and ideologies that subjugate people on the basis of class, race, or gender. While egalitarianism may be a near-universal standard, it is not universal; and the value that we put on it, like all other values, is a product of culture. This bias also affects the content of this next article.

Prostitution in South Korea, as in many parts of the world, flourishes because of the discrimination women suffer in patriarchal societies. Prostitution in these societies (including our own) shares a number of features: 1) the prostitute is shunned and ostracized from conventional society; 2) though often illegal (as it is in Korea), law enforcement efforts are nonexistent or ineffective; 3) the prostitute is often exploited, intimidated, and/or coerced by a male pimp; 4) public indignation and law enforcement usually focus on the prostitute, not on the pimp, nor the client; 5) sexual promiscuity in girls is often a precursor of prostitution, perhaps due to a double standard in labeling; that is, a promiscuous girl is labeled a "slut," while a promiscuous boy is labeled a "stud"; and 6) gender-based discrimination occurs in the labor market, and prostitution is much more lucrative than most other jobs available to women.

Sociologists, of course, argue that crime and the criminal are products of society and the way society is structured. Bias notwithstanding, this article clearly illustrates this viewpoint. (Keep in mind that prostitution is illegal in South Korea.)

SOURCE: Robert Heiner, "Prostitution and the Status of Women in South Korea," from the International Journal of Contemporary Sociology, vol. 29 no. 1. (1992) 115–123. Reprinted with permission from the *International Journal of Contemporary Sociology.*

INTRODUCTION

Functionalists have argued that if an allegedly undesirable phenomenon permeates a culture, and if it has always permeated the culture, and if it permeates other cultures as well, then it must exist for a reason. It must serve some useful function for the society. For Durkheim (1947), consensual moral aversion to crime unites a society; and therefore, crime functions to enhance social solidarity. For Erikson (1966), reactions to deviance serve as a means of publicizing those things that are not tolerated in the community; and therefore, the deviant is necessary for boundary maintenance. For Davis (1937), prostitution provides a sexual outlet for the male that does not interfere with his responsibilities to his family; therefore prostitution provides a functional alternative to other sexual outlets, such as having an affair. In this article, it will be argued that prostitution in South Korea does indeed fulfill a function. It functions to perpetuate an extraordinarily patriarchal social structure. Namely, the fear of being labeled a prostitute keeps women dutiful and submissive. This argument will be developed once the situation regarding prostitution and the status of women in South Korea have been discussed.

This examination is based on my experiences and observations having lived for a year (1985–1986) in South Korea, having made it a point to visit a large variety of prostitution districts, having badgered a wide variety of Korean citizens with questions about the trade, and having made contacts with "managers" (pimps) who allowed me to interview their "girls" (in all, nineteen women were interviewed). It should be noted that, due to various cultural, political, and methodological constraints, this research is largely impressionistic in nature. Prostitution is a phenomenon not openly discussed in Korea. Though rampant, it is regarded as shameful; and it is technically illegal. As anyone who has studied Korean culture knows, "Koreans are preoccupied with appearances, especially with foreigners" (Gibbons, 188:234). While in Western cultures it is acceptable to study and write about the seamier side of society, it is much less acceptable in Korean culture. Just as the individual has *face* that must be guarded at all times, so does the nation; and it is considered somewhat of a betrayal to reveal to an outsider those things that might bring shame to the country.

THE HISTORY AND EXTENT OF PROSTITUTION

Prostitution is rampant in many Asian countries today. Other than being Asian and rife with prostitution, what these countries have in common is that they can trace many of their customs back to Chinese civilization which has been fiercely patriarchal and has a long tradition in prostitution. In Chinese history, and in the history of many of its "relative" cultures, infanticide, the selling, pawning, and enslavement of women were all common practices for centuries. Women were of little economic value in these cultures. When they married, they left their parents' home; and they usually married before they could contribute much to the family in terms of their labor. It was, therefore, in the interest of the family (poorer families especially) to rid themselves of the burden of raising female children. Attitudes towards women can also be traced to Confucianism which established a very strict hierarchy of authority between government and subjects, parents and children, and men and women. Writes one *Koreanist*, "Anyone familiar with China reads Korean ethnography with a smothering sense of *deja vu*" (Kendall, 1985:25). Remarkably, Korea has been more strongly influenced by Confucianism than even China (Iyer, 1988). The same history of infanticide, selling, pawning, enslavement, and prostitution of women belongs to Korea. Also, Korea and China have in common extensive histories of tremendous economic and political unrest and social dislocation — conditions often associated with the prevalence of prostitution (cf. Cohen, 1958; Gronewold, 1982). There have been very few periods of economic and political stability throughout the thousands of years of Korean history. This century has been particularly tumultuous with the brutal Japanese occupation, the Korean War, the bifurcation of north and south, and the American "occupation".

Prostitution proliferates in virtually every sector of Korean society. Every city has a prostitution district. Some have a street devoted to the trade. Some have a neighborhood. Some have many streets scattered throughout. Some have many neighborhoods scattered throughout. Virtually every bus and train station has a series of brothels nearby. There are even small towns devoted to the trade, especially those that cater to the American military bases — such as "Silver Town" outside of Kun-san in the south, and Sunyo-ri near the DMZ in the north — that are known as "villes". (However, the impression of those who believe that the presence of the American military is responsible for the majority of prostitution in Korea is simply incorrect. Probably more prostitutes serve Japanese tourists; and most clients are Korean nationals — cf. Kim, 1987).

There are streets and neighborhoods where the prostitutes wait outside and approach all male passersby. More typically, there are streets and neighborhoods where the women, dressed in traditional formal attire, wait together inside rooms with a big window that opens onto the street so men can look in and choose which one they want. There are prostitutes that work all of the large and not-so-large hotels. There are prostitutes who work on the cleaning staffs of innumerable inns. There are prostitutes who work out of the bars. There are prostitutes who work in the restaurants and coffee shops. There are manicurists who ply another trade in dimly lit barbershops. There are prostitutes who work in the many Korean massage parlors. There are even prostitutes who work in the massage parlors located on the American bases. And, most likely, there are other locales where they work of which I have not been informed.

PATRIARCHY AND THE CULT OF THE MALE

The Korean female lives in a society in which it is most advantageous to be male. Sexism and sex discrimination permeate the entire culture. Males are given the best jobs, the better part of the family's inheritance, and the benefit of the doubt. The birth of a son in Korea is always a joyous event, whereas "the birth of a daughter occasions lament" (Kendall, 1980:12). In fact, "given the pressure placed on couples to produce a male heir and the ability to have legal abortions, the [Korean National] assembly [has considered] legislation forbidding doctors from performing tests capable of determining [the sex] of an unborn child" (McBeth, 1987:38). When a male baby is born, its first formal baby picture will be of him sitting spread-eagle, displaying the "family jewels," of which the parents are so proud. As he is growing up, relatives and friends of the family will greet and compliment him by a brisk fondling of the genitals as a way of expressing "my what a man you are!" and of signifying respect for the family for their having a male child. (Koreans planning to travel abroad must spend a day at "passport school" where, among other things, they are strongly advised not to pay their compliments to Western families by fondling their little boys' genitals.) The female will grow up in this cult of the male — in a society where it is considered bad luck if a shopkeeper's first customer in the morning is a woman. She will quickly learn that her role is to serve men.

Eventually, she will probably marry. The routes to marriage are varied: perhaps she will marry out of love; perhaps her marriage will be arranged; perhaps she will marry because her older sisters cannot marry until she is married off; or she may marry because she is approaching her thirties and will soon be over the hill. When she marries, she will find herself subservient to her husband. Traditionally, the man's world is a public one, while the wife's is private. Korean folklore venerates the woman who refuses to flee her burning home. Today, a frequently used expression referring to "wife" is *annae*, meaning "the one inside". Her husband will quite possibly go out every weekend and get rip-roaring drunk. He is very likely to make use of a prostitute on occasion. And there is more than a slight possibility that he will beat his wife with some regularity. In a national survey conducted in 1983, "61 percent of the men queried readily admitted that they beat their wives" (Kim, 1987).

In light of this backdrop, it is probably superfluous to say that sexism plays a major role in Korean prostitution. This phenomenon simply cannot be explained without reference to the patriarchal social structure. Prostitution provides an alternative, though a painful one, to the subjugation imposed by marriage. It also provides an alternative to the subjugation imposed by the legitimate labor market. Writes Elaine Kim:

> The female entertainment industry is particularly attractive to women workers in South Korea, where employment opportunities are limited even for educated women. . . Women's jobs are predominantly in low-wage factory and service occupations. . . Women in South Korea work ten hours a month more than men, averaging 59 hours a week, the longest in the world (Kim 1987:135).

In fact, the widespread employment of women in the factories for menial wages is one of the factors associated with Korea's current economic success. Their history of being exploited, their willingness to accept low wages, and "the Confucian expectations of a woman — that she be morally strong, self-sacrificing and submissive to men — [have] played and continue to be significant factor[s] in the economic development of the nation" (Yoo, 1985:840).

It is hardly surprising, then, that many young women are drawn to prostitution. While the average monthly salary for working women in Korea was less than 150,000 won (about $170 in 1986), the average salary for the prostitutes I interviewed was about 800,000 won (about $900). Kim writes, "It is said that it is hard to find pretty bus girls or housemaids any longer, since the good-looking women are all working in the hospitality trade" (1987:136).

FACE AND FAMILY

The most striking paradox of Korean prostitution is that it is so rampant in a society where the worst of all human existences is one involving shame, where there is so much emphasis on keeping face, and where prostitution is seen as such a cause of shame and loss of face. We might expect that a cultural priority emphasizing honor would keep most people honorable; however, such a strong demand for honor has the opposite effect. It provides a standard that is often unrealistic, and those who do not meet this standard are cast out. As labeling theory holds, once labeled and cast out, an honorable existence becomes all the more problematic.

The concept of face is inextricably connected to the Korean concept of *kibun*, perhaps best translated as "harmony of self and others". Paul Crane describes this concept:

> Perhaps the most important thing to an individual Korean is recognition of "selfhood". The state of his inner feelings, his prestige, his awareness of being recognized as a person — all these factors determine his morale, his face, or self-esteem, essentially his state of mind, which may be expressed in Korean by the word *kibun* (Crane, 1978:25).

If everyone in a social interaction can keep their face intact (honor), then there is *kibun* (harmony). Koreans will go out of their way to preserve harmony.

This emphasis on honor and harmony very often has a destructive influence on family relations. It is truly remarkable to live in Korea and hear the continuous litany on the importance of the family, and yet find that family members almost never confide in one another. Things that people are likely to confide are also things that are likely to threaten the family's honor and disrupt the family harmony. Many of the women who find their way into prostitution are women who have already felt themselves to be shamed, who could not confide in their families or who did so with disastrous consequences. A norm that is only recently beginning to change is the one requiring women to be virgins on their wedding night. (The extent to which this expectation has changed is unclear; it almost certainly depends upon the family and their place of residence.) But many of the women I interviewed, at least half (many chose not to answer my questions on the subject), were women who were sexually involved before they left home. They left because they were ashamed to admit it; or because they were prohibited from seeing their lover again; or because the tension created by their indiscretion had become unbearable. As in American society (but more so), when the child does something shameful, she or he brings shame onto the whole family. Many of these women were disowned before they turned to prostitution; and many have been disowned after they turned to prostitution.

THE SPOILED IDENTITY OF THE PROSTITUTE

To be a prostitute is to lose face; to lose face is to be an "unperson". Because of the loss of face associated with prostitution, to have a background in prostitution is to have a *spoiled identity*. If those with whom she interacts know of her background, then her identity is *discredited*; if they are not aware of her background, then her identity is *discreditable* (Goffman, 1974). Worse yet, in Korea to associate with an "unperson" is to compromise one's own face, one's own personhood. It is, therefore, important to the Korean to be always on guard, ready to discredit the discreditable.

It is difficult to overstate how attuned Koreans are to the social background of another. As big as America is, having once been a dumping ground for England's criminals, and with as much social mobility that has taken place here, it is difficult for Americans to imagine a country in which one cannot escape one's background. In Korea, it is not so easy. Crane addresses this problem of no-escape in his discussion of social relationships gone sour:

In a tight little country surrounded by water and a hostile boundary to the north, there is no place to escape from the wrath of the enemy. For most people, this means that they must endure when they are under attack or go and hide until the heat subsides. . . Rarely does a foreigner get more than a peep into the seething, bubbling cauldron of hates and fears and subtle attacks that pressure the average person in Korea, who lacks the mobility of most Americans (Crane, 1978:31).

Even in the large and populous country of China a hundred years ago, Gronewold says that it was almost impossible to escape one's background (Gronewold, 1982). Communities were tight-knit; and the newly arrived stranger, whose true background was unknown, was assumed to have the worst of backgrounds.

Koreans are acutely aware of any signs of suspect status. The labeling of deviance is easily facilitated under such conditions. As Lofland points out (1969), when there are a "large number of alternatively sufficient indicators," people can be successfully labeled when they meet one of any number of criteria. Flashy dress, employment on an American base, employment as an actress or in other fields of entertainment, employment in certain neighborhoods, living alone without family coming to visit, unfeminine behavior — these are just a few of the conditions that might eventuate in the label of "prostitute". As labeling theory holds, whether or not one engages in deviant behavior is less important than whether or not one is labeled deviant, because once one is labeled, he or she *is* deviant (Schur, 1971).

Prostitutes in Korea suffer all the conditions associated with stigma described by Goffman (1974). The more salient of these include the following. First, they are regarded as less than human by those who are aware of their spoiled identity. Second, their discreditability drives a wall between them and their family and their past. Separating them from their past, their stigma, in effect, means the reconstitution of their entire identity. Third, they live in fear that one day in the future, after they have left the "business" and thought they had "passed" as normal, someone will denounce them. (Many of the women I interviewed expressed hopes of one day getting married, but explained that they were terrified that one day their past would be discovered by their future husbands.) Finally, when they are interacting with someone who does not know of their discreditability, they are aware of the unsettling fact that this person would not like them if he or she knew the truth about their background.

AND THE PATRIARCHY GOES ON

There are, of course, an intricate variety of means by which patriarchal domination is maintained and enhanced in Korea, as in all other patriarchal societies. One of these means in Korea is through the institution of prostitution. Prostitution involves the exploitation of women in the service of men. This position has been well established. However, *prostitution in Korea is also a means of subjugating all women, not just those involved in the trade.* The fact that so many women are involved makes it all the more feasible that any particular woman is or has been involved. In order to stave off the suspicion of their involvement, it becomes necessary for women to strictly adhere to their assigned (submissive) roles in society. To stray from this role is to invite the label of "prostitute", which means reconstitution of herself, for the worst. If she divorces her husband, he will probably get the kids, and she will have to reestablish herself by herself. A woman living alone invites suspicion. If a woman works on an American base or as an entertainer, she might be exposed to ideas that would challenge male domination; but she will also be inviting the label. If she behaves in an "unladylike" manner, she will, by definition, be challenging the norms governing relations between men and women; but she will also be inviting the label. Aside from prostitution, most of the things a woman could do that might eventuate in the label "prostitute" are things that, in one way or another, pose a challenge to patriarchal relations between men and women.

If prostitution is critical in maintaining the moral/patriarchal boundaries in society as I have argued, then, according to Erikson (1966), reactions to deviance that allegedly discourage it will, in actuality, encourage it. Indeed, this is the case. Many might suppose that the defamatory nature of the label "prostitute" would act to discourage prostitution. However, the ease with which this label is meted out acts as a propellent rather than a repellant. Korean culture has set a vicious cycle in motion. Insistence on adherence to strict ethical principles has led to the "fall" of multitudes of women. The existence of multitudes of "fallen" women has given rise to a situation in which all women are possibly suspect. When all women are possibly suspect, people become even more attuned to moral strictures in order to identify the status of another, or to demonstrate their own virtuous status. The result is an insistence on adherence to strict ethical principles, which leads to the "fall" of multitudes of women. And thus, a steady supply of deviant women is insured. To paraphrase Erikson: the prostitute is not a bit of debris spun out by faulty machinery, but an integral component of patriarchal domination.

➤ DISCUSSION QUESTIONS

According to this article, how does prostitution figure in the oppression of all South Korean women? Would the situation for Korean prostitutes (or for Korean women, in general) be improved if prostitution were legalized? What parallels do you see between Korean prostitution and American prostitution?

REFERENCES

Cohen, Yehudi 1958 "The sociology of commercialized prostitution in Okinawa." *Social Forces*, 37. December. 160–168.

Crane, Paul 1978 *Korean Patterns*. Seoul, South Korea; The Royal Asiatic Society and Kwangjin Publishing Co.

Davis, Kingsley 1937 "The sociology of prostitution." *American Sociological Review*, 2. 744–755.

Durkheim, Emile 1947 *The Division of Labor in Society*. trans. by G. Simpson. New York: Free Press.

Erikson, Kai 1966 *Wayward Puritans*. New York: John Wiley.

Gibbons, Boyd 1988 The South Koreans. *National Geographic*. 174(August), 232–257.

Goffman, Erving 1974 *Stigma: Notes on the Management of Spoiled Identity*. New York: Prentice-Hall.

Gronewald, Sue 1982 *Beautiful Merchandise: Prostitution in China, 1860–1936*.

Institute for Research in History and Haworth Press.

Iyer, Pico 1988 "The yin and the yang of paradoxical, prosperous Korea." *Smithsonian*, 19(August). 45–58.

Kendall, Laurel 1980 "Suspect saviors of Korean hearths and homes." *Asia*. 3(May/June). 12+.

Kendall, Laurel 1985 *Shamans, Housewives, and other Restless Spirits: Women in Korean Ritual Life*. Honolulu: University of Hawaii Press.

Kim, Elaine 1987 "Sex tourism in Asia: A reflection of political and economic inequality." In E. Yu and E. Phillips. eds. *Korean Women in Transition*. pp. 127–144. Los Angeles: Center for Korean-American and Korean Studies, California State University.

Lofland, John 1969 *Deviance and Identity*. Englewood Cliffs, N.J.: Prentice-Hall.

McBeth, John 1987 "A family feud for Confucians and women." *Far Eastern Economic Review*, 135(26) February. 38–41.

Schur, Edwin 1971 *Labeling Deviant Behavior: Its Sociological Implications*. New York: Harper and Row.

Yoo, Ok-Za 1985 "Korean women in the home and the work place." *Korea and World Affairs*, 9(Winter). 820–872.

ARTICLE 7

Women and Crime in Europe

■ *FRANCES HEIDENSOHN*

INTRODUCTORY NOTES

The statistics throughout much of the world indicate that the vast preponderance of crime is committed by males. Likewise, the works of most criminologists focus on male criminals and their crimes. Heidensohn notes, however, that by studying female crime, we might learn more about male crime. Indeed, until the last decade or so, criminologists have neglected this insight. Most criminologists who did examine female criminality (almost all of them male), working from knowledge of the fact that most crime is committed by males, have started with the question, "What is it that female criminals have that makes them more like men?" Early theories addressing female criminality almost inevitably compare female criminals to men. Whereas, of course, theories of male criminality rarely even mention women. Adler's theory (discussed in this article)—that as women's liberation makes women more aggressive, we can expect to see more female criminality—is just a more recent version of the theory that women become criminals when they become more like men.

The feminist critique of such theories is that "male traits" are always used as the standard for understanding criminality. Perhaps a more fruitful angle would be to examine "female traits" as a standard for understanding the *absence* of criminality—in other words, start from the question "What is it that male criminals have that makes them less like women?" This approach may seem alien and even insulting to many males because it implies that if they are law-abiding then they are somewhat like women. But inasmuch as this is insulting, it is only because ours is a patriarchal society and so-called male traits have been valued while so-called female traits have been devalued. However, these traits are for the most part—if not entirely—learned as part of our gender-specific socialization; and we might have far less crime if our socialization were not so gender-specific.

INTRODUCTION

Of all the developments in modern society changes in the perceived position of women have perhaps been the most remarked upon. Women in the majority of western nations have fewer than half the number of children their great-grandmothers did at the start

SOURCE: Frances Heidensohn, "Women and Crime in Europe," from *Crime in Europe*, F. Heidensohn and M. Farrell, eds. (London: Routledge, 1991), ch. 5, pp. 55–71 (edited). Reprinted with permission from the publisher.

of the twentieth century. Many now work in paid employment outside the home after, as well as before, marriage. Political and economic rights have been gained by women, often following considerable struggle, in most countries.

There is thus, at the end of the twentieth century, a climate of change in relation to women's roles. It is an international phenomenon with its source, like a rogue hurricane, in the USA, but prevailing winds have blown it across Europe. Issues related to women thus have a much higher profile today, both as policy matters and as subjects of analysis in the social sciences—which have themselves been much affected by these climatic changes. This then is the background to any study of women and crime in Europe today.

WOMEN AND CRIME

How then does the topic of women and crime fit into the concerns with sexual inequality and oppression? The links are not, at first, perhaps obvious. Crime is certainly a field of endeavor in which women could be said to have underachieved. One of the earliest observations made when systematic criminal records were first kept was that convicted male offenders far exceeded females in number.

For much of the twentieth century, little or no work of substance was carried out on this topic. Only with the arrival of feminism, and especially "feminist criminology" has this state of affairs been altered (Heidensohn, 1985; ch. 8). Simply put, conceptual changes in the ways in which problems were perceived and analyzed made it possible to address key issues in new and rewarding ways. Subjects which had been literally "invisible" could be seriously addressed. As a result a new, much more socially and historically grounded study of the topic was instituted. Extensive accounts of these developments exist elsewhere (Heidensohn, 1985; Naffine, 1987). In brief, three major aspects of crime and women have become matters of interest and study. The first of these is the criminality of women, its trends and patterns, both as subject *per se* and in comparison with the criminality of men. Second is the criminology of women's crime, an area in which there have been significant developments and significant not merely to that topic. Finally there have been important and related changes to the agenda of concerns over crime and penal policy: that agenda has become a "gendered" list. It is on these three aspects that I shall concentrate in this chapter.

Women and Crime in Europe

One of the very few international comparisons of female crime groups western Europe and North America together as regions with similar levels of crime (Adler, 1984). This is misleading. Although some accounts do add crime figures from different nations together to produce continental or hemispheric rates, this is a very dubious practice. Almost certainly, different things will be counted in each country. Adding European to North American rates also creates major distortions since the USA reports strikingly higher incidences of most offenses than Canada (Hagan, 1977) or Europe (Archer and Gartner, 1984). There does appear to be something of a crime convergence between major European nations (van Dijk, 1991). However, since male offenders dominate all national crime figures, how far are there similarities in trends and patterns in female crime?

Only 10 Per Cent of the Trouble?

An English commentator once observed that if men behaved like women the courts would be idle and the prisons empty. To a quite remarkable degree, crime is still an activity overwhelmingly dominated by men in all European countries. In France in 1986, of 809,059 persons *mises en cause* (i.e. dealt with in criminal proceedings) 81.27 per cent were male and 18.73 per cent female (*La Documentation Francaise*, 1987). In England and Wales in the same year, 83 per cent of offenders found guilty or cautioned for indictable offenses were male and 17 per cent female (Home Office 1986). In the Federal Republic of Germany in 1986, of those suspects proceeded against 79.5 per cent were male and 20.5 per cent female (Bundeskriminalamt, 1987). (These figures do *not* of course measure the same stage of judicial proceedings.)

Reported figures for other nations differ somewhat, but do not vary greatly from this benchmark. "Irish criminal statistics show that the vast majority of those convicted are male" (Burke *et al.*, 1981). In the Netherlands the female share of crime suspects has historically been about 10 per cent (Bruinsma *et al.*, 1984) of persons charged by the police. For Norway in the same year, the ratio was 10.7 men to one woman (Central Bureau of Statistics of Norway 1988: 53) while in Italy convictions of women were 19 per cent of the total in the early 1980s. Scandinavian countries show similarly modest female contributions to the totals of crime at about 8 per cent for Finland (Antilla, 1984) and Norway (Jensen, 1984).

These are global figures and do not give a detailed or dynamic picture. Once we examine trends over time, type of offense, and so on, a more complex pattern is reflected. Nevertheless, the figures above fairly indicate the relatively modest contribution made by women.

Historically trends in female criminality have at several periods moved in opposite ways from those of men. Thus in England and Wales a higher proportion of those convicted in the early nineteenth century were female (Mannheim, 1965) and this was also true of Denmark and Germany (Feest, 1985) in the 1800s. In the twentieth century, whereas crime rates in general have risen, female criminality has stabilized, or at times fallen. In Austria, for instance, female criminality fell between 1953 and 1957 by 6 per cent whereas there was an overall rise of 10 per cent. During this period the proportion of convicted men to women rose from 5.2:1 to 7.4:1. In England and Wales the rates of convictions for indictable offenses fell slightly during the 1950s. Stable and at times decreasing rates of female crime were described for Norway for various years during the 1970s and early 1980s (Jensen, 1984). The most remarkable example, however, of decline in female criminality comes from Poland, where there was a "steady and substantial decrease of female convictions in the 1960s and 1970s, a far more significant decrease than that experienced by men" (Plenska, 1984). In fact, convictions of women fell 250 per cent between 1951 and 1977. Many of the nations which took part in the two World Wars saw relatively sharp rises in female crime and delinquency in these periods, nevertheless the relative rate of increase has often been slower for women than for men.

Such longer term analyses have proved important in the debates about the liberation-causes-female-crime hypotheses which have been discussed since the 1970s. Surveying figures for 1935–75 in England and Wales, Smart not only observes the "law-abiding" period of the 1950s mentioned above but also notes "women offenders to be increasing at an overall faster rate than men" (Smart, 1979; 54) except between 1965 and 1975 (although there are inconsistencies in the figures on violent offenses [Austin, 1981; Box and Hale, 1983]). The "new female offender" has been alleged to have become an internationally recognized phenomenon in the late twentieth century and to have sufficient impact to alter the direction of crime rates. Observations in various European countries suggest two kinds of patterns. In the first, typified by Finland and the Netherlands, female crime rates have risen, but not as fast as male rates. In others, notably France, the Federal Republic of Germany, and England and Wales, there is some evidence of relatively sharp increases in female rates. Comparing 1976 and 1986 there has clearly been a larger rise in female than male rates in the period. The Federal Republic of Germany has recorded some reduction in the numbers of suspected persons, but this has been much less in women than men. For England and Wales, the faster rate of increase for women has already been observed. Between 1985 and 1986 there was an overall decline in numbers found guilty or cautioned "mainly accounted for by males but the percentage decrease was equal for males and females" (Home Office, 1986). The pattern for rates in relation to population was similar. What is striking about both the stable and the rising shares trends is that they both show that female crime rates move broadly in step with male crime rates (Box and Hale, 1983: 43).

Modest Contributions?

Aggregating crime figures is a dubious task at best: the old adage about summing apples and pears applies forcefully to frauds and assaults. It is done to satisfy political and public demand for crime audits and accounts. More appropriate are breakdowns by types of offenses: do women commit the same kinds of offenses as men and as often and how similar are the patterns in different parts of Europe?

We have already seen that women commit comparatively little crime. Women, like men, are mainly accused and convicted of property offenses. While definitions of crimes vary across judicial systems it is clear that the commonest crime committed by women is theft, very often in the form of shoplifting (Middendorf and Middendorf, 1984; Feest, 1985; Heidensohn, 1985; Cario, 1987). Fraud and forgery generally follow as the next commonest offenses. It is important to stress that the offenses most often committed by women are not necessarily those in which their *share* is greatest. Motoring offenses are the largest category of all, but the female share is modest. After traffic violations and property crimes, drug-related offenses have become more prevalent. Violent crimes are committed much less often by women, although there have been increases among some younger age groups. Nevertheless, women do contribute to the tariff of all such crimes, including homicide.

The relative lack of female specialization in crime is well illustrated in a summary table on four Scandinavian countries (Antilla, 1984) showing no female participation rate above 50 per cent for any category of crime and none below 2 per cent. There are, of course, a few offenses whose definition makes them specifically sex-linked in most jurisdictions. Rape is one obvious example: usually only men can be convicted of it, although women may be charged as accessories. Male but not usually female (except in Austria) homosexuality was widely criminalized in Europe until the 1960s and 1970s. Infanticide and self-induced abortion are female-only crimes. Most of these latter offenses always appeared rarely in records and have now either been decriminalized or have minute rates.

Prostitution is one area where criminal laws may be said to be operated in a sex-related way. There is, however, great variety in definitions of offenses related to prostitution and these are not always reported as fully as serious offenses are. I have therefore included discussion of the topic in a later section.

Most commentators agree on two additional attributes of female offenders. First, they commit fewer crimes and thus more of them are likely to be first offenders when arrested or tried than are men; second, very many fewer of them are professional criminals.

In summary, all European nations report a marked predominance of men in their criminal justice systems. Men figure as the most frequent suspected or convicted offenders both in total and for almost all offense and age groups. Women commit more crimes than they did earlier this century, but still far fewer than men, less often and less violently. These conclusions are drawn from administrative data from the criminal justice systems concerned. There have been attempts to find a larger iceberg-base of submerged female crime which would alter these findings. Various self-report studies and victim surveys have provided estimates of hidden female crime. They have not located excessive rates which would compensate for the major underrepresentation of women in official data. Most studies do find "hidden" female crime, but they also find more "dark-figure male" crime, so that the picture is modified, but not dramatically so. Dutch studies show more hidden offenses by females under 18 (Bruinsma, 1984) but do not alter adult ratios. One English study showed that males were more likely to indulge in undetected shoplifting and to steal more valuable goods (Buckle and Farrington, 1984). Studies in Scandinavia have also revealed hidden female crime but not enough to raise the visible rates to male levels (Elmhorn, 1969; Aromaa et al., 1970). The modest and marginal contribution made by women to offending has aroused criminological interest in the past twenty years and is discussed more fully below.

THE EXPERIENCES OF FEMALE OFFENDERS

It is perhaps not surprising that with such characteristics, very few female offenders are imprisoned in most European countries. Legal and penal policy changes have led to fluctuations and in general a decline in the numbers and the rate of female imprisonment in the twentieth century. In Norway and Finland (Jensen, 1984; Antilla, 1984) in the 1970s women comprised about 3 per cent or less of the prison population, for the Federal Republic of Germany the figure was 3.7 per cent (Einsele, 1981). In France there has been a decline in numbers of women in prison and the female share of the prison population since 1946. During the 1970s fewer than 1,000 women were imprisoned at any one time and they represented under 3 per cent of the total. By 1985 both figures had risen somewhat to 1,400 and 3.4 per cent respectively (Bibal et al., 1985: 76–8). Remarkably similar figures are reported for England and Wales (although it should be noted that a significant proportion of these are untried or unsentenced prisoners not subsequently sentenced to custody).

In smaller countries the numbers of women in custody are correspondingly tiny. In such instances, the lack of appropriate provision for them may not seem culpable. However, in practice, reports from almost all countries highlight problems and deficiencies in penal provision for women which sound remarkably similar notwithstanding very varied administrative systems. Three major themes emerge as concerns: problems due to the small, scattered numbers of women (the "too few to count" argument), the double or triple deviance issue, and the question of paternalism.

Too Few to Count?

Women offenders do not, on the whole, benefit from their exclusive numbers. On the contrary, they suffer in several ways. Special provision is rarely made for them as they are so few: in England there is a specialized psychiatric prison, Grendon Underwood, for men, but no such provision is made for women. In Germany, because of its federal structure, young women are invariably housed in adult women's prisons—at best in specialized units while young males can be separately housed (Einsele, 1981: 6). Genders and Player (1986) report the same mixing in England and Wales. In centralized systems, the problem is usually one of few units widely scattered where women will be far from family, friends and home. Cario vividly describes the isolation of long-term prisoners in France in the sole Centre Penitentiaire Féminin which is in Rennes in Brittany (Cario, 1985: 313ff). Osborough (1975) points out that girls sentenced to Borstal training (the predecessor to youth custody) in Northern Ireland used to have to go to Scotland to serve their sentences.

Some rungs of the sentencing tariff may not be provided for women: detention centers were provided only briefly for young women in England and Wales. In Switzerland work and education centers have been provided for young men but not women (Einsele, 1981: 62).

Double Deviance

Personal accounts by convicted women (Carlen, 1985; Heidensohn, 1985) as well as an array of research findings insist that female offenders are perceived and treated as doubly deviant: they have transgressed society's rules by their crimes and by defying conventional norms of femininity. They thus feel peculiarly stigmatized and are also subject to particularly censorious and repressive treatment in the penal system.

Ida Koch (1983) has described the effects of this very vividly in her study of Denmark's coeducational prison. She points out that fellow male prisoners' censorious behavior and attitudes were very much an additional punishment to women in this situation. The Dobashes in their study of Cornton Vale, the only prison for women in Scotland, noted that the inmates there felt "a strong sense of shame and stigma" (Dobash *et al.*, 1986:187). Kersten in a comparative analysis of the treatment of young people in the Federal Republic of Germany concluded "Girls in institutions have even less elbow-room as far as expectations of gender role conformity are posed [than boys]. In the event that they obviously 'misbehave', the grasp of control becomes more forceful" (Kersten, 1989: 143). An experimental integration of young male and female offenders at Eboli prison in Italy culminated in "a full-scale revolt" in which girls took full and leading parts. The researchers reporting this suggest that this was due to the failure to address the conventional, feminine roles which the regime imposed on staff and on female inmates (Ferrari-Bravo and Arcidiacono, 1989).

Gender Roles and Paternalism

There is notable congruence in numerous descriptions of institutions for women as explosive and dangerous places. While on the outside, women are generally perceived as the more conforming sex, inside prison they are said to be far more difficult to manage, more violent and more prone to need tranquilizers and other psychotropic drugs. Recent research and reports from several European countries have reassessed such accounts.

Institutions for women in the FRG (Federal Republic of Germany), for example, are described as having "an unrealistic institutional ethos, based on a moralistic assessment of behavior" (Einsele, 1981: 70). This finding is precisely paralleled in studies in women's prisons in England and Scotland. Women in these institutions were much more tightly controlled than in men's prisons, were reported for more trivial offenses, and given less work and education than men (Carlen, 1983; Dobash, *et al.* 1986; Mandaraka-Sheppard, 1986). What emerges very clearly from these researches is the oppressive, gender-stereotyped nature of the regimes in women's prisons:

> A female who does wrong even in the slightest detail must be made into a proper woman (who by definition does not do wrong) and this can be achieved through a therapeutic regime that seeks to reach even the most minute behavior or motivation. (Dobash *et al.*, 1986: 158)

Cario depicts an almost identical system at the CPF at Rennes: "It perpetuates the values which our society attributes to the female role by the notable emphasis in the discipline system on obedience and submission and on educational activities of a traditionally feminine kind" (Cario, 1985: 350—my translation).

A further aspect of such paternalism reported from France concerns the system of conditional release. Reports on the characteristics qualifying women for this focus especially on submission, repentance, order, and hard work with a particular emphasis on family ties (Faugeron and Rivero, 1982: 86–7).

In contrast, most institutional treatment for girls and women offers them far less than their male counterparts. In the FRG girls have "a very narrow offering compared with boys' institutions, in the sector of work employment, leisure and adventure . . . this lack of offered pathways to social and economic independence" (Kersten, 1989: 140).

THE CRIMINOLOGY OF FEMALE CRIME

It is by definition very difficult for distinct criminal justice and social control systems to coordinate themselves and converge. That is indeed one of the major issues for such agencies in Europe after 1992. Cultural and intellectual barriers can often be more easily breached. It is clear from the account outlined above that there have been many comparable developments in female criminality across Europe. Concerns about women's penal treatment have converged even more closely. This is not just coincidence. In surveying the growing criminological literature on women it becomes clear that the new consciousness which I mentioned at the beginning of this chapter has had considerable impact on parts of European criminology.

The amount of work in this area has already grown considerably (Cain, 1989). More significantly, however, than the growth in volume has been the direction in which discussions have run: they have for the most part taken a transatlantic turn.

Much of the key work in this field has been done in the USA and this has, inevitably perhaps, formed the foundations for most debates elsewhere, even when these have developed lives of their own. From a flourishing harvest I can pick out only a selection of choice products which illustrate richness as well as both convergence and diversity. This is not a comprehensive choice but is, I hope, reasonably representative.

Rates and Rises

Only one approach to female criminality has ever managed to penetrate popular consciousness and thus become instantly recognizable. This is the "liberation causes female crime" argument proffered by Adler (1975) and in modified form by Simon (1975). Adler endeavored to explain allegedly rapid rises in female crime rates by linking them to the women's movement. She argued that the latter had spawned a new kind of female criminal who was tough, aggressive and violent, preferring to rob banks rather than to mind babies. Adler's statistical analyses as well as her arguments have been extensively criticized and her thesis refuted (Smart, 1979). What is instructive to note is the way in which discussions about women's crimes in Europe have centered around this hypothesis.

That British studies should do so is perhaps not surprising, given the common language and close cultural and academic ties. There were also, as in most of Europe, certain phenomena to explain, notably faster rises in female than male crime. Feminist criminology had had, however, an early and distinctive start in Britain (Heidensohn, 1968; Smart, 1977; Gelsthorpe and Morris, 1988) and while engaging somewhat in the rates, rises and new female criminal debates, other issues have also been on the main agenda. One of the most important has been that of altering the assumptions of mainstream criminology to see that sex and gender are no longer neglected issues (Carlen and Worrall, 1987; Heidensohn, 1987). In the long run the most important result of studying female crime may lie in what we learn about all, especially male, crime.

Many papers on female crime in Europe take on the task of refuting Adler's relevance to their territory (Feest, 1985) including several in a volume edited by her (Jensen, 1984). In some areas this has also involved tackling the one distinctive manifestation of female criminality in the twentieth century: the female terrorist. Acts of political terrorism featured particularly in Europe in the 1970s and 1980s, although they have a long history. In Ireland, Italy, the FRG, France and Britain there were bombings, kidnaps, assassinations and sieges. The ideologies claimed by the perpetrators were very diverse and spanned from far left to far right yet nearly all had a significant representation of women amongst active members and leaders. Some of these, especially in the FRG, became very well known. Attempts to explain the female terrorist have been rather limited, at best highly individualist descriptions of cases. One German commentator notes the sexism of such accounts which "seem incapable of seeing women as human beings who can be violent criminals or even politically active". She points out that no female terrorist has ever claimed allegiance to the women's movement (Einsele, 1981: 60).

Marginalization and Female Crime

While the debate on liberation and crime can be seen as a damaging diversion, in refuting the arguments criminologists have had to explore other explanations of features of female crime. In doing so they have helped to bury another moribund argument, concerning the sexualization of female criminality. It can sometimes seem to the experienced student of this subject that someone is always trying to glamorize it. In the earlier version of this transformation, crime-prone Cinderella's behavior was attributed to her hormones, the stages of her generative cycle, her sexuality or lack of it. In the emancipation era, power and liberty replaced sex as causative factors. Both these interpretations distort by glossing over the observed characteristics of female offenders.

Studies of imprisoned women in Britain show their poverty, lack of education, and of skills or work record. Many have children, few have stable partners and most report a lack of choice, autonomy and order in their lives (Genders and Player, 1986; Carlen, 1983, 1985). Research and the activities of prostitute women themselves have represented prostitution as an economic, not a primarily sexual activity, through which women earn cash to keep themselves and their families (McCleod, 1982; Heidensohn, 1985). Several contributors to a symposium on girls and social control in Europe note the importance of economic factors in determining both their deviant behavior and, during the recession of the 1980s, the "increasingly punitive response by our European penal systems" (Cain, 1989).

Another version of this approach has developed in Scandinavia. In an influential article, Cecilie Hoigard analyzed Norwegian figures on female crime and concluded that explanations related to liberation changes in gender patterns or the new opportunities for women to commit crime at work were not adequate. Instead she put forward a theory of "expulsion", arguing that the relationship between gender and class has altered in modern society so that gender has become more important. Women offenders are recruited from those at the bottom and margins of society (Hoigard and Snare, 1983; Folgesvold and Dullum, 1988). Gender analysis has also characterized a number of studies of young delinquent women and girls involved in a variety of deviant activities (Cain, 1989).

Chivalry

One debating topic set by American criminology has been widely debated across Europe. This is the "chivalry" debate. Criminologists in the past often asserted that the police and the courts favored women, treating them more leniently than men. Such assertions were usually based on lower female crime rates and even lower imprisonment rates. The consensus from a series of West German studies seems to be that "the theory that the crime prevention authorities treat women better and that women are less thoroughly investigated, more frequently released and less harshly judged can be taken as disproved" (Steffen, 1983:12). Similar findings are reported from Austria (Einsele, 1981).

In one French study comparing the treatment of male and female offenders, the chivalry hypothesis is only one of the possible explanations considered. The authors nevertheless acknowledge its importance as a focus of discussion. They observe that there is some differential treatment and ambiguity in the treatment of women offenders in France (Faugeron and Rivero, 1982). A number of empirical studies in Britain have been reviewed by Lorna Smith (1988), who highlights some problems of definition: does *equal treatment* for men and women mean the *same* treatment? At least one British researcher found that women were more likely to be treated leniently by the courts than men (Allen, 1987). Europeans have adapted and developed American ideas for their own use in analyzing female crime. The adaptations have generally proved fruitful and successful, although it is often clear that the framework of the debate is what the French call "anglo saxon". There are also of course many distinctive local concerns of which discussions about women and social control are perhaps the most notable.

The New Crime Agenda

In Europe and in most developed countries there is a new agenda for social control agencies and for the general public. Priorities for policing have been redefined and policies and practices altered. There are a number of common characteristics on this agenda: these include an emphasis on crime control, a focus on the victims of crime and a redefinition of a number of crimes as having gender links. While all three are to some extent linked, it is the third point which has most salience for our purposes.

With the worldwide growth of victim movements (Shapland *et al.* 1985), the role and position of crime victims has been increasingly acknowledged and supported. Fear of crime is now recognized as a major inhibitor of freedom, especially in some inner city areas. One aspect of this has been recognition of significant gender differences. Thanks to a series of feminist and related studies, it is clear that while young men are often the victims (and the perpetrators) of street violence, women are the main victims of domestic violence, child sex abuse and rape (Stanko 1984). Most European countries have responded by providing shelters and support for victims and by altering policing priorities. These are small steps so far, but they are Europe-wide, even if they have their own forms in each nation, and they represent the internationalizing of certain concepts of social problems. There are doubts about how these concerns may be manipulated but not about the importance of the issues.

CONCLUSIONS AND PROPOSALS

Patterns and trends of female crime in Europe do seem to parallel each other very closely. Low recorded levels, modest crimes, little recidivism and no specialization characterize most nations. Approaches to the understanding of these issues are also linked by common themes, and these often have an American or Anglo-American tone. These are, however, the characteristics of nation states, not of the whole continent. Is there a truly European dimension to female crime?

Several crime trends do cross national barriers very readily, most notably, in this field, substance abuse and prostitution. Women's contribution to the first is growing. Prostitution also seems to be attracting more participants not only because of the number of drug users who need to finance their habit, but also, with high unemployment and high divorce rates, because more women are forced to sell their bodies to support their families.

It is interesting to observe that several historic Europe-wide "crime" waves have involved women. The persecution of witches in the sixteenth to eighteenth centuries killed off large numbers of women, especially in Scotland and Germany (Larner 1981). In the nineteenth century there was an international movement to outlaw prostitution and its state regulation. It was founded in Britain and spread to France, Germany and Switzerland (Petrie 1971). More recently, women have been strongly associated with terrorism in Europe. Can we draw any conclusions from these historical accounts? From the first and last perhaps, to be wary of moral panics which can often involve women and to their detriment. From the second we may conclude that power may sometimes be successfully used by women to help each other. The International Association cut across national and class barriers to achieve its aims.

Proposals

This chapter represents one attempt to make comparisons across Europe. In order to achieve future results in this field two aims have to be achieved. First, the key message of feminist criminology must strike home: acknowledge gender everywhere. There are still too many sets of data without sex breakdowns. Research studies are still published which ignore or omit females or, worse still, are unclear on the point. Second, more comparative data need to be made available and in usable form. This is as true of research findings as of official figures. It is a great pity that many studies are not more widely available, either translated into a major language or in fully published form. My impression in working on this chapter has been of dealing with a samizdat subculture.

Comparative study has much to offer any criminologist: cultural differences can provide instant control groups (as well as complications). For policy-makers there is the chance to learn about other solutions to the same problems—and failed experiments. Comparisons involving women are even fewer than those dealing with men. They should, I believe, be encouraged not only for the obvious general reasons, but also for certain specific ones.

First, the crime agenda has changed. Women played some part in achieving that change and are involved in monitoring many of the new agenda's projects. They can no longer be ignored in this nor in other areas. There are many lessons to be learned about topics as diverse as child sex abuse and the diversion of women in the criminal justice system. Finally, there is an important possible gain for work on crime in general. As I have tried to demonstrate, there is remarkable consistency in European crime patterns. Across a range of cultures, climates and histories women conform and men commit crime. If crime is a major European problem, we must surely be able to learn something from studying this Europe-wide situation.

➤ DISCUSSION QUESTIONS

The vast majority of crime in the world is committed by males. What factors explain this phenomenon? And does knowledge of these factors offer any hope for reducing crime in the world?

ACKNOWLEDGEMENTS

Many people helped me in the preparation of this piece sending me tables, reports and research studies. I am most grateful to Robert Cario, Jane Dullum, Lionel Fontagné, Claude Faugeron, Brit Nora Folgesvold, Ida Koch, Arno Pilgram, René Van Swaningen and Hartmut Weber.

REFERENCES

Adler, F. (ed.) 1984. *The Incidence of Female Criminality in the Contemporary World*. New York: New York University Press.

Adler, F. 1975. *Sisters in Crime: The Rise of the New Female Offender*. New York: McGraw Hill.

Allen, H. 1987. *Justice Unbalanced*. Milton Keynes: Open University Press.

Antilla, I. 1984. "Female criminality in Finland—what do the statistics show?" in F. Adler (ed.) *The Incidence of Female Criminality in the Contemporary World*. New York: New York University Press.

Archer, D. and Gartner, R. 1984. *Violence and Crime in Cross-National Perspective*. New Haven, Conn.: Yale University Press.

Aromaa, K., Toinudd, P., and Wartioraana, K. 1970. *Department Store Shoplifters*. Helsinki: Patrik Institute of Criminology.

Austin, R. L. 1981. "Liberation and female criminality in England and Wales." *British Journal of Criminology*, 21. 4:371–4.

Bibal, D., Fize, M., and Menis, D. 1985. *Les Femmes en Prison*. Paris: Ministry of Justice.

Box, S. and Hale, C. 1983. "Liberation and female criminality in England and Wales". *British Journal of Criminology*, 23. 1: 35–49.

Bruinsma, G.J.N., Dessaur, C.I., and Van Hezewijk, R.W.I.V. 1984. "Female criminality in the Netherlands", in F. Adler (ed.) *The Incidence of Female Criminality in the Contemporary World*. New York: New York University Press.

Buckle, A. and Farrington, D. 1984. "An observational study of shoplifting". *British Journal of Criminology*, 24. 1: 63–73.

Bundeskriminalamt (ed.) 1985. *Ausgewahlte Zahlen fur die Rechts pflege Reihel*. Wiesbaden: Bundeskriminalamt. 1987. *Polizeiliche Kriminalstatisik 1986*. (English summary). Wiesbaden: Bundeskriminalamt.

Burke, H., Carney, C., and Cooke, G. (eds.) 1981. *Youth and Justice*. Dublin: Turoe Press.

Cain, M. (ed.) 1989. *Growing Up Good*. London: Sage.

Cario, R. 1985. "La Criminalite des femmes: approche differentielle". Universite de Pau et des Pays de L'Adur, these pour Dr d'Etat, 22 Fevrier.

Cario, R. 1987. "Contribution a la commissance et a l'explication de la criminalite des femmes". *Revue Internat de Criminologie et de Police Technique*. 3:306–30.

Carlen, P. 1983. *Women's Imprisonment*. London: Routledge & Kegan Paul.

Carlen, P. 1985. *Criminal Women*. Cambridge: Polity.

Carlen, P. and Worrall, A. (eds.) 1987. *Gender, Crime and Justice*. Milton Keynes: Open University Press.

Central Bureau of Statistics of Norway 1988. Oslo: Criminal Statistics 1986.

Dobash, R.P., Dobash, R.E. and Gutteridge, S. 1986. *The Imprisonment of Women*. Oxford: Blackwell.

Einsele, H. 1981. "Female criminality in the Federal Republic of Germany". Strasbourg: Council of Europe.

Elmhorn, K. 1969. *Faktisk Brottslighet Bland Skolbarn*. Stockholm: Statens Offentliga Utreduingar.

Faugeron, C. and Rivero, N. 1982. *Femmes libierees sous condition*. Paris: Ministere de la Justice.

Feest, J. 1985. "Fraunenkriminalitat" in G. Kaiser et al. (eds) *Kleines Kriminologisches Worterbuch*. Heidelberg: Muller.

Ferrari-Bravo, G. and Arcidiacono, C. 1989. "Compounded misunderstanding: relations between staff and girls in an Italian prison", in M. Cain (ed.) *Growing Up Good*. London: Sage.

Folgeswold and Dullum 1988. Personal communication.

Gelsthorpe, L. and Morris, A. 1988. "Feminism and criminology in Britain". *British Journal of Criminology*, 28. 2: 93–110.

Genders, E. and Player, E. 1986. "Women's imprisonment: the effects of youth custody". *British Journal of Criminology*, 26. 4:357–71.

Hagan, J. 1977. *The Disreputable Pleasures*. Toronto: McGraw-Hill.

Heidensohn, F.M. 1968. "The deviance of women: a critique and an enquiry". *British Journal of Sociology*. 19 (2): 160–75.

Heidensohn, F.M. 1985. *Women and Crime*. London: Macmillan.

Heidensohn, F.M. 1987. "Women and crime: questions for criminology", in P. Carlen and A. Worral (eds.) *Gender, Crime and Justice*. Milton Keynes: Open University Press.

Hoigard, C. and Snare, A. 1983. *Kvimers Skyld*. Oslo: Bakgater.

Home Office. 1986. *Criminal Statistics*. London Home Office.

Jensen, A. 1984. "Norwegian women in court", in F. Adler (ed.) *The Incidence of Female Criminality in the Contemporary World*. New York: New York University Press.

Kersten, J. 1989. "The institutional control of girls and boys", in M. Cain (ed.) *Growing Up Good*. London: Sage

Koch, I. 1983. "Krinder i faengsel", in C. Hoigard and A. Snare (eds) *Kvinners Skyld*. Oslo: Bakgater.

La Documentation Francaise. 1987. *Aspects de la criminalite et de la delinquance constitues en France en 1986*. Paris: Ministry of Justice.

Larner, C. 1981. *Enemies of God*. Chatto & Windus.

McCleod, E. 1982. *Women Working: Prostitution Now*. London: Croom Helm.

Mandaraka-Sheppard, A. 1986. *The Dyamics of Aggression in Women's Prisons in England*. Aldershot: Gower.

Mannheim, H. 1965. *Comparative Criminology*. London: Routledge & Kegan Paul.

Middendorf, W. and Middendorf, D. 1984. "Changing patterns of female criminality in Germany", in F. Adler (ed.) *The Incidence of Female Criminality in the Contemporary World*. New York: New York University Press.

Ministry of the Interior 1987. *La Documentation Francaise*. Paris: Ministry of the Interior.

Naffine, N. 1987. *Female Crime*. Sydney: Allen & Unwin.

Osborough, N. 1975. *Borstal in Ireland*. Dublin: Institute of Public Administration.

Petrie, G. 1971. *A Singular Iniquity: The Campaigns of Josephine Butler*. London: Macmillan.

Plenska, E. 1984. "Female crime in Poland", in F. Adler (ed.) *Incidence of Female Criminality in the Contemporary World*. New York: New York University Press.

Shapland, J., Wilmore, J., and Duff, P. 1985. *Victims in the Criminal Justice System*. Aldershot: Gower.

Simon, R.J. 1975. *Women and Crime*. Toronto/London: Lexington Books.

Smart, C. 1977. *Women, Crime and Criminology: A Feminist Critique*. London: Routledge & Kegan Paul.

Smart, C. 1979. "The new female criminal: reality or myth?". *British Journal of Criminology* 19. 1:50–9.

Smith, L. 1988. "Images of women—decision-making in the courts", in A. Morris and C. Wilkinson (eds) *Women and the Penal System*. Cropwood Papers no. 19. Cambridge: Cambridge Institute of Criminology .

Stanko, E. 1984. *Intimate Intrusions*. London: Routledge & Kegan Paul.

Steffen, W. 1983. *Intensitat und Perseveranz Krimineller Verhaltensweisen*. Munich: Bayerisches Landeskriminalamt

Van Dijk, J. 1991. "More Than a Matter of Security: Trends in Crime Prevention in Europe," in F. Heidensohn and M. Farrell (eds.) *Crime in Europe*. London: Routledge.

Japanese Social Structure and White Collar Crime: Recruit Cosmos and Beyond

■ *HAROLD KERBO*
■ *MARIKO INOUE*

INTRODUCTORY NOTES

When Americans think of "the crime problem" they are most likely thinking about lower class street crime, not about white collar crime. It is, however, arguable that white collar crime does society more harm than street crime in terms of both its financial costs and the likelihood of physical injury. The financial costs of activities such as embezzlement, price fixing, and insider trading are inevitably passed on to the public. As for physical injury, the harm done by pollution, workplace safety violations, and the sale of dangerous products can be enormous.

This article makes a number of points worthy of note. First of all, the authors deal with the theory that the fierce individualized competition fostered by capitalism promotes white collar crime. They argue that, though this theory may apply to Western societies, the concept of "individualized competition" must be replaced by the notion of "group competition" in order to explain white collar crime in Japan. The article goes on to discuss the group orientation for which the Japanese are famous and which is often associated with the low crime rates in Japan. Paradoxically, this group allegiance can also foster criminal activity, namely white collar crime.

Another point the authors make is that white collar crime is more likely to be an individual act in the U.S. (such as embezzlement), whereas it is more likely to be a collective act in Japan (such as the Recruit Scandal).

On a related matter, while the authors question the claim that the Japanese sense of social responsibility significantly suppresses the crime rate, they assert that this sense of responsibility may affect the character of white collar crime. Though the group orientation may encourage rather than suppress crime, the Japanese, it seems, are less likely to engage in white collar crime that is injurious to societal welfare than are their American counterparts.

SOURCE: Harold R. Kerbo and Mariko Inoue, *Deviant Behavior,* vol. 11 (1990): 139–54, Taylor and Francis, Inc., Washington, D.C. Reproduced with permission. All rights reserved.

When testing most theories in the social sciences about conditions such as crime, family organization, inequality, or the influence of religion, social scientists are usually forced to limit their observations to either industrial nations or some category of developing nations. So many differences exist between industrial and developing societies that a mixing of these nations in any test of a theory could make the results difficult to accept with any confidence. But a problem remains when limiting observations to industrial nations: until recently all advanced industrial nations have had common European roots. If social scientists find support for a particular theory they cannot firmly rule out the possibility that capitalism or industrialization in general is less the cause than is some other common characteristic of Western nations that only happen to also be industrialized. Japan, as the first advanced capitalist industrialized society with an absence of any European traditions, provides social scientists with an opportunity to test theories of the independent effects of capitalism and/or industrialization on many aspects of society.[1]

A comparative analysis of crime, of course, is fraught with the old problems of comparable definitions, statistics, or even concepts of the subject matter. In the case of Japan, for example, it may be next to impossible to answer even the simple question of whether or not Japan has more white collar crime than other capitalist countries such as the United States. But even in the face of these problems, social scientists have much to learn about the nature and causes of white collar crime in the United States and Japan by attempting a comparative analysis. By looking at a subject such as white collar crime in the United States and Japan social scientists are often able to return to that subject in their own country with a fresh perspective and insights.

In the present paper the focus will be Japan, and more specifically how aspects of Japan's social structure (including the corporate structure) and values shape the opportunities and motivations for white collar crime. As a vehicle for this analysis the paper will begin with a summary of the recent Recruit Cosmos stock scandal to bring out themes and issues to be discussed in the following examination of Japanese social structure and values. This short paper will not attempt anything like a general theory of the causes of white collar crime in Japan. Rather, the intent is simply to call attention to major aspects of the Japanese social structure which are in contrast to those of the United States to provide the groundwork for such a theory or theories, and a fresh look at the subject in the United States.

RECRUIT COSMOS: A SUMMARY OF THE SCANDAL

Recruit Cosmos is a new real estate firm and subsidiary of the larger Recruit Company founded by Hiromasa Ezoe, the principal figure in the stock scandal. Ezoe's Recruit Company began as an information service firm, primarily publishing magazines with information on job placements and opportunities. With rapid growth in its early years, Ezoe expanded into many other activities, including telecommunications, real estate, and finance. By 1988 the overall Recruit Company had annual sales of over 183 billion yen ($1.3 billion), with 5,600 employees, and 27 subsidiaries.[2]

The scandal centered around the sale of 12 million shares of unlisted stock in the Recruit Cosmos firm (in some cases even arranging low cost financing to buy the stock) to 76 people in 1984, including politicians, government bureaucrats, and other businessmen. The stock was originally sold at 1,200 yen (about $9) per share and the price per share went to about 5,000 yen (about $35) when it was first publicly traded two years later. Many of the people able to buy the stock two years earlier quickly sold their stock holdings in Recruit Cosmos and made as much as 100 million yen (about $8 million) in profits.

Many politicians were among the 76 involved in buying this stock, but only one senior LDP (the ruling Liberal Democratic Party) official was indicted. The common pattern was that aids or junior associates of the senior politicians bought the stock, thus keeping the names of the senior politicians technically clear. For example, former Prime Minister Takeshita's secretary bought 2,000 shares, two of former Prime Minister Nakasone's secretaries bought 25,000 shares, a business associate of the Finance Minister (Kiichi Miyazawa) bought 10,000 shares, and a secretary of the head of the LDP (Shintaro Abe) bought 2,000 shares.

At about this time the Recruit Company was receiving favors from the Nakasone government in the areas of employment recruitment, resort development, and the buying and selling of communications equipment, and Mr. Ezoe himself was appointed to four government advisory commissions.

High officials in the ministries of Education and Labor became involved in these stock transactions, and also gave favorable treatment to the Recruit Company in their capacity to regulate recruiting in universities and employment agencies.

The most important businessman outside the Recruit Company to become involved was Hisahi Shinto, the former chairman of Nippon Telegraph and Telephone Company, the largest company in the world in terms of total assets. The business tie between Recruit and NTT was Recruit's favorable treatment allowing them to sublet expensive high speed digital communication lines to smaller corporations after the stock was bought by the head of NTT.

An outcome of the scandal was the resignation of 53 officials and the indictment of 19 others on charges ranging from bribery to conspiring to conceal evidence. Related to the stock scandal was the discovery of violations of campaign disclosure laws by the recruit company and the politicians involved. In 1989 the LDP lost its majority in the upper house elections for the first time since 1955 (though the LDP held its majority after the February 1990 lower house elections). Opinion polls at the time indicated, however, that the Recruit Stock scandal was somewhat less important in this loss than the new consumption tax passed by the LDP in 1988.

This summary of the Recruit stock scandal will conclude by stressing three points. First, the Recruit stock scandal was unprecedented only in the widespread nature of bribes and insider stock trading. Even the Lockheed bribery scandal which brought down Prime Minister Tanaka in the mid-1970s did not involve so many people in high places. All commentators seem to agree, however, that such activity has been rather common in Japanese corporate and political relations (see especially, van Wolferen, 1989). It should also be stressed that this scandal was the first to involve top bureaucratic officials (such as the vice-minister of education and the head of the formerly government controlled communications giant NTT), who until now have had an almost saintly reputation as the guardian of the national interest and morality. And it is perhaps this, along with the widespread nature of the corruption, that has angered so many Japanese.

Secondly, the Recruit scandal shows how the in-group in Japan will attempt to protect its leaders (e.g., the example of Prime Minister Takeshita's private secretary who committed suicide allegedly to hide evidence, as did Prime Minister Tanaka's driver). As this paper will attempt to show below, the importance of small group organization and its characteristics may at times provide social support for the rationalization of white collar crime in Japan, as well as carrying it out in a way that is more difficult to detect.

Finally, it must be stressed that the primary goal of the Recruit insider stock trading was an attempt by a new, but rapidly rising company and its founder to gain influence among a closed circle of elites in Japan (Yayama, 1990). Any attempt to understand the most important cases of white collar crime in Japan must consider the nature of its elite networks. And it is here that this paper will begin its structural analysis, with Japan's power elite.

THE POWER ELITE IN JAPAN

Most Japanologists agree there is a powerful triumvirate of elites in Japan (Tsurutani, 1977; Woronoff, 1986; also see Kerbo, 1990, chapter 13). This configuration is in line with C. Wright Mills' (1956) view of three interlocked elites, but somewhat different in make-up. Most important in this triumvirate are corporate elites and national bureaucratic elites, with the Liberal Democratic Party (LDP) making up the weaker third group.

The power of the top corporate elites is relatively easy to understand from the American experience. There is extensive corporate concentration in Japan and these executives sit on top of the most powerful economic organizations in Japan, and the world for that matter. These corporate elites are interlocked in many ways, especially through intercorporate control of corporate stock, though the practice of interlocking directorates is rare in Japan, because few corporate board members are outside directors (Clark, 1979; Abegglen and Stalk, 1985). The intercorporate control of corporate stock in Japan has gone further than in the United States (Kerbo and Della Fave, 1983), with about 70 percent of all corporate stock in Japan owned by other corporations rather than private individuals (Dore, 1987:112). These top corporations typically form tight groups of firms called *keiretsu* that can be mapped by these stock control patterns.

Equally important for corporate power are the big business organizations, especially *Keidanren,* which is commonly referred to as "the main temple" with its president called the "prime minister" of the corporate elite (Vogel, 1979:113; Woronoff, 1986:152). This organization is made up of the top executives of the more than 800 major corporations that account for more than 40 percent of all the profits and 50 percent of all corporate assets in Japan. The Keidanren organizes business pressure and political activities to an extent probably considered illegal in the United States, and in many ways can exert strong pressure on the ruling LDP.

The next power member of the triumvirate is less understandable from the American experience. The national bureaucracy of government ministries is actually rather independent of political control by the parliament (Diet). For example, these career bureaucrats actually write about 80 percent of the laws which pass the Diet and they are then responsible for the administration of these laws (Kishimoto, 1986:66). The top ministers of these government agencies are political appointees, but it is agreed that it is the lower ranking career bureaucrats, and especially vice-ministers, who actually run the government.[3]

The power and status of the bureaucratic elite, as well as the interlocked nature of the Japanese power elite can be seen in the practice called *amakudari*, which literally translated means "descended from heaven." A high position on the national bureaucracy brings considerable power and respect, but a relatively low income. However, these bureaucrats can expect to retire early (in their 50s) to "descend from heaven" and become top corporate executives or powerful politicians (where income can be obtained in more innovative ways). One study has estimated that from 30 to 40 percent of all top corporate executives are amakudari (descended from the bureaucratic elite, see MacMillan, 1985:129). If we look at the most powerful ministries, such as MITI (Ministry of International Trade and Industry), we find that all of the vice-ministers have descended to top corporate positions since World War II (Johnson, 1982:72). As for the movement in the Diet from the government bureaucracy, over 30 percent of the LDP Diet members and over 80 percent of prime ministers in Japan since World War II have been former top bureaucrats (Tsurutani, 1977:77).

The Liberal Democratic Party has been the ruling party in Japan since 1955, but must still be regarded as the junior member of the triumvirate. As seen above, it is dominated by the bureaucracy and led by former bureaucrats. To this must be added that 90 percent of the LDP's funds come from the corporate elite (Woronoff, 1986:161) to understand its junior status.

Final consideration must be given to the backgrounds of this power elite to understand their unity. There is little of what can be called an old upper class of family wealth in Japan since the old *zaibatsu* was eliminated (or at least greatly reduced) during the occupation reforms soon after the War. (Only 27 percent of corporate stock is owned by individuals, Dore, 1987:113). And it must be noted that compared to the U.S. corporate elite, their Japanese counterpart has come up from relatively humble origins (MacMillan, 1985:129). But it is sponsored mobility that is channeled through elite universities. The "old school ties" are extensive and more important than in the United States. One study found that 32 percent of all corporate elites graduated from Tokyo University (Mannari, 1974; MacMillan, 1985:131), while another study estimated that almost half of the top 3,000 corporate executives came from either Tokyo University, Kyoto University, Hitotsubashi University, Keio, or Waseda (Woronoff, 1980:133). The old school ties are even more extensive among the bureaucratic elite. Of all government bureaucratic officials holding the position of section head or above, over 60 percent came from one of the above elite universities (Rohlen, 1983:91). And at the most important ministries, such as MITI and the Ministry of Finance, the percent with elite university backgrounds is higher, often as high as 80 percent.

In many respects, C. Wright Mills' (1956) idea of a power elite fits modern Japan better than it does the United States (Kerbo, 1990, chapter 13). And because the Japanese are prone to establish tight cliques (Woronoff, 1980), as will be discussed below, it can be argued that Japan's power elite is especially difficult to break into. This is one reason claimed to be behind the Recruit scandal: The second level of smaller business executives are locked out of the big money deals and find the competition more in line with what Adam Smith had in mind for capitalism. It was Recruit Cosmos' attempt to break into this elite circle that brought on the trouble.

This also seems to indicate that Japan's power elite has relatively little formal pressure to make them accountable to other groups in the wider society. Some Japan watchers claim that white collar crime is rampant in the higher circles (Woronoff, 1980: 286; van Wolferen, 1989), but there is less hard evidence of this claim than can be found in the United States. And even what would be defined as white collar crime in most industrial societies has not been defined as such in Japan, which is rather understandable given the interlocking power of the corporate and political elite described above. It must be noted that most of what occurred during the Recruit scandal was actually legal,[4] and the political resignations only occurred because of the popular criticism that was believed to be harmful to the Liberal Democratic Party in the next elections.

It is common when studying Japan to find situations or conditions that do not seem to fit, or appear to be contradictory to Americans. At this point it will be useful to at least briefly note some of these with respect to the subject matter of this paper. Given what seems to be the overwhelming power of corporate elites in Japan, the fact that they receive much less income and hold much less personal wealth than their counterparts in the U.S. seems contradictory. And as it will be seen below, some people claim that clearly socially harmful or irresponsible acts by the corporate elite are relatively less common in Japan than in the U.S. To consider this it is time to turn to group structure in Japan, and a value system that may restrain some socially harmful behavior.

THE NATURE OF THE GROUP IN JAPAN

In Western sociology, theories of crime and white collar crime in particular tend to have an individualist bias. In theoretical discussions on the causes of white collar crime we read about the personality of the offender, the different kinds of financial motivations for white collar crime, individual rationalizations for involvement in crime, and the culture of competition. True, space is also given to subjects such as organizational crime and organizational conformity as a cause of white collar crime in certain situations (see Coleman, 1985:193–232). But the point is, the latter is more of an afterthought in the dominance of individualistic theories of white collar crime. The following quote by Edwin Schur (1969:187) provides a useful example:

> It is difficult not to conclude that American society has what might be termed capitalism with a vengeance—a reverence for the values of individualism, competition, and profit of such intensity as to provide incentives to crime that go well beyond a level that must be considered inevitable in a modern complex society, even a basically capitalist one.

Edwin Schur may well be correct in the context of the American society, though even in the U.S. it can be argued that this individualistic perspective on the causes of white collar crime can be taken too far and the group context has been neglected. In Japan it is clear that Schur's statement would have less meaning. But if one replaced the term "individualism" with "group competition", the statement can be used with equal validity in Japan. As Ford executives working with Mazda in Hiroshima or U.S. executives anywhere else in Japan know, they must also face capitalism with an equal vengeance, but of the group variety, which is perhaps more difficult to face.

The point is that individual motives for white collar crime in Japan are relatively less prevalent than white collar crime for the benefit of the group. And anyone who has taken an introductory course in sociology or psychology should recognize that group support and justifications of collective deviance can be quite powerful. It is for this reason that this paper must now consider some of the important characteristics of group structure and a collectivist orientation in Japan as they relate to white collar crime.

There is no revelation in the statement that the group is more important in Japan compared to the United States. There is more pressure to fit in, conform, and accept group needs to the neglect of individual needs and desires. Numerous social surveys indicate that Japanese people are more likely than Americans or Europeans to say their work is more important than their private lives; and a recent study of workers found that Japanese people are more likely than Americans to say they feel they cannot disagree with their boss (Naoi and Schooler, 1985). These aspects of Japanese society alone suggest how a group orientation in Japan can effect white collar crime. But there are specific practices in Japanese groups which specify how the individual must fit in or conform which effect white collar crime.

Vertical Organization

Chie Nakane (1970) has made her reputation, in large part, with the idea of the importance of vertical organization in Japan in contrast to other societies. The theory is that in Japan groups are organized more vertically, and with relatively fewer horizontal social relations than in the U.S. Group structure is said to be made up of stacks of inverted "V's", each attached to another above and below, all pointing upward toward the final leader of the wider group. It is said that this form of group structure reduces class conflict by making the vertical attachments more important than relations within classes. And it is said that this form of group organization enhances the authority of leadership.

Nakane's ideas have been criticized extensively, but the importance of attachments between the senior and junior members of the group in Japan is clearly important. In short, one needs a senior sponsor or a mentor, without which the junior member is at a disadvantage. In schools, clubs, and many organizations the relation between the younger member and his/her mentor/sponsor is called *kohai* (junior) and *sempai* (senior sponsor or mentor) (Hendry, 1987; Nakane, 1970). In preindustrial Japan and preMeiji times, the samurai without a lord (daimyo) for sponsorship and protection was called a *ronin* and, like the junior worker without a senior sponsor, in a very vulnerable position. And it must be stressed that this relationship is rather long-lasting, for a person seen changing sponsors easily when the fortunes of one or another sponsor goes up or down would have little respect in Japan, and [would be] unlikely to find a new sponsor. Thus, the reputation and position of the leader is to be protected, for if the leader falls, the careers of the attached junior members will likely be permanently damaged. This aspect of group structure was responsible for the continued support for former Prime Minister Tanaka by most Diet members in his faction of the LDP even after his conviction on bribery charges in the Lockheed scandal and until his retirement in 1990.

For the study of white collar crime in Japan this means the leader will be protected and his/her crimes hidden by subordinates. And further, this suggests that group efforts in illegal activity which enhance the leader's position will also enhance the whole group of sponsored individuals.

Ringi System

Much has been written about the Japanese management technique of creating consensus and "democratic decision making" in which ideas are circulated by higher managers or section leaders for group input and discussion before decisions are actually made. There is information suggesting this system, known as *ringi* does work to create consensus among workers and a feeling that they have "had their say" in decisions that have been made (Clark, 1979; Abegglen and Stalk, 1985). However, it is also charged that the system is not really democratic, with decisions that will be made anyway only given the appearance of having been made in a democratic manner. And, most importantly for the present paper, this process also spreads the feeling of responsibility and blame to a wider group if the decision is wrong or leads to illegal behavior (Woronoff, 1980:45).

The possible implications of the ringi system for white collar crime seem clear. It could be that this decision making process results in better decisions, or at least decisions that do not violate the law or ethical standards. However, given other factors discussed above and below, it can also be argued that pressure on the group to compete and succeed could result in decisions involving illegal activity. In this case the whole group now feels responsible and even accomplices to the crime. In other words, there are unlikely to be many "whistle blowers" in the group because of the ringi system and other factors discussed here.

In-Group vs. Out-Group Conflict

As already noted, group competition in Japan is fierce. This group competition starts with the smallest unit group, for example a work group within a larger corporate division, and continues to the largest out-group, the rest of the world. But for the present subject the most significant out-groups are competitor companies (Abegglen and Stalk, 1985). This out-group conflict or competition can at times go to the extreme. In Hiroshima, for example, if a person wants to tour the Mazda factory, a background check is first required which takes about two weeks to insure that the person has no connection with a competitor such as Nissan or Toyota. And at the Mazda test track at Miyoshi (a few miles from Hiroshima) the hotels close by have their windows facing this track closed and blacked out.

The "functional conflict" theorists such as Coser (1956; 1967) and Simmel (1905;1955) tell us how extensive out-group conflict usually results in greater pressure to conform, support the leader of the in-group, and make renegades of anyone who dissents within the group. Again, the possible implications for creating pressure to participate in and hide white collar crime from this aspect of group structure in Japan seem clear.

The Status Order

While Japan has the lowest income inequality of all industrial nations, there is evidence that status inequality is greater, or at least status ranking is more important in Japan than in the United States (Kerbo, 1990, chapter 13; Kerbo and McKinstry, 1987; Kerbo and Sha, 1987). It can be argued that the importance of this status order would make corporate executives or anyone else in a position to participate in white collar crime more cautious about doing so because a loss of status/honor would result if they are caught.

However, there is a counter force in operation through this status order. Unlike the United States where occupational prestige goes primarily with the type of job one has achieved (e.g., doctor, lawyer, etc.) in Japan the more important status marker is the group a person is attached to: the company one works for, and so forth (Clark, 1979:108; Reischaur, 1988; Vogel, 1979; Dore, 1987). And the individual status of each worker is tied to how well the company is doing in competition with others.

Thus, the subject comes back to "group competition with a vengeance" and the pressure to achieve as a group which, under certain circumstances, could lead to group redefinitions of norms and pressure to succeed through illegal activity. And when individual illegal activity is found within a Japanese company that places that company and/or work group in danger because it is likely to be detected, to save the status of the group, the person or people most involved are commonly dismissed quietly and the crime covered up (Clark, 1979:172; Taylor, 1983:82).

JAPAN'S VALUE SYSTEM

Criminologists naturally look at a country's or subculture's value system as a restraining or promoting mechanism when studying crime, and the same must be done with Japan. In the case of Japan, however, an attempt to outline the country's value system and its effects is loaded with controversy and problems. Japanese sociologists themselves are divided into two schools of thought on the subject of whether or not Japanese values are unique or not so different from those of Western nations (Tominaga, 1987; Dale, 1986). And it is clear that Japan's value system is changing with industrialization. Thus, other than saying that the value placed upon the group in Japan remains rather strong and must have some effect on crime in Japan, social scientists must be skeptical that a focus on values (with one exception noted below) will help us understand much about white collar crime in Japan. But this paper must at least point to some possible, though controversial, value differences that may be important to the causes of white collar crime in Japan.

Guilt vs. Shame

One of the most controversial claims of value differences can be traced back at least to the classic work by Ruth Benedict, The *Chrysanthemum and the Sword* (1946). A major point of her analysis is that the Japanese culture lacks a tradition of social control by guilt, in comparison to Western nations. In contrast, the concept of shame is more important for social control in Japan. And it is especially shame a person may bring to the group that is a restraining force. Thus, because there is no absolute "right or wrong" instilled in the person to be carried as guilt if violated, and because detection is the key to shame, it is said that Japanese people are more likely to violate norms when the violation is unlikely to be detected or condemned by others. This also suggests that a group which becomes somewhat isolated, either geographically or socially, from the dominant Japanese society is more likely to break norms when they can be situationally redefined by the isolated group. In particular, this description of Japanese values was used by Benedict (1946) and others to explain the inhumane behavior of the Japanese military outside of Japan during World War II.

Research on the existence of guilt versus shame in modern Japan is badly needed for many reasons. But, its relevance to the causes of white collar crime, if correct, is obvious.

Traditional Social Responsibility

Japan's group orientation has had a positive side with respect to restraining anti-social behavior. The in-group versus out-group relation is always relative, but because the Japanese population is about 97 percent racially and ethnically Japanese, the in-group is always to some extent the nation as a whole. This is one reason why some writers describe Japan as a huge clan. Thus, because the group orientation specifies that group needs and interests should not be harmed, anti-social behavior at times has been restrained.

This is one explanation for Japan's low crime rate, and can be cited as a possible restraining influence on white collar crime more specifically (Hendry, 1987:193). This value has also been used to help explain why Japan has one of the lowest levels of income inequality among industrial nations (Kerbo, 1990, chapter 13), and the income gap between corporate executives and new workers is only approximately 7 to 1, compared to 37 to 1 for the United States (Abegglen and Stalk, 1985:192; *Wall Street Journal*, April 18, 1984). Along these lines it is interesting to note that the name for merchant and businessperson in preindustrial Japan had a negative connotation of selfishness, so a new term was invented during industrialization by the new Meiji elites (Dore, 1987:116). Because of this value of social responsibility there is extensive pressure on anyone in an elite position to resign if their company or agency has harmed the society in some way.[5] And it is this value of honor and social responsibility which is said to account for the very low level of corruption among the national bureaucratic elite.

An explanation such as this is necessary if social scientists are to understand why the corporate elite has such low income in face of its power outlined in the first section. However, it is known that values are often subject to varied interpretations, which perhaps must be recognized to explain the 100 to 1 income gap, instead of 7 to 1, that existed only 50 to 60 years ago in Japan (Hane, 1982:11). And there are already common claims that the value of social responsibility is rapidly breaking down in modern Japan to be replaced by the "religion of materialism" (Woronoff, 1980:69, 246). And C. Wright Mills (1956) warned of the "higher immorality" due to corporate elite redefining American values of social responsibility to their own advantage.

In short, social scientists should remain skeptical about the extent of the influence of norms of social responsibility on restraining white collar crime in Japan. This is especially so when "group competition with a vengeance" is mixed with capitalism and the possible ability of elites to redefine values in ways that justify the illegal behavior to benefit their more immediate reference group. However, with the reality that Japanese people do have a sense of their nation as an extended clan, it is likely that there is greater pressure on elites to be socially responsible, and we therefore caution that research is needed before we can dismiss this possible restraint on white collar crime.

CONCLUSION

There is, of course, no reason to believe that Japanese people are by nature any more or less selfish and materialistic than people in other capitalist industrial societies. But to the extent that any human nature brought out by capitalism or industrialization leads to white collar crime, there are aspects of Japanese society that shape the types and extent of white collar crime in Japan. It may be reasonable to conclude that white collar crime is at least as extensive in Japan as in the United States, and possibly higher because it may be easier to hide white collar crime in Japan. This paper has described the massive extent of the Recruit stock scandal that brought down many political and corporate elites in Japan, including Prime Minister Takeshita (though the new sales tax was also a cause for his resignation). But the tentative nature of this claim of more white collar crime in Japan must be stressed given the massive Pentagon bribery scandal and HUD scandal occurring in the United States at about the same time as the Recruit stock scandal.

A second major, and perhaps more important point is that there is most likely less individualistic white collar crime in Japan, but more white collar crime to benefit the group. The Recruit stock scandal again reflects this view. The top executive at Recruit (Ezoe) was not simply bribing politicians and ministry officials for his own enrichment, but to benefit his company more generally because it was locked out of the "old boy network" of power elites in Japan. For example, it seems likely that individualistic forms of white collar crime such as embezzlement are lower in Japan compared to the United States. It has been noted that when considering Japan, U.S. theories of white collar crime seem to have a strong individualistic bias. Certainly differing aspects of group structure must be considered in the causes of white collar crime in Japan, and perhaps through reexamination of Western theories in the context of Japan social scientists may find even an individualistic bias in these theories when applied to the United States as well.

This paper will close with a call for more comparative research on the subject of white collar crime, difficult and fraught with mine fields as it no doubt will be. And in particular, of course, this paper has called for comparative research on Japan. Many theories claim that aspects of capitalism, and even industrialization more generally, shape white collar crime. But at present, only in the case of Japan can social scientists find an advanced capitalist industrial society without Western traditions and values (particularly individualism) which also influence the extent of white collar crime in the nation. The ideal would be a theory of white collar crime which is complete enough to explain the varying levels and causes of white collar crime in both Western and Asian capitalist societies.

➤ DISCUSSION QUESTION

Compare and contrast white collar crime in the U.S. and Japan. What cultural features (political, social, and economic) help to account for the differences?

NOTES

1. It should be noted further that Japan and Thailand are the only Asian countries without a long period of disruption through colonization. Added to this list are the countries of Taiwan and South Korea, which were colonized, but not by a Western power. Thus until Korea and Taiwan can be called advanced industrial nations, Japan provides us with the best test of material influences of capitalism and industrialization (in the absence of value or cultural effects) on many aspects of a society than would Hong Kong, China or Singapore.

2. Information in this section comes from various mass media sources in Japan, but most can also be found in the leading English newspaper in Japan, *The Japan Times*. There is also some information on the details of the Recruit stock scandal in Yayama (1990), though this is a translation of an article expressing political opinion originally published in Japan, which may not otherwise be helpful to social scientists in the United States.

3. As an example of the lack of the Diet's power, only 30 percent of the laws initiated there ever pass the Diet, and Diet members have almost no staff to investigate issues, gather information, and write these laws (Woronoff, 1980:196–206).

4. Specifically, it was not illegal to provide stock at very low prices before it went on the open market, even when the loans to buy the undervalued stock were provided at low interest by the Recruit corporation, unless some exact benefit was given by a person in political office to the company as a result of the stock transaction (in other words, a bribe). It was only this situation that brought the few convictions in the stock scandal.

5. For example, in 1985 the crash of a Japan Airlines jumbo jet led the chief executive of the airline to resign, and in 1988 when a Japanese submarine hit a fishing boat in Tokyo Bay killing less than 10 fishermen, the head of the self defense force (Japan's secretary of defense) resigned. Many resignations, of course, followed the Recruit stock scandal. The main point is that this is a very common occurrence with a long tradition in Japan, which in the past was usually followed by suicide as well.

REFERENCES

Abegglen, James C. and George Stalk, Jr. 1985 *Kaisha: The Japanese Corporation*. New York: Basic Books.

Benedict, Ruth 1946 *The Chrysanthemum and the Sword: Patterns of Japanese Culture*. New York: Houghton Mifflin.

Christopher, Robert 1983 *The Japanese Mind: The Goliath Explained*. New York: Simon and Schuster.

Clark, Rodney 1979 *The Japanese Company*. Tokyo: Tuttle.

Coleman, James W. 1985 *The Criminal Elite: The Sociology of White Collar Crime*. New York: St. Martin's Press.

Coser, Lewis 1956 *The Functions of Social Conflict*. New York: Free Press.

Coser, Lewis 1967 *Continuities in the Study of Social Conflict*. New York: Free Press.

Dale, Peter N. 1986 *The Myth of Japanese Uniqueness*. New York: St. Martin's Press.

Doi, Takeo 1986 *The Anatomy of Self: The Individual Versus Society*. Tokyo: Kodansha.

Dore, Ronald 1987 *Taking Japan Seriously*. Stanford: Stanford University Press.

Hane, Mikiso 1982 *Peasants, Rebels, and Outcasts: The Underside of Modern Japan*. New York: Pantheon.

Hendry, Joy 1987 *Understanding Japanese Society*. London: Croom Helm.

Johnson, Chalmers 1982 *MITI and the Japanese Miracle*. Stanford: Stanford University Press.

Kalleberg, Arne L. and James R. Lincoln 1988 "The structure of earning inequality in the United States and Japan," *American Journal of Sociology*, 94:5121–53.

Kerbo, Harold R. 1990 *Social Stratification and Inequality: Class and Class Conflict in Historical Perspective* (2nd edition). New York: McGraw-Hill.

Kerbo, Harold R. and L. Richard Della Fave 1983 "Corporate linkage and control of the corporate economy: new evidence and a reinterpretation," *Sociological Quarterly*, 24:201–18.

Kerbo, Harold R. and John McKinstry 1987 "Social stratification in modern Japan: a comparative analysis," paper presented at meetings of the Western Society of Asian Studies, Oct. 1987, Tucson.

Kerbo, Harold R. and Meika Sha 1987 "Language and social stratification in Japan," paper presented at meetings of the Eastern Sociological Association, May 1987, Boston.

Kishimoto, Koichi 1988 *Politics in Modern Japan: Development and Organization* (3rd Edition). Tokyo: Japan Echo Inc.

Lincoln, James R. and Arne L. Kalleberg 1985 "Work organization and work force commitment: a study of plants and employees in the U.S. and Japan," *American Sociological Review* 50:738–60.

MacMillan, Charles J. 1985 *The Japanese Industrial System.* New York: Walter de Gruyter.

Mannari, Hiroshi 1974 *The Japanese Business Leaders.* Tokyo: Tokyo University Press.

Mills, C. Wright 1956 *The Power Elite.* New York: Oxford University Press.

Nakane, Chie 1970 *Japanese Society.* Berkeley: University of California Press.

Naoi, Atsushi and Carmi Schooler 1985 "Occupational conditions and psychological functions in Japan," *American Journal of Sociology,* 90:729–52.

Reischaur, Edwin O. 1983 *The Japanese.* Cambridge: Harvard University Press.

Rohlen, Thomas P. 1983 *Japan's High Schools.* Berkeley: University of California Press.

Schur, Edwin M. 1969 *Our Criminal Society: The Social and Legal Sources of Crime in America.* Englewood Cliffs: Prentice-Hall.

Shimizu, Ryuei 1980 *The Growth of Firms in Japan.* Tokyo: Keio Tsushin Ltd.

Simmel, Georg 1905/1955 *Conflict and the Web of Group Affiliations.* ed. Kurt H. Wolff and Reinhard Bendix. New York: Free Press.

Smith, Robert J. 1983 *Japanese Society: Tradition, Self, and the Social Order.* Cambridge: Cambridge University Press.

Taylor, Jared 1983 *Shadows of the Rising Sun: A Critical View of the "Japanese Miracle".* Tokyo: Tuttle.

Tominaga, Ken'ichi 1987 "Problems of viewpoint in interpreting Japanese society: Japan and the West," Donald Treiman and Ken'ichi Tominaga (eds.), *Social Stratification and Mobility in Japan and the United States.* Princeton: Princeton University Press.

Tsurutani, Taketsugu 1977 *Political Change in Japan.* New York: David McKay.

Van Wolferen, Karel 1989 *The Enigma of Japanese Power,* New York: Knopf.

Vogel, Ezra 1971 *Japan's New Middle Class,* Berkeley: University of California Press.

Vogel, Ezra 1979 *Japan as Number One: Lessons for America,* Cambridge: Harvard University Press.

Woronoff, Jon 1980 *Japan: The Coming Social Crises,* Tokyo: Yohan Lotus Press.

Woronoff, Jon 1986 *Politics the Japanese Way,* Tokyo: Lotus Press

Yayama, Taro 1990 "The Recruit scandal: learning from the causes of corruption," *The Journal of Japanese Studies* 16:93–114.

The Ideology of Terrorism

■ *WILLIAM D. PERDUE*

INTRODUCTORY NOTES

At what point does a grievance justify war? And if your grievance does justify going to war, what do you do if you are at a severe military disadvantage? Surely our pre-revolutionary American ancestors thought their grievances against British colonial rule were very legitimate; but, early on, they were not organized for a military offensive. Episodes like the Boston Tea Party were likely to be seen by the British as "terrorist" actions; but Americans were likely to see them as legitimate acts of rebellion. "One man's terrorist," the saying goes, "is another man's freedom fighter."

This leads us to the question: What if, in the global scheme of things, Muslim fundamentalists have legitimate grievances with Western governments, or The Irish Republican Army has legitimate grievances with the British government? What are either of these factions to do when "talks" fail to address their grievances? At what point are "guerilla"/"terrorist" tactics justified? The "statist" position is that "terrorism" is never justified. (For one thing, it usually involves the killing of innocent people. But what about the U.S.

raids on Libya or Panama: did those not involve the killing of innocent civilians?)

Relatively recent terminology for "terrorism" includes the phrases "low intensity conflict" or "low intensity war.". Such terminology has an advantage because it acknowledges that in "war" there are almost always civilian casualties; and in "war" both sides feel that their cause and their tactics are legitimate. The term "terrorism," however, is a politically laden term that suggests that your side's cause and tactics are legitimate while the other side's are not. There has never been a war where each side did not try to delegitimate the other. And the use of the word "terrorism" is one method of delegitimation, often used by the side that has the military advantage.

The following article elaborates this challenge to the popular conceptualization of "terrorism." Perdue adds another slant to this critique, however, by suggesting that it is those acts that threaten structured global inequalities—both international and intranational inequalities—that receive the label "terrorist."

The United States must be able to deal with terrorists as brutally and as deviously as they deal with it.

Raymond Price, former member of the Nixon administration, quoted in the *International Herald Tribune*, November 9, 1985.

SOURCE: William D. Perdue, "The Ideology of Terrorism," from *Terrorism and the State*, chapter 1, pp. 1–16 (abridged). Reprinted with permission of Greenwood Publishing Group, Inc., Westport, CT. Copyright© 1989 by William D. Perdue.

Calling for terror to oppose terror represents well the polemic that dominated U.S. international policy during the 1980s. Yet the question of terrorism, both in terms of events and ideology, is clearly not the invention of one nation, one administration, or one decade. As shall be demonstrated, its dilemmas and controversies have a history and, one fears, a future. It is the nature of our time, however, that some appear ready to yield to barbarism in the name of antibarbarism. Yet, the *problematique* of terrorism transcends the political, tactical, and philosophical questions of how to respond. Even those who wish to take the "high moral ground" (by opposing the position exemplified by Raymond Price), still assume that a "civilized" nation must not stoop to "brutal and devious" measures. So framed, the terrorism debate in Western nations is often over tactics of international social control. Such a focus pits the moralists, who favor diplomatic and other political approaches, against the realists, who opt for forms of coercion ranging from economic sanctions to military action.

Realism is a much abused term, but as a kind of "statespeak," it means that holders of power must deal with the world as it is, not as "we" might wish it to be. This position assumes, of course, that "we" are not part of the problem. C. Wright Mills (1959: 356) unkindly referred to this blindness, which emanates from the elite but that spreads through the lower echelons of power, as "crackpot realism." Ironically, whatever their differences on means, tacticians agree on ends. Both hold to the rightness of their position while attributing brutality to the other side. To assume the superiority of one's own political culture is perhaps a simple modification of a more general ethnocentrism, and such influences are clearly evident in many pronouncements on terrorism. Still, there is more to the terrorism debate than the brutality of tactics or the phenomenon of culturally induced blindness.

INTERNATIONAL TERRORISM IN THE 1980S: THE BUSH REPORT

Terrorism for most people is captured more in images than in words. In the West, high-impact media portrayals feature personal and dramatic accounts of victims and their families, with the signature of the terrorist written in blood. In the 1980s, a cornerstone of U.S. foreign policy became its "low-intensity" war on terror, legitimated by the imagery of senseless, brutal, and random violence. It is in this spirit that the *Public Report of the Vice President's Task Force on Combatting Terrorism* proclaimed in 1986 that "terrorism is a phenomenon that is easier to describe than define." Undeterred, the Bush report cites: "the unlawful use or threat of violence against persons or property to further political or social objectives. It is generally intended to intimidate or coerce a government, individuals, or groups to modify their behavior or policies." This cabinet-level attempt at definition also specified the methods of terrorism, including "hostage-taking, aircraft piracy or sabotage, assassination, threats, hoaxes, indiscriminate bombings or shootings." And finally, the document portrayed the targets of terrorism as innocent, noting that "most victims of terrorism seldom have a role in either causing or affecting the terrorist's grievances." (1986: 1)

Having defined the undefinable, the vice-president's task force constructed a profile of the terrorist, followed by a listing of likely targets.

> The motivations of those who engage in terrorism are many and varied, with activities spanning industrial societies to underdeveloped regions. Fully 60 percent of the Third World population is under 20 years of age; half are 15 years or less. These population pressures

create a volatile mixture of youthful aspirations that when coupled with economic and political frustrations help form a large pool of potential terrorists. Many terrorists have a deep belief in the justice of their cause. They are tough and vicious and may have little regard for their own lives or those of their victims in attempting to achieve their goals. Others may even be hired assassins. . . . Middle East terrorist groups have three main targets: Israel; Western governments and citizens . . . and moderate Arab governments and officials. (1986:1–2)

These targets were allegedly at risk from several sources. While European organizations (such as the Italian Red Brigade, French Direct Action, German Red Army Faction, and the Provisional Irish Republican Army) were duly noted, the report held that: "the most deadly terrorists continue to operate in and from the Middle East. In 1985, they were involved in roughly 50 percent of the total worldwide terrorist incidents. The two main sources are militant Shi'ites from various Middle Eastern countries, especially Lebanon, supported to varying degrees by Iran or Syria; and radical Palestinian elements, principally offshoots of the Palestine Liberation Organization (PLO), often with direct support from Libya, Syria or Iran." In Latin America, the document declares, "Nicaragua and Cuba have been implicated in terrorist activity . . ." (1986: 1–3).

Taken as a whole, the excerpts convey the official story of terrorism. The statist standing of the document and the extent to which its themes have entered public perception qualifies it as an exemplar of the dominant ideology of terrorism. By this set of interrelated ideas, the legitimation of a particular view of world order is constructed through claims made about the nature of terrorism. This idea-system identifies what terrorism is, which methods terrorists employ, and who the terrorists and their victims are. From this viewpoint, terrorism (whether employing action or threat) is unlawful, intended to advance a political or social agenda, and its first targets are Western and other friendly governments.[1]

POWER RELATIONS

To begin to demystify terrorism then, is to raise the question of power relations. One might begin simply by noting that powerless groups often employ guerrilla methods to compensate for their military disadvantage; tactics ordinarily decried by powerful forces as uncivilized. The hit and run tactics of native tribes in North America were called "savage" by European colonials, who then used them later against the British in the American Revolution. The guerrilla forces of Pancho Villa and Emiliano Zapata were similarly denounced by the privileged patrons during the Mexican revolution. Today, the African National Congress, a resistance movement that advocates armed struggle against white minority rule, is termed "terrorist" by the South African government. (Perhaps the ANC would prefer to use air and naval forces against the apartheid government of South Africa if they were available.) All of this is not to argue that powerless groups are incapable of acts of violence that betray whatever cause they claim. The point is that the guerrilla tactics of the powerless are more apt to be labeled terrorist than martial force on the part of an established state.

Second, a focus on power relations goes beyond tactics to ask why some forms of political violence are described as terrorist, while others that bring greater human loss do not invite that label. If parties in conflict do not have equal standing, a double standard of terrorism may be expected to emerge. Thus the definitions of terrorism that prevail reflect such forces as the influence of office, access to the highly sophisticated and pervasive international media, and the "audience appeal" of common values, stereotypes, and symbols. A presidential address on terrorism will have a vast media audience, many of whom are predisposed to respond favorably to the symbols of office, the appeals to nationalistic imagery and the attribution of terrorism to ethnic, ideological and religious forces that already carry negative stereotypes.

Finally, differences in power on the international stage often obscure the reality of institutional terror. To focus on institutional terror means to critically analyze violent and coercive patterns that coalesce around fundamental human purposes, such as meeting material needs and resolving the questions of political rule. It poses the plausible yet disturbing thesis that people face grinding conditions of fear rooted in the very arrangements that promise to safeguard and better their lives. These arrangements are not confined to the societal level, nor do they recognize lines drawn on maps.

To this point, an international economic order may quite "normally" reproduce inequality on a world scale, quite efficiently and systematically transferring wealth from the southern to the northern hemispheres. In the lives of ordinary people, this means 450 million severely malnourished people, the deaths of 15 million children yearly from hunger or hunger-related illness (George, 1984: 3), and in the poorest countries, the death of one child in four before the age of five (Brandt Commission, 1980: 32). On another level, the political organization known as the modern state may be used alone or in alliance with others to advance or protect that order. In the name of security, it offers missiles; in the name of freedom, war; in the name of antiterrorism, terrorism. In the lives of ordinary people, the corruption of state power may be expressed in the knock on the door, mass arrests, disappearances, and summary execution. It may be a device for diverting water, occupying land, and sponsoring its settlement. It may mean capital punishment for those "without the capital," especially if the victims are of some ethnic or racial minority group.

IDEOLOGIES OF DOMINATION

Ultimately, terrorism is a label of defamation, a means of excluding those so branded from human standing. When applied in a one-sided fashion to those who struggle against established political structures, it is a means of organizing both the perceptions and reactions of others in the world community. Once so defined, those affected may become international lepers. Hence the nature of their movement; its objectives, ideology, and historical reason for being will be dismissed out of hand. Paradoxically then, the very label of terrorism has of itself assumed a terrifying power.

Those ideas that interpret the nature and dimensions of human behavior do not arise in a historical vacuum. They are created, formed, and shaped in the minds of people who participate in and respond to the conditions of their age. Yet not all who would define the nature of terrorism exist as equal contributors to the debate. For the ideological construction of terrorism is a function of power, of the ability to control events and to impose one's ways upon others against their will. It follows from the preliminary and sensitizing argument to this point, that power consists of more than overt force and coercion. Within its nature must be found an ability to define events, and to broadly disseminate the official view.

Historically, colonial powers plundered the human and natural resources of their territories. The great plantations of the new world were built by the Africans, wrested from their native land, stacked like timber in the holds of slave ships, then broken from tribe and family and sold into bondage. This conversion to chattel meant more than the death of millions in passage; it also meant that survivors and their descendants would know the negation of their humanity, while the African continent would suffer the devastation of its labor force and thus of its productive future. Even with the decline of the slave trade, the nations of the northern hemisphere continued to transform the vast riches of the south into finished products the original providers of primary resources still find difficult to purchase.[2] And the labor in the north was provided by workers who owned neither factory nor mill, their tools nor their machines, their time nor their jobs.

No doubt, had they been asked, victims then and now would define such conditions as those of constant dread and fear. However, the ideologies that prevailed proved to be those of the master not the slave, of the colonizer not the colonized, of the owning class, not those who sold their labor for a wage. Hence the ideas of racism legitimated the conversion of human beings into chattel, those of colonialism portrayed the native as primitive, and those of social Darwinism argued that the class system was a form of merited inequality. These ideologies of domination were routinely offered academic legitimation. For example, William Graham Sumner joined the faculty of Yale in 1872 and three years later offered one of the first sociology courses on the continent. Drawing from the "principle of noninterference" (social, political, economic *laissez-faire*) of Britain's Herbert Spencer, he reproduced the darker side of the age of imperialism. In this context, the social world, as the natural, was an orderly creation obeying the prime directive of all life: a struggle in which the fit survive and the unfit perish.

> The sociologist is often asked if he wants to kill off certain classes of troublesome and bewildered persons. No such inference follows from any sound sociological doctrine, but it is allowed to infer, as to a great many persons and classes, that it would have been better for society and would have involved no pain to them, if they had never been born. (Sumner, 1963: 25)

The Aryan myth was nurtured in the works of Arthur de Gobineau (1816–82) and H. S. Chamberlain (1885–1926) and others. It remained for Karl Pearson (a turn-of-the-century mathematician who pioneered in the area of correlation) to succinctly demonstrate the power of racism as an ideological tool for political and economic domination. In one paragraph, he offered a defense of the colonization of Africa, the superiority of the white race, and the survival of the fittest component of social Darwinism.

> How many centuries, how many thousands of years, have the Kaffir or the negro held large districts in Africa undisturbed by the white man? Yet their intertribal struggles have not yet produced a civilization in the least comparable with the Aryan. Educate and mature them as you will, I do not believe that you will succeed in modifying the stock. History shows me one way, and one way only, in which a high state of civilization has been produced, namely in the struggle of race with race, and the survival of the physically and mentally fitter race. (Quoted in Sorokin, 1964: 260)

Supremacist thought from the age of imperialism served only to disguise and legitimate the institutional terror of slavery, forced labor among the colonized, the exploitation of the industrial working class, child labor, and ultimately, patterns of genocide. The historical functions of such myths are clearer today. But the contemporary question is whether new or reformulated patterns of inequality have given rise to modern myths of legitimation and defamation.

THE DOMINANT IDEOLOGY OF TERRORISM

In the dominant view, those who perpetrate outsider violence are often portrayed as irrational or crazed, exercising a twisted thirst for blood. For example, Claire Sterling writes in her prologue to *The Terror Network:* "My own conclusion was that, Black or Red, right or left, there are no good killers and bad killers—only killers" (1981b: 2). This conclusion effectively magnifies, depoliticizes, and delegitimates all violence on the part of outsiders. And from a somewhat less polemical author:

> It is clear that those who attempt bizarre, ostensibly political actions with uncertain or irrational outward motivations do so for what are internal, personal reasons. . . . Those who act out their fantasies by murdering the mighty are only one variant in the pool of psychotics whose acts can threaten transnational order. (Bell, 1975: 10)

The dominant ideology of terrorism as known in the West is more than content, it also reflects a particular style. Specifically, the nature of terrorism is privatized as are attempts to explain it. History is reduced to the behavior of notorious persons (whether good or evil) locked in an international morality play. Institutions (such as the state) and movements that oppose those institutions are downplayed or ignored as social forces respectively committed to order and change. There is instead an emphasis on enemy ideologies, conspiracies, and shadowy organizations. Expressed polemically, the good guys are free enterprisers, democratic, Christian, and civilized. The bad guys are communists, Marxists, Islamic fundamentalists, and assorted crazies.

Demonology and Solidarity

Questions of content and style should not obscure the consequences of ideological imagery. Human beings live in a symbolic universe, and symbols represent the medium of social interaction. The most intricate of symbolic systems is language, and the use of complex and highly expressive languages distinguishes the human species. Of course, all words represent some level of symbolism, but in considering the properties of political language certain words are more equal than others. This is not simply because of the precise definitional content (what the word denotes) but also because of the inherent emotional impact (what the word connotes). The argument again is that the term terrorism unleashes powerful imagery with clear societal and intellectual consequences.

Symbolism and allegory are ideological devices that intensify what the Arab social philosopher Ibn Khaldun termed solidarity: a collective sense of oneness or cohesion among the members of a given social order. Through imagery and intricate political fables, those who have alternative visions of society or a changed international order are defined as irrational. Combined with appeals to nationalism, faith, and other traditional symbols, the war on terror unites the social audience against the forces of barbarism and heresy. However, from the standpoint of the state, it is useful to magnify the threat and to weave a pattern of conspiratorial power in order to make a credible foe. This pattern will necessarily involve the identification of a cast of higher demons. The following quotation features the magnification of the threat, the use of imagery (ironically drawn from the history of crime in the speaker's nation), and an appeal to grandeur and unmerited persecution.

> So, there we have it: Iran, Libya, North Korea, Cuba, Nicaragua—continents away, tens of thousands of miles apart, but the same goals and objectives. I submit to you that the growth in terrorism in recent years results from the increasing involvement of these states in terrorism in every region of the world. This is terrorism that is part of a pattern, the work of a confederation of terrorist states. Most of the terrorists who are kidnaping and murdering American citizens and attacking American installations are being trained, financed, and directly or indirectly controlled by a core group of radical and totalitarian governments—a new international version of "Murder Incorporated." And all of these states are united by one, simple, criminal phenomenon — their fanatical hatred of the United States, our people, our way of life, our international stature." (From Ronald Reagan, "The New Network of Terrorist States," an address to the American Bar Association, Washington, D.C., July 8. 1985)

The use of the term *terrorism* to delegitimate those who oppose the West is not an invention of the 1980s. During the post–World War II period of political decolonization in Africa, various national liberation movements were described as terrorist by the affected European states. Only a few examples include the Mau-Mau uprising against the British in Kenya; the FLN (Front de Liberation Nationale) opposed to French colonial rule in Algeria (Hutchinson, 1978) and the Simba forces that battled the Belgians in the Congo (Waggoner, 1980). More recently, ZANU (Zimbabwe African National Union) and ZAPU (Zimbabwe African People's Union), which ended white settler rule in Zimbabwe, and the African National Congress, which battles the RSA, were labeled "terrorist" by Ronald Reagan (Danaher, 1984: 61). Of course, the use of the term to delegitimate national liberation movements has not been confined to Africa. Predictably, as the United States became increasingly mired in Southeast Asia in the 1960s, its leader sought to rally public support by denouncing "Viet Cong terror tactics in South Vietnam."

> Look for a moment at the record of the other side. Any civilian casualties that result from our operations are inadvertent, in stark contrast to the calculated Viet Cong policy of systematic terror. Tens of thousands of innocent Vietnamese civilians have been killed, tortured, and kidnapped by the Viet Cong. There is no doubt about the deliberate nature of the Viet Cong program. One need only note the frequency with which Viet Cong victims are village leaders, teachers, health workers, and others who are trying to carry out constructive programs for their people. Yet the deeds of the Viet Cong go largely unnoted in the public debate. (Lyndon B. Johnson, quoted in United States Department of State, 1968)[3]

It is clear that the war on "Viet Cong terror" reflected not simply opposition to national liberation movements but a continuing obsession with the threat of communism. The paradox is that the decline and fall of the Johnson presidency, as well as the U.S. defeat in Vietnam, was not a consequence of communism, but a paranoid style of anticommunism projected on a world scale. Of course, this record is not confined to a single presidency or to the executive branch. For example, the House Committee on Internal Security (charged with the control of "Communist and other subversive activities affecting the internal security of the United States") (U.S. Congress, Committee on Internal Security, 1974, Part 3: v) held hearings in 1974. These focused on the threat of domestic terrorism and supposed links to "foreign communist terrorists" (1974a: 3915).

However, in the recent past, terrorism has taken on a new and, I think, a more sinister complexion. This new terrorist phenomenon, particularly as applied to organized groups, poses extremely serious problems to our law enforcement agencies and also to our national security. From the testimony and evidence ... it has become more and more apparent that Marxist, Leninist, and Maoist forces operating within worldwide networks do play a dominant role in promoting international terrorist incidents. (House Committee on Internal Security, 1974 (2): 3085)

That the ideological war on terrorism has been historically linked with the war on communism is further evidenced in hearings conducted by the Senate Internal Security Subcommittee of the Senate Committee of the Judiciary on the "Trotskyite Terrorist International."

In previous hearings. it has been established that the Communists, despite their repeated declarations that they do not engage in terrorist activities, do in fact provide training and logistical and financial support for terrorist groups.... This is true of the Moscow Communists, the Maoists, the Trotskyists and the Castro Communists. Indeed, a majority of those groups which are actively engaged in terrorism consider themselves Marxist-Leninists of some kind. (United States Senate, 1975: 1)

The process of constructing the greater meaning of terrorism is further evidenced in more recent congressional hearings on *narcoterrorism*. The argument follows a familiar conspiratorial theme, with a familiar demon.

Then, in the early 70's, the international terrorist community struck on a brilliant, new quick-buck scheme. Drug sales. It was a natural. As terrorism expert, Michael Ledeen of the Georgetown Center for Strategic and International Studies said in a recent article: "Running drugs is one sure way to make big money in a hurry. Moreover, the directions of the flow are ideologically attractive. Drugs go to the bourgeois countries where they corrupt and where they kill, while the arms go to pro-Communist terrorist groups in the Third World." It has worked like a charm. (U.S. Congress, Senate Committee on Labor and Human Resources, 1984: 2)

The statement of former Senator Paula Hawkins of Florida went on to name various "terrorist" groups in Latin America, Malaysia, Burma, while implicating Bulgaria in the use of narcotics to "destabilizing NATO's easternmost flank," and accusing the Vietnamese government of selling opium to resolve that nation's economic problems. The effect of this argument is to blame the huge U.S. narcotics market on an international communist conspiracy that employs terrorism to realize its objectives. (Such a position implicitly denies that the appetite for drugs reflects problems *within* the demand society, while ignoring the historical role of U.S. government agencies and/or allies in narcotics trafficking originating in Southeast Asia (McCoy, 1972: 149–217), and Latin America.

Perhaps most revealing in a context of continuing anticolonial struggle is the conceptual (as opposed to polemical) linkage of terrorism and revolutionary movements. To wit:

1. Terrorism is a systematic and purposeful method used by a revolutionary organization to seize political power from the incumbent government of a state.

2. Terrorism is manifested in a series of individual acts of extraordinary and intolerable violence.

3. Terrorism involves a consistent pattern of symbolic or representative selection of its physical victims or objects.

Terrorism is deliberately intended to create a psychological effect on specific groups of people . . . in order to change political behavior and attitudes in a manner consonant with the achievement of revolutionary objectives. (Hutchinson, 1978: 21)

Considering this definitional attempt, it is evident that the term *revolutionary,* when added to *terrorism* once again expands the scope of the problem and makes evident its political direction. It is also clear that this aspect of the dominant ideology of terrorism ignores the role of the state. It is certainly plausible that incumbent governments may be implicated both in the conduct of terrorism and in the creation of those conditions that give rise to a reactive form of "extraordinary and intolerable violence." Also ignored or understated in this fear of the left is the terrorism of the right, whether on the part of friendly regimes that may support the interests of "national security" or on the part of counter-revolutionaries seeking to restore a lost order.

THE WESTERN ACADEMIC CONSTRUCTION OF TERRORISM

Most Western academic contributions to the terrorism debate evade the question of institutional domination through fear. Mention has already been made of some intellectually dubious efforts dealing in sensationalism and conspiracy. Other work in what might be called an order paradigm of terrorism is clearly committed to a control perspective. The Rand Corporation, routinely supported by funding from the U.S. government, has generated a great deal of literature dealing with such topics as the terrorist environment, terrorist "mindsets," government responses, and the future of terrorism (Jenkins, 1982). Similar approaches view terrorism as a challenge to the state, or a weapon of political agitation (Lodge, 1981; Thornton, 1964). Whether or not by explicit design, these works (and many others) are rooted in the assumption that the Western state is the political expression of a societal consensus, and that terrorism is primarily (if not exclusively) the practice or threat of nongovernmental public violence (see Krieger, 1977).

Other less "tactical" works consider how terrorism represents a threat to democratic or liberal states, while probing how counterterrorism can be balanced with civil liberties (Wardlaw, 1982: Wilkinson, 1977). One well-known historical study (Laqueur, 1987) finds "different terrorisms" (p. 9) and while not disputing that "crimes committed by governments" (p. 11) have been historically more deadly, continues to focus on "terrorism from below" (p. 11). Ironically, in centering on "movements that have used systematic terrorism as their main weapon" (p. 12), this inquiry transfers the emphasis on "system" from its acknowledged historical connection with the Jacobin *régime de la terreur,* to outsiders who threaten existing orders.

A recent and more conceptually sophisticated comparative inquiry provides some sense of proportionality on the scope and effectiveness of outsider violence, while casting serious doubts on the question of an "international revolutionary terrorism" (Gurr, 1988). Another distinguishes between legitimate guerrilla warfare and the generalized terror directed toward innocents (Wilkinson, 1977: 52). *Caveats* notwithstanding, the prime focus of these and more historically oriented orderist literature on terrorism remains with antistate forces.

Certainly, some of the literature goes beyond the tacit admission of state coercion through fear, seeking to analyze regime terror (Parry, 1976: 187–243, passim). However, there is a recurring tendency to specify notorious regimes, such as the Jacobins, the Nazis, the Stalinist, and so on, and to avoid placing such regimes in historical and global context. One effort to study a regime of terror (as opposed to a "siege" of terror by outcasts) ties terrorism to fear induced by government violence and even includes certain acts of war (Walter, 1969: 6). However, the thesis of this book is explored through a study of what the author terms "primitive" African communities, with the exemplar of the terrorist regime being the early 19th-century Zulu state under Shaka. (To the ideological point, no mention is made of the British armies who were involved in perhaps 50 major colonial wars in the same century (Giddens, 1985: 223). Absent from this entire type of inquiry is an analysis of Western state violence, much less the global relations that give it form.

The more critical literature on terrorism is sparse and often suffers from mechanical and instrumental conceptions of the nation-state. However, the argument has been made that regime terror is a means of insuring the social "stability" required to secure loans from Western-dominated "multilateral" lending institutions (such as the International Monetary Fund) (Pion-Berlin, 1984), and to attract multinational corporate investment (Chomsky and Herman, 1977). Thus, regime terror is driven by more than Caesaristic ambition. It is routinely directed at opposition movements and leaders who threaten the maintenance of systemic inequality, between nations and more specifically between classes (Carleton, 1988). And it is frequently the result of training and financing provided by core states, who otherwise may resort to both overt and covert programs of intervention and counterrevolution. To this specific point is a study of the sponsorship and support of "National Security States" by the United States (Herman, 1982: 119–37; McClintock, 1985).

That the definition of terrorism by U.S. officials and the mainstream media routinely masks state (wholesale) terrorism has been argued eloquently by some (see especially Chomsky, 1986a). St. Augustine's morality tale (in which the emperor that uses a fleet to intimidate and plunder is judged by different standards than a pirate with a single ship) is heuristic. Also instructive is an examination of terrorism, the "Red menace," and the legitimation of the post–World-War II Truman Doctrine of "containment" in the United States. The case that real terror involves land owners, death squads, and malnutrition tied to a developmental model structurally designed for permanent peripheral dependency has been made well, if only rarely (Herman, 1982).

A political economy of terrorism must take note of such efforts, probing theoretically the structure of ideological systems, and placing these in a material context. Beyond this, a political economy of terrorism must place statist behavior in a world system context. However, terror is not confined to purely instrumental linkages between specific nation states and the misdeveloping world. The internal dynamics of the national security economy, with its expression in nuclear and other forms of warfare misproduction, cannot be separated from the New Global Security Economy. This misproductive system is marked by its traffic in arms and military sales and its needs for strategic resources. It is also an employer, not only of national and military support personnel but of an indigenous workforce to help maintain worldwide bases, to provide local "security" and to manufacture weapons systems and military supplies.

And finally, the dominant ideology of terrorism has arisen dialectically in conflict with rival visions of societal transformation and alternative development. It is not enough to document and critique abuses of world market power. It is also necessary to examine fledgling movements and new attempts at institutional formation to further understand why they have been targeted for negation by core powers.

➤ DISCUSSION QUESTIONS

An ideology is a set of beliefs that justifies certain political and economic practices. This article is about the effect of ideologies on definitions of "terrorism." What ideologies are being discussed in this article? And how might these or other ideologies effect definitions of, or responses to, other types of crime?

NOTES

1. The actual loss to life and property for U.S. citizens does not appear to match the publicity surrounding the issue throughout the 1980s. To illustrate, by the reckoning of the Task Force, 23 U.S. citizens lost their lives to international terrorism in 1985, and 2 were victims of the domestic variety. This compares with 18,980 domestic homicides in the same year (*World Almanac*, 1987: 786).

2. This phenomenon of declining terms of trade reveals the permanence of "unequal exchange." When a country's terms of trade decline, which is the case for many in Africa, Latin America, and Asia, the value of exports (routinely raw materials) is artificially low compared to the cost of manufactured or finished imports. The exchange gap widens, ever exacerbating the relations of dependency (Debt Crisis Network, 1985: 19–20).

3. Of course, as was to become distressingly clear to the American people, U.S. trained allies in Vietnam were no strangers to the practice of state torture. And the tactics of that war of terror, with its saturation bombings, napalm, white phosphorous, search and destroy missions, free-fire zones, and ecocidal chemicals, were not lacking in terror.

REFERENCES

Bell, J. Bowyer 1975 *Transnational Terror*, Stanford, Calif.: Hoover Institution on War, Revolution and Peace.

Brandt Commission 1980 *North-South: A Program for Survival*. Report of the Independent Commission on International Development Issues. Cambridge, Mass.: MIT Press.

Carleton, David. 1988 "The New International Division of Labor and Repression in Latin America." In George A. Lopez and Michael Stohl (eds.). *Development, Dependence, and State Repression*. Westport, Conn: Greenwood.

Chomsky, Noam. 1986 "Libya in U.S. Demonology." *Covert Action 26*. Summer, 15–24.

Chomsky, Noam, and Edward S. Herman. 1977 *The Washington Connection and Third World Fascism*. Boston: South End Press.

Danaher, Kevin. 1984 *In Whose Interest? A Guide to U.S.–South African Relations*. Washington, D.C.: Institute for Policy Studies.

Debt Crisis Network. 1985 *From Debt to Development: Alternatives to the International Debt Crisis*. Washington, D.C.: Institute for Policy Studies.

George, Susan. 1984 *Ill Fares tge Kabd: Essays on Food, Hunger, and Power*. Washington, D.C.: Institute for Policy Studies.

Giddens, Anthony. 1985 *The Nation-State and Violence*. Berkeley and Los Angeles: University of California Press.

Gurr, Ted Robert. 1988 "Some Characteristics of Political Terrorism in the 1960's." Pp. 31–58 in Michael Stohl (ed.), *The Politics of Terrorism*. New York and Basel: Marcel Dekker.

Herman, Edward S. 1982 *The Real Terror Network*. Boston: South End Press.

Hutchinson, Martha Crensaw. 1978 *Revolutionary Terrorism: The FLN in Algeria, 1954–1962*. Stanford, Calif.: Hoover Institution Press.

Jenkins, Brian. 1982 *Terrorism and Beyond*. An International Conference on Terrorism and Low-Intensity Conflict. Santa Monica, Calif.: The Rand Corporation.

Krieger, David M. 1977 "What Happens If? Terrorists, Revolutionaries, and Nuclear Weapons." *The Annals of the American Academy of Political and Social Sciences,* 430: 44-57.

Laqueur, Walter. 1987 *The Age of Terrorism*. Boston: Little Brown.

Lodge, James. 1981 *Terrorism: A Challenge to the State*. Oxford: Martin Robertson.

McClintock, Michael. 1985 *The American Connection: State Terror and Popular Resistance in Guatemala*. Boston: Zed Press.

McCoy, Alfred W. 1972 *The Politics of Heroin in Southeast Asia*. New York: Harper and Row.

Mills, C. Wright. 1959 *The Power Elite*. New York: Oxford University Press (1956).

Parry, Albert. 1976 *Terrorism from Robespierre to Arafat*. New York: Vanguard.

Pion-Berlin, David. 1984 *Ideas as Predictors: A Comparative Study of Coercion in Peru and Argentina*. Ph.D. Dissertation, University of Denver.

Public Report of the Vice President's Task Force on Combatting Terrorism. 1986 Washington, D.C.: U.S. Government Printing Office, February.

Sorokin, Pitirim. 1964 *Contemporary Sociological Theories*. Harper and Row.

Sterling, Claire. 1981 "Qaddafi Spells Chaos." *The New Republic*, March 7.

Sumner, William Graham 1963 *Social Darwinism: Selected Essays of William Graham Sumner*. Englewood Cliffs, N.J.: Prentice-Hall.

Thorton, Thomas. 1964 "Terror as a Weapon of Political Agitation." Pp. 71-99 in H. Eckstein (ed.) *Internal War*.

U. S. Congress, Committee on Internal Security, House of Representatives. 1974 *Terrorism,* Parts l, 2, 3, and 4. Washington, D.C.: U.S. Government Printing Office.

U. S Congress, Committee on the Judiciary, U.S. Senate. 1975 *Trotskyite Terrorism International.* Washington, D.C.: U.S. Government Printing Office.

U. S. Congress, Committee on Labor and Human Resources, United States Senate. 1984 *Drugs and Terrorism*. Washington, D. C.: U.S. Government Printing Office.

U. S. Department of State. 1968 Office of Media Services, Bureaus of Public Affairs. *Viet Cong Terror Tactics in South Vietnam* (No. 7). U. S. Government Printing Office.

Waggoner, Fred E. 1980 *Dragon Rouge: The Rescue of Hostages in the Congo*. Washington, D.C.: U.S. Government Printing Office.

Walter, Eugene Victor. 1969 *Terror and Resistance: A Study of Political Violence*. London: Oxford Press.

Wardlaw, Grant. 1982 *Political Terrorism: Tactics and Countermeasures*. Cambridge: Cambridge University Press.

Wilkinson, Paul. 1977 *Terrorism and the Liberal State*. London: Macmillan.

World Alamanac. 1987 New York: Pharos.

Conceptualizing Hate Crime in a Global Context

■ *MARK S. HAMM*

INTRODUCTORY NOTES

In recent years more and more attention has been given to a category of offense commonly known as "hate crime." Racist and ethnically inspired violence is no stranger to the U.S. nor, for that matter, to many countries throughout the world; but a number of events during this century (not the least of which was the Nazi Holocaust) have sensitized much of the world to this phenomenon.

Furthermore, several events in the past decade seem to have precipitated a number of such violent incidents, and threaten even more. The fall of the Soviet Union is one such event. Before the fall, the Soviet government managed to keep ethnic hostilities in check. With the fall of the Soviet Union also came severe economic strife throughout its former territories; such strife seems to exacerbate ethnic clashes in that one ethnic group often tends to scapegoat the other, blaming the outgroup for its economic problems.

A related event was the reunification of Germany, bringing to the birthplace of Nazism a whole host of economic problems, especially unemployment. Compounding these problems has been the influx of refugees to countries throughout the world, making available a target for economically frustrated racists.

The problem for legislators, law enforcement officials and criminologists, however, is in defining "hate crime." When making and enforcing law, an inexact definition can threaten the civil liberties of everyone.

The author engages in a good deal of polemics, using words such as "lunatic," perhaps exaggerating the problem, and seeming to advocate draconian methods of law enforcement. Most readers will be vehemently opposed to neo-Nazi violence; but it is important that we remain circumspect when we encounter such impassioned criminological prose because, when social control measures are concerned, civil liberties are at stake.

Though "hate crime" (as defined in this article) accounts for only a small proportion of violent crimes in the U.S., this type of criminal activity does deserve the attention of American criminologists because it could very well escalate in the near future. As the author notes, this type of crime is of further interest because, operating as a form of "domestic terrorism," it seems to have swayed immigration policies in Germany (in the direction favored by neo-Nazis); and it has the potential to affect other public policies elsewhere in the world.

Look at the liars and the propagandists among us, the skinheads ... here at home, the Afrikaners Resistance Movement in South Africa, the radical party of Serbia, the Russian Black Shirts.... We must stop the fabricators of history and the bullies as well. Left unchallenged, they would still prey upon the powerless, and we must not permit that to happen again.

U.S. President Bill Clinton Upon Dedication of the United States Holocaust Museum Washington, D.C.
April 22, 1993

Since the collapse of the Soviet empire and the destruction of the Berlin Wall, more than two million poor immigrants from Eastern Europe have crossed borders to the countries of Western Europe. Another one million immigrants, truly disadvantaged men and women from third-world nations, have also crossed these borders seeking political and economic asylum.

This migration has been tragic for many émigrés, especially in Germany—the birthplace (let us never forget) of national socialism. Since 1990, an estimated 4,000 immigrants from Albania, Bosnia-Herzegovina, Bulgaria, Croatia, Romania, Turkey, Algeria, Morocco, Pakistan, Nigeria, Uganda, Mozambique, and Vietnam became victims of violence committed by German neo-Nazi skinheads and other young extremists. Yet this is an official statistic; it is estimated that the frequency of violent attacks against foreigners may actually be closer to 80,000. This violence has been wretchedly brutal, ranging from gang beatings to firebombings and murder. Currently, an average of 60 immigrants are harassed, beaten, or firebombed each day by highly organized groups of young males who often revere the memory of Adolf Hitler and Nazism. Forty-seven years after the allied liberation of Nazi Germany, this youthful convolution of violence also includes a distinct anti-Semitic dimension: Skinheads have recently desecrated dozens of Jewish cemeteries and attacked concentration camp memorials at Satchsenhausen, Ravensbrueck, and Dachau. Among German government officials, police, and researchers, this catastrophic social problem is referred to as *right-wing violence*.[1]

But Germany is not the only country to suffer from political violence in the post-communist era. Racist skinheads and other neo-Nazi youth collectives also exist in Belgium, Britain, Denmark, France, the Netherlands, Norway, Sweden, Switzerland, and in former Eastern bloc countries such as Hungary and Poland. These groups have committed some 4,000 violent attacks against Eastern European, Pakistani, East Asian, and third-world immigrants—including more than 25 murders, and dozens of firebombings and desecrations of Jewish and Muslim religious institutions. In Belgium, the Netherlands, and Norway this crime is defined by government officials and researchers as *racist violence*. In Britain and France, it is called *racial violence*.[2]

In North America, skinhead youth gangs have been implicated in the murder of more than 100 young African-Americans and third-world immigrants; at least four homicides against gay men; nearly 400 assaults against black males; more than 300 cross-burnings; 14 firebombings of African-American churches; more than 200 assaults against gays and lesbians; some 40 desecrations of Jewish cemeteries; and nine acts of violence perpetrated against worshipers at Jewish synagogues, including one attempted mass murder in Dallas, Texas (Hamm, 1993; Klanwatch, 1991; Thornburgh, 1990). Because Canada's share of the problem is so small, government officials and researchers have yet to reach a consensual definition for this type of crime. But not so in the United States. Here, we suffer from an excess of definitions.

In the United States, attacks by white neo-Nazi youth against African-Americans, immigrants, gays, and religious institutions have been referred to with such diverse terms as *hate crime, hate-motivated crime, bias crime, bias-motivated crime* and *ethnoviolence* (e.g., Berk, 1990; Bensinger, 1991; Garofalo & Martin, 1991; Weiss, 1991). Because the use of these various terms often feeds community divisiveness, especially in racially charged times, several urban police departments have even created the label *possible bias crime* in an effort to contain media attention and hostile reactions from special interest groups (Fritsch, 1992). Finally, politicians and feminist scholars from all points on the ideological spectrum have argued that rape should also be included in the hate crime category (Buchanan, 1990; Miller, 1992; Renzetti, 1993).

In summary, crimes motivated by a victim's race, ethnicity, or religion are defined at least nine different ways in seven different nations around the world.[3] These diverse definitions of a common criminal event suggest the need for a global definition of the social problem at hand. Such a definition would serve two important functions. First, it would create common language for social scientists with an interest in the problem. The failure of doctrines associated with the teachings of Engels, Marx, and Lenin has taught us that "human imagination driven by an improper use of language is vulnerable to extreme errors" (Ostrom, 1990:245). In the same way, erroneous cognition of a criminal phenomenon can produce social control doctrines that yield greater errors in magnitude than the problems they are meant to solve. In Germany, this would likely exacerbate a social problem that is already catastrophic.

Second, a global definition is necessary because the crime is a global problem. The fall of communism has brought with it "a growing interdependence of nations for their economic progress and political stability" (Chambliss, 1992:1). A global definition promises to help scholars and policymakers better understand how the emergence of a global economic and political system effects the emergence of a particularly insidious social problem.

TOWARD A GLOBAL CONCEPTUALIZATION

Globally, hate crime (alternatively referred to as right-wing violence, racist violence, etc.) must be conceptualized as an international youth movement toward racism. This is so because it is *racism* (not homophobia, and certainly not misogyny) that fuels the fires of neo-Nazi skinhead violence from Rostock to London, from Amsterdam to Paris, and from Stockholm to Dallas. Across international contexts, three features remain constant. According to the overwhelming body of evidence gathered since the fall of the Berlin Wall:

1. Eastern European, Asian, Pakistani, and third-world immigrants are the most frequent victims of hate crime;

2. Groups of young white males are most often the aggressors; and

3. Among these aggressors, neo-Nazi skinheads are responsible for the most egregious acts of violence in the world today.[4]

Therefore, the neo-Nazi skinheads present a worst-case scenario. Yet this also makes them an identifiable target for social scientists who wish to understand the criminology and control of hate crime in the post-communist era.

Neo-Nazi Skinheads

The study of hate crime begins like any other problem in criminology: With an examination of the motives that lead certain individuals, under certain circumstances, to commit crime. Yet with the neo-Nazi skinheads we are not interested in all crime. We have no interest, for example, in the number of robberies, extortions, or larcenies committed by skinheads because skinheads do not commit these crimes (Anti-Defamation League of B'nai B'rith, 1989; Hamm, 1993; Seidel-Pielen, 1991). Globally, we are only interested in their violence against racial and ethnic minorities.

I argue that if we want to make better social policies to control hate crime, we should pay less attention to broad generalities, and more attention to the growing volume of specific examples of hate crime being committed around the world. Instead of constructing macro-level sociological treatises on hate crime, generalizing hate crime to other victims, or devising more elaborate definitions of hate crime, we must focus on patterns that lead certain white neo-Nazi youths, under certain conditions, to commit violence against social outgroups. It is only through an understanding of these patterns that we can achieve a global definition for the hate crime phenomenon. I am suggesting that a criminology of hate crime—based on facts about the most extreme and essential cases—must be articulated before any global definition can be reached; and long before any social policy is justified.

THE CRIMINOLOGY OF HATE CRIME

I begin with the meditations of Holocaust scholar Hannah Arendt:

> Racism, as distinguished from race, is not a fact of life, but an ideology, and the deeds it leads to are not reflexive actions, but deliberate acts based on pseudo-scientific theories. Violence in interracial struggle is always murderous, but it is not "irrational," it is the logical and rational consequence of racism (1963:42).

Following this insight we may assume two theoretical tenets concerning the most violent form of hate crime as it exists in the world today (i.e., the brutal victimization of thousands of immigrants by German neo-Nazi youths). First, this form of crime is grounded in an ideology of racism. The motivation toward hate crime does not exist in the abstract world where randomness and chaos prevail; rather, it lies in a structured philosophical system of simple, traditional beliefs called *neo-Nazism* that features racism as its defining characteristic (Hamm, 1993; Mucke, 1991; Protzman 1992a). From this perspective hate crime can be considered globally. By conceptualizing the phenomenon in terms of a circumspect yet international youth movement toward lunatic extremism, it becomes isolated. Thus, it forms a concept package for researchers (right-wing extremism) and a target set of subjects to investigate: neo-Nazi youth—wherever they exist around the globe. To reemphasize, in its most violent form, hate crime is always ideological.

Second, because it is ideologically motivated, hate crime is rational. In the minds of neo-Nazi skinheads, hate crime is not irrational nor is it "magical." To the contrary, hate crime is premeditated violence carried out in heroic ecstasy. Inspired by the social and political brio of skinhead "Oi" music, this *sensuality of violence* is used by youths as a tool to advance group goals, to maintain order within their community, and to punish those who threaten the well-being of each tiny neo-Nazi skinhead cell from Munich to El Paso. The organized use of sensual violence continues to draw a growing number of youths into a thrill-seeking cult of right-wing lunatics throughout Europe and the United States (Hamm, 1993). Today, the heartbeat of this lunacy can be heard most loudly in Germany (Protzman, 1992a–d).

THE ATTEMPTED SOCIAL CONTROL OF HATE CRIME

"The skinheads," writes William Chambliss, "are a world unto themselves. The more they are attacked, the stronger grow the internal ties" (1993:xiv). Until recently, state responses to neo-Nazi skinhead violence have been fairly tame. Throughout Europe and the United States, federal prosecutors have kept clear of cases involving skinhead attacks; preferring instead to let these cases be handled by local jurisdictions where violent skinheads have typically been charged with no offense more serious than disturbing the peace (see Benjamin, 1992; *The Economist* 1992; Witte, 1992). Even in murder cases, light sentences have been handed down to the German skinheads (Kinzer, 1992d). Yet this approach seems to be changing.

In December of 1992, the German Ministry of Justice made two broadsweeping changes in the nation's justice system to deal with the rising tide of violence against foreigners. First, it is now illegal for youths to join organizations that question the democratic principles of the German republic. Recently, for example, memberships in the Nationalistic Front and the German Alternative Party—both dominated by young skinheads —have been banned (Kinzer, 1992c; Lane & Breslau, 1992). German Interior Minister Rudolf Seiters has charged that the Nationalistic Front is "an active fighting organization aimed at disposing our democratic order" (quoted in Fisher, 1992:2a); about the German Alternative Party, he proclaimed that "the disgusting work of these rabble-rousers must be stopped" (quoted in Toomey, 1992:21). Second, it is now a crime to sell, manufacture, and distribute skinhead Oi music in Germany. It is also a crime for Oi bands to perform in public. The German Parliament has declared that "there is a direct connection between the texts of their songs, which glorify Hitler and call for the murder of foreigners and Jews" (quoted in Protzman, 1992b:A16). Similar attempted control policies have been advanced in Poland, Britain, France, Canada, and the United States (see Protzman, 1992c; Hamm, 1993; Ross, 1992, Chapter 6; Witte, 1992). Like the German approach, these attempted control policies feature an immeasurable amount of censorship and suppression of freedom of expression.

The more skinheads are attacked, the stronger grow their internal ties. The stronger the internal ties, the more skinheads attack. Since the Ministry of Justice outlawed skinhead Oi music, it is now available only through clandestine channels. Within German society, these channels lead straight to Nazism and violence. Oi records, cassettes, and compact discs are now available only on the black market. The first group of entrepreneurs to fill this demand were the owners of army and weapons stores (Protzman, 1992b). Hence, Oi music—recently described by *Newsweek* as "the emblem of an international underground of haters"—has become aligned with German militarism and weaponry. *Newsweek* warned that a " head-on attack [against Oi music] could backfire" (Masland, 1992:53). Perhaps it is for this very reason that the Ministry of Justice recently announced to the 80 million people of Germany that "the right-wing trail of death has just begun" (quoted in Kelly, 1992:2A).

Shortly following this extraordinary statement, *The Economist* observed the tragic fact that:

> Violence against foreigners . . . is not unique to Germany. Britain, Sweden, France, Italy and now Spain have all seen it. No government seems to know what to do (1992:55).

A GLOBAL DEFINITION: DOMESTIC TERRORISM

The definition of any crime must clearly delineate the individual and social nature of the phenomenon at hand. The exercise serves an important purpose far beyond the concerns of academic theorizing. If clearly defined, a crime becomes comprehensible to social control agents and implicates the state institutions that should deal with the problem. A clearly defined crime also identifies the social importance of the problem and the potential public resources that can be marshaled to enhance problem-solving capabilities. More than simply reflecting the individual and social nature of a crime, a clear definition also attracts attention to its causes and control.

Because hate crime is ideological and rational, it satisfies the criterion for most definitions of *domestic terrorism*. Between 1941 and 1989, government officials and researchers in Europe and the United States published more than 100 definitions of domestic terrorism (Gurr, 1989; Laqueur, 1987). Domestic terrorism is, on balance, one of the most thoroughly defined crimes in all of international criminology. Ironically, it is also one of the least understood because international criminology is altogether void of original research on the subject (Laqueur, 1987; Ross, 1992; Wilkinson, 1986).

Definition of Domestic Terrorism

Perhaps the most global and rigorous definition of non-state domestic terrorism has been advanced by Jack Gibbs who stipulates that "in all instances [i.e., in all settings and across all social contexts] . . . terrorism is illegal violence or threatened violence directed against human or nonhuman objects" (1989:330, 337) provided that such violence or attempted violence meet five criteria.

1. It was undertaken with a view to maintaining a putative norm in at least one particular territorial unit.

2. It had secretive, furtive, and/or clandestine features that were expected by the participant to conceal their personal identity.

3. It was not undertaken to further the permanent defense of some area.

4. It was not conventional warfare.

5. It was perceived by the participant as contributing to the normative putative goal (described in point "1") by inculcating fear of violence in persons other than the immediate target of the actual or threatened violence and/or by publicizing some cause.

Globally, there are now tens of thousands of examples of neo-Nazi skinhead violence, which if examined under a sociological microscope, would meet Gibbs' rigorous definition of domestic terrorism. If only they were examined. The data are not hard to come by. They can be gathered from interviews with neo-Nazi skinheads themselves; from their living victims; and from court transcripts, police files, and the international print media. Yet given these diverse data sources, we would expect the applicability of Gibbs' definition to vary because of differences in research methodology, the accuracy and completeness of available evidence, geographical variation in the crime, and variations in the seriousness of the crime across samples and time frames. With these caveats firmly in mind, below I offer four brief case studies—drawn from such data sources—that demonstrate the usefulness of Gibbs' global definition.[5]

The Portland Case Study

At about 1:30 A.M., November 13, 1988, three teenage skinheads—heavily intoxicated with beer—encountered three Ethiopian immigrants on a rainy backstreet in Portland, Oregon. The skinheads had never met the immigrants before and vice-versa. Unprovoked, the skinheads singled out one immigrant named Mulugeta Seraw, a slightly-built 27-year-old employee of Avis Rent a Car and father of one son. They set upon Seraw with a baseball bat and steel-toed boots, beating him savagely and shouting, "Die nigger, die!" When they were finished, the skinheads had fractured Seraw's skull in two places, killing him. Twenty-four hours later, Portland police searched the three-room apartment shared by the skinheads. In the first room, they found baseball bats and clubs wrapped in barbed wire. In the second room, they found racist propaganda published by a Southern California organization known as the White Aryan Resistance. And in the third room, they found a small library on the rise and fall of Nazi Germany (Hamm, 1993).

The Wuppertal Case Study

On the evening of November 14, 1992, five skinheads, aged 14 to 18, entered a pub in Wuppertal, Germany—a tiny western village near the Dutch border. Intoxicated with beer, they began a heated argument with a 53-year-old butcher named Karl-Heinz Rohn about immigration policy in unified Germany. At the end of the argument Rohn called the skinheads a gang of "Nazi swine."

One hour later, the five skinheads met Rohn several blocks away from the pub. They brutally beat Rohn with baseball bats and steel-toed boots, killing him. Then they doused his body with schnapps and set him afire. Assisted by the owner of the pub where the argument originated the skinheads then loaded the burned corpse into a car trunk and crossed into the Netherlands where they dumped Rohn's body in a canal outside the village of Venlo.

On arrest and interrogation, one of the skinheads said he thought Rohn was Jewish. He was not. Rohn died for another reason: Because of his support for German immigrants (*Chicago Tribune*, 1992; Meyer, 1992; *The Economist*, 1992).

The Mölln Case Study

At about 1:00 A.M., November 23, 1992, two skinheads approached the home of a 51-year-old woman named Bahide Arslan in Mölln—one of western Germany's most prosperous cities located near Hamburg in the state of Schleswig-Holstein. Arslan was a Turkish immigrant who owned a successful grocery business and lived with her

10 children and four grandchildren in a modest three-story house in Mühlen Street
—a home she had occupied for the past 25 years. At 1:00 AM., November 23, the
Arslan family was asleep.

The two skinheads were Michael Peters, a 25-year-old unemployed high school
dropout, and Lars Christiansen, a hard-working 19-year-old grocery store clerk.
Both were members of the Free German Workers' Party, a newly organized grouping
of neo-Nazi skinheads and other violence-prone rightists. Both carried firebombs
made out of rags stuffed into a canister of gasoline (known in the United States as a
Molotov cocktail). They lit their firebombs and smashed them through the windows
of the Arslan home. Then they fled in Peters' Volkswagen.

In the ensuing fire, Bahide Arslan was burned to death as she lay atop her grand-
son, protecting him from the smoke and flames. Another child, Arslan's grand-
daughter Yelitz Arslan, age 10, also burned to death in the blaze along with her
cousin, 14-year-old Ayse Tuknaz, who was visiting from Carsamba, Turkey. Six other
family members were hospitalized for severe burns and smoke inhalation.

Just after the firebombs were thrown, Peters anonymously telephoned the Mölln
fire department and shouted: "It's burning in Mühlenn Street! Heil Hitler!" This was
followed by a series of extraordinary events.

Later that morning (November 23), the German Parliament began its daily session
with a moment of silence for the Arslan family. Chancellor Helmut Kohl then issued
his most forceful and genuine denunciation of right-wing violence since the fall of the
Berlin Wall.

> What has appeared here is an act of brutality that for every humane sensibility is incom-
> prehensible. The German government [will invoke] every legal step to combat violence
> and political extremism (quoted in Benjamin, 1992:44; Masland, 1992:53).

By noon, Chancellor Kohl's office was flooded with faxed condemnations of the
killings from international civil rights groups, and from the heads of states of Israel,
Turkey, and Italy who threatened to pull economic interests from Germany unless the
government got a grip on its catastrophic social problem. Meanwhile, some 10,000
protesters gathered on the streets of Hamburg in silent mourning for the Arslan family. Then the most significant events transpired.

For the first time in the history of unified Germany, a federal prosecutor from the
Ministry of Justice took jurisdiction of a case involving right-wing violence. Because
of the Holocaust, Germany has an arsenal of federal law for use against political
extremism. The strongest laws cover terrorism. On the same day, the president of the
Opel car company offered the Ministry of Justice 100,000 Deutsche marks ($62,000)
towards an award for help in finding the Mölln killers. Opel, like the German government, was interested in protecting its export-based economy.

And so, the German government—in collaboration with the private sector—
mounted an aggressive manhunt for Peters and Christiansen. Using the full force of
the mighty German law and economy, these powerful interests were not looking for
delinquents who were guilty of disturbing the peace. Now they were after a couple
of terrorists. "Brutally put," reported the London *Observer,* "a neo-Nazi murder was
useful to galvanize the country" (Catterall, 1992:13).

For the next two days, police throughout Schleswig-Holstein conducted an aggressive investigation of the far-right. Focusing on skinheads, they raided more than 100
houses—uncovering caches of weapons, neo-Nazi propaganda, and Oi music. This
intense response resulted in the arrest of Peters and Christiansen on November 26.

They were officially described as members of a "terrorist organization formed to pursue rightist, extremist and xenophobic aims through violent action on foreigners living in Germany" (quoted in Catterall, 1992:13) and were charged with three counts of murder, nine counts of attempted murder, arson, and breach of the peace. (They *were not* charged with terrorism.) Peters and Christiansen were immediately taken to Lubeck prison, 30 miles north of Mölln. After being placed in his cell, Christiansen slashed his wrists with broken glass in a suicide attempt (Benjamin, 1992; Kinzer, 1992e, 1992f, 1992g; Protzman, 1992c; *The Economist,*1992; *The New York Times,* 1992).

The Hereford Case Study

On the night of February 18, 1991—at the height of the Persian Gulf War—four skinheads approached a Lebanese refugee camp near Hereford, England. They were all members of a London-based neo-Nazi group called the Anti-Pakki League, and they were intoxicated with beer. Each youth carried a homemade bomb made out of rags stuffed into a bottle of gasoline. The skinheads jumped a security fence and fire-bombed the camp barracks, injuring more than 20 immigrants. Among these victims was a 12-old-girl; one bomb struck her bed as she lay sleeping. As a result most of the skin was burned from her body. Three days later she died a horrible and agonizing death (Bauerlein, 1992; field notes).

APPLYING GIBBS'S GLOBAL DEFINITION OF DOMESTIC TERRORISM

In summary, each skinhead gang committed its homicide as an expression of intolerance and contempt for immigrants. Because the United States, Germany, and Britain all assume tolerance and respect for immigrants through liberal or moderate immigration laws (and because laws reflect dominant norms of democratic societies), then the murder of immigrants and their supporters can be viewed as a violent act *undertaken with a view to maintaining a putative norm* of the neo-Nazi skinhead movement. And because four different skinhead groups committed four separate homicides in four different geographical locations, each crime was committed in *one particular territorial unit.* Moreover, the available evidence surrounding each case study satisfies Gibbs's first criteria for domestic terrorism.

Each case also satisfies Gibbs's second criteria: the four homicides had *secretive, furtive, and/or clandestine features that were expected by the participants to conceal their personal identities.* Each murder was carried out in the dead of night by individuals who were affiliated with a group, thus concealing their personal identities. In Portland, these individuals were members of the East Side White Pride, a hybrid neo-Nazi cell created by the White Aryan Resistance. Each skinhead was known by a street name. (For example, the skinhead who wielded the baseball bat, Kenneth Murray Meiske, was known as "Ken Death".) Though we know little about the skinheads who murdered Rohn in Wuppertal, the facts that they immolated his body, transported it across international borders, and then disposed of it in a canal strongly suggest that these secretive and clandestine features of the crime were intended to conceal their personal identities. Furthermore, the Wuppertal skinheads, like Meiske and his accomplices, did not publicly claim responsibility for their murder. Likewise, the Free German Workers' Party skinheads of Mölln—who fled the murder scene immediately—used an anonymous phone call to conceal their personal identities; and the Hereford skinheads, all members of the clandestine Anti-Pakki League, did not publicly claim responsibility for their deadly firebombing.

Gibbs's third criteria is also satisfied. The Wuppertal and Hereford homicides were the first and only crimes committed by these particular skinhead groups against immigrants (or their supporters) in their respective areas. Although the East Side White Pride had been involved in several other beatings of minorities in the Portland area prior to the Seraw murder, and although the Mölln skinheads were involved in the firebombing of an asylum hostel in nearby Kollow, these groups *were not seeking a permanent defense of their areas*. At the time of the Seraw murder, the East Side White Pride had been in existence for less than six months; Peters and Christiansen had known each other for only a few months when they killed Arslan and her children. Accordingly, these skinhead collectives had little time to even prepare for a permanent defense of their areas.

Gibbs's fourth criteria is quickly satisfied across all four cases: baseball bats, steel-toed boots, schnapps, and gasoline firebombs *are not conventional weapons of war.*

With respect to Gibbs's fifth criteria, available evidence suggests that the motive for each crime was to strike out against immigrants and their supporters—the enemy *(contributing to the putative norm)*—thereby *inculcating fear of violence in persons other than the target of the actual violence.* In each case, anti-immigrant prejudice motivated specific acts of violence designed to capture the attention of a larger human audience—the Governments of the United States, Germany, and Great Britain. In other words, these acts of violence were exercises in what Gibbs refers to as *attempted deterrent vicarious social control*. I shall refer to this notion with the shorter, "vicarious social control."

Vicarious Social Control

Gibbs defines domestic terrorism as a case where:

> the first party [i.e., the terrorist group] attempts to punish the third party [i.e., victims of terroristic violence] ... always presuming that such action will influence the second party's [i.e., the government's] behavior [e.g., by attempting to control the third party] (Gibbs, 1989:337).

Figure 1 presents the notion of vicarious social control. As applied to the evidence reviewed here, the motives of the "first party" were grounded in neo-Nazism. From Kenneth Meiske's portentous library in Portland to Michael Peters' refrain of "Heil Hitler" recited to the Mölln fire department, a belief in modern Nazism served as the common denominator for these four acts of domestic terrorism. And as history tragically reminds us, Nazism represents a *sustained and violent campaign* against certain segments of the civilian population in the pursuit of political and social objectives that defile human morality. This is the first party's ultimate blackmail vicariously posed to Gibbs's "second party"—the governmental structures of the world today. Following the massacre of Turkish immigrants in Mölln, for example, the Minister of Justice charged that the skinheads were attempting "to reestablish a National Socialist dictatorship in Germany" (quoted in Lane & Breslau, 1992:30).

FIGURE 1: The Global Application of Gibbs' Theory

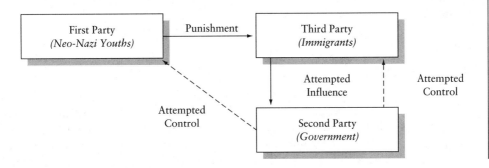

Figure 1 shows how the first party (neo-Nazi youths) punishes the third party (immigrants) in an attempt to influence the second party's (the government's) behavior, *presuming that such violence will lead to increased control of the third party through laws enacted by the second party to deter immigration.* Hence, the skinhead slogan "Foreigners Out!" is not only a battle cry for terrorism, it is also a literal and imaginative expression of vicarious social control over the state. The skinheads exert this control by threatening government with a harsh return to national socialism; with lunatic extremism.

Finally, Figure 1 outlines the role of the state in responding to domestic terrorism. "Because nonstate terrorists resort to violence," argues Gibbs, "they are certain to be targets of attempted control by the police and/or *the military*" (1989:338, emphasis added).

DISCUSSION

Although neo-Nazi skinheads are not responsible for all hate-motivated crime in the world today, they are responsible for the most violent attacks against racial and ethnic minorities. Globally, however, these attacks are defined more than half a dozen ways. There is, then, no coherent sociological definition for a global phenomenon which has been referred to as "potentially the major social problem of the next century" (Chambliss, 1993:xiii).

I have attempted to fill this void by invoking what Paul Wilkinson refers to as the "mental reenactment of terrorist thought in each tiny terrorist group" (1986:97). Through my brief reenactment of skinhead violence, I have endeavored to show that this international social problem can be defined through reference to Gibbs's (1989) global definition of the phenomenon: Wherever in the world neo-Nazi youths use violence or the threat of violence against persons because of their race or ethnicity, this crime is properly defined as *domestic terrorism.*

Thus, terms such as right-wing violence, racist violence, racial violence, hate crime, hate-motivated crime, bias crime, bias-motivated crime, possible bias crime, and ethnoviolence are all irrelevant sociological abstractions because they do not adequately capture the true meaning of the individual and social content of the crime at hand. Accordingly, the social scientific use of these terms is counterproductive to enhancing problem-solving capabilities in the area. "There is a danger," warns Vincent Ostrom, "that names (symbols, words) may be incorrectly associated with referents." If so, erroneous definitions of a social problem "can yield greater errors in magnitude than simple ignorance" (Ostrom, 1990:244).

CONCLUSIONS

The world is currently linked together by the malaise of change. In Europe, the heart of this change is in Germany, where there also beats the heart of a catastrophic social problem. Each day, scores of foreigners are harassed, beaten, or firebombed by young German males who strive to fulfill the hidebound dreams of Nazism. This violence is carried out heroically with baseball bats, brass knuckles, knives, and beer bottles; with gasoline, Oriental throwing stars, starter pistols, steel-toed boots, and schnapps. Such wildcat Aryanization of the general populace has gone on before in Germany's history—bringing with it catastrophic impacts on the moral sensibilities of the Western world.

This same social entropy is now at work in the form of skinhead youth gangs who loiter around subway stations, housing projects, pubs, and public parks in German cities and villages. The post-communist rise of such vitriolic neo-Nazism (at a time when most thought it a remote possibility) has been described as nothing less than "a ball and chain dragging down Germany and all Europe with it" (Lewis, 1992:15A) . . . For the first time since Spain's democratic rebirth, swastikas have recently appeared on walls in Madrid. The tolerant Canadian and Dutch Parliaments have begun to complain about immigrants and refugees seeking asylum in their countries.

Mainstream politics begins to walk lockstep with the bloody boots of Nazism. Swastikas begin to appear on sidewalks around the Holocaust Museum in Amsterdam, and near the synagogues of Old Montreal. In Austria the far-right populist Jorg Haider becomes a candidate for the nation's presidency, advocating a referendum against foreigners; and soon, swastikas appear in the streets of Vienna. In the United States, Republican Presidential candidates Patrick Buchanan and David Duke make nativism a key element of their campaigns, charging that new immigrants would "dilute" the nation's European character. In their 1992 Convention, the Republican Party introduces a plank calling for "a barrier—a wall or trench—along the border with Mexico." And as President Bush signs an executive order forcing the repatriation of Haitians fleeing their country by boat, immigrants across the land begin to feel the brunt of a growing hostility.

Attacks on newly arrived immigrants become a routine occurrence in New York City public schools, as skinheads in the South Bronx start to accost Asian immigrants, spray-painting their faces black. In Houston, two skinheads stomp a 15-year-old Vietnamese boy to death. In Carbondale, Illinois, police begin an investigation of skinhead links to a mass murder of five Asian students. In Great Barrington, Massachusetts, a teenage skinhead goes on a killing rampage with an automatic assault rifle, leaving two dead and four seriously wounded. And in Patterson, New Jersey, a skinhead gang called the "Dotbusters"—named for the dot, or bindi, that some women wear on their foreheads—emerges to terrorize a growing population of East Indian women (see DePalma 1992; Sontag, 1992).

Meanwhile, the human ravages of "ethnic cleansing" continue in Bosnia-Herzegovina and threaten to spread north through the Baltics, to Central Europe and south through Albania, perhaps to Greece.

Highly consistent with this global trend toward xenophobia, the ruling conservatives in the German Parliament recently led the way for a wide-bodied capitulation to the demands of the terroristic neo-Nazi youth gangs of their country. On December 18, 1992, the Parliament passed a law making it harder for asylum-seekers and refugees to enter Germany. In effect the new law bars immigrants from most nations of Eastern Europe, and calls for the repatriation of thousands of immigrants from Vietnam and Romania. Moreover, the skinhead battle cry of "Foreigners Out" has been incorporated into public policy.

This new law has been criticized by left and right alike as the most serious threat to European democracy and peace since the fall of the Berlin Wall. "It must be a matter for the gravest reflection, that for violence in the streets, [Germany's immigration problem] would have continued to mount" wrote conservative analyst William Buckley shortly after its passage (1992:12). Members of Germany's liberal Green Party have described the new immigration law as "a surrender to street fighters who have attacked refugees and the homes where they live" (quoted in Kinzer, 1992h:A6). In sociological terms, the first party vicariously controlled the second party through a sustained campaign of violence against the third party.

This terroristic strategy, therefore, has now proven effective in changing the course of public policy on immigration in Germany, the heart of Europe, if not the world. If domestic terrorists can effectively change immigration policy, then they can also change policies in criminal justice, health, education, welfare, and most important— in the military direction of nation-states.

The Global Control of Domestic Terrorism

All of this can change through democratic leadership provided by men and women of goodwill and courage who have the resolve to get control of Gibbs's first party— neo-Nazi youth wherever they exist around the world today. The social institutions exist to effect such change. On this point, history is extremely clear.

During the 1970s and early 1980s, the German Federal Republic showed their ability to impose harsh social control against the violence of such leftist groups as the Baader-Meinhof Red Army Faction. Beginning in the early 1970s and extending up to 1992, the British have employed draconian measures to control the anarchist terrorism of the Angry Brigade and the leftist terrorism of the Irish Republican Army. To this day, the British government combats IRA guerrillas with an elite cadre of anti-terrorist commandos. These agents wear suits of full body armor and are specialists in firearms, explosives, and dog handling; their tactics include state-of-the-art electronic surveillance and routine stop and checks of any vehicle traveling in the Greater London area which might be linked to the IRA. Similarly, American police and federal law enforcement officials moved swiftly and decisively to bring down such leftist groups as the Black Panthers, the Symbianese Liberation Army, and the Weathermen.

This same measure of public energy must now be brought against the far-right. More than simply taking away their rock music and forbidding them to join clandestine groups (thus causing new problems), public officials can begin to view the young neo-Nazis for what they truly are. Since these youths are known to commit violence against persons because of race or ethnicity, they are *terrorists*. They are much more than delinquents involved in boys' pranks. According to Gibbs, these terrorists can only be controlled by throwing the full weight of the state against them.

In Germany—at the epicenter of the international youth movement toward racism —this calls for the use of such law enforcement and military tactics as saturation patrol, stakeouts, electronic surveillance, follow-up investigations, improved crime reporting, and permanent international intelligence machinery designed to remove these youths from the public sector and incarcerate them in prison where they belong. Under any normative definition of democracy, terrorists ought not be entrusted with the power and privilege to shape public policy.

Immediate legal remedies for prosecuting domestic terrorists are available under the federal civil rights laws of all nations (Dees, 1991; Padgett, 1984; *The Economist,* 1992), and methods for their treatment and rehabilitation are described in the international literature of correctional education (Hamm, 1991). In the emerging European community, the alternative to a domestic terrorism approach is simply more of the same: A dangerous social entropy of assaultive violence, profound fear, anxiety, isolation, restricted mobility and, especially among the poor immigrants of Western Europe and Africa, fatalistic despair—the feeling that prudent behavior is unavailing because criminal justice systems are inadequate to the task of providing law and order.

To be reversed, this condition demands the wisdom to change. This process can begin with a global definition that attracts attention to the real causes and control of the problem.

➤ DISCUSSION QUESTIONS

Imagine two cases of assault. Both cases involve a white man assaulting a black man; both occur in the same situations; both result in the same degree of injury. But in one of the cases, the assailant issues a racial slur while inflicting the injury. Certain hate crime statutes being proposed would provide for a more severe penalty for the assailant using a racial slur. What do you think of such a statute? What civil liberties issues are involved?

NOTES

1. Official statistics on right-wing violence come from Germany's Federal Office for Protection of the Constitution reported in Fisher (1992), Jackson (1991), Kelly (1992), Kinzer (1992a; 1992b), Marshall (1992), Protzman (1992a), and Whitney (1992a). The estimate of 80,000 attacks since 1990 is based on calculations contained in British Home Office studies that show an overall reporting rate of between only two and five percent among victims of racial harassment and assault (see Bowling, 1990, Chapter 1; Brown, 1984; London Borough of Newham, 1986). The organization of German neo-Nazi skinhead groups and their allegiance to the memory of Hitler is reported in Douglas (1993), Jackson (1991), Kinzer (1992b, 1992c), Lane and Breslau (1992), Mücke (1991), Protzman (1992a, 1992b), and Seidel-Pielen (1991). The "catastrophic" nature of this violence was voiced by Chancellor Helmut Kohl's government and reported by the Associated Press in the *Bloomington Herald-Times* (1992a, 1992b). The definition of the crime phenomenon is reported in Cartner (1992), Haberman (1992), Kinzer (1992a, 1992b), Protzman (1992a), Seidel-Pielen (1991), and Whitney (1992a, 1992b).

2. The dimensions and definitions of these problems are reported in Bauerlein (1992), Björgo Chapter 3, Bowling (1990; Chapter 1), Brown (1984), Cooper (1989), Coplon (1989), Gordon (1990), Hamm (1993), Hunt (1992), Hiro (1991), Lane and Breslau (1992), Saulsbury and Bowling (1991), *The Economist* (1992) and Witte (1992).

3. Only in the United States are crimes motivated by a victim's sexual orientation included in the crime definition and only in the United States has it been suggested that rape be included in the definition.

4. For evidence of this trend in Germany, see Note 1. For evidence in other parts of Europe and Britain, see Note 2. For evidence in the United States, see Anti-Defamation League of B'nai B'rith (1989, 1990), Center for Democratic Renewal (n.d.), Clarke (1991), Klanwatch (1991), and U.S. Department of Justice (1989). The U.S. studies show that young American-born black males are the most frequent victims of hate crime (Labaton, 1993; Meddis, 1993) and that neo-Nazi skinheads are responsible for nearly two-thirds of these racial attacks (Hamm, 1993; Herek & Berrill, 1992; Klanwatch, 1991).

5. There is well-established precedent within the terrorism literature for using single case studies for purposes of illustration, as demonstrations of hypotheses and for theory building (e.g., Crenshaw, 1981; Laqueur, 1987; Gibbs, 1989; Wilkinson, 1986).

REFERENCES

Anti-Defamation League of B'nai B'rith 1990 "Neo-Nazi Skinheads: A 1990 Status Report." *Terrorism,* 13: 243–275.

_____ 1989 *Skinheads Target the Schools.* New York: ADL.

Arendt, H. 1963 *Eichmann in Jerusalem: A Report on the Banality of Evil,* New York: The Viking Press.

Bauerlein, M. 1992 "The Right Rises in Europe." *Utne Reader,* March/April: 34–38.

Benjamin, D. 1992 "Cracking Down on the Right." *Time,* Dec. 14: 43–45.

Bensinger, G.J. 1991 "Hate Crime: A New/Old Problem." Paper presented at the annual meeting of the American Society of Criminology, San Francisco, November.

Berk, R.A. 1990 "Thinking About Hate-Motivated Crimes." Journal of Interpersonal Violence, 5: 334–349.

Bloomington Herald-Times 1992a "Germans Face Another Night of Ethnic Violence." Aug. 8: A8.

_____ 1992b "Kohl Vows Crackdown on Neo-Nazis." Aug. 28: A3.

Bowling, B. 1990 "Racist Harassment and the Process of Victimization: Conceptual and Methodological Implications for Crime Surveys." Paper presented at the Realist Criminology Conference, Vancouver, B.C.

Brown, C. 1984 *Black and White Britain: The Third PSI Survey.* London: Heinemann.

Buchanan, P. 1990 "African Women Are Real Victims of Hate Crime." *Terre Haute Tribune-Star,* March 8: A6.

Buckley, W.F. 1992 "Fuel to the German Fire." *National Review,* Dec. 28: 12.

Cartner, H. 1992 "Foreigners Didn't Cause German Violence." *The New York Times,* Sept 6: A16.

Catterall, T. 1992 "Heil Hitler Slayings Spark Bout of Hysteria." *The Observer,* Nov. 29: A13.

Center for Democratic Renewal (n.d.) *Skinhead Nazis and Youth Information Packet.* Atlanta, GA: CDR.

Chambliss, W.J. 1993 "Foreword." In M.S. Hamm *American Skinheads: The Criminology and Control of Hate Crime.* Westport, CT: Praeger.

_____ 1992 "Call for Papers." Program announcement for the 1993 annual meeting of The Society for the Study of Social Problems.

Chicago Tribune 1992 "Neo-Nazi Bomb Shames German Town," Nov. 24: A1

Clarke, F.I. 1991 "Hate Violence in the United States." *FBI Law Enforcement Bulletin,* January: 14–17.

Cooper, M.H. 1989 "The Growing Danger of Hate Groups." *Editorial Research Reports,* 18: 262–275.

Coplon, J. 1989 "The Skinhead Reich." *Utne Reader,* May/June: 80–89.

Crenshaw, M. 1981 "The Causes of Terrorism." *Comparative Politics,* 13: 379–399.

Dees, M. 1991 *A Season for Justice: The Life and Times of Civil Rights Lawyer Morris Dees.* New York, NY. Charles Scribners Sons.

DePalma, A. 1992 "Questions Outweigh Answers in Shooting Spree at College." *New York Times,* Dec. 28: A1.

Douglas, M.C. 1993 "Auslander Raus! Nazi Raus! An Observation of German Skins and Jugendgagen." *International Journal of Comparative and Applied Criminal Justice* 16: 1–15.

Fisher, M. 1992 "Germany Cracks Down on Neo-Nazis." *Washington Post,* Nov. 28: Al.

Fritsch, J. 1992 "Police Vow New Caution in Labeling Bias Crimes." *The New York Times,* Dec. 22: A11.

Garofalo, J. & S.E. Martin 1991 "The Law Enforcement Response to Bias-Motivated Crimes." In Taylor (ed.) *Bias Crime:The Law Enforcement Response.* Chicago, IL: Office of International Criminal Justice.

Gibbs, J.P. 1989 "Conceptualization of Terrorism" *American Sociological Review,* 54: 329–340.

Gordon, P. 1990 *Racial Violence and Harassment.* London: Runnymede Trust.

Gurr, T.R. 1989 "Political Terrorism: Historical Antecedents and Contemporary Trends." In TR. Gurr (ed.) *Violence in America* (Vol. 2). Newbury Park, CA: Sage.

Haberman, C. 1992 "An Anxious Israel, 2 Germans, a Riveting Tableau." *The New York Times,* Nov. 19: A3.

Hamm, M.S 1993 *American Skinheads: The Criminology and Control of Hate Crime.* Westport, CT: Praeger.

_____ 1991 "Confronting the Appeal of White Extremism Through Correctional Education." In S. Duguid (ed.) *The 1991 Yearbook of Correctional Education.* Burnaby, B.C.: Simon Fraser University.

Herek, G.M. & K.T Berrill 1992 *Hate Crimes: Confronting Violence Against Lesbians and Gay Men.* Newbury Park, CA: Sage.

Hiro, D. 1991 *Black British White British: A History of Race Relations in Britain.* London: Grafton Books.

Hunt, S. 1992 "Fascism and the 'Race Issue' in Britain." *Talking Politics,* 5: 23–28.

Jackson, J.O. 1991 "Unity's Shadows." *Time,* July 1: 6–14.

Kelly, J. 1992 "Refugees, Jews Targets of Neo-Nazis." *USA Today,* Nov. 11: A1.

Kinzer, S. 1992a "Germany Blocks a Big Neo-Nazi Rally Near Berlin." *The New York Times,* Nov. 16: A3.

_____ 1992b "Youths Adrift in a New Germany Turn to Neo-Nazis." *The New York Times,* Sept. 28: A3.

_____ 1992c "Neo-Nazi Front Will Fight Its German Banning in Court." *The New York Times,* Nov. 30: A6.

_____ 1992d "Light Sentences Against Germans Who Killed Foreigner Stir Debate." *The New York Times,* Sept. 16: A4.

_____ 1992e "Germans Arrest a Neo-Nazi, 19, In Bombing That Killed 3." *The New York Times,* Dec. 1: A6.

_____ 1992f "Germany Outlaws Neo-Nazi Group." *The New York Times,* Nov. 11: Al.

_____ 1992g "A Look Into the Violent World of a Young Neo-Nazi." *The New York Times,* Dec. 12: A4.

_____ 1992h "Germans in Accord on a Law to Limit Seekers of Asylum." *New York Times,* Dec. 8: Al.

Klanwatch 1991 *The Ku Klux Klan: A History of Racism and Violence.* Montgomery, AL: The Southern Poverty Law Center.

Labaton, S. 1993 "Poor Cooperation Deflates FBI Report on Hate Crime." *The New York Times,* Jan. 6: A8.

Lane, C. & K. Breslau 1992 "Germany's Furies." *Newsweek,* Dec. 7: 30–31.

Laqueur, W. 1987 *The Age of Terrorism.* Boston, MA: Little, Brown and Co.

Lewis, F. 1992 "Europe's Champagne Goes Flat." *The New York Times,* Dec. 5: A15.

London Borough of Newham 1986 *The Newham Crime Survey.* London: LBN.

Marshall, T. 1992 "German Jews' Exodus is Small but Ominous." *Los Angeles Times,* Nov. 28: A4.

Masland, T. 1992 "Muffling the Music of Hate." *Newsweek,* Dec. 14: 53.

Meddis, S.V. 1993 "Race Biggest Factor in Hate Crimes." *USA Today,* Jan. 5: Al.

Meyer, K.E. 1992 "The Ghosts of Weimar." *The New York Times,* Dec. 1: A14.

Miller, S.L. 1992 "Misogyny Masquerading as Ordinary Violence: Counting Hate Crimes Against Women." Paper presented at the annual meeting of the American Society of Criminology. New Orleans, November.

Mucke, T. 1991 "Bericht uber das Project—Miteinander Statt Gegeneiandeer." *Jervental:* 38–47.

Ostrom, V. 1990 "Problems of Cognition as a Challenge to Policy Analysts and Democratic Societies." *Journal of Theoretical Politics,* 2: 243–265.

Padgett, G.L. 1984 "Racially Motivated Violence and Intimidation: Inadequate State Enforcement and Federal Civil Remedies." *Journal of Criminal Law and Criminology,* 26: 591–625.

Protzman, F. 1992a "German Attacks Rise As Foreigners Become Scapegoat" *The New York Times,* Nov. 11: Al.

_____ 1992b "Music of Hate Raises the Volume in Germany." *The New York Times,* Dec. 2: Al.

_____ 1992c "Germany to Ask Court to Revoke Some Civil Rights of 2 Neo-Nazis." The New York Times, Dec. 10: A6.

_____ 1992d "Germany Moves to Ban a Second Neo-Nazi Party." *The New York Times,* Dec. 11: A9.

Renzetti, C.M. 1993 "Bias Motivated Violence and Hate Crimes Against Women: They Just Don't Count." Paper presented at the annual meeting of the Academy of Criminal Justice Sciences. Kansas City, March.

Ross, J.I. 1992 "Radical Right-Wing Violence in Canada: A Quantitative Analysis." *Terrorism and Political Violence,* 4: 72–101.

Saulsbury, W. & B. Bowling 1991 *The Multi-Agency Approach in Practice: The North Plaistow Racial Harassment Project.* London: Home Office.

Seidel-Pielen, E. 1991 *Krieg im den Stadten.* Berlin: Rotbuch, 34.

Sontag, D. 1992 "Across the U.S., Immigrants Find the Land of Resentment." *The New York Times,* Dec. 11: Al.

The Economist 1992 "Germany Looks at Itself, and Winces." Nov. 28: 55–56.

The New York Times 1992 "2 Germans Admit Arson Attack That Killed 3 Turkish Nationals." Dec. 2: A6.

Thornburgh, R. 1990 Address before the Simon Wiesenthal Center. Chicago, March 5.

Toomey, C. 1992 "Women Dreaming of Fourth Reich Swell neo-Nazi Ranks." *The Sunday Times,* Dec. 13: 21.

U.S. Department of Justice 1989 *Terrorism in the United States 1989.* Washington, DC: U.S. Dept. of Justice.

Weiss, J.C. 1991 "Ethnoviolence: Impact and Response in Victims and the Community." In N. Taylor (ed.) *Bias Crime: The Law Enforcement Response.* Chicago, IL: Office of International Criminal Justice.

Whitney, C.R. 1992a "Germans Emphasize Non-Rioters at Berlin Rally." *The New York Times,* Nov. 10: A6.

———— 1992b "350,000 in Germany Protest Violence Against Migrants." *The New York Times,* Nov. 11: Al.

Wilkinson, P. 1986 *Terrorism and the Liberal State.* New York: New York University Press.

Witte, R.B.J. 1992 "State Response to Racist Violence: A Theoretical Framework." Paper presented at the annual meeting of the American Society of Criminology. New Orleans, November.

PART TWO

The Police

The Royal Ulster Constabulary: A Law Unto Themselves?

■ *DERMOT WALSH*

INTRODUCTORY NOTES

The police in the U.S. operate under considerable legal constraints; the police we see on the streets we know are usually from the lower ranks; and we know that they are not likely to be well paid; it's easy to forget, then, just how powerful these individuals are. Not only is a police officer authorized to administer lethal force, but perhaps more important, a police officer has the power to instantaneously deprive you of your freedom.

Jurisprudents have argued the question of just when is a person "under arrest," not legally, but practically speaking. Practically speaking, it can be argued that you are under arrest whenever you are in the immediate presence of a police officer— because you are being deprived of your freedom *by virtue* of being in his or her presence. You cannot, for example, suddenly start to run in the opposite direction or do anything else that might cast suspicion on you. In fact, in a police officer's presence, we feel compelled to act normally, and often with the utmost respect. Now that's power!

Further establishing the officer's power over you is the fact that she or he can exercise a great deal of discretion in the exercise of her or his duties. It is usually at the officer's discretion whether or not to put you under surveillance, whether or not to stop you, whether to simply warn you or "take you in," and whether or not to fire upon you. In a very real sense, the police officer's power means more to the "person on the street" than the power of any other agent of the criminal justice system. For this reason, it is very important that the power of the police should be constrained.

It is the police officer's ability to deprive individuals of their freedom—both legally and practically speaking—that makes the police a frequent weapon of tyrants. In fact, while we have come to take the presence of the police for granted, the development of British and American police forces in the nineteenth century at first received

SOURCE: Dermot Walsh, "The Royal Ulster Constabulary: A Law Unto Themselves?" from *Whose Law and Order? Aspects of Crime and Social Control in Irish Society,* Mike Tomlinson, Tony Varley and Ciaran McCullagh (Belfast: The Sociological Association of Ireland, 1988): 92–107 (abridged). Reprinted with permission.

very little popular support. The British had a history of tyrants using the criminal justice system for their own ends (e.g., Charles I and Oliver Cromwell); and many Americans saw a police force as being inherently undemocratic.

While not always defending tyrants, the police do, almost invariably, defend the status quo. If they are here to ensure "law and order," we might ask "whose order"? They work for the state, so it's safe to assume they defend the state's idea of order—the status quo. They are an inherently conservative institution, defending the state's interests and often deployed for the express purpose of preventing change. (A good example is the way the police were used against civil rights protesters in the South in the early '60s.) And this is another reason that the power of the police—as agents of the state—needs to be constrained.

The following article provides one illustration of the use of the police to defend the status quo and the interests of the state. In this case—Northern Ireland—there has been ongoing violent strife between the largely Protestant (British) government and its Catholic constituency, especially the Irish Republican Army. From this example, and others, we might draw a simple hypothesis: the greater the threat perceived by the state, the less compelled it will be to constrain its police.

INTRODUCTION

To the average citizen a uniformed police officer often represents a figure of authority. If s/he says stop, the citizen will stop; if s/he asks a question, the citizen will feel constrained to answer; if s/he requests the citizen to go to the police station to assist with further enquiries, the citizen will feel obliged to cooperate. If such instructions or requests were issued by an ordinary individual the citizen may comply out of simple curiosity or from a desire to be helpful or for some other reason, but s/he is unlikely to feel under any obligation.

There are many possible explanations for the deference afforded a police officer. Not the least of these is a fear that failure to obey a police officer's direction is punishable by a legal sanction. Indeed, as the law stands today, there are real grounds for this fear. Although conceived originally as nothing more than a citizen in uniform, the police officer in Ireland and Britain has acquired such numerous and diverse powers over the centuries that the similarity between his/her office and that of the citizen is tenuous to say the least. Unlike the latter s/he has the power, in certain circumstances, to stop individuals in the street without arresting them; to search individuals and private property; to take breath, blood and urine samples; to detain suspects in a police station; to control the movement of traffic, pedestrians and demonstrations; and much more besides (Leigh, 1985). In fact the powers of the police officer are so wide-ranging and complex that it can be difficult for police officers to know the exact limits of their powers in any given situation. To make matters worse parliament can add to these powers whenever and in whatever manner it sees fit.

Simply because a police officer enjoys wide-ranging powers, it does not follow that s/he is all powerful in dealing with the citizen. One fundamental feature that they share in common is that both are subject to the law. If the citizen exercises his/her freedom in a manner which contravenes the law then s/he is liable to prosecution or civil action. Exactly the same applies to the police officer. It is true that his/her freedom of action is much broader than that of the citizen because of extra powers, but s/he does not enjoy a general power to do whatever is necessary to maintain law and order. When a police officer moves to curtail the freedom of the individual s/he must be in a position to justify his/her action on the basis of a specific legal power vested in his/her office. If the officer is unable to bring his/her actions within any such power then his/her infringement of a citizen's freedom will be unlawful and liable to legal sanction, just as if s/he was an ordinary citizen.

That, at least, is the theory. If the example of Northern Ireland is anything to go by, the practice is quite different. Between 1969 and today individuals and groups who have opposed the British presence there by violent and non-violent means have found it extremely difficult to secure protection and redress in the courts against police excesses. A remarkable feature about their lack of success is that the abuses have been high profile, substantial in volume and severity, and sustained in frequency over the years.

RUC PRACTICES

Five phases can be identified. The first concerns the RUC's handling of civil rights demonstrations in the late sixties and early seventies, many of which ended in violent confrontation between opposing factions and ultimately between the marchers and the police. Extensive media coverage of these events revealed excessive force being employed by the RUC, sometimes to restore public order but on other occasions to break up unlawful but peaceful demonstrations. Official inquiries into the events made no secret of their findings that the RUC had exceeded their powers, usually by applying more force than was reasonably necessary in the circumstances to effect arrests and maintain public order (Cameron, 1969; Scarman, 1972). Despite these findings, the evidence of video recordings and eye witnesses and loud protestations from many quarters, no police officer was prosecuted in respect of these matters.

The second phase began in 1971 following the internment operation. RUC officers subjected a number of internees to excessively oppressive interrogation techniques in an effort to gather intelligence. The methods used included subjection to "white noise," long periods of standing and food and sleep deprivation. An official inquiry found that these methods were almost certainly in breach of United Kingdom law (Parker Report, 1972). The European Court of Human Rights, in a case brought by the Irish government against the United Kingdom government, ruled that the methods constituted inhuman and degrading treatment and, therefore, were in breach of the European Convention on Human Rights. Nevertheless, no prosecutions were instituted against any of the officers involved, although it is understood that out-of-court awards of compensation have been made to many of the victims.

Interrogation also forms the basis of the third phase. In the mid-seventies, special interrogation centers were established at Castlereagh and Gough barracks, Armagh. At this time the RUC was under intense pressure to secure convictions against suspects in the Diplock courts. The officers responded, by resorting frequently to physical beatings, threats, verbal abuse, intimidation and generally oppressive treatment in an effort to extract confessions from suspects in the interrogation centers (Taylor, 1980). In response to increasing public disquiet at these practices Amnesty International was persuaded to carry out an investigation in 1978 which concluded that "maltreatment of suspected terrorists by the RUC has taken place with sufficient frequency to warrant the establishment of a public inquiry to investigate it". The United Kingdom government was not willing to pursue such an inquiry and plumped for the soft option of setting up an inquiry into interrogation procedures. Nevertheless, even this inquiry felt compelled to voice its opinion that prisoners had received injuries in police custody which were not self-inflicted. Despite the volume of evidence and formal complaints lodged,[1] and the fact that these practices prevailed over four or five years, no RUC officer was prosecuted (Bennett Committee, 1979). In only one case did the authorities set up an investigative tribunal and even that was thwarted by the refusal of the RUC officers involved to cooperate and the lack of any legal compulsion on them to cooperate.[2] Nor have there been any successful civil actions against police officers in respect of these practices.

The fourth phase takes over in 1980 where the third phase leaves off. It concerns the current arrest practices of the RUC. Since 1980 they appear to be following a policy of arresting individuals not because they believe that they are actually engaged in criminal activity but because they want information. This information can range from details of the individual's personal life to recent incidents in the area in which s/he lives. The apparent purpose is to build up and maintain comprehensive intelligence on individuals and whole communities. The scale of the operation and the likelihood that innocent persons are being dragged into the net is indicated by the fact that in the first 10 months of 1980 no less than 4,029 were arrested under emergency powers and, of these, only 11% were ultimately charged. Normally one would expect this figure to be about 90%. A survey (Walsh, 1982:37) reveals that many of these "suspects" were not even questioned about criminal activity.

The fifth phase consists of the "shoot-to-kill" policy. There have been many occasions in the past 18 years when innocent individuals, some of them young children, have been shot dead by the security forces using real or plastic bullets. In the last few years, however, the RUC would appear to have been following a policy of using maximum force—a synonym for shooting dead—against suspects in situations where a lesser degree of force is an option. So far no police officer has been convicted for an offense arising out of these incidents. Although a top-level police inquiry was initiated (firstly under Stalker and then Sampson), this became subject to lengthy delays and has been shrouded in controversy. In January 1988, the British Government announced that it would be "against the national interest" to prosecute RUC officers for perverting the course of justice, as alleged in the Stalker/Sampson report.

It would appear from these five phases that the RUC have exceeded their powers regularly in their dealings with republican individuals and groups. More recently, members of the loyalist community have also been victims of the RUC stretching their powers beyond the limits of the law. This prompts the question why there has not been a much greater volume of prosecutions, convictions and successful civil actions against police officers in Northern Ireland. There can be little doubt that if individuals or organized groups of civilians stretched their legal powers in a similar manner the outcome would be very different.

CONCLUSION

A police force is an essential component of modern society. It would be difficult to envisage how the person and the property of the individual could be protected without such a policing mechanism. A police force, however, would be counter-productive if its powers and resources were not limited and subject to the rule of law. A force which enjoyed the capacity to act beyond the law would carry the potential to threaten as well as protect the individual (Goldstein, 1977). This paper has attempted to show that, at least since the outbreak of communal violence in 1969 in Northern Ireland, the RUC has been such a force in that it has been able to overcome the normal, legal restrictions applicable to police forces in modern, civilized and democratic countries. An inevitable consequence is the insecurity of individuals in those communities most likely to suffer from police excesses. Not only are their persons and property exposed to the normal risks of modern society but they are exposed also to attack from those whose official role is to protect them. That in itself is a recipe for instability, conflict and violence.

▶ DISCUSSION QUESTIONS

Throughout the world and throughout modern history, urban riots have often been triggered by repressive and/or abusive police actions. In this sense, the rioter and the terrorist may have much in common. In what ways are they similar? In what ways are they different? (You may want to refer to the introductory notes to Article 9.)

NOTES

1. Between 1976 and 1980 (inclusive) there were 1,690 complaints of assault in police custody.

2. Under section 13(2) of the Police Act (Northern Ireland) 1970 the police authority has the power to refer a complaint against an RUC officer to an independent tribunal for adjudication. On the first and only occasion that the authority exercised this power the RUC officers involved withdrew from the hearing. The High Court ruled subsequently that the tribunal had no powers to compel the attendance of witnesses.

REFERENCES

Bennett Committee 1979 *Report of Committee of Inquiry into Police Interrogation Procedures in Northern Ireland*, London: H.M.S.O. Cmnd. 7497.

Cameron, Lord 1969 *Disturbances in Northern Ireland. Report of the Commission Appointed by the Governor of Northern Ireland*, Belfast: H.M.S.O., Cmnd. 532.

Goldstein, H. 1977 *Policing a Free Society*, Cambridge, Massachusetts: Ballinger.

Leigh, L. H. 1985 *Police Powers in England and Wales*, 2nd Edition, London: Butterworths.

Parker Report 1972 *Report of Privy Councillors Appointed to Consider Authorised Procedures for Interrogation*, London: H.M.S.O. Cmnd. 4901.

Scarman, Lord 1972 *Report of Tribunal of Inquiry into the Violence and Civil Disturbance in Northern Ireland in 1969*, Belfast: H.M.S.O. Cmnd. 566.

Taylor, P. 1980 *Beating the Terrorists? Interrogation in Omagh, Gough and Castlereagh*, Harmondsworth: Penguin.

Walsh, D. P. J. 1982 "Arrest and Interrogation in Northern Ireland," *Journal of Law and Society*, 9(1): 37–62.

"Extraordinary" Police Operations in Venezuela

■ *TOSCA HERNÁNDEZ*

INTRODUCTORY NOTES

Of all the articles in this volume, the following article perhaps states the neo-Marxist argument most explicitly. Neo-Marxist criminology (also called "radical" or "critical" criminology) bases its understanding of crime on a critique of economic structures, namely capitalist economic structures. Accordingly, the elite are able to use the tools at their disposal (i.e., the government, the media, religious institutions, and the educational system) to assure their continued domination. Crimes committed by the lower class are seen as a result of their oppression; and crimes committed by the upper class (which can be far more damaging to the society) are deemphasized by the very institutions that are under its control.

Juxtaposed with Marxism, "social constructionism" is also introduced in this article.The problem of crime is socially constructed. This is to say, the shaping (i.e., "construction") of crime into a problem of public concern—no matter how much crime is actually being committed—is a social process that, in this case, is a function of political and economic arrangements. When the status of the elite is being threatened by an economic or political crisis, the elite are able to muster the forces (namely, the media) to construct a crime problem and instigate "law and order" campaigns. These campaigns cause the public to tolerate greater forms of repression—in the name of crime control. Law and order campaigns also serve as a diversionary tactic of the elite, focusing the attention of the poor and middle classes on the exaggerated threat of crime, and diverting their attention from the economic structure that is an even greater threat to their well-being. The middle and lower classes come to think of the criminal—and not the elite—as the enemy. Further, in that the media and law enforcement tend to focus their attention on lower class criminals, law and order campaigns serve to alienate the middle class from the poor, causing the middle class to fear the poor and preventing the two classes from uniting against the elite.

SOURCE: Tosca Hernández, "'Extraordinary' Police Operations in Venezuela," (originally "Los operativos policiales 'extraordinarios' en Venezuela: Dos acercamientos reflexivos al problema"), *Anuario del Instituto de Ciencias Penales y Criminologicas*, no. 9 (1984–1985). Reprinted with permission.

In Venezuela since 1965, a period that includes the so-called democratic period, no government has failed to use "extraordinary" police operations. These have included police dragnets, and roundups and beatings, usually by Venezuela's Metropolitan Police. Increasingly, such police operations have included actions coordinated by the Metropolitan Police, the Intelligence Police (DISIP), the Judicial Police (PTJ), and the National Guard (FAC), with the ostensible objective of ending the "underworld's explosive growth."[1] These roundups have resulted in the detention of large numbers of suspected criminals. Such dragnets have created a feeling of personal insecurity in cities.

Initially extraordinary police operations had the facade of exceptionality. They were thought of as "extraordinary" because they were implemented only at specific times of the year—on weekends, Carnival, Holy Week, and Christmas. Today these operations have become part of the formal judicial apparatus, with official status and institutional labels. In effect, "extraordinary" police operations have become less exceptional; they are now used throughout the year.

The object of this chapter is to understand the social and political significance in Venezuela of "extraordinary" police operations. They have resulted in the detention of massive numbers of suspected criminals. A central premise of this analysis is that extraordinary police operations cannot be dissociated from perceptions about crime and the social problem of crime.

LEGISLATIVE FOUNDATIONS OF "EXTRAORDINARY" POLICE OPERATIONS

In Venezuela, mass arrests are made possible by the "Law Concerning Vagrants and Habitual Criminals."[2] Under this law a person can be arrested on a written order issued by an authorized official. Since such an arrest does not necessarily result from commission of a punishable act, no arrest report is available, and there are no grounds for defense at the time of arrest. This law is aimed not at punishing criminal acts but at conduct manifesting a "social danger."[3]

People arrested under the Vagrancy and Habitual Criminals Law and tried directly by the Executive (civil authorities, governors, and the Ministry of Justice) have three days to present witnesses, without the mandatory defense attorney (although Article 68 of the Venezuelan Constitution guarantees "that defense is an inviolate right in all levels and degrees of the criminal process"). These circumventions of the Constitution are possible because the suspect is not accused of a crime. The accused will be sentenced within fifty days of arrest, possibly up to 5 years in prison.

Extraordinary police operations are characterized by selectivity in terms of the "criminals" against whom they are directed. These operations are carried out primarily in the "marginal zones" of our cities, where they undoubtedly will net "socially dangerous characters." In these poor barrios the unemployed (vagrants) abound, not by choice but as a product of the social system. (Such unemployment exists in spite of the Venezuelan Constitution's guaranteeing every citizen the right to work.) It is in the poor barrios where police "roundups" are constantly carried out. Such roundups provide the raw material for police "rap sheets," which establish criminal histories and profiles. These can be used by the police during other normal or extraordinary police operations.

The Venezuelan police use extraordinary operations to pull in those convicted two or more times of crimes against property, or people accused two or more times of crimes against property who are in possession of false or altered keys. But such an arrest rationale is clearly unconstitutional: The Venezuelan Constitution does not allow police to target someone for arrest just because that person has a record of having committed a particular type of crime. That is, under Venezuelan law the police may not institute a street sweep against presumed criminals—usually defined as people who have committed a crime against property, often accompanied by crimes against persons—on the assumption that anyone with a past record of having committed such crimes or having been detained in past police roundups is fair game under the Vagrancy and Habitual Criminals Law.

The utility of this law for extraordinary police operations becomes evident when we contrast it with police action allowable under the Venezuelan Penal Code. The Law against Vagrants and Habitual Criminals is highly flexible and effective: It assures speed of arrest and trial, and ensures the arrested person's total lack of defense. When extraordinary police operations are carried out, the Law Concerning Vagrants and Habitual Criminals takes precedence over legally mandated repressive practices, in spite of the law's being an administrative expedient rooted in exceptional legal principles. In fact, police action in defense of the "social order" dominates during extraordinary police operations. Criminal law, which should normally inform the repressive apparatus, is relegated to second place, thus resulting in *de facto* suspension of constitutional guarantees for specific segments of the population.

CRIME, SOCIAL PERCEPTIONS, AND THE MEDIA

Extraordinary police operations are justified and legitimated by the perceived existence of a "crime wave" whose reality is usually confirmed by a dramatic crime that stirs public opinion through the victim's importance or the violence of the criminal act. The mass media play an important role in shaping public images about crime and criminals. The information given the public about a "crime problem," and the way such information is organized, are decisive factors in problematizing crime and creating a feeling of personal insecurity.

Here we are referring to public perceptions of a crime wave, not so much the reality of one. Police and court statistics, as reliable as they may be (which is not the case in Venezuela), are not a mirror of crime's objective reality. Police statistics can be considered an expression of official insecurity: They vary in accordance with selective and massive arrests, not with the commission of crimes. Judicial statistics reflect the action of social control institutions. Such statistics thus signify what the criminal justice system has designated as pernicious and reprehensible. Criminal statistics give insight into the operation of the police and larger criminal justice system. They selectively identify what is illegal (through criminalization) and designate the population considered criminal.

Whether a crime wave is real or not, it can be perceived as real. Perceptions about crime can justify the use of "extraordinary" police operations. Criminologists—as well as police and government institutions—know that extraordinary police operations do not stop crime, particularly not the common crimes against which they are directed. For as Nagel has concluded, "The massive use of jailing has not significantly contributed, nor will it contribute, to stopping crime or correcting imperfections within our social fabric."[4] In Venezuela, in recent years, the frequent use of extraordinary police operations lends credibility to Nagel's statement. In fact, it is possible that such operations actually instigate crime.

The Law Concerning Vagrants and Habitual Criminals has facilitated the arrest and jailing of many Venezuelan citizens, even though they have committed no crime. Such State action has the immediate effect of substantially increasing prison crowding. Convicts are eventually returned to a society that holds negative attitudes toward them. These attitudes make their reincorporation into society difficult. The "social rejects" may thus be pressured into committing new crimes.

Extraordinary police operations also involve the police in crime. Increasingly, and without always being clearly conscious of it, the police become involved in a tremendous amount of illegitimate violence against citizens. This violence is a "normal" reaction to the stress placed on police during extraordinary police operations. Demanding that police act within legal limits while insisting upon highly productive arrest action (e.g., mass arrests) places the police in a fundamental contradiction.[5] Practicing excesses against supposed criminals leads the police to lose sight of the legal limitations on their action. Citizen murders are carried out in the name of ending crime!

In earlier periods, extraordinary police operations were short-lived and the negative consequences resulting from them were more limited. In February 1981, the government of Venezuelan President Luis Herrera instituted the Union Plan, which has become the basis for ongoing police operations that are no longer "extraordinary." The Union Plan involves coordination between the police and National Guard. These ongoing police operations were baptized Security Act 84 by the Jaime Lusinchi government.

However, large-scale police street sweeps and arrests are ineffective against common crime. In contemporary Venezuela the most important "common crime" is organized and, therefore, cannot be effectively attacked through large-scale street sweeps—a fact constantly pointed out by many Venezuelan police specialists and criminologists. If street sweeps are ineffective against organized crime, why have such operations been utilized by various Venezuelan governments?

We can initially propose that such extraordinary police operations are in some sense "successful" precisely because they have been repeated so frequently. Their success seems to lie in the mass arrest of supposed criminals. The police obviously concur with this assessment. In an introductory preface to the Union Plan's 1981 statistical summary of crime, it was noted that in 1981 "The measures implemented (by the Union Plan) brought satisfactory results for the community in general, making 31,714 arrests, of which 19,973 were by the Metropolitan Police, 1,321 by the DISIP (Intelligence Police), 4,463 by the PTJ (Judiciary Police) and 5,957 by the FAC (National Guard)."[6]

The simplistic assumption that seems to lie behind and to sustain extraordinary police operations is that increases in crime call for increased arrests, which, in turn, will reduce the number of criminals. The assumption is also made that criminals are easily identifiable and detectable. Another associated assumption is that crime waves are quantifiable; they are statistical realities created solely by criminal action. Within this framework, the problem of crime ceases to be social and becomes technical: Criminal actors must be controlled.

But the real "success" of extraordinary police operations lies in their ability to satisfy illusorily the social desire to end crime. This logic is not held only by police officials; it is also ingrained in society's common sense: If more people (presumably criminals) are arrested and jailed, society will have greater personal security because fewer criminals will be on the street. The public establishes a logical relationship between the number of criminal acts and the number of criminals. Such an identification feeds the subjective construction of "criminal types" and "criminal acts," and objectifies the link between the two. We need to be clear that behaviors defined, represented, or appraised as crime are socially constructed; one of the elements in that construction is police action.

Criminals are people with socially constructed characteristics that *represent* them as "criminal types." These characteristics are stereotyped into social intersubjectivity. An important element in the social construction of criminality is selectively generated police action that, in the case of Venezuela, involves enforcement of the Law Concerning Vagrants and Habitual Criminals. In order to understand why extraordinary police operations are used, we need to examine (a) their social significance, which is indistinguishable from societal perceptions of crime, and (b) the connections between extraordinary police operations and the sociohistorical situations into which they are inserted.

SOCIAL PROBLEMS AND LEGITIMATION

Crime, social perceptions of it, and feelings of personal insecurity are intertwined. This represents the crime creation dimension. This interrelated and socially constructed configuration, in turn, becomes part of the justification for carrying out extraordinary police operations. This justification represents the social legitimation dimension. Let us draw this out further.

In the crime creation dimension we include perceptions of crime and feelings of personal insecurity. These create pressure to employ extraordinary police operations. In the process of carrying out extraordinary police operations, those operations come to be legitimated. This is the social legitimation dimension. While these two elements of criminological analysis can be separated analytically, they are connected in reality. Citizen perceptions about crime and their feelings of insecurity constitute elements in the legitimation and justification of extraordinary police operations. In fact, extraordinary police operations and the processes legitimizing them are two sides of the same coin.

The Italian criminologist Allesandro Baratta,[7] in a reference to Kitsuse and Spector,[8] pointed out that crime as a social problem exists both in social consciousness and in state organization. It results from a definition and an evaluation that are part of the process of communication and social interaction. Crime is not only socially constructed, it is also part of society's symbolic universe. The mass media play a fundamental role in creating and fostering social symbolization within this universe. The media are major producers and shapers of public opinion, and therefore play a role in the social construction of crime and in its problematization.[9] Crime as a social phenomenon is ambiguous: It marks a point of convergence between subjective (cultural) and material (structural) realities. The judicial system classifies only certain behaviors as criminal. This classification represents the cultural component of crime. The system of objective social relations (the material sphere) includes the behavior of individuals defined as criminal. According to Baratta, an analysis of the material sphere of crime should be integrated into its subjective sphere.

In the social construction of crime, action by the mass media (the press in particular) is fundamental. The media can create social concerns, amplify them, and establish the relative location of an issue on the subjective scale of social problems. The media do this through propaganda strategies and techniques. They not only make crime public, they also publicize the action of social control agents. The mass media's discourse, therefore, mediates social interaction.

When extraordinary police operations are used, and become news, we learn something about the material foundations of crime. For example, according to Baratta, "law and order" campaigns are promoted by ruling political elites to distract the public from problems that threaten the foundations of elite privilege. We have seen this in Venezuela, where there appears to be a relationship between social and political crises and the use of extraordinary police operations. Such police operations usually have been carried out at times of economic or political crisis: spiraling food or gasoline prices, elevated unemployment, or political turmoil (government scandal, riots, strikes). The public is led to believe that extraordinary police operations will eliminate societal problems by doing away with common crime. These police operations serve the function of deflecting public consciousness from more pressing social and police problems. They place "common crime" in an elevated position within social consciousness.[10] Extraordinary police operations are part of the State's political arsenal for manipulating citizen perceptions about societal shortcomings. They represent moments in which a government confronts and neutralizes threats of state delegitimation.

Both extraordinary police operations and the media blitzes that publicize them push crises of state legitimacy into the background. They do so by thrusting safer (and well selected) socioeconomic and political problems into social perception. Extraordinary police operations, through the arrest of massive numbers of "criminals," illusorily satisfy (albeit provisionally) demands for the protection of life and property and neutralize the poor, marginalized, and exploited groups whose dissatisfaction with the system could seriously threaten the legitimacy of the existing order.

CRIME AND SOCIAL INEQUALITY

Crime serves a legitimizing function for the State by helping to mobilize consensus. In fact, according to Baratta, the making of crime into a social problem fulfills two State legitimation functions. First, criminal stereotypes are created. In most Latin American societies this involves the image of criminals as almost exclusively from the least favored social strata. This stereotype helps to reinforce social barriers; it reproduces social inequality.

Second, the social stigma provoked by criminalization reinforces a societal consensus in support of the existing power structure. That is, social stigma produces social distance that discourages solidarity with the "criminal," and fosters public disapproval of criminal acts and of the lower-class marginals who supposedly (exclusively) commit crime.

These processes isolate small segments of the population and hold them responsible for everything that is negative in society. The "silent majority's" fictitious cohesion is enhanced through exclusion of a socially distinct and marginalized minority. Those who honor the "social pact" have a community of common interest. This helps to legitimize the existing order of domination, which includes a social barrier between those whose rights are guaranteed and those whose rights are not.

Police action, based on the Law Concerning Vagrants and Habitual Criminals, plays an important role in social construction and legitimation. The carrying out of extraordinary police operations defines the social groups (always the least favored) who are "criminals," and who will be the object of future police action. This helps to reinforce forms of social marginalization and reproduces social relations of inequality. The media's reporting of such police action makes public the "criminal threats." By concentrating responsibility for all that is negative in society on the poor who are criminalized, extraordinary police operations hide the State's inability to satisfy basic needs guaranteed all citizens. Extraordinary police operations help to legitimize further repressive State action, thus reinforcing social consensus and avoiding questions that might delegitimize the existing structure of domination.

CONCLUSIONS

Certain conclusions can be drawn about the Venezuelan State's use of extraordinary police operations, the latter having a juridical base in the Law Concerning Vagrants and Habitual Criminals. A central conclusion is that extraordinary police operations are part of the social problem of crime, a short-run political solution to it, and a source of State legitimation. The social problem of crime is part of the symbolic sphere where a synthesis is formed between the material facts of crime and its symbolic side. According to Baratta, the material realities of crime should be integrated into analyses of its subjective sphere.

The mass media, particularly the press, play a fundamental role. They amplify social concerns and publicize law-and-order campaigns. Law-and-order campaigns become social facts in Venezuela through extraordinary police operations. News about such police operations is fundamental to the problematization of crime: Such operations make public the behavior considered negative and reinforce public perceptions about crime.

Extraordinary police operations highlight historically recognized social needs whose realization has been blocked or threatened. We can, therefore, propose that one of the functions of extraordinary police operations is to stave off crises of legitimacy by substituting one social problem—"crime"—for other, more serious ones.

➤ DISCUSSION QUESTION

Does Hernández's argument about law-and-order campaigns in Venezuela apply to the United States as well? Explain your answer.

NOTES

1. *Desbordamiento del hampa* in the original.

2. *Ley sobre vagos y maleantes*, in the original text.

3. For more information about this law and its consequences, see Tosca Hernández, *La ideologización del delito y de la pena* (Caracas: Instituto de Ciencias Penales y Criminólgicas, UCV, 1977).

4. William Nagel, "On Behalf of a Moratorium on Prison Construction," *Crime and Delinquency,* 23, no. 2 (April 1977): 156.

5. See Maureen Cain, "Trends in the Sociology of Police Work," *International Journal of the Sociology of Law* 7, no. 2 (May 1979): 143–67.

6. Venezuela Policía Metropolitana, "Plan Union Uno" (2-13081, 3-16-81) (Caracas, Departamento de Estadística, 1981), p. 1.

7. Allesandro Baratta, "Problemi sociali e percezione della criminalitá," *Dei delitti e delle pene,* no. 1 (1983).

8. J. Kitsuse and M. Spector, *Constructing Social Problems* (Menlo Park, Calif.: Cummings, 1977).

9. Rodríguez Ibá ñ iez confirms this. He believes that the mass media do not merely "describe or paint reality a definite color, but ... substantiate it ... suggesting the same plan of daily action by means of [a given] emphasis and [with] silences." J. Rodríguez-Ibáñiez, *El sue ñ io de la razón* (Barcelona: Ediciones Taurus, 1982), pp. 133–34.

10. In Venezuela, several research projects have examined the media's role in creating criminal stereotypes. They include Xiomara de Valbuena and Marta Colomina de Rivera, "Los medios de comunicación de masa en una sociedad capitalista. El caso venezolano," in *Los rostros de la violencia,* Vol. I (Maracaibo: Instituto de Criminología LUZ, 1976); and, more recently, Audelina Tineo, "El estereotipo del delincuente en Venezuela" (Maracaibo: Instituto de Criminología LUZ, n.d.). (Mimeograph.)

Why Us and Why? Some Reflections on Teaching Ethics to Police

■ *DAVID MASSEY*

INTRODUCTORY NOTES

The following article is about an Australian program which requires police and police recruits to take ethics courses at the university level. This is an interesting idea that is not likely to garner overwhelming support from American police officers, police administrations, nor the public. For one reason, there has long been a tradition of anti-intellectualism in the United States (*see* R. Hofstadter, *Anti-Intellectualism in American Life,* 1963), and perhaps we expect to find even less of this quality in our police officers. We expect theirs is a job that requires them to respond on a more visceral, instinctive level.

When faced with the suggestion that police officers should be required to study subjects such as psychology, problems of the underclass, or ethics, it is not unusual to hear law enforcement students respond something to the effect of, "When somebody is pointing a gun at me, I don't have time to think about why they are doing it, or whether it is right or wrong." However, it can be argued that an ethical response could become as automatic as any other. Besides, somebody is not always pointing a gun at a police officer; and in regard to their other duties, an ethical, social science, or liberal arts training may improve their performance.

The way the media present the crime problem to us—as random, savage violence, where the guilt of the perpetrator is usually obvious—it is not surprising that the public rarely concerns itself with the frequently dubious legal and ethical practices of the police. While the media is telling us that crime is escalating—whether in fact it is or not—the public is all the more willing to give up their constitutional rights. These become mere "technicalities"; they know the guy is guilty of obscene brutalities, and whatever Arnold Schwarzenegger or Clint Eastwood have to do to bring him to justice is—just that—justice.

Crime is a serious problem; but a force of police personnel, authorized to carry arms, to deprive a citizen of his or her freedom, and to use deadly force represents a potential problem of which we as a public should be ever-mindful.

SOURCE: David Massey, "Why Us and Why? Some Reflections on Teaching Ethics to Police," *Police Studies,* vol. 16, no. 3 (1993): 77–83. Reprinted with permission from Anderson Publishing Co. and the author.

A recent initiative in police education in Queensland, Australia is the development of courses, for both serving officers and recruits, which involve academic studies at university which are designed to enhance the educational standards of the Queensland Police Service. Police recruits now engage in six months of academic studies at university followed by six months of academic study and practical training at the Queensland Police Academy. Serving police officers are able to enroll in Arts degrees that are specifically designed for practitioners who work or intend to work in the justice system. This initiative, to a significant extent, was triggered by the Fitzgerald (1989) inquiry, a Commission of Inquiry into possible illegal activities and associated police misconduct in the state of Queensland. An important component of these new courses, which have been established at Griffith University and the Queensland University of Technology, is a focus on ethics. In his report, Tony Fitzgerald QC advocated the revision of police education to take account of ethical considerations and argued, furthermore, that "ethical education ... should help groups of employees to establish a supportive atmosphere within which it would be harder for corruption to flourish." (1989:133)

In commenting on these developments Preston (1990:6) questioned "whether academics, senior police and certainly government officials know what they mean and what they want when they plan to include ethics in these courses." On the basis of my own involvement in the teaching of the ethics subject, *Social Ethics and the Criminal Justice System,* in the BA (Justice Studies) course at Queensland University of Technology, it soon became apparent that the students, too, held differing views about the need for and value of ethical education. The purpose of this article, therefore, is to describe some of the views expressed by the students and, in responding to them, to seek to contribute to the necessary conversation about the teaching of applied ethics. This is particularly important given the renewed interest in ethics, what Charlesworth (1991) described as a "renaissance of ethics," and the emergence of courses in applied ethics in many institutions over recent years (Preston, 1991; Isaacs, 1992; Jordan, 1992).

The views of the students were expressed in lectures and tutorials, and at meetings of the Subject Advisory Committee, which was chaired by the author and consisted of lecturers, tutors and student representatives. I do not claim that the views expressed are representative of all the students but I think they are significant beliefs that warrant a response.

WHY US?

One of the questions asked by some students, particularly serving police, was why do *we* need to study ethics? The view expressed by these students was that they were already ethical and therefore did not need a university subject to teach them to be ethical. The predominant belief of these students was that they were required to study ethics because it was assumed they were not ethical. In other words, they believed their integrity was being questioned and that the reason for studying ethics was to purge them of their evil and corrupt ways, to be "reeducated." This belief, to a significant extent, may be attributed to the climate within the Queensland community following the Fitzgerald inquiry. Some police believed that the community thought all 'cops' were crooked and were concerned that they were being unfairly labeled and stigmatized. They claimed that although some police may be corrupt, a fact they acknowledged, that did not mean all of them were. It is pertinent to note that this belief is consistent with what Scheingold (1984) claims is a characteristic of police cultures: the view that police are victims of public misunderstanding and scorn.

My response to this issue is to suggest that police and police recruits are not encouraged to study ethics because they are regarded as unethical, just as prospective doctors and nurses are not required to study illness and disease because they are regarded as unwell themselves. Rather, people study medicine because the community values people who are able to assist and support those who are unwell and who are able to promote human well-being. Similarly, people study ethics because the community values people who are able to promote goodness and who can respond appropriately and effectively to practices that are malevolent, wicked, corrupt or unethical. The community also values those who are able to assist the victims of such practices, although it should be noted that the criminal justice system for far too long has tended to ignore the predicament of victims (Shapland, Willmore & Duff, 1985; Donatiu, 1992).

I maintain that if one is to promote goodness, and is to contribute to the making of a better society, it is important to understand what constitutes goodness (justice, compassion, empowerment, authenticity) and what is required in order to enhance it. Studying ethics, I suggest, provides students with the opportunity to extend their ethical understandings, dispositions and competencies through, inter alia, examining the ethical beliefs of others, particularly those with ethical 'expertise' (Singer, 1991), as well as clarifying and scrutinizing their own beliefs, values and practices. This would include an examination of the beliefs, values and practices of police cultures, for the ethical challenge needs to be seen primarily as a cultural rather than an individual challenge. I do not believe, however, that ethical education can make people ethical: if people wish to be "do badders" no course in ethics can prevent this. It may have a positive impact, and hopefully it will, but one could not guarantee it. What I believe ethical education can do, however, is equip people who do have a commitment to goodness (justice, freedom, compassion, equity) with the understandings, dispositions and competencies that will enable them individually, but most importantly collectively, to first of all recognize evil (injustice, coercion, violence, discrimination), and then to confront it more effectively, thus making it "harder for corruption to flourish." (Fitzgerald, 1989: 133).

While it is important and necessary to confront corruption and other unethical practices and structures, I think it is important to recognize also that a world without corruption, coercion or discrimination is unlikely. As T.S. Eliot (1961) observed:

> The world turns, and the world changes,
> But one thing does not change.
> In all of my years, one thing does not change.
> However you disguise it, this thing does not change:
> The perpetual struggle of Good and Evil.

There is a need, therefore, to recognize the presence and possibility of wickedness for, as Midgley (1988:308) argues, "People often treat each other abominably. They sometimes treat themselves abominably too. They constantly cause avoidable human suffering." Thus it is important to appreciate that "we are not going to run out of evils" (Midgley: 317) and that there will never be a final solution but only continual struggle. How one might engage most effectively in this struggle is an important issue and should be thoroughly addressed in any ethics course for police, but it is one that is beyond the scope of this paper.

WHY ETHICS?

Another question asked by students was: why should we be required to study *ethics?* Surely, they reasoned, there were more important things for them to learn.

My response to this question is that it is important to study ethics because ethics is intrinsic to the nature of police work, whether you are a Constable or a Commissioner. Furthermore, police work is morally complex and demanding, and most of the work of police involves ethical considerations. Sherman (1982: 1), for example, argued that:

> Few vocations offer as much moral complexity as criminal justice. Few occupations are as ethically demanding or as full of moral conflicts. No other occupation requires its members to make moral judgments about how other people have behaved, and then to make and implement moral judgments about how society should respond to them. . . Measured solely by the volume of moral confrontations and judgments, it would seem that the moral boundaries of our society are not set by organized religion, not by school but by the agents of criminal justice.

The kinds of moral issues police are likely to confront include the use of deception, undercover work and entrapment procedures, the use of informants, the use of force and perhaps deadly force, gratuities and corruption (Elliston and Feldberg, 1985). It is pertinent to note that, since ethics is concerned with who we are in our relations with others (Fletcher, 1966; Kitwood, 1990) then police work, because it involves relationships with members of the community as well as one's colleagues, necessarily entails ethical considerations. For instance, a significant proportion of the work of police is involved in service, peace keeping and protection activities (Schaefer, 1978; Cohen and Feldberg, 1991), work that requires police to show respect for the persons they are dealing with: tourists seeking directions, victims of crime seeking support and comfort, persons whose relatives have been critically or fatally injured. Significantly, Doyle claims that police increasingly are required to work with and for community members who may be labeled as socially different and, on that basis, isolated, excluded, intimidated, subordinated or degraded. Thus, "the police have a moral responsibility to ask why the defined differences matter, and to limit as far as possible the injurious effects of these differences on people and the community." (Doyle, 1992:57)

A further reason for studying ethics, I suggest, is that within the criminal justice system in general, and in police services in particular, there is an expectation that police should act ethically and with integrity. For example, Lee Brown (1991: 8), the President of the International Union of Police Chiefs and Commissioner of the New York Police, argues that:

> One value the chief must articulate and demonstrate is the expectation that all members of the department will adhere to the highest ethical standards. . . The chief must initiate and support anti-corruption efforts and hold commanders and supervisors responsible for the ethical conduct of their personnel. . . It is essential . . . that all law enforcement activities also meet the community's standard of ethical behavior.

As Brown's statement intimates, the community also has a strong expectation that the police will uphold the highest ethical standards. The community, in general, values and welcomes the presence of the police, particularly in times of crisis. As Robinette (1991: 44) argues:

> A police officer is an agent of the government to whom the people have transferred their rights in exchange for safety and security. With such authority comes the power to defend the transferred rights, up to and including the use of fatal force.

Given that the police are granted such extensive authority it has been argued that it is "all the more imperative for both the police and the public to subscribe to ethical standards that can effectively restrain the discretionary power of the police while also encouraging their justified exercise of it." (Doyle, 1992: 52)

While the public is willing to grant the police special powers and responsibilities, in doing so they insist that those powers are not exceeded or abused. For example, they resent police using their powers to promote their own interests rather than acting to protect the public interest, which was clearly demonstrated in Queensland, where the former Commissioner of Police is currently serving an extensive jail term for corruption.

Studying ethics is important, therefore, because police work is ethically complex, the nature of police work is inherently ethical, police services expect their officers to act in accordance with the highest ethical standards, and the community expects police to maintain and promote exemplary ethical standards.

WHY UNIVERSITY?

Acknowledging that we did not regard them as ethically suspect, that they were not being unfairly targeted, and accepting that ethics is perhaps important, the students still raised further concerns. Why can't we learn about ethics from serving police officers? Surely they would have a better appreciation of the ethically difficult situations that arise and how best to respond to them? The view being expressed, the craft approach to education, is one that is familiar to many educators.

I do not wish to argue that serving police officers have no role to play in the education of recruits: in fact, I think they can play a valuable role. However, it is important to recognize that craft or apprenticeship approaches pose many difficulties. One of the problems of a craft approach, or the "sitting with Nellie" approach as it is sometimes referred to (Stones and Morris in Kirk, 1986), is that students are merely trained rather than educated. It can be argued that the hallmark of an education, as distinct from training, is that it promotes understanding rather than merely the ability to master a range of skills and techniques. Thus, educated people, when faced with a novel situation, should be able to analyze, interpret and make judgments about the situation themselves, rather than rely on others to tell them what to do. (I am not suggesting that they should refrain from deliberating and collaborating with others in order to resolve problems and dilemmas.) Moreover, educated people should be able to justify their actions by applying reason and reasonableness rather than appealing to authority to justify their decisions, the familiar and discredited "I was just following orders" argument.

A person who has been merely trained, on the other hand, is more likely to rely on others to tell her/him what to do in a particular situation and is less likely to understand the reasons for doing what they are directed to do. Thus education is intended to promote autonomy and deliberative judgment while training may create dependency, conformity and working to rule. "They train lions, don't they," but do we want to train police? (Williams, 1982)

Another criticism of the craft perspective is that the social and political contexts within which such activities take place are taken as given and are not seen as problematic. Thus the approach is a conservative one because there is "a confounding of experience with necessity" (Buchanan and Schwille, 1982). In other words, it is assumed that the ways things are done is the way things should be done. One of the reasons for locating police education within a university setting was to overcome this very problem, and to provide students with the opportunity to question and appraise current practices without there being any pressure to conform to the prevailing police culture.

It is argued also that the craft perspective adopts a passive view of the student who is expected to absorb the received wisdom but is rarely encouraged to challenge that wisdom (Zeichner, 1983). Furthermore, the relationship between the student and the teacher is one that places a high value on closely following orders (Zeichner and Liston, 1986). Perhaps learning to follow orders is desirable but it is arguably also likely to have dangerous and destructive repercussions, as recent events in the Queensland Police Service show. On this point, it is interesting to note the comment of the Commissioner of the New York Police, who argues that the paramilitary style of police services needs to be questioned, a view I endorse (Brown, 1991).

Finally, it is claimed that craft approaches are not only conservative and uncritical but also are wasteful, inefficient and haphazard, "at best a socialization and induction into the work context ... But at worst ... a haphazard process sustained by a mythology of uninformed judgment and lore" (Kirk, 1986:159). If serving police are to be involved in the education of recruits I think it is important to recognize the problematic situations that may arise so that the educational experience does not become diluted, distorted or subverted.

WHY THEORY?

The final question I would like to respond to is one that is asked, quite rightly I believe, by many students. Why do we have to learn about theory? Why don't you just tell us what is the right thing to do and then teach us to do it? I am sure these are questions that are familiar to many of you.

For example, students often assert that they are not interested in theory. I suggest to them that this claim is inaccurate and that it would be more accurate to say that they are not interested in other people's theories. I base this claim on the now widely accepted belief that all people, and therefore students, are theorists. In other words, all of our observations and interpretations of the world are theory dependent. As Bruner (1990: 32) commented: "Mind is never free of precommitment. There is no innocent eye, nor is there one that penetrates aboriginal reality. There are instead hypotheses, versions, expected scenarios." Thus our reality is dependent on the conceptual framework (theories) we use to look at the world.

Thus my first response to the theory question is to suggest that conceptual frameworks enable us to see: differently or more clearly, for example, and thus overcome what Isaacs (1992) refers to as moral blindness. As Murdoch (1970:91) argues: "It is a task to come to see the world as it is." For example, if one is unfamiliar with the law and legal concepts, one is unlikely to perceive a particular situation or event as having legal significance. Similarly, if one has not been introduced to, or appropriated, theories of justice one is unlikely to see the justice issues that are inherent in so many situations. What, on the face of it, may seem just may, on closer examination with the appropriate frames of reference, raise many justice (or injustice) issues: distributive, retributive or commutative justice. A good example of failing to see is a layperson examining an X-Ray. It requires an expert, one who has learned what to look for, to see what is going on.

Another function of theory is that it can enable us to recognize many everyday events as problematic. Perhaps things are not as simple as they first appear to be. Thus theory may help us to appreciate the complexity and perplexity of situations we encounter and to realize that there may be no easy solutions to many problems. For instance, let us consider the Dirty Harry problem. Klockars (1985: 428) describes it in the following way.

> Policing constantly places its practitioners in situations in which good ends can be achieved by dirty means. When the ends to be achieved are urgent and unquestionably good and only a dirty means will work to achieve them, the policeman faces a genuine moral dilemma. A genuine moral dilemma is a situation from which one cannot emerge innocent no matter what one does—employ a dirty means, employ an insufficiently dirty means, or walk away. In such situations in policing, Dirty Harry problems, the danger lies not in becoming guilty of wrong—that is inevitable—but in thinking that one has found a way to escape a dilemma which is inescapable.

> . . . The only means of assuring that dirty means will not be used too readily or too crudely is to punish those who use them and the agency which endorses their use.

Klockars concludes, however, on a sobering point.

> In urging the punishment of policemen who resort to dirty means to achieve some unquestionably good and morally compelling end, we recognize that we create a Dirty Harry problem for ourselves and/or those we urge to effect such punishments. It is a fitting end, one which teaches us once again that the danger in Dirty Harry problems is never in their resolution, but in thinking that one has found a resolution with which one can truly live in peace. (p. 437)

A further function of theory is that it can illuminate a situation (Fletcher, 1966) and help us see more clearly. It can do this by enabling us to describe and interpret a situation more carefully, more elaborately and with finer discriminations, thus helping us to understand it more fully and in a more discerning manner. If we can see that a person is adopting an egocentric rather than an allocentric stance towards an issue, for example, that will enable us to respond more appropriately to that person. If we recognize that a problem is essentially one of distributive rather than retributive justice, we are better placed to respond to it. Thus one's actions are more likely to be based on understanding and insight rather than ignorance or prejudice.

My second response to the theory question is to suggest that by acquainting oneself with ethical theory (concepts and language) one is enabled to participate in the ethical conversation about issues such as justice, equity, compassion, rights and responsibilities, civil liberties, autonomy, and so on, thus avoiding moral muteness: an inability or unwillingness to engage in ethical deliberations. Ethics is a conversation that has been engaged in for hundreds of years, within all human intellectual traditions (Kitwood, 1990; Singer, 1991). As Wittgenstein (1961: 56) noted: "The limits of my language are the limits of my world." Thus, if our ethical language is limited then our world also is ethically limited. If police officers' worlds are ethically limited there is more likelihood that they will not only fail to see unethical practices but also will be unable to engage in meaningful discourse about matters of ethical significance. Such ethical blindness and muteness is also likely to result in ethical paralysis: a failure to adequately confront and resist unethical practices or promote more ethical practices.

While all students may be theorists, as noted earlier, it is also likely that their conceptual frameworks are taken-for-granted in much the same way that fish take water for granted. Thus they may not examine their own beliefs and may feel uncomfortable if those beliefs are challenged. I suggest to them that while it may not be (so) important for them to scrutinize their beliefs in the private realm, once they enter the public domain, exercising the social role of a police officer, it is most important that they do so. For example, no one would want to be tried in a court of law that was presided over by a judge who had a limited and unreflective understanding of the law and justice. Nor would one wish to be tried by a judge who adopted a legalistic rather than a judicial approach to the law (Fletcher, 1966).

In suggesting that it is important for practitioners to critically examine their own theories I am not arguing that their theories will necessarily be inferior to those generated by "experts" only that they may be and that they should be subjected to the same intensity of scrutiny. It is perhaps pertinent, however, to take account of Russell's (1960: 1) comment that "What passes for knowledge in ordinary life suffers from three defects: it is cocksure, vague, and self contradictory." I am also arguing that it can be helpful to appropriate and use the theories of "experts," which does not mean you should accept them uncritically. There is an increasing amount of evidence to show, however, that it is valid to make a distinction between novices and experts (Chi, Glaser and Farr, 1988). Thus the educational process can be seen as one that seeks to promote forms of reflection that are characteristic of experts: elaborate and systematic rather than casual and superficial; critical and questioning rather than conservative, dogmatic and taken-for-granted; and collective rather than personal. Thus if a police officer wishes to provide the best service possible to the public, s/he "must learn to be critical of the tribal customs and tribal beliefs that are generally accepted among his neighbors." (Russell, 1952: 78).

I also think it is helpful to make a distinction between reflection-inaction, reflection-in-action and reflection-for-action. Often when we talk of reflection we mean reflecting on our actions, in retrospect. For example, Shulman (1987:19) argues that reflection is "what a teacher does when he or she looks back at the teaching and learning that has occurred, and reconstructs, reenacts, and or recaptures the events, emotions and accomplishments. It is that set of processes through which a profession learns from experience."

A form of reflection that Schon (1987) has focused on is reflection-in-action, in which the emphasis is upon what happens in the action rather than the thinking about the action. I do not want to elaborate on his arguments here other than to suggest that how one reflects-in-action will be influenced by how one has reflected-for-action. Often students claim that theory is irrelevant because, when faced with a novel and complex problem which requires an immediate response, there will be no opportunity for reflection. I claim that to the extent that one has had an opportunity to reflect on one's own actions as well as the actions of others, and has had the opportunity to reflect for the actions they are likely to engage in, one will be able to respond more effectively and appropriately when one is engaged in action. Iris Murdock (1970:37), I believe, sums it up well: "At critical moments of choice most of the business of choice is already over." One of the goals of education for police, therefore, should be to enhance their ability to theorize: for practice, in practice and on practice. It also follows from what has been argued earlier that the content of such theorizing should include not only technical considerations but also ethical ones.

CONCLUSION

In this paper I have sought to respond to questions raised by students, many of them police and police recruits, enrolled in ethics subjects in the BA (Justice Studies) at Queensland University of Technology. My reason for sharing my responses with you is to extend the debate about police education in general and ethical education for police in particular. An important component of any police education program is the ethical domain, given the desires of the community, the expectation of police services and the inherently moral nature of police work. Numbers of students, however, are dubious of the value and necessity of studying ethics and of the ways ethics is taught. I think it is important to respond to these concerns rather than reject them or acquiesce to the students' wants in a bid for popularity. What is required, I believe, is to engage the students in an interdependent learning encounter in order to establish a dialogue which takes account of the needs of society, learners (police) and the subject matter, in this case ethics, so that the integrity of all stakeholders is preserved and enhanced. I hope the ideas I have shared with you will contribute to that ongoing dialogue and lead to the development of even better educational programs for police.

➤ DISCUSSION QUESTIONS

At each step along the "criminal justice process" (from arrest to arraignment to prosecution to conviction to incarceration) important decisions are being made about whether or not to deprive a person of her or his freedom. This article argues that the police should be required to take a course in ethics. Do you agree? Do you think there are other people in the criminal justice system who should be required to take an ethics course? Do you think an ethics course should be required of criminology and/or criminal justice majors?

REFERENCES

Brown, L. 1991 Law enforcement and police brutality. *The Police Chief*, May 6.

Brown, L. 1991 Responding to a changing environment. *The Police Chief*, March 20–23.

Bruner, J. 1987 Life is narrative. *Social Research*, 54, 11–32.

Buchanan, M. & Schwille, J. 1982 Education: the overcoming of experience. ERIC document: ED228195.

Charlesworth, M. 1991 Ethics in Public life. The Annual Ethics and Public Life Lecture, Brisbane: QUT.

Chi, M., Glaser, R. and Farr, M. (eds) 1988 *The Nature of Expertise*. Hillsdale: Lawrence Erlbaum.

Cohen, H. and Feldberg, M. 1991 *Power and Restraint: The Moral Dimension of Police Work*. New York: Praeger.

Donatiu, P. 1992 Towards a restorative model of criminal justice. *Social Alternatives*, 11 (3), 31–33.

Doyle, J.F. 1992 Empowering and restraining the police: how to accomplish both. *Criminal Justice Ethics*, 11 (1), 52–57.

Eliot, T.S. 1961 *Choruses from "the Rock"*. Chorus 1. Selected Poems. London: Faber.

Elliston, F. & Feldberg, M. (eds) 1985 *Moral Issues in Police Work*. Maryland: Rowman and Littlefield.

Fitzgerald, T. 1989 *Report of a Commission of Inquiry Pursuant to Orders in Council*, Brisbane: Queensland Government Printer.

Fletcher, J. 1966 *Situation Ethics*. Philadelphia: The Westminster Press.

Isaacs, P. 1992 Ethics and education in the 90's: Context, culture and challenge. *New Horizons in Education*, 86,12–21.

Jordan, T. 1992 Ethical education after Fitzgerald. *Social Alternatives*, 11 (3),17–22.

Kirk, D. 1986 Beyond the limits of theoretical discourse in teacher education: Towards a critical pedagogy. *Teaching and Teacher Education*, 2 (2), 155–167.

Kitwood, T. 1990 *Concern for Others. A New Psychology of Conscience and Morality*. London: Routledge.

Klockars, C.B. 1985 The Dirty Harry Problem. In F.A. Elliston and M. Feldberg (eds.) *Moral Issues in Police Work*. New York: Rowman and Littlefield Publishers, pp. 428–438.

Midgley, M. 1988 The reality of human wickedness. In D.M. Rosenthal and F. Shehadi (eds). *Applied Ethics and Ethical Theory*. Salt Lake City: University of Utah Press.

Murdoch, I. 1970 *The Sovereignty of the Good*. London: Routledge.

Preston, N. 1990 Fitzgerald, ethics and higher education. Paper presented to the Law and Society Conference. Griffith University, Brisbane.

Preston, N. 1991 Applied ethics: A challenge for Australian universities. *Social Alternatives*, 10 (3), 56–59.

Robinette, H.M. 1991 Police ethics. Leadership and ethics training for police administrators. *The Police Chief*, January 42–49.

Russell, B. 1952 *Human Society in Ethics and Politics*. New York: New American Library.

Russell, B. 1960 *An Outline of Philosophy*. Cleveland, Ohio: The World Publishing Co.

Schaefer, R. 1978 Law enforcer, peace keeper, servicer: Role alternatives for policemen. *Journal of Police Science and Administratior*, 6 (3), 324–335.

Scheingold, S. 1984 *The Politics of Law and Order*. New York: Longman.

Schon, D. 1987 *Educating the Reflective Practitioner: Toward a New Design in Teaching and Learning in the Professions*. San Francisco: Jossey-Bass.

Sherman, L. 1982 *Ethics in Criminal Justice Education*. New York: Hastings Center.

Shulman, L.S. 1987 Knowledge and teaching: foundations of the new reform. *Harvard Educational Review*, 57, 1–22.

Singer, P. (ed.) 1991 *A Companion to Ethics*. Oxford: Basil Blackwell.

Williams, J.E. 1982 They train lions, don't they? *Journal of Teacher Education* 33 (3), 31–34.

Wittgenstein, L. 1961 *Tractatus Logico-Philosophicus*. London, Routledge.

Zeichner, K. 1983 Alternative paradigms of teacher education. *Journal of Teacher Education*, 34 (3), 3–9.

Zeichner, K. & Liston, D. 1986 An inquiry-oriented approach to student teaching. *Journal of Teaching Practice*, 68 (1), 5–24.

Community Policing in Canada: A Review of Some Recent Studies

■ *ANDRÉ NORMANDEAU*

INTRODUCTORY NOTES

One of the most recent trends getting attention from policymakers and criminologists around the world is the move toward community policing. "Community policing" means lots of different things to lots of different experts; but, generally, it means a move from the more standard form of reactive policing with which most of us are familiar to a more proactive form of policing—with the involvement of the community.

In reactive policing, crime control is largely a matter of responding (reacting) to reports of crime: Someone calls the police to report a crime, the police react. Ultimately reactive measures, at best, contain crime; they do little to prevent crime, as might proactive measures.

In the proactive model, the police do more to interact with the community, and they do not restrict their activities to matters involving crime. One such measure is the transition to the foot patrol, where the police officer does not spend the majority of her or his time looking for crime, but focuses on establishing a rapport with the people in the community. In so doing, the officer makes his or her presence known, makes the people feel someone is looking out for them, and picks up tips from them about likely trouble spots and troublemakers. The officer can then monitor potentially troublesome situations and let the potential troublemakers know that they are being watched.

Besides the proactive emphasis, another advantage to community policing is its apparent effect on reducing the fear of crime. Members of a community often feel more secure, knowing that someone they know is taking care of their neighborhood. To a police administrator, fear of crime can be as important as crime itself. If a community that was once highly fearful is now considerably less fearful, the administration will often get the credit.

The following two selections address the issue of community policing. The first outlines some of the details of what it involves. The second provides an example of such a program in Germany.

SOURCE: André Normandeau, "Community Policing in Canada: A Review of Some Recent Studies," from *American Journal of Police*, vol. 12, no. 1 (1993): 57–73. Reprinted with permission from Anderson Publishing Co. and the author.

THE PRINCIPLES OF COMMUNITY POLICING

The future of policing in Canada, the United States, England, France and elsewhere in Europe, is associated more and more with a contemporary model of policing called: "Community Policing." The literature on the subject is abundant, from the book of Herman Goldstein: *Policing a Free Society* (1977), to the book of Trojanowicz and Bucqueroux: *Community Policing* (1990). Two authors have synthesized American projects in this field (Skolnick & Bayley, 1986, 1988) and we have presented a Canadian version of the model in general (Normandeau & Leighton, 1990, 1991) and with regard to ethnic minorities (Bellemare, Normandeau et al., 1988; Normandeau, 1990).

We do not intend to give an account of this literature here. However, because we wish to submit the community police model to the test of a number of empirical studies of an evaluative nature, we shall briefly outline the essential points of this model.

In the first place, considering our consultations with 586 Canadians on the subject of their view of "the future of policing" for the year 2000 (Normandeau & Leighton, 1990), we found a growing consensus among elected officials, police officers, academics as well as other involved citizens that enables us to describe community policing as follows:

Theoretical Elements of Community Policing

1. The mission of the police is basically to act as peace officers; the police officer, in his work, respects democratic rights and freedoms.

2. The police adopt a crucial strategy: systematic consultation with the community and its associations.

3. The attitude and behavior of the police are always proactive and interactive (police-community).

4. The police devote their energies in part to the solution of problems linked with crime and social disorder; in collaboration with the appropriate partners, they try to solve the causes of certain problems, at least partially, by prevention as much as by law enforcement.

5. The police, together with other major public and private services, help to improve the quality of life; by their community prevention programs, they try not only to contain and reduce crime but also to reduce the fear of crime and promote a true feeling of community safety.

6. Front-line police officers are generalists rather than specialists, and have a high level of responsibility and autonomy, important in a decentralized organization.

7. The obligation to be rigorously accountable to the community and to the legitimate political authorities characterizes a police service of quality.

In the second place, Jean-Paul Brodeur (1991) has described this consensus by the following five traits:

1. *Broadening the mandate of the police:* the need to maintain public order and solve problems has assumed a clear priority over the mandate to fight crime.

2. *A proactive approach* (in the matter of crime prevention): the police seek solutions by the establishment of a general intervention policy, by a consistent effort to have consultations concerning interventions.

3. *The establishment of a partnership:* first at the general level of the community; then with groups of clients and more specialized agents.

4. *Decentralization:* the police consult the population, particularly at the local level, in order to discover its needs and expectations.

5. *A soft policing:* the action preferred by a community police is persuasion by means of communication; this method is the opposite of the more traditional one of coercion, which is exercised by recourse (if necessary) to "legitimate" force.

In the third place, because the community model is partly a rediscovery of the principles laid down since 1829 in England by the "founding father" of the modern police, Sir Robert Peel, a comparison between the so-called "traditional policing" and "community policing" is interesting. It is well described in a series of bulletins, the result of a prestigious seminar held over the past few years by the United States Department of Justice and Harvard University (U.S. Department of Justice, 1988–90). Sparrow's bulletin (1988) is a résumé of the comparison, even though he simplifies the reality a little for pedagogical reasons.

PRACTICES OF COMMUNITY POLICING

The community police model has been expressed "in action" for several years in a number of practices whose scope and quality vary from one police service to another, from one project to another, and even from one period of time to another within the same service. However, the essential elements are usually the following:

Practical Elements of Community Policing

1. A multitude of projects of community crime prevention under the leadership of the police and community organizations, often in partnership with other public and private services. The list of projects is comprehensive, much more than in the past (Normandeau & Ouellette, 1980). It comprises some well-known prevention programs, such as "neighborhood watch," which became widespread during the 1980s in Canada (Jubinville, 1989; Gabor, 1990), in the United States (Rosenbaum, 1988), in England (Bennett, 1989; Bottoms, 1990), and elsewhere in Europe (Waller, 1988). The French model of crime prevention is slightly different (Borricand, 1991), but in its own way is in line with the others.

2. An increased police presence through the opening of community mini-stations (sub-station, neighborhood station) in the four corners of the city or even a neighborhood, depending on the demographic and geographic dimensions. Often cited on this subject is the historical example of the city of Detroit, Michigan, in the mid-seventies, and more recently that of the Japanese "Kobans:" "police counters" in the neighborhoods where the police and volunteers inform the citizen (in matters of prevention, for example), direct him to other public and private services if necessary (victims of crime, for example),

and patrol the district while maintaining direct contact with the children, the storekeepers, the elderly . . .

3. Additional police visibility is also reinforced by the return to the neighborhood of police foot patrols, attached (preferably) to the mini-stations.

   Sometimes the police officer does his work on foot and sometimes by car; more and more on foot, however, depending on the circumstances. The historic example of this return to the sources is that of the city of Flint, Michigan, also during the mid-1970s, and the practice of "ilotage" (neighborhood policing) in France and in Europe. Certainly the expansion and quality of this practice is of particular importance.

4. The setting up of citizens' consultation committees to the police service at the level of the city as well as neighborhoods is an important element. In a way, it is the equivalent of a Board of Directors, first advisory and then, who knows, partly directive. The partnership takes its true meaning here—with the representatives of the associations and pressure groups of the city and its neighborhoods.

5. The active participation of the local elected officials in a public security council (municipal police board or local commission) is of the essence. Elected officials, in the security councils where they assume normal democratic authority, control the police service's budget but are also involved in directing the general policies of the service in the matter of repression and prevention, by concentrating on certain targets (thefts with violence, for example) or certain groups (vulnerable persons such as children and the elderly). A distinction should be made here between this legitimate involvement and inappropriate political interferences.

All in all, the five practical elements of community policing can be expressed as well by the image of two "orthodox" styles of police (Brodeur, 1991:23):

1. *A police of proximity:* from the mini-station to the foot patrol and neighborhood policing.

2. *A police of animation:* mobilization of the citizens through projects of community prevention, citizens' consulting committees and public security councils.

EMPIRICAL EVALUATION OF COMMUNITY POLICING

Evaluation studies on the impact of community policing programs usually use two main criteria of efficacy: the rates of crime and the extent of citizens' feelings of security. A list of the research done in this field would be very long. Therefore, we refer the reader to the appropriate bibliographies of certain key authors who have recently written a synthesis on the subject (Bottoms, 1990; Rosenbaum, 1988). On the whole, the rates of crime have not changed significantly although the feeling of insecurity has: the more complete and operational the community police model is, the more the feeling of insecurity diminishes for the citizens as a whole (or for certain groups) in a city or neighborhood.

Considering that this account had been based on American and British studies, we decided to look at some recent Canadian evaluation studies, in particular:

1. A study in *Montreal* (Rizkalla, 1990): an urban community of 2 million inhabitants; 4,500 police officers.

2. A study in *Edmonton* (Hornick, 1990): a city of 750,000 inhabitants; 1,050 police officers.

3. A study in *Halifax* (Clairmont, 1990): a city of 150,000 inhabitants; 265 police officers.

4. A study in *Victoria* (Walker & Walker, 1989, 1991): a city of 75,000 inhabitants; 150 police officers.

The community police program was developed in one form or another in 1985 (Halifax), 1986 (Montreal), 1987 (Victoria) and 1988 (Edmonton). The evaluation studies cover a period of two or three years. Even though certain methods vary from one place to the other, the aims and objectives are the following.

The Aims (General)

- "To prevent" crime and create a better "quality of life."
- To offer proactive police services that involve "solving problems" rather than responding case by case (individual incidents).
- To offer "community service" as much as law enforcement, in collaboration with the community.

The Objectives (Specific)

- Reduce "real" crime: rate of victimization.
- Reduce "apparent" crime: rate of official crime.
- Reduce the feeling of insecurity (or fear of crime).
- Reduce the number of calls for service by telephone.
- Reduce the number and gravity of complaints against the service and police officers.
- Increase useful information for the prevention and repression of crime.
- Increase the rate of solutions of apparent crime (in general and for certain special offenses, such as burglary in private residences).
- Increase public satisfaction with the police.
- Increase the number and quality of volunteers as well as citizens' consultation committees.
- Increase satisfaction at work of police officers.
- Use more effectively and efficiently (cost/benefit) the time and expertise of police officers as well as the service's budget; new measures of effectiveness in the perspective of community policing; number and quality of the contacts with the citizens, storekeepers, associations, for example.
- Solve certain more complex community problems, in partnership with the citizens and other private and public services: the violence of certain youths, conjugal and family violence, drug-related problems . . .

RESULTS OF THE RESEARCH: SOME SALIENT FACTS

Rate of Official Crime and Rate of Victimization

The rates of official crime have not been thoroughly analyzed by Canadian researchers. The classic criminological reasons of "doubtful" validity and reliability of statistics guided this choice.

On the other hand, the study of victimization (by surveys) in Victoria, for example, shows that the citizens under community policing had been victims of violence or theft half as often (50 percent) as the citizens under the traditional model in time ("before and after" community policing) and in space (neighborhoods inside or outside the community model). The perception of a reduction in crime is of the same order for the two groups (Walker & Walker, 1991).

Two critical questions are in order. The first concerns the phenomenon of the "displacement of crime" from one city to another, or one neighborhood to another, depending on the prevention programs and type of police in action. This subject has already been studied in detail by Gabor (1990) and others who generally found some displacement. But the research is still going on this important topic.

The second, raised by several authors, among them Raymond Gassin (1990) is summarized by some question marks: How is it that evaluation studies on community policing make little use of the classic criterion of the rates of official crime, despite the limitations of the official statistics? Are we afraid of results that, as in the United States and England, sometimes show no significant difference regarding "before and after" community projects? Is it skepticism about the validity and reliability of the statistics? Is it the difficulty of collecting, analyzing and systematically comparing the results? The four Canadian studies, unhappily, have not directly tackled these important issues.

The Feeling of Insecurity (Fear of Crime)

"Feeling of insecurity" is the European (especially French) expression for "fear of crime." The feeling of insecurity on the part of the public, as measured by surveys, diminishes considerably in time and in space in a city or neighborhood under community policing. The reduction is from 25 to 50 percent (Bottoms, 1990; Rosenbaum, 1988), save exceptions, when the community model is actually in force. Some police services now say that their main objective will be to increase the citizens' feeling of security as a mark of the quality of community life. The famous article by Wilson and Kelling (1982) on "broken windows" and community policing has warranted this approach by valorizing the "fight against disorder and petty crime" to mobilize the citizens and increase a feeling of security.

A community police service is by nature a community relations service, although it is "more than that." If the quality of the "relations" and the tandem "community-police" is of a high level, the "fear of crime" should normally diminish, due to the increased visibility of the police, the increased citizen confidence in the police, the increased self-assurance of volunteers, and even the population at large of a particular neighborhood, in their own ability to prevent crime. In fact, in our opinion we should use rates of crime and victimization as well as rates of insecurity ("fear of crime") in a complementary manner, to evaluate police and citizen's programs.

Public Satisfaction

Measured by surveys and multiple indicators, the indices of satisfaction with community policing are higher in time and in space, by 25 to 35 percent (Hornick, 1990), than in the case of traditional policing. The detailed study in Edmonton on the subject shows, for example, that this kind of additional satisfaction applies to the "perceived" efficiency of the police service, the visibility and availability of the police, confidence in the quality of the follow-up and the quality of prevention programs. The Montreal study also shows a high degree of citizen satisfaction with about a dozen dimensions of police work.

Community policing has adopted what is called in private enterprise a "client approach." A certain "marketing" is necessary. There is more and more concern for the citizen, so it is not surprising that the citizen is relatively satisfied. Thus, this instrument of evaluation is useful but should be used judiciously, taking into account all the gamut of measures.

Satisfaction at Work of Police Officers

Psycho-sociology of work and industrial relations have been using this instrument of evaluation for a very long time, not only for private enterprise but also for major public services. Police public services have escaped it, however, with few exceptions.

The Halifax study, in particular, has taken this approach. The key concept is "the quality of life at work" (QLW). The study in time and in space clearly shows the scope of the organizational change:

- greater general and specific satisfaction of the police officers for their work;
- a considerable enrichment of their tasks and functions;
- greater participation in decisions within the framework of a "participative management" model;
- more room for professional autonomy, personal and collective initiative, creativeness, innovative projects, etc.

A symbolic but significant sign is an increase in productivity of 20 percent, using, for example, the criterion of the reduction in sick days (Clairmont, 1990).

The Edmonton study, with the aid of a scale of more than 50 indicators, shows that the community police officer is significantly more satisfied with his work than the traditional police officer. The satisfaction is specifically reflected in the following:

- the general "climate" at work;
- personal motivation at work;
- personal involvement in the work;
- personal and professional growth;
- quality of the policies, directives and supervision;
- the system and criteria of promotions and careers;
- material conditions of work;
- communications and collaboration with citizens.

The studies in Victoria and in Montreal, while also showing the satisfaction of the community police officers, point out that the officers would appreciate a more thorough training in order to take up the challenge of the "community approach."

Obviously this instrument of measure must be calibrated. It is natural that the enthusiasm for a new police model, especially considering the community element, casts a positive light on the daily work of the police. It's new. It's valued by both the elected officials and the citizens. It's a challenge. Why not? They play the game. They are very satisfied, at first. Psycho-sociology calls this phenomenon "the halo effect." Usually, this effect diminishes, depending on events. This initial satisfaction, then, must be strengthened, for the police officer's satisfaction at work is of the essence for testing this change from a traditional police service to a community police model.

THE FUTURE OF COMMUNITY POLICING

In the difficult economic context of the 1990s, it is obvious that a community police will not be developed on a large scale unless a permanent evaluation study of quality makes it possible to specify and correct its range and methods as needed. Generally speaking, research on community policing is still underdeveloped (Tremblay & Rochon, 1991).

The future of community policing also depends on a certain number of questions that must be satisfactorily answered. Two recent books make a survey of these (Greene & Mastrofski, 1988; Klockars & Mastrofski, 1991). For example:

1. Will the "resistance to change" (misoneism) be as strong as that which has been opposed for a long time to community corrections? Will the ideal of community policing be complementary to the ideal of community social reinsertion?

2. Should we plan the changes from the point of view of an incremental approach or use a strategy of rapid change? Reform by small doses or reform in one large step? It is a question of "real politik."

3. To attain the objectives of community policing, how can one judiciously use: a) police management and police unions; b) public opinion; leaders and opinion makers; elected officials; associations and pressure groups?

4. How can we channel or circumvent the three serious constraints mentioned by Clairmont (1991): a) the police subculture; b) the citizens' desire to be able to call the police at any time and for almost any problem, crime-related or not; perhaps we should "demarket the 911," the almost universal call number in America; c) the historical evolution toward specialization when community policing promotes generalists?

5. What are the criteria by which to evaluate a community police service? What are the criteria to assess the productivity of a police officer? As Brodeur (1990) points out, "How can the performance of a solver of social problems be evaluated?"

CONCLUSION

In the field of community policing there are some very interesting projects in Canada, the United States and Europe. These projects are the door to the future. Community policing is the "wave" of the future in the matter of public safety. This, for three main reasons (Bayley, 1991).

1. Everyone knows by now that the traditional police system just "doesn't work" anymore! According to criminological research, police patrols by automobile, the speed of intervention and police investigations have not had any significant effect on the rate of crime and the rate of crimes solved. This is particularly so in certain North American urban centers and European suburbs.

2. Budgets for the police have reached a relative ceiling point for the foreseeable future. The only way to generate new resources for the police and public safety is by the mobilization of inside and outside human resources. In other words, a new way of working, in partnership with the community and with the other public and private services.

3. Community policing is the only system that can combat the main fear in the mind of both the police and citizens of urban centers. What the people fear most is the potential collective violence on the part of socioeconomically disadvantaged groups in urban communities, often along lines of racial and ethnic demarcation.

The community police model is the only system that makes it possible for the police to meet with disadvantaged groups, cultural communities, rebellious youths, etc.

The keynote of all this must be a show of respect, determination, collaboration, humanity and a regard for individual rights, without condescension.

Alone, the police cannot restore the fabric of urban social life, eliminate or even considerably reduce crime and the general feeling of insecurity. In partnership, however, much can be done.

➤ DISCUSSION QUESTION

This and the following article are both highly positive evaluations of the benefits of community policing. Why might the conflict theorist and the civil libertarian be more skeptical about this trend?

REFERENCES

Bayley, D. 1991 "Community Policing: The International View." *Criminology Australia,* 5(1):19–22.

Bellemare, J. and A. Normandeau 1988 *Committee of Inquiry on the Relations Between the Police and Ethnic Minorities.* Montréal: Quebec Human Rights Commission.

Bennett, T. 1989 *Evaluating Neighborhood Watch.* Aldershot, England: Gower.

Borricand, J. 1991 "Les contrats de ville: un nouvel outil de prevention de la délinquance en milieu urbain." *Problemes actuals de science criminelle IV.* Aix-en-Provence: Presses universitaires d'Aix-Marseille: 87–116.

Bottoms, A. 1990 "Crime Prevention Facing the 1990's." *Policing and Society,* 1(l):3–22.

Brodeur, J. 1990 "Police et sécurité en Amérique du Nord." *Les Cahiers de la sécurité intérieure.* 1(l):203–240.

Brodeur, J. 1991 "Policer l'apparence." *Revue canadienne de criminologie,* 33(3–4):285–332.

Clairmont, D. 1991 "Community-based Policing: Implementation and Impact." *Canadian Journal of Criminology,* 33(3–4):469–484.

Clairmont, D. 1990 *To the Forefront: Community-based Zone Policing in Halifax*. Ottawa, Canada: Canadian Police College.

Gabor, T. 1990 "Crime Prevention." Special issue of the *Canadian Journal of Criminology,* 32(1):1–212.

Gabor, T. 1990 "Crime Displacement and Situational Prevention." *Canadian Journal of Criminology,* 32(1):41–73,

Gassin, R. 1990 *Criminologie*. Paris, France: Dalloz.

Goldstein, H. 1977 *Policing a Free Society*. Cambridge, MA: Ballinger.

Goldstein, H. 1990 *Problem-Oriented Policing*. New York: McGraw-Hill.

Green, J. and S. Mastrofski, (ed.) 1988 *Community-Based Policing: Rhetoric or Reality?* New York: Praeger Publishers.

Hornick, J. et al. 1990 *An Evaluation of the Neighborhood Foot Patrol Program of the Edmonton Police Service*. Ottawa, Canada: Solicitor General of Canada.

Jubinville, R. (ed.) 1989 Safer Communities and Crime Prevention in Canada." Special issue of the *Canadian Journal of Criminology,* 31(4):359–579.

Klockars, C. and S. Mastrofski (eds.) 1991 *Thinking About Police*. New York: McGraw-Hill.

Normandeau, A. and C. Ouellette 1980 "Les programmes de prévention de la délinquance." *Crime et justice,* 8(2):119–123.

Normandeau, A. 1990 "The Police and Ethnic Minorities." *Canadian Police College Journal,* 15(l):215–229.

Normandeau, A. and B. Leighton 1990 *A Vision of the Future of Policing in Canada: Police-Challenge 2000*. Ottawa, Canada: Solicitor General of Canada/Supply and Services Canada.

Normandeau, A. and B. Leighton (eds.) 1991 "Police and Society in Canada." Special issue of the *Canadian Journal of Criminology,* 33(3–4):239–585.

Rizkalla, S. et al. 1990 *La prévention communautaire du crime á Montréal*. Montréal, Canada: Société de criminologie du Quebec, 3 volumes (115, 110 and 112 pages).

Rosenbaum, D. 1988 "Community Crime Prevention: A Review and Synthesis of the Literature." *Justice Quarterly,* 12(5):323–395.

Skolnick, J. and D. Bayley 1986 *The New Blue Line: Police Innovation in Six American Cities*. New York: The Free Press.

Skolnick, J. and D. Bayley 1988 "Theme and Variation in Community Policing." In N. Morris and M. Tonry (ed.), *Crime and Justice: A Review of Research* (volume 10). Chicago: University of Chicago Press.

Sparrow, M. 1988 *Implementing Community Policing* (Perspectives on Policing). Washington, DC: National Institute of Justice, U.S. Department of Justice.

Tremblay, P. and C. Rochon 1991 "D'une police efficace á une police informeé: lignes directrices d'un programme global de traitement de l'information." *Revue canadienne de criminologie,* 33(34):407–420.

Trojanowicz, R. and B. Bucqueroux 1990 *Community Policing*. Cincinnati, OH: Anderson Publishing Co.

U.S. Department of Justice 1988–90 *Perspectives on Policing*. Washington, DC: National Institute of Justice.

Walker, C. and S. Walker 1989 *The Victoria Community Police Stations: An Exercise in Innovation*. Ottawa, Canada: Canadian Police College.

Walker, C. and S. Walker 1991 *Evaluation Project: The Victoria Police Station*. Victoria, Canada: The Victoria Police Department.

Waller, I. 1988 *Current Trends in European Crime Prevention.* Ottawa, Canada: Ministry of Justice of Canada.

Wilson, J. and G. Kelling 1982 "Broken Windows: The Police and Neighborhood Safety." *Atlantic Monthly,* March:29–38.

Neighborhood Policing in West Berlin

■ *JOHN BROWN*

INTRODUCTORY NOTES

Until the 1930s, the police did their patrolling by "walking their beats." Afterwards, and especially after World War II, almost all police patrol has been done by automobile. Recently, however, more and more communities in the U.S. are experimenting with community-oriented policing, putting police officers back on foot patrol.

While these experiments are going on, none of these programs in the U.S., to the editor's knowledge, give the officer the kind of latitude afforded by Germany's neighborhood policing program. While the German *KoB* may have little discretion in terms of the decision to make an arrest, he does have a great deal of leeway in terms of his work schedule and the performance of his duties. Note that in this article Officer Melitz acts not only as a law enforcement officer, but also as a social worker, and primarily as a "contact officer." The same can be said of U.S. police, but to a far lesser extent. As contact officer, Herr Melitz acts as a liaison between the people on his beat and agencies such as the Civil Engineering Department, the Housing Office, the Gas Board, the Health Office, the schools, and other social services.

In serving such a broad range of his constituents' needs, it seems likely that he is able to forge a bond of trust between the police and the public—an important goal of community policing. In this manner, the community takes greater responsibility for crime control and cooperation with the authorities.

The system of neighborhood policing in West Berlin derives from a critical revaluation of police organization and methods in the early seventies. As in most industrialized countries, reported crime, public order, and traffic problems had risen rapidly there from the mid-fifties; and as demands on limited police man-power increased, so police turned increasingly to motorized "fire-brigade" styles of policing. This in turn brought in its train increasing demands from the public for more police on the streets and for closer contact between police and citizens.

From October 1974, the West Berlin police were reorganized with the uniform and detective branches under unified central command *(Landespolizeidirektion),* and in five newly-established *Direktionen* (divisions) comprising 31 *Abschnitts* (sub-divisions).

SOURCE: John Brown, "Neighborhood Policing in West Berlin," *Police Studies,* vol. 5, no. 4 (1983): 29–32. 1983. Reprinted with permission from Anderson Publishing Co.

The main objectives of the reorganization were to increase police presence on the streets and to improve crime suppression through the greater involvement of the uniform branch. As a result of the reorganization, more officers and H.Q. personnel were returned for field duty, and the Berlin police were then able to establish and man 756 foot-beats below the Abschnitt level (722 city beats, 18 water police beats, and 16 mounted police beats). The size of each of the 756 beats was determined by a formula which took into account some 50 factors, particularly the numbers of people in the area, reported crime rates, public order and traffic problems, shopping and leisure facilities, business activities, and other special characteristics (e.g., foreign embassies, concentrations of aliens, etc.). The average size of each beat is 0.5 square kilometer, the biggest being about 2 square kilometers, and the smallest (the Europa shopping center) approximately 0.1 square kilometer. Each of the beats is assigned to an area foot patrol officer within the *Kommissar* (inspector) range. Each officer is required to be at least 40 years of age, to have a highly rated confidential report and substantial experience (including at least 3 years service as *Polizeihauptmeister*—Senior Sergeant), and to have completed a 6-month advance course preparing him for the job.

Each officer is responsible for the policing of his own area in ways and at times he himself determines within a 40-hour week frame of reference. His main functions are contact with the public, environmental control, crime suppression, traffic control (including accident prevention), and assistance to other agencies (including registration matters). In fulfilling these functions, he acts not only on his own initiative, but also as a mobilizer of police and public resources to ensure the overall safety and security of his patch, taking a central role when other police units carry out operations on that patch.

Policemen operate from their own Abschnitt, where they have their own desks, large scale maps of their own areas, and files containing comprehensive information on local people, places, and activities. Reports of all incidents and offenders on each beat are also on file, so that each officer can rapidly identify what and where local crime and other problems arise. This is regarded as an important factor by the West Berlin police, since their research shows that 80% of all crimes of medium and minor importance are committed by offenders within 5 kilometers of their own places of residence.

In terms of crime suppression, the main functions of the beat officer are:

i) to stimulate flows of criminal intelligence from public to police;

ii) to provide advice and support for Criminal Investigation Department (C.I.D.) activities, including assisting in searches for wanted and missing persons and for stolen goods;

iii) to alert the C.I.D. to developments of criminal activity in the area and to suggest local assignments;

iv) to provide crime prevention counselling within the area (police research has shown that in 60% of 1,000 cases, citizens took precautions as a result of counselling of that kind);

v) to serve warrants for arrests.

Preliminary research by the West Berlin police suggests that the delegation of responsibility to individual beat officers has done much both to improve police initiative and effectiveness and to relate it to public acceptability. Perhaps the most significant statistical evidence relates to street crime offenses in West Berlin since 1974. (This includes theft in cars, theft from vending machines, sex offenses in public, burglary of building sites, kiosk breaking, summer-house breaking, burglary of one-family and multiple dwellings, burglary of shops and display-windows, factory breaking, and robberies.) This represents a fall of 11.2% in street crime between the years 1974 and 1980.

This paper reflects the experience of a neighborhood beat officer in Kreuzberg, a traditional working-class area of West Berlin, now in process of renewal and redevelopment, covered by Abschnitts 52 and 53 within Direktion 5. Kreuzberg has a high population density and major concentrations of foreign residents—20% in Abschnitt 22, 30% in Abschnitt 53. (Just over a quarter million foreigners live in West Berlin as a whole—about 12% of the total population of 2.1 million. Half of them are Turks.)

Gerhard Melitz, married, age 53, holds the rank of *Polizeihauptkommissar*. His beat in Abschnitt 52 (total population 74,000) comprises six or seven streets near Kreuzberg Town Hall, with an estimated population of 2,000. Enthusiastic and committed to his work, Herr Melitz has already served 4 years on his beat, and looks forward to continuing there until retirement at age 60.

Walking his beat with him leaves no doubts about his acceptability to local people. He is greeted by those of all ages in the most friendly way. Turkish children run up to shake his hand. Old men hail him from across the street. Men and women cross the street to consult him. In all the shops, bars, banks, garages and other businesses we visit, he is plainly welcome. Now in a launderette to reassure the manager, who has had trouble from tramps. Now in a bar shaking hands with young unemployed Turks amongst the pinball machines (unemployment doubled in Germany during 1981, and young foreigners are particularly at risk). Now asking garage hands to look out for certain stolen cars. (He passes by a sex shop. Sometimes they have a live show, and he doesn't want to embarrass the clients.) Now at a coffee and hamburger stall, to tell the woman serving there that he has circulated a description of the man who recently held her up at the point of a gun. And so on around the streets, Herr Melitz consulting, explaining, investigating, contacting—clearly knowing his patch and his people like the back of his hand.

Youth problems are of particular concern to him: 80% of reported crime in West Berlin is committed by young people under 25. Patterns of youth crime there are similar to those found in North Rhine-Westphalia where recent research established that 33% of reported youth crime is committed by 5% of young offenders. At the time of writing (March 1982) gangs of punks and rockers cause a great deal of damage and create a great deal of fear. Herr Melitz therefore visits a local pub used by punks as a meeting place to make contact with them, talk things over, calm things down.

YEAR	STREET CRIMES
1974	58,450
1975	62,230
1976	57,821
1977	58,526
1978	50,293
1979	48,711
1980	51,896

Problems of squatting are also of major concern in West Berlin as a whole as well as on Herr Melitz's patch, where properties are falling vacant prior to demolition or renovation. (Renovation creates additional difficulties of its own since in its train come striking increases in house rents, exacerbating accommodation problems for poorer families.) As squatting involves the offense of trespass, police are required to take action under the German principle of legality, which leaves them with no discretion in the matter. And action to evict squatters is a frequent trigger for protest, confrontation, political polarization, and violence, with the police in the middle. In the 14 1/2 months between December 1980 and the end of February 1982, 150 demonstrations following evictions of squatters led to injuries to 895 West Berlin policemen, involving 3,875 offenses.

For the police, the bitter irony is that these squatters do not in themselves represent a significant problem. In March 1982 police records showed that 139 houses in West Berlin were occupied by some 1,200 squatters, most of them students or young migrant workers from other parts of Germany, drawn to West Berlin by its labor shortage, or members of the "Green Movement." Apart from a few criminal groups moving from squat to squat, most squatters live in communal peace; in the words of one senior police officer, "communality of this kind may well represent real hope for our society."

Yet once the legal requirements for the eviction of squatters have been met, the police have almost no freedom of action. They know that wherever they have to take on this unenviable and largely unwanted role, they will be liable to attack by conservationists and radical interests, just as they also know that if they seek a *softly, softly* approach, they will be liable to widespread and bitter criticisms from an increasingly conservative public. (Indeed, this highly emotive issue played a significant part during the West German elections of 1981, when the Social Democrats and their allies were replaced by the Christian Democrats as the party of Government.)

Herr Melitz is therefore punctilious to ensure that evictions from squats are carried out to the letter of the law, and with minimum disturbance. He points out a house recently cleared of squatters prior to demolition. Before police moved in, he made sure that the owner had first made an official complaint against the squatters, was physically present with a demolition order in hand, and had demolition workers standing by to go into immediate action. The police then asked the squatters three times to leave voluntarily. Most did. A few had to be carried out. But for the most part, peace was preserved. As soon as the squatters left, the demolition workers went to work with their steel ball. And that was that.

Herr Melitz sees his role as contact man between police and community; his official visiting cards designate him as *Kontactbereichsbeamter* (Contact officer)—*KoB* for short. The more he involves himself in the community and the more he identifies himself with it, with its welfare and security, the wider and more effective his range of contacts becomes. He liaises—for example—with the Civil Engineering Department at the Town Hall over broken pavements that cause hazards for pedestrians; with the Housing Officer over neglected premises or falling masonry; with the Gas Board over the marking of street excavations; with building contractors over piles of broken concrete left near places where children play; with the Health Officer over rat-infested premises; with Social Services about old people needing help or support; with shopkeepers over car parking facilities (in one area he had unnecessary restrictions removed); with schools over the cars and control of children, etc.

Many of these activities are not strictly "police business," but Herr Melitz believes they do much to create public trust and confidence in the police, and to enhance the police image in society: "For instance, I make a point of stretching out my hand and shaking hands with every kid on my beat, because my contact with him might be decisive later in life—when, later on, for example, he's told about this 'fucking snooper,' he may say 'they're not all that way. I knew a *KoB* who was very nice and friendly.'"

Herr Melitz's place in the community is reinforced by his contacts both with those who make complaints against the police and with victims of crime. As the first to visit complainants and to talk things over with them, he does much to mollify their attitudes to police. His visits to victims of crime not only do much to calm and reassure them, but also to improve police-community relations. He also gives advisory talks to those whose homes have been broken into or who have been robbed, to advise them how to prevent further dangers. In some instances, he himself has fixed preventive devices for them, e.g., window clamps for an old lady living in a ground floor flat who had been robbed several times.

Through his contacts in every corner of the community, and with ears and nose constantly close to the ground, a *KoB* soon becomes both the servant of the people on his patch and a rich source of criminal intelligence, keeping tabs on offenders, spotting potential offenders, and picking up hints of crime and disorder far more quickly than car patrol officers could do. Much of the information gathered by the *KoB* is passed onto the C.I.D. or to the special plainclothes squads set up by the West Berlin police to tackle particular categories of crime or to work in particular locales. (C.I.D. and uniform branch officers work together on these squads, each of 20 men divided into five teams of four, a degree of integration probably unique in West Germany.) Examples: a *KoB* report about a local rash of thefts from cars leads to the arrest of two drug addicts; another report about drug dealing in a youth club leads to the arrest of two drug addicts; another report about drug dealing in a youth club leads to the arrest of three or four dealers.

As in other major cities, hard drug dealing and abuse (mainly of heroin) are a growing concern to the West Berlin police; increasing numbers of crimes, ranging from shoplifting to break-in offenses and robberies, are found to be hard-drug related. About 90% of the major hard-drug dealers that come to police attention are aliens, 60% of them Arabs, 30% of them Turks, though, at the time of writing, the Turkish connection is tending to diminish as the military government in Turkey cuts off lines of supply. (A main supply line runs through East Berlin; the authorities there show little readiness to cooperate to halt this source of infection to the West.)

The involvement of aliens in the drug scene is also a source of hostility between Berliners and the foreigners in their midst ("Them" and "Us"), and this hostility is exacerbated—especially amongst the youth—by the current context of growing unemployment. Herr Melitz is particularly concerned on this score. He is old enough to know from direct experience what race hatred means, and he takes it upon himself to point out any racial graffiti he finds on his beat.

Despite—and certainly also because of—the many community problems in which he is involved, Herr Melitz is wholly committed both to his own role and to the *KoB* system of policing: "For the public, the police could not have done better than set up the *KoB* system. And for me, the best thing is that I have sole responsibility for my beat and can act on my own discretion."

But to what extent is Gerhard Melitz's work representative of the *KoB* system as a whole? How do his functions compare with those of other *KoBs* in high and low crime areas and in areas of high and low concentrations of ethnic minority groups in West Berlin? What are the ranges and effects of the networks created by *KoBs* amongst local communities and with other social agencies in such areas? What is the operational standing of *KoBs* in the eyes of other police units? By what criteria does police management assess the effectiveness of the *KoB* system? By what criteria do community groups assess the effectiveness of their *KoBs*? What problems do *KoBs* find in reconciling the demands made upon them by the police with the demands made upon them by community? To what extent are *KoBs* able to link police effectiveness to public acceptability? These and many other questions remain to be answered by more comprehensive research.

Yet first impressions certainly suggest that the *KoB* system has done much not only to improve relationships between police and community in West Berlin, but to protect life and property, to prevent and detect crime, and to keep the peace. This has been achieved by devolving police responsibility and accountability to local patch levels, and by giving a new primacy to local contact functions, thus giving considerable reality to the hoary—and all too often empty—rhetoric that "the most important man is the man on the beat."

For police in other parts of Europe concerned to improve the quality of their operational contact with the public and their relationship with local communities, the Berlin *KoB* model is almost certainly of key relevance. As such, it merits further study and more detailed assessment.

➤ DISCUSSION QUESTIONS

What are the advantages of the *KoB* model of policing? What are its disadvantages?

PART THREE

Conceptions of Justice and Societal Reactions

The Maori and the Criminal Justice System: A New Perspective— *He Whaipaanga Hou*

NEW ZEALAND

■ *MOANA JACKSON*

INTRODUCTORY NOTES

When we speak of societal responses to crime, it is easy to overlook the fact that the work of criminologists constitutes one such response; and like the other responses, it is subject to the influence of culture. In that the work of the criminologist is a product of the culture that she or he is trying to explain, in some sense it serves to perpetuate that culture. In that the criminologist is subject to the biases of her or his culture, she or he may carry on the very biases that are in part responsible for the genesis of crime. The criminologist may be unwittingly complicitous in the perpetuation of crime.

In this article, Jackson explains how certain theoretical responses to crime often take the "system" for granted. By focusing on the offender or on the offense, attention is taken away from the system that is the cause of the offense. Though it seems that American criminology is less culpable of this sort of obfuscation than New Zealand's criminology (as described by the author), American criminology has not put the degree of emphasis on the integrity of the offender's subcultural point of view that is advocated by Jackson.

This article addresses a very important issue in criminology: the ofttimes higher crime rates among ethnic minorities—a problem experienced in the U.S. as well as in many other countries. This article, dealing with the Maori in New Zealand, is of particular interest. The Maori, much like Native Americans in the U.S., were overrun by the British before the turn of the century. Similarly, tribal societies all over the world are being overrun by the spread of industrialization. As these indigenous peoples are being displaced and their cultures overwhelmed, we can expect to see more of such crime problems.

SOURCE: Moana Jackson, "The Maori and the Criminal Justice System: A New Perspective—*He Whaipaanga Hou*" Study Series 18, Part 1, (Policy and Research Division, Department of Justice, Wellington, New Zealand: 1987): 25–51 (abridged). Reprinted with permission.

MGA TAHU WHAKAMARAMA I NGA—THE THREADS OF COMPARISON

Comparative analysis is a frequently used research tool and has been much applied in studies of Maori crime and imprisonment. The Maori has been compared to the Pakeha [the Maori word for whites] on the basis of many criteria (sex, age, socio-economic status), and for many subject purposes (rate of offending, arrest, sentencing).

Several important questions arise from the results of this research and the assumptions which underlie it. From a strictly analytic viewpoint, what are the bases of comparison used in these studies and are they valid? Are societal biases reflected in the concentration on comparative research and what is its empirical and etiological value? What limitations does the methodology impose, and what possible explanations does it present to "render intelligible" the behavior of the Maori offender and the systemic consequences of his behavior? From a broader Maori perspective, the comparative approach raises interrelated issues: how culturally valid are the assumptions made in comparative research, and do the findings achieve anything other than a reaffirmation of a positive-negative dichotomy within society?

Anthropologists and sociologists have long been aware of the extreme difficulty in making accurate cross-cultural comparisons. Because each culture is unique, the behavior exhibited by its members has certain unique characteristics. No members of a culture can be understood in isolation from the cultural forces which shape them, and no culture can be understood unless account is taken of the attitudes, expectations, beliefs and values on which it is based. Any index of behavior across cultural boundaries must acknowledge these different values and attitudes and interpret them within their own cultural context. Unfortunately, many researchers' understanding of other institutions and values

> . . . has often been obscured by over-facile interpretation of them in terms of their own institutions.[1]

This has led to a misunderstanding of certain phenomena and the consequent wrongful imputation of motive on alleged cultural grounds—what has been termed the "social imputation of causality of social action."[2]

A specific example of this is found in criminal research. Some researchers hold that disparity in Maori/non-Maori offending rates may be accounted for to some extent by differences in the perception of property. It is asserted that

> . . . the Polynesian attitude to property is less personal than the European and . . . sanctions against theft differ markedly.[3]

or that

> . . . the Maori is not nearly as preoccupied by the concept of private ownership of chattels as the European.[4]

Unfortunately these assertions are culturally inaccurate. Traditional Maori society imposed many sanctions for theft and there were clear guidelines for acceptable and unacceptable behavior. The strictures imposed are recorded in oral and written history. *I nga ra o mua* (in the days gone by) legends tell how Kae stole the whale Tutunui and paid dearly for his crime. Tribal stories tell of many sanctions imposed for theft, as when Ira-tu-moana killed a man for stealing fish. Written records tell of a thief being ordered by his chief to forfeit all his goods to a Pakeha from whom he had stolen a rope.[5]

The Maori drew a clear distinction between sharing with *whanaunga,* and taking from a stranger, which they classified as theft. A "help-yourself" philosophy was

> . . . far from being a true picture of Maori views with regard to property. Maoris do recognize individual rights of possession.[6]

Attempts to explain Maori/Pakeha disparities on this basis are therefore fallacious. However they are indicative of the broader problem inherent in comparative research across cultural lines: ethnocentrism.

Although two cultures may coexist within one wider society, as do the Maori and Pakeha, they continue to exhibit perceptions and insights which are frequently at variance. These differing perceptions will affect the theoretical base a researcher might adopt to assess cross-cultural behavior. They will also influence the subsequent interpretation the researcher places upon that behavior.

In New Zealand, the construction of this theoretical base is shaped by European ethnocentrism which implies that differences between Maori and Pakeha can be standardized to produce valid comparisons: an assumption that cultural differences are in fact irrelevant to the particular study. If the differences are actually deemed to be relevant, they are interpreted from a European perspective in terms of non-adaptational conflict.

This approach views cultural difference in terms of a conflict in which Maori cultural values have not adjusted or adapted to the dominant Pakeha value system. Its roots lie in an ethnocentric belief that assimilation is the path to true 'progress' and a Victorian equation of 'civilization' with technological advance. It leads to judgements, about what behavior is acceptable, being made according to the dominant Pakeha values. Reasons for non-normative behavior by members of the minority culture, the Maori, are sought in instances of non-assimilation, or in specific cultural mores of the Maori; they are not sought in the cultural norms of the Pakeha which are impacting upon Maori people. Thus an explanation of the high rate of Maori theft was sought, albeit incorrectly, in an alleged Maori value. It was not sought in a questioning of the relevant Pakeha values or systems.

In order to seek explanations behind the descriptions it is necessary to consider the various untouched threads of research and so set up a framework which will enable an understanding of both the Maori offender and the system which seems so often to impact inequitably upon him.

NGA TAHU KAORE ANO I KITEA—THE UNTOUCHED THREADS

The inability of research to offer substantive explanations of Maori offending is a consequence of the accent placed upon descriptive methodology, and the inherent, if unwitting, sociocultural bias involved in cross-cultural analyses. Another consequence is that certain relevant areas of research have been largely untouched while an inappropriate emphasis has been placed on others.

A 1981 study summarized the proffered reasons for the disproportionate representation of the Maori as being due to factors ranging from the

> . . . comparable inequities of a characteristically Anglomorp society favoring a particular group, namely European, to ambiguities in the process of law enforcement.

The paper then outlined how manifestations of these factors included arguments that

> . . . the problem of Maori offending can be attributed to the lower socioeconomic status of . . . the Maori (and) the process of attrition whereby Maoris are more likely to be disfavored by the process of law.[7]

This is an accurate distillation of much of the research but its generalized nature illustrates how research has tended to describe certain perceived phenomena without adequately explaining them.

A less definitive summary was propounded the following year :

> It is unclear whether the high crime rates for Maoris means that (1) they commit more crimes than Europeans; (2) they are less sophisticated offenders, and hence are more frequently detected, apprehended and convicted; (3) they are the recipients of differential policing by virtue of their powerlessness and cultural vulnerability; or (4) by a combination of all or some of these processes.[8]

The uncertainty evinced in this summary is an honest but nevertheless inevitable consequence of inherent sociocultural bias. The inability to be more definitive flows from the fact that the research has misinterpreted certain phenomena, asked the wrong questions, or been prevented by its own constructs from scrutinizing all relevant contributory factors. A consideration of three specific areas of analysis will illustrate these points and isolate a number of untouched research threads.

The most obvious instance in which research is hindered by its own ethnocentricity is in its search for "cultural correlates" of crime. One such correlate which has been found to have profound cultural, social, and economic consequences for the Maori people is the post-war urban shift.

This movement of nearly 70% of the Maori population from rural to urban areas in the last 30 years has been the result of economic and land use policies implemented by successive governments. Its consequences for the Maori people have been a physical and emotional separation from their ancestral roots and a consequent dislocation of traditional kinship ties. As well, there have been the social and psychological difficulties involved in any adaption to a new environment. These consequences have been labelled as the "cause" of much Maori behavior, ranging from failures in education to criminal offending. This imputation of causality has convincingly placed the "blame" on Maori inability to adapt and excluded consideration of the rationale behind the original policies, or the factors within it which have led to so much cultural disruption. Instead, research has simply focussed on the fact that

> . . . differences in the whole network of values and behavior associated with the urban environment seem likely to increase the probability of offending.[9]

The increased risk of non-normative behavior therefore arises because the Maori is perceived to be incapable of adapting to the new urban environment. The cultural appropriateness of the urban milieu itself is not considered; neither is the rapid pace of the upheaval. It is assumed that with time the Maori people will adapt, the spread of urbanization will slow down, and the crime rate will decline:

> . . . we cannot realistically expect a significant improvement in the Maori crime rate until the process of urbanization has slackened . . . [10]

It is clear from a Maori viewpoint that the pain and loss caused by separation from one's *papakainga* and *whanaunga* have many emotional and behavioral consequences. However the explanation of these consequences lies not in the pain, but in the situation which created it. An evaluation of the causes of particular behavior should be sought not in the outward manifestations of loss, but in the societal forces which have occasioned it. Many Maori people would in fact argue that the difficulties associated with the urban shift are due in part not so much to their "cultural vulnerability" as to the inability or unwillingness of society to cater to their different kinship structures within an urban setting.

The emphasis in urban-drift research has therefore been misplaced. The extent and effects of tribal and *whanau* dislocation do need to be understood. However they need to be understood as the consequences of particular policies, not just the cause of certain behavior. Indeed, if one accepts that

> . . . the urban milieu itself spawned the brown proletariat. . .[11]

then explanations for that alienated group's behavior will be found largely in the structures of the urban environment itself.

In specific investigative terms this means that factors identified as "cultural correlates" of crime need to be reassessed. There needs to be a clear distinction drawn between the specific cultural mores which shape the Maori offender and the wider social forces which act upon those mores. Such a reassessment will require that different factors be emphasized and different questions be asked in relation to the effect of phenomena such as the urban shift. Thus because not all young Maori men commit crime, it is necessary to first ascertain whether the undoubted sense of cultural loss consequent upon urban migration is in fact greater among urban Maori offenders than it is among urban Maori non-offenders. If it is not, then clearly any attempts to link cultural "inadequacy" or non-adaptability to criminal offending would be hard to validate. However, if it is, the emphasis should not immediately be upon assuming that cultural loss per se is a contributory factor in offending. Rather the loss should be perceived as a consequence of the shift itself and hence of accumulated economic pressures and social attitudes which impact upon young Maori in particular ways. It is these pressures which need to be considered, and questions asked as to how they prevent a Maori retaining the basic foundations of his *tikanga* Maori and how they might also create situations which predispose him to commit crime.

The second area in which a different research emphasis is required is in the relationship between SES and offending. Maori/Pakeha differences have been correlated and

> . . . it is possible that the differences in the Maori and non-Maori rates of offending reflect differences in the socioeconomic distribution rather than cultural or other differences between the two groups.[12]

Although not all of the disparity can be attributed to socioeconomic difference, it is postulated that a reduction in Maori crime may come from

> . . . improvements in the relative socioeconomic position of Maoris (although) improvements in socioeconomic status are unlikely to lead to a reduction . . . unless they are sufficiently large to advance the position of Maoris compared to non-Maoris.[13]

This presumption posits the rather simplistic belief that money and time will ameliorate the inequality and hence the offending. It is consistent with the monist perspective that crime differentials will be lessened when the process of Europeanization has promoted the Maori to an appropriate level of material security. It maintains that integration/assimilation will help reduce offending since the "causes" of Maori crime are basically comparable to the "causes" of Pakeha crime.

This view does not explain the disparities in offending at comparable socioeconomic levels and is inconsistent with findings which indicate that improved Maori SES does not reduce offending to a degree comparable with the Pakeha. However it does uphold the validity of existing socioeconomic structures and so effectively precludes their examination. It maintains the inherent "potential for equality" in the system and prevents an analysis of the ways in which the structures themselves might confine Maori people to lower socioeconomic levels.

Clearly there are several questions which can arise from this approach. If disparities in socioeconomic levels do not account entirely for the higher Maori offending and imprisonment rates, is it possible to identify other contributory factors within the broad social or economic structures? If so, how do they affect Maori people, and in what ways can they be interpreted as increasing the likelihood of criminal offending? If not, where can the other factors indicated by research be found? Are they within the particular processes of the justice system itself?

The "process of attrition" within the justice system results in obvious differences in rates of conviction and imprisonment. Where research has proffered explanations for this it has concentrated on issues such as prior offending: the Maori is in jail more because he offends more. There are almost Alice in Wonderland tones of circumlocution to this statement but the approach which it represents has effectively prevented any detailed consideration of systemic or procedural operations which might contribute to higher Maori imprisonment rates. Apart from begging the obvious question of "why does the Maori offend more?", the focus is safely placed on a descriptive actuality borne out by statistics. The possible existence of unfair or even prejudicial practices, within or outside the justice system, is not contemplated.

The lack of quantifiable data for each stage of the justice process has meant that there is no comprehensive analysis of how the system works vis-à-vis the Maori offender. In the place of analysis, there has simply been an assumption that the system operates towards all people equally, as if the concept of equality flowed from one culturally impartial norm. In fact, of course,

> . . . we use (the term) equality in law . . . without realizing that we are surreptitiously asserting diverse and sometimes conflicting moral and legal norms.[14]

There are many specific questions left untouched by such an assumption: how are various discretionary powers exercised by justice functionaries in relation to Maori people; what criteria are applied in bail and remand decisions; how culturally sensitive or appropriate are justice processes? Consideration of these and similar questions should be an essential component of any research into offending and imprisonment. They are particularly apposite when the application of a system is across cultural lines.

It is now necessary to draw together the relevant strands of research with the untouched threads of analysis and create a new fabric of perspective.

TE WAHANGA TUATORU   *NGA TAHU HOU: THE NEW THREADS*

Kotahi ano te kohao hei urunga atu mo te miro ma, te miro whero me te miro pango.

The white, the red and the black threads are drawn together through the single eye of the needle.

The new weave of research arises from several interrelated strands of enquiry. Some have been extracted from existing research, others have developed as a result of its shortcomings. All have interlocking hypotheses.

The first supposition is that research must view the Maori offender as an entity quite distinct from the Pakeha offender. He is a person who is shaped by cultural forces which are unique to his being Maori, and who is subject to particular influences which are consequent upon that sense of Maoriness. Any behavior which manifests itself in this context requires an "ethno-specific" base of understanding.

Such a base means that research must analyze the specific complex of factors which may predispose certain young Maori men to commit crimes and to scrutinize the systemic responses to that behavior. It is an "ethno-specific" approach in that it seeks to render intelligible the "causes" of his offending as distinct from the "causes" of Pakeha offending. It presupposes that while Maori and Pakeha young people may have much in common and may share the apparently similar facades of youthful bravado, they are also different, and the reasons for their offending are different. It seeks to ascertain whether responses to that offending are also different, and endeavors to avoid the descriptive pitfalls and sociocultural biases of comparative analysis.

The corollary of this supposition is that the behavior of any person must be understood within the parameters of a distinctive cultural milieu. For the Maori offender this means that he is a product of formative influences which are best interpreted from within the same cultural framework and from insights rooted in the same values and cultural experiences.

One researcher has compared a people's culture to a set of books which an outsider

. . . strains to read over the shoulders of those to whom they properly belong.[15]

Existing research on Maori crime has either misread the "books", not consulted them at all, or ethnocentrically judged them by their covers. It has therefore failed to isolate the particular characteristics of the Maori offender and the special features which separate him from the Pakeha offender.

A closely linked supposition is that a person's cultural esteem is unavoidably affected by the wider social perceptions of that culture's worth. Entrenched ideas of cultural superiority may deliberately or unwittingly demean another culture and hence a person's perception of his worth and the worth of his heritage. Any analysis of Maori behavior needs to accept that there are many historic and contemporary pressures which challenge the value of Maori ideals. These may manifest themselves in overt bigotry, institutional racism, or ignorant insensitivity. Whatever their manifestation, they are an inextricable part of the sociocultural fabric impacting upon the Maori. Any efforts to understand the Maori offender need to consider how these pressures might influence his sense of self-esteem and consequent behavior patterns.

The final supposition is that an understanding of Maori crime and imprisonment is possible only if the operation of systemic responses to an alleged Maori offender is available for analysis. The untouched threads of research in this area have hindered the understanding of offender-system interaction and hence the whole phenomenon of the Maori crime rate. This has led to a clear methodological need to analyze justice processes which arises from the Maori belief that one gains an understanding of a problem only by considering all of the parts which contribute to the whole. It is an attitude to knowledge and understanding which is essentially holistic: it seeks not merely to describe, but to seek out seeds of understanding. Its relevance to an analysis of Maori crime is perhaps best illustrated by way of analogy.

Customary Maori thought conceived of good health as a state in which the inter-related parts of one's being were in harmony. The body *(te tinana)* was never divorced from the state of mental well-being *(te taha hinengaro)* or from one's spiritual aspect *(te taha wairua);* they were interrelated parts of a functioning whole which in turn was part of an interdependent community and natural world. Illness occurred when one or more parts of a person's being were in disharmony with the other parts which shaped his existence. The subsequent diagnosis and treatment depended upon a holistic assessment of this totality.

The Maori offender or prisoner of today can only be understood or "diagnosed" if his total existence is similarly assessed. He is shaped by various internal and external forces which are interrelated. The functioning of the internal forces is a complex cultural and socio-psychological process. The functioning of the external forces is an interactional exercise of power in the name of the wider community of which the justice system is an integral part. The existence of a phenomenon such as the disproportionate number of Maori men within the prison system indicates a state of social disharmony. To render it intelligible the total interaction between the internal and external forces at work upon young Maori men must be reviewed. To concentrate on the "offender-based" indices while ignoring "system-based" influences such as the judicial process is to give an incomplete diagnosis. To consider them both is to point the way to a meaningful prognosis.

Based on these suppositions, this research will address several issues, ask different questions, and seek different perspectives.

Because most research to date has been by Pakeha people its monocultural framework has resulted in "top-down" research which has tended to preclude consultation with the group most affected. The basic thread of methodology in this research will attempt to remedy this and will be based on a process of consultation with Maori people. While it will naturally be necessary to also consult a wide range of Pakeha people involved within justice processes, the key consultative guide will be Maori. It is essential to draw out from the diversity of Maori opinion the hitherto largely untapped wisdom and perceptions which may render intelligible both the behavior of Maori offenders and the systemic responses to that behavior.

The information gained from this consultative process will be difficult to quantify and impossible to fit within traditional Pakeha methodologies. However it is the contention of this paper that the recorded perceptions and views will be developed within a Maori framework which is equally valid. It is a framework of *whakawhitiwhiti whakaaro* (shared thoughts) which encourages input from both old and young and then relies on accurate and impartial assessment to draw out the major issues of concern. It is a framework which needs to be taken to tribal, not court, districts, and to be held in the forums which each tribal group deems appropriate. Most importantly, it is a framework which will allow for a synthesis of Maori views.

The methodology is therefore specifically Maori. The information gathered in the course of the research will consequently need to be gathered in a way which is also specifically Maori. This is best done by conducting unstructured and open-ended "interviews" in a way and in a forum which are culturally appropriate.

Normally this is a more "public" forum than the term "interview" implies in a Pakeha situation, because it becomes talk in a *marae* situation where others are present. The collection, analysis, and interpretation of the material elicited in this situation requires an understanding of the cultural forces and attitudes at play.

It is a methodology which is valid in a cultural sense and which therefore needs to be recognized as equally valid in an analytic and research sense. It draws its validity not from preset surveys or questionnaires, but from a form of input determined by the particular tribal, *hapu,* or other group concerned. It is input based on an oral, rather than a written transmission of information.

In specific terms, the research draws heavily on the traditional structure of decision-making and requires consultation with appropriate elders, *Kaumatua* and *Kuia,* to provide an accepted base for consultation with the wider Maori community. It also requires an acceptance of the need for such research by the researcher's own tribe and *whanaunga.*

This consultation, and the concurrent discussion with staff inside the justice system, will enable the welding together of both "offender-based" and "system-based" analyses. The former will be an ethno-specific deduction based on the views of Maori people, both offenders and non-offenders. The latter will be a qualitative and quantitative assessment of judicial structures and processes arising from the issues considered important by Maori people.

Preliminary consultation on the offender-based indices indicate a need to investigate such factors as the causes and effects of tribal dislocation on Maori offenders. This could perhaps be done through a controlled comparison with a group of Maori non-offenders. There is also a clear need to monitor increasing Maori unemployment and the continuing consequences of cultural stereotype and denigration. Each of these issues must of course be seen as a part of the much wider historic and social fabric of institutional and cultural racism which impact upon Maori people.

Preliminary consultation on the operation of the justice system has highlighted areas which Maori people perceive to be unfair or unjust. These areas cover all steps in the process from arrest and apprehension procedures through to sentencing. An analysis of administrative guidelines and procedures operating in those areas would elicit whether this perception of unfairness arises from systemic or aberrational prejudice. A quantifiable evaluation of a limited set of cases in particular districts would indicate specific patterns in Maori arrest, conviction, and imprisonment, and would also indicate whether those patterns were due to the monocultural structure of the system or other factors. A qualitative analysis of courtroom processes based on non-participant observation would enable a more structured interpretation of court behavior to be aligned with the perceptions drawn from the consultative process.

This amalgam of consultation and analysis is the specific research which will flow from and be concurrent with the recorded perceptions of the Maori community. The total project will not illuminate all of the "causes" of criminal offending by young Maori men. However it will give new insights into the behavior of the Maori offender and enable the justice system to see itself through the eyes of the community from which most of its defendants come.

➤ DISCUSSION QUESTION

"Cultural diversity" and "multiculturalism" have become increasingly important in college curricula today. Part of this emphasis comes from a realization that our understanding of the world and its history have been slanted by a male eurocentrist bias. Our history has been written by white Western European males and it, therefore, reflects their biases. For example, our history books tell us that Columbus "discovered" America, whereas the indigenous peoples of North and South America are more likely to use the word "conquest" rather than "discovery." The use of the word "discovery" implicitly takes the superiority of European culture for granted. Just as history can reflect a white eurocentric bias, so can theory; and locating the cause of Maori crime in their failure to adapt to the Pakeha (white) culture implicitly takes the Pakeha culture for granted. Discuss this article in terms of its contribution to a multicultural understanding of crime. How might such an understanding contribute to American criminology?

NOTES

1. Beattie, J., "Other Cultures". Routledge and Kegan Paul, Ltd. 1964. (p. 117)

2. O'Malley, P., "The Amplification Maori Crime: Cultural and Economic Barriers to Equal Justice in NZ". In "Race" 15. 1973. (pp. 47–57)

3. McDonald, C., Maori and Non-Maori Imprisonment Rates: An Outline of Previous Studies. Department of Justice. (in press)

4. "Crime in NZ". Justice Department. 1968. (p. 397)

5. Hunt, F., "Twenty-five years in NZ and the Chatham Islands". 1886. Quoted in "Economics of the NZ Maori" R. Firth. Government Printer. 1973. (p. 347)

6. Metge, J., "The Maoris of New Zealand". Revised ed. Routledge and Kegan Paul. 1976. (p. 217)

7. Minority Group Involvement in the Criminal Justice System. A Statistical Analysis. Justice Department. 1981. (p. 3)

8. Gidlow, B., "Deviance". In "NZ Sociological Perspectives". Eds P. Spoonley, Pearson, Shirley. Dunmore Press. 1982. (p. 334)

9. McDonald, C., *ibid* (p. 13)

10. Te Punga, R., "Maoris and Crime". In "Essays on Race Relations and the Law in NZ". Ed. W. McKean, Sweet and Maxwell. 1971. (pp. 40–56)

11. Walker, R., "The Lost Tribes". In "Korero", NZ Listener, March 1984. (p. 42)

12. Fergusson, D., et al., "The Effects of Race and Socio-Economic Status on Juvenile Offending". Statistics Research Report No. 2. Government Printer. 1975. (p. 10)

13. Fifield, J. and Donnell, A., *ibid* (p. 52)

14. Estern, P., "The Empty Idea of Equality". Harvard Law Review. vol. 95. 1982. (p. 537)

15. Geertz, C., "Myth, Symbol and Culture". W.W. Norton, 1974. (p. 47)

Criminal Law and the Legal System in Iran

■ *NADER ENTESSAR*

INTRODUCTORY NOTES

The criminal justice system is a product of culture. That is, a full understanding of a society's criminal justice system requires an understanding of its culture which, in turn, requires an understanding of its political, economic, religious, and social heritage.

Politics and religion figure very strongly in this next article about the criminal justice system in Iran. This system is a product of a religious political movement—namely, Islamic fundamentalism. In the U.S., the First Amendment requires that we take great effort to separate religion and the government ("church and state"); in Iran they take great effort to unite the two.

To an extent, the separation of religion from the law in the U.S. is a myth, as our laws—especially those governing sexual and marital behavior—reflect a definite Judeo-Christian influence. (In the U.S., for example, where we are assured "freedom of religion," a person whose religion permits him or her to have more than one spouse is not free to practice that aspect of his or her religion.) We also see the influence of religion in our penitentiary system, the development of which is credited to the Quakers in the latter half of the eighteenth century who were reacting to the brutality of corporal and capital punishment, and striving to unite their beliefs in "penance" and forgiveness with the goals of criminal justice.

Iran's response to crime is, by the standards of most Western societies, quite draconian. While the American public may be clamoring for get-tough policies, and while I often hear my students speak wistfully of the tough Iranian criminal justice system, few Americans would opt to live in a society where the government wields such enormous power.

SOURCE: Nader Entessar, "Criminal Law and the Legal System in Revolutionary Iran," from *Boston College Third World Law Journal* vol. 8, no. 1 (1988): 91–102 (abridged). Reprinted with permission.

INTRODUCTION

The purpose of this article is to analyze the penal code of the Islamic Republic of Iran and to examine the methods by which the administration of justice is exercised in post-revolutionary Iran.

The Iranian Revolution of 1978-79 was the culmination of a long struggle between the modern secularist trends that had engulfed Muslim societies for many decades and Islamic revivalist movements. The latter had contended that in order to save Muslim societies from internal decay, socio-political degeneration and Western domination, one would have to eschew Western secularist values and return to those of the early period of Islam. Perhaps no single manifestation of Western secularism in Muslim societies has been as disturbing to the revivalists as those reflected in the modern legal systems of Muslim countries. A return to *shari'a*, or Islamic law, has become the battle cry of Muslim revivalists from Tunisia to Egypt, and from the Levant to the Persian Gulf. In fact, a regime's adherence to the *shari'a* has become the litmus test of its Islamic solidarity and commitment to Islamic values.[1]

For Ayatollah Khomeini and the Islamic militants who participated in the overthrow of the Pahlavi monarchy in Iran, the monarchical justice system was the primary channel for spreading corruption, inefficiency, and foreign political and cultural domination of the country. Offering a simple alternative to the notoriously slow and ineffective method of conflict adjudication during the Shah's reign, Khomeini stated:

> ... the method established by Islam for enforcing people's rights, adjudicating disputes, and executing judgments is at once simple, practical, and swift. When the juridical methods of Islam were applied, the *shari'a* judge in each town, assisted only by two bailiffs and with only a pen and an inkpot at his disposal, would swiftly resolve disputes among people and send them about their business. But now the bureaucratic organization of the Ministry of Justice has attained unimaginable proportions, and is, in addition, quite incapable of producing results.[2]

In his political *magnum opus*, written before the Revolution and published under the tide of Islamic Government, Ayatollah Khomeini severely criticized the European origin of Iran's legal system.[3] He claimed that although some Islamic precepts had been added to the country's laws just to "fool the people," the anti-Islamic nature of the monarchical legal system was due to the overwhelming influence of French and Belgian jurisprudence.[4] A further impetus for Ayatollah Khomeini to call for the replacement of Iran's judicial system with an Islamic one came from his conception of justice. As Khomeini contended, all secular governments, be they monarchical or republican, communist or capitalist, rely on man-made laws to govern their affairs.

In contrast, an Islamic government would rely on God-given laws, as enumerated in the holy Quran, which are infinitely more just than man-made laws even under the best of circumstances.[5] In other words, justice as the expression of Divine Will should become an integral part of an Islamic society. The exercise of Divine Will is performed by the Prophet Mohammad and his rightful successors, or *Imams* as they are called in Shi'a branch of Islam, which is the dominant belief system in Iran. It is incumbent upon the believers to obey the Prophet and his successors who execute God's Sovereign Will.[6] The two major divisions in Islam, the Sunni and the Shi'a schools, concur on the principle that either a member of the Prophet's family or a member of his tribe can exercise the Divine Sovereign Will for the Muslim community. The Shi'as contend that the Divine Sovereign Will can be exercised in a just manner only by a member of the Prophet's family. The Sunnis, on the other hand, have argued that "membership in the larger circle of the prophet's tribe was quite adequate for the requirements of political justice ."[7] This doctrinal difference between the Sunnis and the Shi'as has led to the latter's acceptance of the legitimacy of the principle of Imamate as the sole vehicle for establishing a just socio-political system. That is, the acceptance of Ali, the Prophet's son-in-law, as the first rightful successor to Mohammad, followed by Ali's male descendants in direct line, is for the Shi'as a *sine qua non* for establishing a just political order. However, according to the Twelver Shi'ism (the dominant sect in Iran), the Twelfth Imam went into occultation and will return at some time in the future in the person of the Mahdi, or Messiah, when he will once again establish justice on earth.[8] In the absence of the Twelfth Imam, the *ulema,* or religious scholars, would guide the Shi'a community on a righteous path.

As secular rulers gradually enhanced their power *vis-à-vis* the *ulema,* the religious authorities in the Shi'a communities were pushed to the fringes of the political order. As a consequence, the *ulema* became mere dispensers of opinions on religious exegeses and provided guidance for the believers on issues of faith. Ayatollah Khomeini introduced a radical dimension to this long-standing role performed by the Shi'a *ulema.* Khomeini argued against the notion that the duty of the *ulema* was simply to render advice to believers. Instead, he maintained that when the advice of the *ulema* is disregarded by secular rulers, as was the case in Pahlavi Iran, the *ulema* are obligated to "take over authority and put an end to corruption and injustice."[9] In order to accomplish this task in monarchical Iran, it was incumbent upon the *ulema* to establish an Islamic government under the guardianship of *velayat-e faqih* (government of the just jurist) and institute the *shari'a* as the only source of law in the country.[10]

THE POST REVOLUTIONARY JUDICIAL STRUCTURES

The Iranian Constitution of 1979 not only terminated more than 2,500 years of monarchy in Iran, but it has also uniquely entrusted supreme power in the hands of Ayatollah Khomeini in his capacity as *velayat-e faqih.* Article 5 of the new Constitution states that in the absence of the Twelfth Imam, all political and legal power emanates from a "just jurist" whose leadership has been recognized by the majority of the Iranian people.[11]

In his capacity as supreme *faqih,* or jurist, Ayatollah Khomeini issued *fatwahs* (juridical declarations) declaring all pre-revolutionary laws null and void. Furthermore, Articles 4 and 170 of the Constitution have placed a ban on all laws deemed to be "un-Islamic" by proper judicial and religious authorities of the country.[12] In the absence of qualified judges who were trained to interpret Shi'a principles of law, the Supreme Judicial Council (the country's highest judicial body) instructed the Islamic courts to "refer to the judicial views *[fatwas]* of the Ayatollah whenever they were doubtful or unclear about a law."[13]

Moreover, the Council of Guardians, a body of jurists established by the 1979 Constitution with the power to veto the laws passed by the Parliament, informed the Supreme Judicial Council on April 16, 1981 that constitutionally only the Council of Guardians has the authority to pass final judgment on the propriety of any new law or the validity of any pre-revolutionary legislation. This apparent conflict of authority contributed to the confusion in implementing laws and regulations in the early periods of the Islamic Republic. The confusion became more acute in the administration of the criminal justice system where some degree of anarchy, or extreme diffusion of authority, reigned supreme, resulting in vastly different sentences for people convicted of committing the same type of transgression but living in different parts of Iran. It was not until the centralization of functions of the Islamic judges under the Supreme Judicial Council and the passage of *hudud* and *qisas* laws (to be discussed later) that some degree of uniformity was established in the administration of justice in the country.

CRIMINAL LAW IN THE ISLAMIC REPUBLIC

As was discussed before, the *shari'a* is considered the supreme law over everybody and the government "cannot change the law to suit the ever-changing socioeconomic climate."[14] This is especially true in the area of criminal law, where punishment for certain categories of crime is non-negotiable. Also, the supremacy and permanency of all Islamic laws connote an important principle of the Islamic government: legislative and judicial organs of the state should not *originate* any laws. Their purpose is simply to *codify* and *apply* the *shari'a*. This implies that in cases of conflict between societal changes and the requirements of the Islamic law, the law is not to be interpreted in such a way as to meet such societal changes. Rather, it is the society that needs to adapt itself to the requirements of God's Will as contained in the *shari'a*.[15] As Joseph Schacht has observed, the rules of the *shari'a* become valid "by virtue of their existence and not [necessarily] because of their rationality."[16]

The concept of criminal law in Islam differs from the Western notion of the law, not just because it is religiously derived but because in many instances the subject of law is not the person but his family. For example, murder is viewed not as an offense against the society but as a crime against the victim's family. The punishment for murder, therefore, is designed to not only deter crime but also to "compensate" the family of the victim. Hence, retribution and "blood money" have been an integral part of the Islamic punishment for murder. This, in effect, is akin to the concept of *wergeld* practiced by Western European nations from the 5th century to the advent of feudalism in the 9th century.

Notwithstanding the harsh methods of punishment in the Islamic criminal justice system, the Muslim judicial system was much more benign than the legal systems of Europe. For example, under the Islamic criminal law, only mentally sound adults were fully responsible for criminal acts they committed, whereas minors and the mentally ill were not responsible for many criminal transgressions.[17] Furthermore, as I.P. Petrushevsky has observed:

> Muslim law does not allow the use of torture (which several European countries employed as late as the eighteenth century) nor does it countenance 'the diving decision' whether in the shape of the *ordalia*, the ordeal by fire and water, or of the legal duel between plaintiff and respondent, as practised in Western Europe and Russia in the Middle Ages .... Its [Islamic] procedure was marked by speed and expedition and was innocent of the judicial delay, ... which characterized European and Russian courts in the last century.[18]

Whereas Islamic criminal law remained unchanged for centuries, reforms and alterations in much of Western law have incorporated safeguards and guarantees of protection for the accused; they have also adapted the law to reflect societal mores and changing values.

The Quran deals only with a few categories of crime with specific punishment for each. These transgressions include adultery, consumption of alcohol, fornication, theft, brigandage, and accusations of unchastity. According to the dominant Shi'a doctrine, as well as some Sunni schools of law, apostasy and rebellion against a righteous Islamic government also fall into the category of crimes with Quranic punishments, which range from flogging to execution. The apparent incongruity of such punishments as public floggings, mutilations and stoning to death, with the modern and internationally accepted norms of conduct, is lost on the proponents of the literal application of Quranic punishment, as they argue that only such public spectacles will deter the occurrence of future crimes.[19]

In general, the Islamic Republic's penal code has divided crimes into the four categories of *hudud*, *qisas*, *ta'zir*, and *diyat* based on the type of punishment for each category of offense. *Hudud* crimes are acts prohibited by God and punishable by mandatory penalties defined by the Quran.[20] Although Islamic jurists differ on the precise nature of *hudud* crimes, the Iranian penal code considers the following as *hudud* offenses: theft, robbery, adultery, apostasy, drinking of alcoholic beverages, and rebellion against Islam as interpreted and defined by the religious authorities and legists in Iran.

Since *hudud* crimes are specific and their penalties are specified in the Quran, the judge exercises no discretion as to the type of punishment imposed. The harshness of the punishment of *hudud* crimes, such as the amputation of hands for theft or stoning to death for adultery, have cast a negative image on revolutionary Iran's administration of justice. However, the Iranian authorities rebut Western criticism of their country's system of justice by claiming that lawbreakers should not be seen simply as sick individuals, and their punishment as a form of treatment for their sickness. As the Islamic Republic's Chief Justice, Ayatollah Mussavi Ardabili, has contended: "Islam teaches us that it is equally important to punish a lawbreaker, as a punishment is considered to have three purposes—repentence of the crime, admonition to not repeat it, and a lesson to others."[21] In the same vein, Ayatollah Khomeini, responding to domestic critics of Iran's new penal code, stated: "When a measure of punishment is carried out, it teaches the person concerned a lesson and this is beneficial for the nation . . . . It is a sin to be merciful to someone who should be receiving a certain measure of punishment. In fact, it would be damaging to the person concerned . . . ."[22]

Of all punishments of *hudud* crimes, severance of thieves' hands has become the most frequent method of punishment under Iran's Islamic penal code. The authorities have, in fact, boasted that they have developed a perfect device for the speedy amputation of hands, which is carried out primarily by the Judicial Police inside the prisons. According to Abbas Hashemi Ishaqpour, the head of the Judicial Police, several persons from the Ministry of Health, Coroner's Office, and Tehran and Beheshti Universities Medical Faculty have been consulted to develop a "safe and speedy" method of amputation of arms and hands.[23]

Qisas crimes include murder, manslaughter, battery and mutilation. The Islamic law regards such offenses as acts against the victim and his family and allows for "inflicting on a culprit an injury exactly equal to the injury he inflicted on his victim."[24] The decision to inflict retribution on the culprit rests with the victim and the victim's family in case of murder. Although retribution in kind and vendettas are allowed under the *Qisas* crimes and punishment, it is important to note that both the Quran and the Iranian penal code recommend forgiveness, because the act of forgiving pleases God.[25] On numerous occasions, Ayatollah Khomeini has chastised the clerical authorities for their zealous advocacy in encouraging retribution and vendettas in *qisas* cases.[26]

The practice of *qisas,* more than any other aspect of Islamic criminal law, had its origin in pre-Islamic Arabia, where acts of vengeance and blood feuds pitting one Bedouin tribe against another were accepted practices of conflict resolution. With the advent of Islam, the practice of taking vengeance against the whole tribe was reduced to acts of retribution against the culprit alone and not his family or tribe. Also, the family of the victim was allowed to ask for alternatives, such as blood money, or even forgiveness of the slayer, rather than physical acts of vengeance.[27]

Ta'zir offenses are those for which no specific penalties are mentioned in the Quran or *hadith*. Therefore, the punishment of *ta'zir* is left to the discretion of the Islamic judge, who should take [into account] the public interest and changing requirements of the time to mete out an appropriate punishment.[28] However, the judge's discretionary power is not boundless. In the Islamic penal code, the range of punishment of *ta'zir* crimes has been determined and codified in law, which ranges from admonition, to fines, to seizure of property. Such punishments also include public flogging, which has become a common *ta'zir* punishment in the Islamic Republic of Iran for such offenses as "immoral behavior," "immodest clothing," public drunkenness, and the like.

Diyat punishment is not strictly a separate category of punishment under the Islamic law. It refers to a form of compensation, or blood money, which is to be paid to the victim or his family as reparation for an injury or murder.[29] In other words, *diyat* becomes a form of punishment if a victim or his family (in case of unintentional manslaughter) choose to forego their right of retribution under *qisas* and instead demand blood money from the perpetrator of the crime. The Iranian penal code has extensively codified the nature of *diyat* for various types of crimes and the time element required in payment of *diyat* in each case.

SPECIAL CRIMINAL COURTS

A number of ad hoc "courts" emerged on the scene shortly after the revolution to mete out immediate punishment to the "offenders of the Islamic mores" and "enemies of the Islamic Republic." The *Komiteh* (Committee) Courts and the Revolutionary Courts are prime examples of these special courts.

A. *Komiteh* Courts

Shortly after the victory of the Revolution, some residents of each neighborhood in major cities set up committees to guard the security of their neighborhood in the wake of the virtual collapse of the Shah's police force, and to enforce "fundamentalist moral and religious standards upon the residents in their neighborhood."[30] These committees have performed quasi-independent judicial functions and have interfered with the legally instituted judicial organs.

> They have flogged individuals found drinking in the confinements of their own private homes; have physically punished youths holding the hand of a girlfriend; and have shown no respect for privacy or individual freedom; even playing Western music has occasionally resulted in arrest and punishment . . . . [31]

Although the semi-anarchic nature of the *Komiteh* Courts has been changed and many of them have been amalgamated into the Revolutionary Courts, they occasionally revert to their earlier status as self-appointed guardians of Islamic moral codes.

B. Revolutionary Courts

Islamic Revolutionary Courts were first established in 1979 in the immediate aftermath of the Iranian Revolution as a temporary means to try to speedily punish hundreds of officials of the deposed Pahlavi regime. The authority of the Revolutionary Courts was derived from the Islamic Revolutionary Council, the secretive body that governed the country in the early months of the Revolution.[32] From their limited early jurisdiction, the mandate of the Revolutionary Courts has been vastly expanded and now includes jurisdiction over the following categories of offenses: (1) all crimes against Iran's security, (2) waging war on God and corruption on earth, neither of which has been defined by law, and hence are left to the discretion of the judge in a Revolutionary Court, (3) narcotics smuggling, (4) attempts on the lives of the country's political and religious authorities, (5) plunder of the public treasury, (6) hoarding and profiteering, and (7) acts that are designed to consolidate the remnants of the Pahlavi monarchy and/or help other opponents of the Islamic Republic.[33]

According to Article 4 of the Administrative Regulations Governing the Revolutionary Courts and Public Prosecutor's Office, the sweeping judicial powers of the Revolutionary Courts are exercised by a three member panel. The panel consists of a religious judge (appointed by Khomeini), a civil judge (nominated by the Ministry of Justice and approved by the Court's religious judge), and an individual "trusted by the people" (and approved by the aforementioned religious judge). In practice, however, the Revolutionary Courts have become dominated by the religious judge, and in political cases, the Revolutionary Court "may well consist of a one-person tribunal, namely a religious judge."[34] The overwhelming number of executions carried out since 1979 have been the result of the decisions of the Revolutionary Courts whose decisions are final with no right of appeal.

C. Special Criminal Courts for the Clergy

A new set of criminal courts has been set up since mid-1987 for the purpose of trying persons accused of "counter-revolutionary and anti-clerical crimes."[35] The judicial scope of these criminal courts has been ill-defined by law and remains vague. In fact, in the opinion of many observers, these special courts were established to oust clerics who were not supportive of the Islamic Republic's policies. Irrespective of the motives behind their establishment, these courts have pursued a sustained policy of handing down decisions against several clergymen in the country. The first execution of a clergyman by the order of a criminal clerical court occurred on October 13, 1987 when Ali Shahidi, a junior cleric convicted of narcotics violations, consumption of alcohol, and "spreading corruption," was stoned to death in Tehran.[36]

CONCLUSION

The foregoing discussion of the legal system in the Islamic Republic of Iran raises a number of disturbing issues. [Among them,] the application of many types of penalties imposed for criminal offenses, such as public flogging and stoning, has come into direct conflict with the accepted procedures of public international law and international human rights standards. The Islamic Republic's authorities have tended to dismiss summarily the conflict between the punishments imposed under Iran's penal code and the generally accepted international standards of criminal prosecution and punishment. The Iranian authorities have consistently asserted that divine laws supersede any international man-made standard, and that Islamic law is always supreme over "both customary and conventional international law."[37] Consequently, protestations of and/or inquiries made by such human rights organizations as Amnesty International or the International Commission of Jurists have been disregarded by the Iranian authorities as either irrelevant or as sinister attempts by the secular West to undermine the institutions of the Islamic Republic.[38]

Finally, the jurisdictional competence of the so-called special criminal courts, such as the *Komiteh* and Revolutionary Courts, and their exercise of *de facto* extrajudicial authority, have cast a dark shadow over the fairness of trials in such courts. The largely undefined categories of crimes, such as *mofsed-e fil arz* (corrupt on earth) or *mohareuh ba Khoda* (enmity to God), both of which carry the death penalty, have allowed the judges of the special courts to exert an undue amount of arbitrary power over the criminal procedures and have removed any semblance of impartiality in criminal trials in the Islamic Republic of Iran.

➤ DISCUSSION QUESTIONS

One cannot fully understand the criminal justice system in a society without understanding the culture that influenced its development; and a critical aspect of culture is, of course, religion. How does religion influence criminal justice in Iran? What religious influences are detectable in our criminal justice system? How might one's religion influence one's stance on various issues in criminal justice?

NOTES

1. See Mayer, "Islamic Law", in *Islam* 240–41 (M. Kelley ed. 1984).

2. H. Algar, *Islam and Revolution* 58–59 (1981).

3. R. Khomeini, *Islamic Government* 12–13 (1971).

4. *Id.*

5. *See id.* at 52–55.

6. M. Khadduri, *The Islamic Conception of Justice* 14–20 (1984).

7. *Id.* at 16.

8. A. Sachedina, *Islamic Messianism* 78–79 (1981).

9. M. Khadduri, *supra* note 6, at 225. *See also* J. Cole and N. Keddie, *Shi'ism and Social Protest* 1–29 (1960).

10. *See* H. Algar, *supra* note 2, at 40–49.

11. H. Hamid, *The Complete Text of the Iranian Constitution* 23–24 (1983).

12. *Id.* 23, 87–88.

13. H. Amin, *Commercial Law of Iran* (1986).

14. *Id.* at 32.

15. See Y. Noori, *Islamic Government and Revolution in Iran* 11–74 (1985).

16. J. Schacht, *An Introduction to Islamic Law* 203 (1964).

17. I. Petrashevsky, *Islam in Iran* 135 (H. Evans trans. 1985).

18. *Id.*

19. Mayer, *supra* note 1, at 242.

20. G. Hojati-Ashrafi, *The Complete Collection of the Penal Code and Criminal Regulations* 3M–4M (1986). *See also* I. Petreshevsky, *supra* note 17, at 136–38; Al-Alfi, *Punishment in Islamic Law,* in *The Islamic Criminal Justice System* 227–28 (M. Bassiouni ed. 1982); M. El-Awa, *Punishment in Islamic Law* 23–24 (1982).

21. *Iran Times* August 9,1985, at 1, col 1.

22. *Id.*

23. Kayhan, November 21, 1984, at 4, col. 2; *Iran Times,* December 7, 1984, at 4, col. 2. The first usage of the "amputation machine" occurred in February 1985 when a thief's hands were amputated in Tehran's Qasr prison. See *Iran Times,* February 15, 1985, at 1 col. 2

24. M. El-Awa, *supra* note 20, at 69.

25. See G. Hojati-Ashrafi, *supra* note 20, at 14M–23M; *Iran Times,* October 1, 1982, at 12, col. 1.

26. See *Iran Times,* September 7, 1984, at 5, col. 3.

27. I. Petrashesky, *supra* note 17, at 136; M. El-Awa, *supra* note 20, at 69–77.

28. See *Al-Afi, supra* note 20, at 227–28.

29. *Official Gazette* (Tehran), December 29, 1982, at 2, col. 1.

30. H. Amin, *Middle East Legal Systems* 136 (1985).

31. *Id.* at 136–137.

32. S. Bakhash, *The Reign of the Ayatollahs* 59–63 (1984).

33. *Official Gazette* (Tehran), May 10, 1983, at 11, col. 1.

34. Amnesty International, *Iran: Violations of Human Rights* 29 (1987)

35. *Iran Times,* July 17, 1987, at 4, col. 2.

36. *Kayhan,* October 14, 1987, at 8, col. 2.

37. H. Amin, *supra* note 13, at 30.

38. Amnesty International, *supra* note 34, at 56–69.

Criminal Justice with Chinese Characteristics

■ *LAWYERS COMMITTEE FOR HUMAN RIGHTS*

INTRODUCTORY NOTES

The following article describes parts of the criminal justice system in the People's Republic of China (PRC). The article was written by an organization of human rights activists and employs a rhetorical style reflecting Western democratic ethnocentrism. The system described would be considered by most Americans as harsh, arbitrary, and dictatorial. However, the Chinese people have had similar relationships with their governmental leaders for millennia. Not only do many of them take this arrangement for granted, but many also see it as advantageous. Far more Chinese expect and respect this style of government than most Westerners would like to believe. To perhaps overstate the case: Tyranny is in the eyes of the beholder.

The problem with this kind of relativist thinking ("tyranny is the eyes of the beholder") is that it makes it very difficult (if not impossible) to identify tyranny and abuses of the criminal justice system. Sociologist Max Weber distinguished between "legitimate" and "illegitimate" power. Legitimate power is wielded by a government that is accepted by the people; illegitimate power is not. In other words, if the Chinese people accept their government's right to use the criminal justice system in the manner described below (as their propaganda would have us believe), then it is legitimate; if they do not accept it (as our propaganda would have us believe), then it is illegitimate. It's an important issue, but difficult to resolve, given our limited access to information. Whatever the case in the PRC, the reader is reminded that the criminal justice system is often the principle tool of tyrants and dictatorships.

The following article refers to both political crime and ordinary criminal acts in much the same way as they are used in common parlance—as though they are easily distinguishable. This, however, is not the case. What we would classify as a political crime in another country may not be seen as such in that country. And what people in other countries would consider to be a political crime in the U.S. may be considered an ordinary criminal act by the U.S. government and its people. It is difficult to distinguish between ordinary crime and political crime because ordinary crime is defined by the law, and lawmaking is a political process. Furthermore, many of the social conditions (e.g., poverty and unemployment) that propel people into criminal

SOURCE: The Lawyers Committee for Human Rights, "Criminal Justice with Chinese Characteristics," from Criminal Justice with Chinese Characteristics: China's Criminal Process and Violations of Human Rights (New York: The Lawyers Committee for Human Rights, 1993): 66–89 (abridged). Reprinted with permission.

activity are the products of political processes. Therefore, while many may argue that there are few, if any, political prisoners in the U.S., the radical criminologist may well argue that a great many of the prisoners in the U.S. are political prisoners because they were poor and unemployed before they landed in prison.

The article begins with a discussion of "administrative sanctions" in China that "theoretically are intended for cases whose level of severity does not merit the intervention of the formal criminal process. Those subjected to administrative procedures are in principle treated as 'non-criminals' and do not obtain a criminal record if their case is not transferred to the formal criminal process." This could very well be a description of "diversion" programs in the U.S.. Diversion takes many forms. A typical example, though, might involve an alleged offender agreeing to undergo alcoholism treatment or agreeing to pay restitution in lieu of going to court and facing more severe penalties. While the Chinese administrative sanctions certainly differ from American diversion programs in terms of the severity of "punishment," the conflict theorist may well see both policies as a form of "net-widening." That is, both administrative sanctions in China and many diversion programs in the U.S. allow the state to circumvent the formality of a criminal trial (and of the determination of guilt or innocence) and thereby exercise more control over its citizenry.

ADMINISTRATIVE SANCTIONS

An analysis of the Chinese criminal justice system and violations of internationally recognized human rights is incomplete without a discussion of the frequently used system of administrative sanctions. The public security authorities have at their disposal a wide array of detention, investigation and sanctioning mechanisms not found in the Criminal Procedure Law (CPL). Administrative mechanisms theoretically are intended for cases whose level of severity does not merit the intervention of the formal criminal process. Those subjected to administrative procedures are in principle treated as "non-criminals" and do not obtain a criminal record if their case is not transferred to the formal criminal process.[1] Through administration sanctions, the public security authorities are able to severely punish alleged criminal and political offenders without regard to the formal criminal process. The minimal and often disregarded protections provided under the CPL do not apply under what is effectively a parallel set of procedures under the discretion of the Communist Party and the public security. These include the right to counsel, the right to be presented before a judicial authority and the right to a fair trial. Even cases that reach the formal justice system often only do so after exceedingly lengthy periods of investigation under administrative mechanisms that are impervious to scrutiny.

A system of administrative sanctioning for petty offenses does not necessarily present a human rights problem. However, public security authorities have extensively used administrative sanctions to take actions against suspected offenders so as to avoid the procedural obstacles that are presented even under the grossly inadequate criminal process. Of particular concern has been the widespread use of administrative sanctions to detain political dissidents from previous periods, such as the 1979 "Democracy Wall" movement, and more recently after the Tiananmen crackdown.[2]

Shelter and Investigation

A notorious form of administrative sanction goes under the innocuous-sounding name of "taking in for shelter and investigation" *(shourong shencha)*. Formal regulations governing this system have never been made public, but internal rules are widely reported to limit the security authorities' use of "shelter and investigation" to transients who commit offenses or who refuse to reveal their identities.[3] These rules also limit the period of "shelter and investigation" to one month, extendable to a maximum of three months. Persons so held are typically detained in public security detention centers.[4]

Available evidence indicates that the few limitations on the use of "shelter and investigation" are easily subverted by the authorities. One legal scholar told the Lawyers Committee that the internal regulations on *shourong shencha* do not in fact impose any time limits on detention. The only principle ever considered by the authorities is that the period of detention be "very short," a vague standard easy to abuse.[5]

In actuality, *shoushen,* as this practice is known in Chinese shorthand, and other administrative sanctions like "detention for investigation" *(juliu shencha),* are frequently used to keep criminal and political suspects in preventive detention for months and even years pending a decision by the security authorities on how to proceed with their case. Numerous persons detained in the wake of the Tiananmen crackdown are believed to have been held under "shelter and investigation." For instance, Liu Qing, the long-time pro-democracy activist, was in 1990 charged with "illegal residence" for staying at his mother's home in Beijing. Although he was no transient and his identity was known, he was detained under "shelter and investigation" for about 180 days before being released.[6]

A number of persons apprehended after June 4th were administratively detained in "guest houses" under public security supervision while their cases were being investigated. One rubric used in such cases is "supervised residence" *(jianshi juzhu),* a term from the CPL for suspects whose danger to society does not require detention pending trial.[7] This seems to have occurred in the case of Qian Liyun, a 26-year-old activist, who was arrested on September 1, 1992 with Shen Tong, a student leader who had returned to China from the U.S. in August 1992 to set up an office of the Boston-based Democracy for China Fund. Qian was detained in the Red Flag Hotel in Beijing for one month and then moved to a prison. Qian told *United Press International* that she was released on October 30, 1992 "out on guarantee awaiting trial." She reported that the public security "said I could leave my house, but not leave Beijing."[8]

Professor Yu Haocheng recounted to the Lawyers Committee his experience of being held under "supervised residence." After the Tiananmen crackdown he was picked up by the public security authorities who provided neither a warrant nor any other legal document. He was taken to a location in the Beijing suburbs for "investigation" and held for 18 months. During this time he was only allowed to visit his family twice and his letters to relatives were censored.[9] Shanghai lawyer and journalist Zhang Weiguo was held for three weeks in the summer of 1991 under "supervised residence," after an earlier longer period of administrative detention in a *shourong shencha* detention house.[10]

The grounds for release from administrative detention are as vague as those for apprehension. In some cases, individuals held administratively are eventually simply released and handed a document from the public security authorities indicating that their investigation has been "completed." This was the case with Professor Yu, noted above. Professor Yu, like others whose investigations were terminated after a period of administrative detention, did not get a criminal record, but as a retired official of the Ministry of Public Security, received administrative penalties of a reduction in rank and salary.[11]

In cases where the public security is satisfied that it has met the standards for formal arrest and prosecution, the case may be transferred into the formal criminal process. At this time the rules on criminal detention—as opposed to administrative detention—are set in motion, but *after* the individual has already been detained for a lengthy period.

Administrative detention methods such as *shourong shencha* date back to the 1950s. A 1980 State Council ruling called for *shoushen* to be phased out and for relevant offenses (minor crimes and offenses by transients) to be handled under the administrative sanction of "reeducation through labor," discussed below.[12] However-er, subsequent to that ruling, a number of further internal provisions on *shoushen* have been issued by the public security agencies that clearly provide for its continued use and it has been applied frequently since Tiananmen.[13]

Interestingly, official sources in both the procuracy and the Justice Ministry have criticized the public security agencies' continuing resort to these practices, which are impervious to intervention or supervision by other agencies. An August 1991 article in the procuracy's official journal, while recognizing the utility of *shourong shencha*, proposed as an "urgent" matter that this method be integrated into the formal criminal process with legal standards for its use. Supervision (presumably by the procuracy) over its application was also recommended.[14]

Legal scholars in the PRC have extensively discussed the problems of administrative detention. Some have argued that methods of detention such as *shourong shencha* should be abolished altogether. Others contend that detention for minor infractions is necessary but that the procedures should be incorporated into the CPL to provide checks on its use.[15] Not surprisingly, the public security authorities are resistant to giving up their administrative detention authority. Scholars and lawyers interviewed by the Lawyers Committee in China were very pessimistic about the prospects for reform in this area.[16]

In the meantime, the PRC courts have granted indirect recognition to administrative detention practices by giving defendants credit in their sentences for time served in administrative detention prior to formal arrest. This occurred, for example, in the cases of Bao Tong, Wang Juntao and Chen Ziming. This practice is not inconsistent with the CPL, which provides for criminal sentences to be shortened by one day for each day spent in "custody" prior to the sentence, without making any distinction between administrative and formal criminal detention.[17] While the result is clearly to be welcomed, it reflects the ambiguous boundaries between legal mechanisms and administrative policy in the PRC and the arbitrariness of their application, both of which undermine the protection of due process rights.

Reeducation through Labor

The other major component of the PRC's system of administrative sanctioning is the process of "reeducation through labor" *(laodong jiaoyang* or *laojiao)*. This term is to be distinguished from "reform through labor" *(laodong gaizao)*, a system of punishment applied to individuals sentenced under the formal criminal process. The sanction of *laojiao*, officially introduced in 1957 regulations, grants the public security agencies wide authority to send violators of minor offenses not meriting a trial to "reeducation" camps for indefinite periods.[18] Significantly, these regulations were reissued and supplemented just prior to the publication of the new codes of criminal law and procedure in 1979,[19] as if to assure the security authorities that the new procedural system would not unduly constrain them in dealing flexibly with offenders.

Under the 1979 rules, *laojiao* was subjected to new restraints. These included a three-year limit on a "sentence" of reeducation, extendable by one year; the creation of "reeducation through labor" committees that theoretically add the participation of labor and civil affairs authorities to that of the police in rendering *laojiao* decisions; and provisions granting the procuracy some control over the locations where those administratively detained are sent.[20]

These legislative changes have had no measurable impact on the power of the public security authorities to determine jurisdiction and period of detention under "reeducation through labor." The public security retains unfettered discretion to impose administrative sanctions upon persons who have no recourse to a hearing, the right to counsel or other protections found, if often not enforced, under the criminal process.[21]

To make matters worse, the authorities frequently only impose *laojiao* after a lengthy period of administrative detention pursuant to the *shourong shencha* system. This process is sometimes called *jiaoyang shencha* ("investigation for reeducation"), under which the security authorities detain an individual to consider whether to proceed through *laojiao* or the formal criminal process.[22] If *laojiao* is decided upon, the individual is supposed to receive credit in his or her term of *laojiao* for time previously spent under investigative detention.[23]

The case of Zhang Youshen, 65, a leader of the unofficial Catholic community in Baoding, Hebei province, is illustrative. In March 1991, shortly after the authorities had obtained a copy of an unpublished article he had written criticizing the official Catholic Church organization, he was ordered to the public security bureau. That day his family learned unofficially that he was being held for "shelter and investigation." In April 1991 the public security searched his home for religious books and articles printed by the underground church, which the authorities labeled "illegal printed matter." More than three months later, on July 2, 1991 Zhang was administratively sentenced to three years' "reeducation through labor" and sent to Hengshui labor camp in Hebei.[24]

"Reeducation through labor" in political cases has been frequently documented in the past thirteen years. Hundreds, if not thousands, of persons detained for their involvement in the 1989 pro-democracy protests nationwide were held under "reeducation through labor."[25] Use of the sanction in political cases has a legislative basis in the provision of the "reeducation through labor" regulations that prescribes the sanction for "those counterrevolutionaries and anti-socialist reactionaries who, because their crimes are minor, are not pursued for criminal responsibility. . ."[26] Evidence since Tiananmen has shown that, as in earlier periods, public security authorities use "reeducation through labor" to avoid the formal criminal process where persons are deemed to have engaged in behavior against the state.

One case concerns Xu Guoxing, a leader of the non-official church in Shanghai. He was initially detained by the authorities on March 14, 1989. On June 16, 1989, after extensive interrogation, he was released without charge. The public security again detained Xu on November 18, 1990. On November 18, 1990, he was administratively sentenced to three years' "reeducation through labor." The authorities determined that he had set up illegal churches in Shanghai and in Anhui, Zhejiang and Jiangsu provinces. He also allegedly "broke social order by stirring up trouble and creating conflicts [and] interfering with and damaging the regular order of religious activities." He was sent to the Da Feng labor farm in northern Jiangsu province.[27] According to Asia Watch, Xu's family refused to petition for his release despite being told to do so by prison camp officials. They believe to do so would make it appear that he was repenting for his acts and was willing to give up his religious work.[28]

Individuals who undergo "reeducation through labor" are not supposed to acquire a criminal record. Nonetheless, according to first-hand observers, their treatment is often difficult to distinguish from those subject to the formal criminal sanction of "reform through labor."[29] "Reeducatees" are often held in the same camps as formal criminals (though, unlike convicted persons, they are in principle paid a nominal amount for their work).[30] As in the case of individuals sentenced criminally to "reform through labor," they may be subject to *defacto* extension of their sentences beyond the formal period. This practice may result from the unwillingness of work units of released offenders to rehire them after their term has ended, forcing them to remain at the camp as "free" workers.

The murky practical distinctions between the criminal punishment of "reform through labor" and the administrative ("non-criminal") sanction of *laojiao* emerge not only from empirical accounts but also from the PRC's own legislation. For example, a 1981 government decision[31] prescribes that individuals who, upon completion of a term of "reform through labor," commit "minor criminal acts not qualifying for criminal sanctions" (sic), be "given the sanction of reeducation through labor [and] in general remain at the camp and be employed." This provision unwittingly illustrates the overlap, both in content and physical location, between the "criminal" and "administrative" approaches to the punishment of offenders, despite great differences in the respective procedures.

The 1990 Administrative Litigation Law provides some measure of judicial review over "reeducation through labor" by virtue of its status as an administrative sanction. The Lawyers Committee is aware of several cases in which an individual sentenced by the public security to a term of *laojiao* challenged the decision in the local people's courts on grounds of unfairness, with as yet no favorable results.[32]

Persons seeking to assert such a claim against a "reeducation through labor" decision face a number of severe obstacles. First, the rules on "reeducation through labor" are so broadly drafted as to make it difficult to successfully assert, as a petitioner is required to do under the Administrative Litigation Law, that the rules were being incorrectly applied in his or her case.[33] Second, the Administrative Litigation Law does not allow for suspension of an administrative decision pending a hearing, unless the court determines that failure to suspend the decision will result in "irreparable damage" and would not harm the public interest.[34] It is doubtful that an individual already consigned to a reeducation camp, which are frequently located in remote areas, and unable to communicate with family or friends, would be able to mount an administrative lawsuit against the public security authorities. Moreover, the ineffectiveness of the Administrative Litigation Law in other cases of political importance[35] provides no grounds for optimism in cases of "reeducation through labor," particularly where it is being used for political reasons.

THE DEATH PENALTY

[In addition to the issues discussed above], PRC legal scholars have also been discussing the use of the death penalty, whose application has been expanded significantly over the past decade through various amendments to the Criminal Law dealing with violent and economic crime. Thousands of persons are judicially executed each year in the PRC. Amnesty International recorded 1,891 death sentences and 1,079 executions in China for 1992 but believes these figures greatly understate the actual number of executions that were carried out.[36] Unnamed sources in China cited by Amnesty International placed the actual number of executions per year at around 20,000. The official number of death sentences is considered a "state secret" and is not made public."[37]

Due process violations that routinely occur in criminal cases in China are exacerbated by the speed with which capital cases are often taken through the courts. This occurs both as a result of expedited legal procedures for "public security offenses"[38] and official pressure for handing down death sentences. The latter is reflected in the increase in the number of death sentences imposed during government "anti-crime" campaigns. Following conviction, death sentences are often announced at mass sentencing rallies in which groups of prisoners awaiting execution are paraded before large crowds of people. It is not uncommon for the prisoners to then be taken directly to an execution ground where they are killed with a single bullet to the back of the head.[39]

An undetermined number of workers were sentenced to death and executed for alleged criminal acts committed in connection with the Tiananmen events. Paradoxically, these cases were typically handled much more quickly than the non-capital political cases involving students and intellectuals, virtually eliminating the minimal procedural safeguards existing under PRC law. One such case, which received international condemnation, concerned workers Bian Hanwu, Xu Gnoming and Yan Xuerong, who were arrested for allegedly setting fire to a train that had gone through a crowd of demonstrators in Shanghai on June 6, 1989. The three men were formally charged on June 11. On June 14 the Shanghai Intermediate People's Court, in a single half-day session, convicted them of "sabotage[ing] means of transportation"[40] and sentenced them to death. Because this is a public security offense, the defendants had only three days in which to file an appeal. On June 20, the Shanghai High People's Court rejected the defendants' appeal and upheld the verdict of the lower court."[41] The three men were executed in Shanghai on June 21, 1989 before at least 1,000 people, a mere two weeks after their arrest.[42]

Roughly one-third of all criminal offenses in the PRC can be punished with the death penalty. A majority of scholars interviewed by the Lawyers Committee favor reduction of the number of offenses to which the death penalty may be applied, some by as much as one-quarter or one-third.[43] There is the greatest support for reduction of the penalty's application in cases of economic crime, and less support for its reduced use in cases involving drug trafficking and violent crimes.

CONCLUSION

Some grounds for optimism may be derived from the fact that members of China's legal community now have greater leeway than ever before to analyze and criticize their system and propose reforms. Through legal publications, conferences and exchanges, these discussions have been able to take place within the PRC legal community and in the company of foreign colleagues. Comparative analysis of the PRC and foreign criminal justice systems is taking place both in China and by Chinese lawyers, judges and scholars studying abroad.

Significant change for the better depends on factors that lie beyond the control of the legal community. Now one can only hope that the current relatively open atmosphere for study, discussion and debate of these crucial issues will continue. The development of legal knowledge and ideas will be crucial to instituting extensive and fundamental reforms in China's legal system when political circumstances make such reforms possible. These reforms are necessary if respect for fundamental human rights in China is ever to be anything but a distant dream.

► DISCUSSION QUESTION

In the introduction to this article, a comparison was made between "administrative sanctions" in China and "diversion programs" in the United States. In what ways is this a fair comparison, and in what ways is it unfair?

NOTES

1. *See*, e.g., Criminal Law, art. 32; Decision of the State Council of the PRC Regarding Problems of Reeducation Through Labor, Aug. 1, 1957 [hereinafter 1957 Decision], art. 1.

2. For an excellent overview of the use of administrative detention, see generally Amnesty International, *China—Punishment Without Crime: Administrative Detention* (London: 1991) [hereinafter *Punishment Without Crime.*]

3. Lawyers Committee interview with Fu Kuanzhi, Beijing, August 6, 1992 [hereinafter Fu Interview.].

4. *See*, e.g., *Zhongguo Fazhi Bao*, Aug. 30, 1986, cited in Amnesty International, *Punishment Without Crime, supra* note 2, at 10.

5. Fu Interview, *supra* note 3.

6. Asia Watch, "Liu Qing: China's 'White Paper' and Guarantees of Human Rights in the Judicial System," Aug. 10, 1992, at 2.

7. CPL, art. 38. See Notice of the State Council Regarding the Merging of the Two Methods of Forced Labor and Taking in for Shelter and Investigation with Reeducation through Labor, Feb. 29, 1980 [hereinafter 1980 Notice], art. 2.

8. See "China Releases Another Student Activist," *United Press International*, Oct. 30, 1992. Qian Liyun is currently living in the United States.

9. Lawyers Committee interview with Prof. Yu Haocheng, Beijing, Aug. 4, 1992 [hereinafter Yu interview].

10. Lawyers Committee interview with Zhang Weiguo, Shanghai, Aug. 1, 1992 [hereinafter Zhang interview].

11. Yu interview, *supra* note 9.

12. 1980 Notice, *supra* note 7, arts. 2–3.

13. See Chen & Zhang, *supra* note 3. According to an official source, the total number of cases of *shourong shencha* was 1,500,000 in 1988. See Mu Yi, *"Shourong Shencha Jixu Zhengdun"* [Urgent Need to Rectify the Work of Sheltering for Investigation], *Remnin Gongan* [People's Public Security], No. 7, 1989, at 18. The Minister of Public Security, in a 1991 speech before the Meeting on Legalization of Public Security Work, said that there were 930,000 cases of *shourong shencha* in 1989, and 902,000 in 1990. Internal PRC document quoted to the Lawyers Committee. A Chinese lawyer attributed the drop in total number of cases largely to widespread criticism of the practice in the media.

14. Miao Yanbo, "Principal Problems Existing in the Implementation of the Criminal Procedure Law and Their improvement," *Zhongguo Jiancha Bao*, Aug. 15, 1991, at 3. A discussion of the need to regularize the system of *shourong shencha* also appeared in the Legal Daily, the official organ of the Ministry of Justice. "Several Problems Regarding Forceful Criminal Measures," *Fazhi Ribao*, Jan. 30, 1992, at 3.

15. Lawyers Committee interview with Fu Kuanzhi, Beijing, Aug. 6, 1992; interview with Li Jinjin, Aug. 3, 1992; and interview with Yu Haocheng Aug. 4, 1992.

16. Yu Interview, *supra* note 3; Lawyers Committee interview with Li Jinjin [hereinafter Li Jinjin]; and Gelatt discussions with various scholars in China, Mar. 1992.

17. CPL art. 42.

18. 1957 Decision, *supra* note 1.

19. Supplementary Provisions of the State Council on Reeducation Through Labor, Nov. 29, 1979.

20. *Id.* arts. 1,3 & 5.

21. See Amnesty International, *Punishment Without Crime, supra* note 2, at 28–30, 48–50.

22. Li Jinjin interview, *supra* note 16.

23. See Notice of the Ministry of Public Security Regarding the Crediting Against Time of "Reeducation through Labor" of Time Spent by Reeducatees Who Have Been Held for Shelter and Investigation by the Public Security Agencies, Gongfa (1979) No. 90, June 23, 1979, in *Compendium of Judicial and Administrative Historical Documents of the People's Republic of China* (1950–1985) (Beijing: 1987) at 326.

24. *See* Asia Watch, "Freedom of Religion in China," Jan. 20, 1992, at 22.

25. See Amnesty International, *Punishment Without Crime, supra* note 2, at 38–48.

26. 1957 Decision, *supra* note 1, art. 1(2) ; Ministry of Public Security, Trial Methods for "Reeducation Through Labor," Jan. 21, 1982, art. 10(1), in *Zhonghua Remnin Gongheguo Falu Quanshu* [Collection of Laws of the People's Republic of China] (Beijing: 1989) at 1583.

27. *See* Amnesty International, Urgent Action, ASA 17/34/91.

28. Private communication from Asia Watch.

29. *See,* e.g. Hongda Harry Wu, Laogai: *The Chinese Gulag* (Westview Press, Boulder: 1992) at 81–104.

30. 1957 Decision, *supra* note 1, art.2.

31. Decision of the Standing Committee of the National People's Congress Regarding the Handling of Offenders Undergoing Reform Through Labor and Persons Undergoing Reeducation Through Labor Who Escape or Commit New Crimes, adopted June 10, 1981; trans. in the *Criminal Law and the Criminal Procedure Law of China, supra* (Foreign Languages Press, Beijing, 1984) p. 220.

32. Gelatt discussions with Zhang Weiguo and U.S. consular official in Shanghai, Mar. 1992 and Mar. 1993.

33. Administrative Litigation Law of the People's Republic of China, adopted Apr. 4, 1989, effective Oct. 1, 1990 [hereinafter Administrative Litigation Law], arts. 53 & 54.

34. *Id.* art 44(2).

35. *See* e.g., the case of Prof. Guo Luoji, discussed in Pitman Potter, "Administrative Litigation and Political Rights in China," *Human Rights Tribune* (Summer 1992) at 4.

36. "The judicial massacre continues,"*Amnesty International Newsletter,* Mar. 1993.

37. "More than a thousand executions in 1991," *Amnesty International Newsletter,* Mar. 1992.

38. See Part 11, Section 9, for discussion of 1983 Decision of the Standing Committee of the National People's Congress Regarding the Procedure for Rapid Adjudication of Cases Involving Criminal Elements Who Severely Endanger Public Security, Sept. 2, 1993, trans. in *The Criminal Law and the Criminal Procedure Law of China* (Foreign Languages Press, Beijing: 1984) p. 246.

39. See generally Amnesty International, "The Death Penalty in the People's Republic of China in 1990, " ASA 17/17/9 1, Feb. 1991.

40. Criminal Law, art. 110.

41. *See Shanghai City Service,* June 20, 1989, as reported in FBIS, June 21, 1989, at 47; *see also,* Part II, Section 9 [of the original report of the Lawyers Committee] for a discussion of the streamlined death penalty review procedures that were applied in this case.

42. *See Agence France Presse,* June 21, 1989 & Kyodo, June 21, 1989; as reported in FBIS, June 21, 1989, at 48.

43. Lawyers Committee interview with Prof. Zhao Bingzhi, People's University of China, Beijing, Aug. 7, 1992. Lawyers Commitee interview with Gu. See Yang and Chen, "Sixing Cunfei yu Renquan Baohull [The Maintenance or Abolishment of the Death Penalty and Protection of Human Rights], 6 *Zhangwai Faxue* (1991) at 57.

Globocop?
Time to Watch the Watchers

THE U.N. AND WAR CRIME

■ *C. DOUGLAS LUMMIS*

INTRODUCTORY NOTES

Criminologists and jurisprudents distinguish between two types of definitions of crime: *mala in se* and *mala prohibita. Mala in se* (wrong in itself) holds that a crime is a crime because it is wrong. Proponents of this definition usually adhere to some concept of "natural law," or "universal law," or "God-given law." *Mala prohibita* (wrong because it is prohibited) holds that a crime is a crime only because it is illegal. The debate generated by the two definitions is an important one that poses a number of ethical, religious, and philosophical questions.

One "God-given law" that is very pronounced in the Judeo-Christian tradition is "Thou shalt not kill." And, yet, many who believe killing to be wrong in itself also believe in such a thing as a "just war" and in capital punishment. They obviously believe that there are exceptions to the injunction of the Fifth Commandment. Critics of the *mala in se* definition ask who is to decide what these exceptions are? Who is to decide which crimes are wrong in themselves, *mala in se?*

On the other hand, millions of people were killed in the concentration camps of the Nazi regime. Many of these people had been stripped of their citizenship and, therefore, had no legal rights. To kill them was not illegal and, therefore, according to the *mala prohibita* definition, not a crime. Critics of the *mala prohibita* definition argue that it ignores that there are human rights that transcend civil rights. Proponents of *mala prohibita* respond, "Who is to decide what these human rights are?"

The use of the term "war crime" usually reflects adherence to the *mala in se* definition of crime because the behavior (later to be termed "criminal") was likely not considered illegal by the regime under which it occurred. The following article reflects the fears a *mala prohibita* proponent would have with allowing someone to decide which behaviors are war crimes—that is which behaviors during war are *mala in se.*

All laws are political by nature. They are the result of a political process, and they represent the interests of some at the expense of others (the prospective criminal). To the extent that we take the laws for granted in our own country, we fail to recognize their political content. However, as you read the following article, take note of the political process and the interests at stake.

SOURCE: C. Douglas Lummis, "Globocop? Time to Watch the Watchers," *The Nation*, vol. 259, no. 9, (September 26, 1994): 302–6 (abridged). Reprinted with permission from *The Nation* magazine. (c) The Nation Company, L.P.

Did you know the United Nations now has a jail? Almost everyone I have asked this question, including newspaper reporters and experts on the U.N., has responded with a startled "No!" When I explain that in connection with the new International Criminal Tribunal for the Former Yugoslavia (I.C.T.F.Y.) the U.N. now has twenty-four cells near The Hague, they say, "Oh, that. Now that you mention it . . ." They knew, but hadn't noticed that they knew. It has been in the papers, usually in the last paragraph of an article about the atrocities being committed in and around Bosnia and Herzegovina. You read about horrors that bring the blood pounding to your ears, and when at the very end it says that the monsters responsible are going to be brought into a court of law, you feel nothing but relief: Human order is to be restored.

"You've got to do something," says my human rights activist friend in Geneva. Yes, and it's easy, when presented with an Actually Existing State of Nature, for the "something" to slide over into "anything." It's hard to care much whether the angel of retribution is Justice or Dirty Harry.

But it is precisely this "something/anything" mood that can lead us into one of the classic political blunders. One of the most succinct and persuasive renderings of the argument for defeating political chaos by establishing "a supreme power which may govern us by wise laws, protect us and defend all members of the association . . . and maintain eternal harmony among us" is followed by the bitter conclusion, "All ran headlong into their chains." This was Rousseau in his "Discourse on the Origin of Inequality"; in his telling, what had been presented as a neutral umpire was in fact a conspiracy of the powerful, "which bound new fetters on the poor, and gave new powers to the rich."

It is appropriate to cite Rousseau here, considering the scale of what is being proposed. If the U.N. takes on the powers to arrest, prosecute, sentence and imprison individuals, it is taking on sovereign powers hitherto reserved to states. Add to this Secretary General Boutros Boutros-Ghali's proposal that the U.N. have its own permanent military arm, and you have the conditions for a full-fledged world state. What we are seeing, in short, is the founding, albeit gradual and half-hidden, of a political entity unprecedented in history. We need to drag our attention for a moment away from the loathsome acts being committed in the former Yugoslavia and take a careful look at the nature of this putative engine of justice, before we rush headlong into it.

Where does the U.N. get the power to prosecute individuals? The I.C.T.F.Y. (are we supposed to pronounce this "icktify"?) was established by Security Council resolutions, but that answers nothing. Where does the Security Council get such power? The legal fiction is that the power comes from Chapter VII of the U.N. Charter. Chapter VII authorizes the U.N. to deploy the armed forces of member states in peacekeeping operations. Stretch the words as you will, you cannot make them say that the U.N. has the power to put people in jail under criminal charges. On the contrary, the Charter, written by representatives of states jealous of their power, falls all over itself to insist that the U.N. may never usurp the sovereign rights of states.

What about the precedent of the Nuremberg and Tokyo trials? There individuals were tried and punished under the authority of "The United Nations." Many experts value these trials as precedents in international law. I have trouble grasping their thinking, as exemplified in a conversation I participated in the other day with some experts in the field:

"The Nuremberg trials were legally flawed. They convicted people under *ex post facto* laws. But there won't be that trouble this time."

"Why not?"

"This time there is a precedent."

"What's that?"

"The Nuremberg trials."

However one thinks of this problem, there is another. The Nuremberg and Tokyo trials were *military* tribunals, carried out by conquering powers in territories under their direct rule. For better or for worse, their authority came from the right of conquest. That's why the tribunals could and did make up law as they went along. (For all their flaws, the tribunals were anyway more law-abiding than Churchill's initial proposal, which was to line up the enemy leaders against a wall and shoot them.) But what is being proposed this time is to give the U.N. power to prosecute individuals from states that still retain their sovereign independence. The legal and practical problems this presents are enormous.

Another possible precedent, often cited in I.C.T.F.Y. documents, is the Genocide Convention, which declares genocide a crime punishable under international law. But detailed comparison between the Genocide Convention and the statute that establishes I.C.T.F.Y. is instructive.

The Genocide Convention is an international treaty, approved by the General Assembly and ratified by the governments of U.N. member states according to their constitutional mechanisms. With all its care for procedure—perhaps because of it—the Genocide Convention did not endow the U.N. with radical new powers. In particular, it does not provide for an international criminal tribunal. This is not an oversight; the idea was proposed, discussed and rejected. Instead, the convention stipulates that the ratifying states make their own laws against genocide, which they themselves should enforce. And, in fact, as Istvan Deak has pointed out, far more war criminals have been punished in this fashion—that is, by states—than by international tribunals.

Although the Genocide Convention was ratified in two years by twenty countries, ratification by the U.S. Senate took four decades. The history of Senate resistance offers a fascinating glimpse into the development of U.S. guilt feelings in the post-war period. In the 1950 hearings, an American Bar Association representative testified that the convention's definition of genocide might apply to racist lynchings, or to a move "to drive five Chinamen out of town." Twenty years later another A.B.A. representative testified that the inclusion of "mental harm" might enable black Americans to make a case that segregation laws had been genocidal. At the same hearing, Senator Sam Ervin, Jr. worried that the convention "would make American soldiers fighting under the flag of their country in foreign lands triable and punishable in foreign courts—even in courts of our warring enemy." This was no empty fear. North Vietnam had been threatening to do just that.

In 1986 the concern had shifted to possible prosecution of Americans by an international criminal tribunal. Senator Orrin Hatch, speaking apropos U.S. actions toward Nicaragua, warned that such international authority "would be disastrous." Now, the convention establishes no such tribunal, but it does mention vaguely that one might be set up in the future. So when the Senate finally did ratify the convention, in 1986, it attached a set of conditions designed to make it virtually impossible for any U.S. citizen ever to be prosecuted under the convention. Among those:

The United States declares that it reserves the right to effect its participation in any such [international penal] tribunal only by a treaty entered into specifically for that purpose with the advice and consent of the Senate.

There has not been the same resistance in the U.S. Senate to the I.C.T.F.Y. proposal. This despite the fact that the statute establishing I.C.T.F.Y.—Security Council Resolution 827 (1993)—grants the U.N. powers that the U.N. Charter and the Genocide Convention pointedly refuse to give it; and that it has not been subject to ratification by member states. This brings us back to the original question: Where does the Security Council get the power to pass such a resolution? The answer was given by Boutros-Ghali himself. In his opening statement to the World Conference on Human Rights in 1993 he said, referring to I.C.T.F.Y.:

In asking the Secretary-General to consider this project, the Security Council has given itself an entirely new mandate.

Actually, the United Nations began "giving itself" these powers even before the I.C.T.F.Y. resolutions were passed. In its issue of January 21, 1993, the *Far Eastern Economic Review* reported that the U.N. Transitional Authority in Cambodia had begun "to arm itself with new powers," announcing that it "would form a special prosecutor's office and court system designed to indict, prosecute, sentence and imprison those deemed responsible for political crimes." Then that June the Security Council called for the arrest, prosecution and trial of whoever killed U.N. peacekeepers in Somalia.

All this took place in the absence of any international criminal law authorizing such arrests. But that primitive stage is in the past: Now such criminal law is being written. By what legislative assembly, you ask? No, not by the General Assembly, or even by the Security Council. The tribunal itself is making the law and—my informant in Geneva assures me—the document will not have to be submitted to any other U.N. organ for approval. They write it, and it's law. Just like that. So much for "consent of the governed."

Of course, the United Nations has never pretended to be a representative democratic organization. This made good enough sense when the U.N. also did not pretend to have the legislative, executive and judicial powers of a sovereign state. But now that the U.N. has begun generating criminal law, it is fair to ask, whatever happened to that cherished tenet of political philosophy that people can be obligated to obey only those laws to which they have consented?

Boutros-Ghali's speech sketches a theory of power that has no need of consent, a theory that is, to my knowledge, new. It is grounded in "human rights."

"Human rights," he says, are "absolute timeless injunctions" and are "truly universal." At the same time, "human rights . . . reflect a power relationship." Although it may be difficult for a dedicated human rights activist to see the problem here, whenever people in high places start weaving together notions of power with notions of "absolute injunctions," watch out. Boutros-Ghali makes quite clear what conclusion he is driving at:

I am tempted to say that human rights, by their very nature, do away with the distinction traditionally drawn between the internal order and the international order. Human rights give rise to a new legal permeability. They should thus not be considered either from the viewpoint of absolute sovereignty or from the viewpoint of political intervention.

This last vagary does not mean that there should be no interventions into sovereign states; on the contrary, it means that we should rid ourselves of the taboo against intervention: "The international community must *take over* from the States that fail to fulfill their obligations." (Emphasis added.) For Boutros-Ghali, "human rights" serve the same function that "divine right" did in the seventeenth century: As absolute injunctions, they generate an authority higher than any other. In the light of this theory, the procedures establishing I.C.T.F.Y. make perfect sense. Consent would only muddle the process.

Despite its undemocratic character, the notion has its attraction. In fact, good-hearted human rights activists are attracted to it. Sure, they argue, formal procedures matter, in ordinary cases. But here we have real devils roaming the earth carrying AK-47s, bringing hell to the lives of the people. You've got to do something. Do you have a better idea?

But the call for a "better idea" presupposes that this is a "good idea"—i.e., that setting up a criminal tribunal counts as "doing something" about the situation in the former Yugoslavia. This is by no means obvious. First of all, I.C.T.F.Y. has neither material means nor legal authority to arrest and indict the big criminals—the political and military leaders. To imprison presidents, Cabinet members, generals, etc., would require a full-fledged, successful invasion, and that does not seem to be on the agenda. The war crimes trials will begin this fall by indicting soldiers and militia members who committed atrocities and then escaped to other countries, where they happened to be identified and arrested. In other words, the powerless small fry.

What effect will these trials have on the situation in the former Yugoslavia? It is argued that they will be good for the victims, giving them the satisfaction of just retribution, and giving the world a moral lesson. This is a strong argument. But if the trials end up prosecuting only the privates and corporals, leaving the military and political commanders free, the long-run effect will be to teach cynicism.

Possibly the trials will deter further atrocities. Certainly they will deter people who committed them from leaving their countries. Just as certainly they will motivate the guilty to support their governments—their chief protection from trial—to the end. Also the trials are likely to obstruct an end to the war. It is common sense that in negotiating a truce, you promise amnesty to the soldiers on both sides. Without that, who will agree to put aside their weapons?

But it may be that the people behind I.C.T.F.Y. are less interested in "doing something" about the situation in the former Yugoslavia than in setting a precedent for a permanent international criminal tribunal. I know that some of the people who are supporting this latter proposal are acting with the best of intentions. But what can we make of the proposal itself? Would such a court be a genuinely impartial umpire? Or would it be yet another instrument to bind new fetters on the poor, and give new powers to the rich?

It is a scandal in contemporary international law, don't forget, that while "wanton destruction of towns, cities and villages" is a war crime of long standing, the bombing of cities from airplanes goes not only unpunished but virtually unaccused. Air bombardment is state terrorism, the terrorism of the rich. It has burned up and blasted apart more innocents in the past six decades than have all the antistate terrorists who ever lived. Something has benumbed our consciousness against this reality. In the United States we would not consider for the presidency a man who had once thrown a bomb into a crowded restaurant, but we are happy to elect a man who once dropped bombs from airplanes that destroyed not only restaurants but the buildings that contained them and the neighborhoods that surrounded them. I went to Iraq after the Gulf War and saw for myself what the bombs did; "wanton destruction" is just the term for it.

. . . I.C.T.F.Y. is not going to develop into a weapon that could someday be used against the United States. One I.C.T.F.Y. supporter told me, "Of course, we know that's a problem. But you've got to set a precedent where you can set a precedent. You begin with what's possible, and then once you've got the legal precedent you can go after the others." Sure. First, you get the big fish to eat the bad among the little fish; then, when you have the precedent established, you go after the bad among the big fish. When I expressed my doubts that this would work, he accused *me* of not understanding *Realpolitik*.

But most of the people supporting I.C.T.F.Y. are not even thinking about going after the big fish. Either by cynical design or by benumbed acculturation to great-power violence, they have no image of a possible defendant other than the middling or the small. Kai Bird let the cat out of the bag when he proposed that countries whose governments commit mass murders should be subjected to a U.S. naval blockade [see "The Case for a U.N. Army," *The Nation*, August 8/15]. Now, how is the United States going to blockade itself? Obviously, the thought, perfectly clear to Sam Ervin in the 1970s, that any U.S. government or military personnel might be brought to trial before an international criminal tribunal never entered his head.

Precisely in this one-sidedness, the movement to establish I.C.T.F.Y. (and perhaps a permanent tribunal) is the true heir to the Nuremberg and Tokyo trials. Robert Jackson, who resigned from the Supreme Court to become the American prosecutor at Nuremberg, was one of the major legal brains behind the proceedings. Of course he was aware that the Nuremberg trials stood on dubious legal foundations; his solution to that problem, given in a report to President Roosevelt, is revealing:

> We can save ourselves from those pitfalls if our test of what legally is crime gives recognition to those things which fundamentally outraged the conscience of the American people and brought them finally to the conviction that their own liberty and civilization could not persist in the same world with the Nazi power . . . . I believe that those instincts of our people were right and that they should guide us as the fundamental tests of criminality.

As it happened, carpet-bombing, firebombing and atomic holocausts perpetrated on residential areas did not outrage the conscience of the American people at that time, so they were not crimes by definition. Similarly, I.C.T.F.Y. is also an institutionalization of selective outrage. More specifically, it seems that what we are witnessing here is a movement not to delegitimize war crimes but to delegitimize one kind of war crimes (poor people's war crimes) and to relegitimize another (rich countries' war crimes). To take Bird's article again, in it he suggests that the U.N. ought to establish "a permanent international strike force—an international posse—authorized to arrest any individual indicted by the international court." We have an example of this in Somalia. The international posse trying to "arrest" General Aidid fired into crowds of civilians, attacked villages with helicopter gunships and all the rest—in short, committed war crimes. Any future "arrest" attempts will require roughly the same methods. But these crimes we are supposed to wink at, as we are supposed to wink at the crimes of Dirty Harry, since they are carried out in the name of justice and "human rights."

What is being founded here is not, after all, a new world superstate but a front for New World Order politics—in other words, G7 rule. We can be confident that only the borders of middling and small countries will show a "new legal permeability." These are the same countries whose borders were always "permeable" throughout the age of colonialism and European continental imperialism: the countries of the Third World and Eastern Europe. However much good might be achieved by, say, Norwegian or Nigerian peacekeepers protecting human rights in Los Angeles or Detroit, it's not something we are likely soon to see.

There is nothing in this that should denigrate the value of human rights watching *per se*. As inspiration for a grass-roots movement, human rights is a vital and precious weapon against the state, the corporation and other organized power. When it raises armies and jailers, however, the time has come to start watching the watchers.

➤ DISCUSSION QUESTIONS

As mentioned in the introductory notes to this article, critics of a *mala in se* definition of crime are concerned with the question of who is going to define which acts are wrong in and of themselves. Why is the author of this article so concerned with this question? Do you think his argument is strong enough to invalidate the U.N.'s prosecution of "war crimes"?

R$_x$ Drugs

■ 60 MINUTES *TRANSCRIPT*

INTRODUCTORY NOTES

An argument that has not been very seriously considered by much of the American public is that illegal drugs should be made legal. It sounds like a radical idea, but more and more intellectuals—both liberal and conservatives—are taking such a stance. They argue that the legalization of drugs will reduce the price of drugs and will, therefore, reduce the property crime that is committed in order to afford the product. It will also take the incentive out of selling drugs and, therefore, reduce the violent crimes committed in the protection of drug territories and reduce the income of organized crime. Furthermore, legalization will reduce the number of drug offenders in the prisons and allow more space for violent offenders. It will allow money currently being spent on law enforcement to be spent on drug rehabilitation. Besides, proponents argue, the war on drugs is not effectively reducing drug consumption.

Opponents argue that present laws do act as a deterrent, and they are concerned that if drugs are made legal, the number of addicts in the U.S. will skyrocket. The experience of other countries that have experimented with decriminalization does not show this to be true. As for the American experience with Prohibition, there was a slight increase in alcohol consumption when Prohibition was repealed; and, while organized crime syndicates did find other legal and illegal outlets, there is little doubt that repeal took a sizable bite out of their profits, and the notorious gangland shootings became a thing of the past.

This next selection is a transcript of a broadcast from the popular television news "magazine" *60 Minutes*. This broadcast addresses a number of issues that should be considered in the legalization debate —namely, that many addicts may be able to stabilize their lives if they are not forced to seek illegal means of obtaining their drug of choice, and that legalization may reduce the incidence of AIDS.

Furthermore, this article describes a prime example of what has come to be known as the "medicalization of deviance." The medicalization of deviance refers to the phenomenon whereby deviance is conceived of as a medical problem, emanating from a physiological disorder, rather than having an environmental source or being the result of free will. (For example, when little Johnny's hyperactivity is seen as the result of a physiological disorder, Johnny's free will and/or his interactions with his family are being diminished as possible explanations for his behavior.) Critics of the medicalization of deviance argue that it represents a rather insidious form of social control in that it is not easily recognized as such and, hence, the public is likely to accept more and more social control in the form of medical treatment.

ED BRADLEY: Can Britain teach us anything about dealing with drug addicts? That remains to be seen, but one thing seems certain, there's little or nothing we can teach them. They tried our hard-line methods back in the '70s and '80s and all they got for their trouble was more drugs, more crime and more addicts. So they went back to their way, letting doctors prescribe whatever drug a particular addict was hooked on. Does it work? If they're ever going to know, Liverpool, where drugs are out of control, is the place to find out.

This is a gram of 100 percent pure heroin. It's pharmaceutically prepared. On the streets, it would be cut 10 to 15 times and sell for about $2,000. But take it away from the black market, make it legal and heroin's a pretty cheap drug. The British National Health Service pays about $10 for this gram of heroin and for an addict with a prescription, it's free.

(Footage of Dr. John Marks sitting at his desk)

BRADLEY: *(Voiceover)* In Britain, doctors who hold a special license from the government are allowed to prescribe hard drugs to addicts. Dr. John Marks, a psychiatrist who runs an addiction clinic just outside Liverpool, has been prescribing heroin for years.

Dr. JOHN MARKS *(Runs Addiction Clinic in Liverpool):* If they're drug takers determined to continue their drug use, treating them is an expensive waste of time. And really the choice that I'm being offered and society is being offered is drugs from the clinic or drugs from the Mafia.

(Footage of a woman dispensing a drug and a patient talking to Dr. Marks, a nurse and a social worker)

BRADLEY: *(Voiceover)* To get drugs from the clinic rather than from the Mafia, addicts have to take a urine test to prove they're taking the drugs they say they are. And unlike most other addiction clinics, where you have to say you want to kick the habit before they'll take you in, addicts here have to convince Dr. Marks, a nurse, and a social worker that they intend to stay on drugs come what may. But doesn't Dr. Marks try to cure people?

Dr. MARKS: Cure people? No. Nobody can. Regardless of whether you stick them in prison, put them in mental hospitals and give them electric shocks—we've done all these things—put them in a nice rehab center away in the country; give them a social worker; pat them on the head. Give them drugs; give them no drugs. Doesn't matter what you do. Five percent per annum, one in 20 per year, get off spontaneously. Compound interested up, that reaches about 50 percent. Fifty-fifty after 10 years are off. They seem to mature out of addiction regardless of any intervention in the interim. But you can keep them alive and healthy and legal during that 10 years if you so wish to.

BRADLEY: By giving them drugs?

Dr. MARKS: It doesn't get them off drugs. It doesn't prolong their addiction either. But it stops them offending; it keeps them healthy and it keeps them alive.

(Footage of Julia pushing her daughter on a swing)

BRADLEY: *(Voiceover)* That's exactly what happened to Julia. Although she doesn't look it, Julia is a heroin addict. For the last three years, the heroin she injects every day comes through a prescription. Before she had to feed her habit by working as a prostitute, a vicious circle that led her to use more heroin to cope with that life.

JULIA *(Heroin Addict):* And once you get in that circle, you can't get out. And I didn't think I was ever going to get out.

BRADLEY: But once you got the prescription . . .

JULIA: I stopped straight away.

BRADLEY: Never went back?

JULIA: No, I've never. I went back once just to see, and I was almost physically sick just to see these girls doing what I used to do.

  (Footage of Julia talking to her daughter)

BRADLEY: *(Voiceover)* Julia says she's now able to have normal relationships, to hold down a job as a waitress and to care for her three-year-old daughter.
  Wi—without that prescription, where do you think you'd be today?

JULIA: I'd probably be dead by now.

Dr. MARKS: OK.

Unidentified Man: OK.

Dr. MARKS: One sixty then . . .

Man: If I can, yes.

Dr. MARKS: . . . of heroin.

  (Footage of a man sitting in Dr. Marks's office)

BRADLEY: *(Voiceover)* Once they've got their prescriptions, addicts must show up for regular meetings to show they're staying healthy and free from crime. But how can anyone be healthy if they're taking a drug like heroin?

Mr. ALLAN PARRY *(Former Drug Information Officer):* Pure heroin is not dangerous. We have people on massive doses of heroin.

  (Footage of Parry talking to Bradley)

BRADLEY: *(Voiceover)* Allan Parry is a former drug information officer for the local health authority and now a counselor at the clinic. So how come we see so much damage caused by heroin?

Mr. PARRY: The heroin that is causing that damage is not causing damage because of the heroin in it. It's causing the br—the damage because of brick dust in it, coffee, crushed bleach crystals, anything. That causes the harm. And if heroin is 90 percent adulterated, that means only 10 percent is heroin; the rest is rubbish. Now you inject cement into your veins, and you don't have to be a medical expert to work out that's going to cause harm.
  OK, George, let's put your leg up. Let's have a look.

  (Footage of George having his leg looked at)

BRADLEY: *(Voiceover)* Many at the clinic, like George, still suffer from the damage caused by street drugs. Allan Parry believes you can't prescribe clean drugs and needles to addicts without teaching them how to use them.

(Footage of George in the office)

Mr. PARRY: *(Voiceover)* The other major cause of ill health to drug injectors is not even the dirty drugs they take; it's their bad technique, not knowing how to do it.

I've seen drug users in the States with missing legs and arms, and that is through bad technique.

Can I have a look at your arms. Have you been . . .

(Footage of George in the office)

BRADLEY: *(Voiceover)* George's legs have ulcerated and the veins in his arms have collapsed. To inject, he must use a vein in his groin which is dangerously close to an artery.

Mr. PARRY: Now when you go in there, you getting any sharp pains?

GEORGE *(Addict)*: No.

Mr. PARRY: If you hit the artery, how—how would you recognize it?

GEORGE: If I hit the artery?

Mr. PARRY: Yeah.

GEORGE: By me head hitting the ceiling.

MR. PARRY: So we show people how to—not how to inject safely, but how to inject less dangerously. We have to be clear about that. You know, stoned people sticking needles into themselves is a dangerous activity, but the—the strategy is called 'harm minimization.'

(Footage of a billboard with the words: Heroin screws you up; police entering a building and a man under arrest)

BRADLEY: *(Voiceover)* In the '70s, the British weren't content with minimizing the harm of drug abuse. They adopted the American policy of trying to stamp it out altogether. Prescription drugs were no longer widely available, and addicts who couldn't kick the habit had to find illegal sources. The result? By the end of the '80s, drug addiction in Britain had tripled. In Liverpool, there was so much heroin around it was known as smack city. And then came a greater threat.

More than anything else, it's been the threat of AIDS that has persuaded the British to return to their old policy of maintaining addicts on their drug of choice. In New York, it's estimated that more than half of those who inject drugs have contracted the AIDS virus through swapping contaminated needles. Here in Liverpool, the comparable number — the number of known addicts infected — is less than 1 percent.

(Footage of a pharmacist Jeremy Clitherow dispensing cigarettes containing heroin)

BRADLEY: *(Voiceover)* In an effort to get addicts away from injecting, Liverpool pharmacist Jeremy Clitherow has developed what he calls 'heroin reefers.' They're regular cigarettes with heroin in them. Whatever you feel about smoking, he says, these cigarettes hold fewer risks than needles for both the addicts and the community.

Mr. JEREMY CLITHEROW: *(Pharmacist)* So we then use this to put in a known volume of pharmaceutical heroin into the patient's cigarette. And there we are, one heroin reefer containing exactly 60 milligrams of pharmaceutical heroin.

BRADLEY: So the National Health Service will pay for the heroin, but not for the cigarettes.

Mr. CLITHEROW: Oh yes. Yes, of course. It's the patient's own cigarette, but with the National Health prescription put into it.

(Footage of the outside of Clitherow's pharmacy and people waiting in line inside the store)

BRADLEY: *(Voiceover)* Addicts pick up their prescriptions twice a week from his neighborhood pharmacy. And how does this affect his other customers?

Mr. CLITHEROW: *(Voiceover)* The patient who comes in to pick up a prescription of heroin in the form of reefers would be indistinguishable from a patient who picks up any other medication.

PAUL *(Heroin Addict):* Good morning.

Mr. CLITHEROW: Hello, Paul. How are you doing?

PAUL: Fine.

Mr. CLITHEROW: All right.

PAUL: Cigarettes next—next week?

Mr. CLITHEROW: That's my sheet. Anything else we can do for you?

PAUL: No, that's fine . . .

Mr. CLITHEROW: The prescription is ready and waiting, and they pick it up just as they would pick up their Paracetamol, aspirin or bandages.

BRADLEY: But with all of these drugs available to—to—to most people, plus the hard drugs which you have here, what's your security like?

Mr. CLITHEROW: Like Fort Knox. But we keep minimal stocks. We buy the stuff in—regularly, frequently. It comes in, goes out.

(Footage of Clitherow filling a prescription)

BRADLEY: *(Voiceover)* And heroin isn't the only stuff to come in and out of here. Clitherow also fills prescriptions for cocaine, and that's 100 percent pure freebase cocaine—in other words, crack.

So in fact when you're putting cocaine in here . . .

Mr. CLITHEROW: Yes.

BRADLEY: . . . you're actually making crack cigarettes?

Mr. CLITHEROW: Yes.

BRADLEY: In America that has a very negative connotation . . .

Mr. CLITHEROW: Mm-hmm.

BRADLEY: . . . but not for you?

Mr. CLITHEROW: It depends which way you look at it. If they continue to buy on the street, whether it's heroin, methadone, crack or whatever, sooner or later they will suffer from the—the merchandise that they are buying. I want to bring them into contact with the system. And let's give them their drug of choice—if the physician agrees and prescribes it—in a form which won't cause their health such awful deterioration.

BRADLEY: And you don't have any problems giving people injectable cocaine or cocaine cigarettes.

Dr. MARKS: No, not in principle. I mean, there are—there are patients to whom I've prescribed cocaine and to whom I've then stopped prescribing the cocaine because their lives do not stabilize. They continue to be thieves or whatever. But there are equally many more to whom we prescribe cocaine who've then settled to regular, sensible lives.

(Footage of Mike)

BRADLEY: *(Voiceover)* Mike is one of those who has settled into a regular, sensible life on cocaine. He has a prescription from Dr. Marks for both the cocaine spray and the cocaine cigarettes. Before he got that prescription, the cocaine he bought on the street cost him $1,000 a week, which at first he managed to take from his own business. But it wasn't long before it cost him much more than that.
So you lost your business.

MIKE: *(Cocaine Addict)* Yeah.

BRADLEY: You lost your—your wife.

MIKE: Yeah.

BRADLEY: You lost the kids.

MIKE: Yeah.

BRADLEY: And the house.

MIKE: Yeah.

BRADLEY: But you kept going after the cocaine.

MIKE: Yeah. That's what addiction is. That's the whole—the very nature of addiction is the fact that one is virtually—chemically and physically—forced to continue that way.

(Footage of Mike sitting in a chair writing)

BRADLEY: *(Voiceover)* Now after two years of controlled use on prescription cocaine, Mike has voluntarily reduced his dose. He's got himself a regular job with a trucking company and is slowly putting his life back together again.

Where do you think you would be now if—if Dr. Marks had not given you a—a prescription for cocaine?

MIKE: I wouldn't be here now talking to you, and you probably wouldn't be interested in talking to me, either. I'd be on the street.

BRADLEY: Dr. Marks, how would you re—reply to critics who would say that you're nothing more than a legalized dealer, a pusher?

Dr. Marks: I'd agree. That's what the state of England arranges, that there's a legal, controlled supply of drugs. The whole concept behind this is control.

(Footage of Bradley talking to Parry while they're walking outside)

BRADLEY: *(Voiceover)* And there are signs that control is working. Within the area of the clinic, Allan Parry says the police have reported a significant drop in drug-related crime. And since addicts don't have to deal anymore to support their habit, they're not recruiting new customers. So far fewer new people are being turned on to drugs.

What do the dealers around the area of the clinic think about it all?

Mr. PARRY: *(Voiceover)* Well, there aren't any around the clinic.

BRADLEY: *(Voiceover)* You—you've taken away their business.

Mr. PARRY: Exactly. There's no business there. The scene is disappearing. So if you want to get rid of your drug problem, which presumably all societies do, there are ways of doing it, but you have to counter your own moral and political prejudice.

BRADLEY: What would you say to people who would ask, 'Why give addicts what they want? Why give them drugs?'

JULIA: So they can live. So they have a chance to live like everyone else does. No one would hesitate to give other sorts of maintaining drugs to diabetics. Diabetics have insulin. In my mind it's no different. It's the same. I need heroin to live.

(Show motif)

(Announcements)

Editor's Postscript: A recent communiqué from the Drug Policy Foundation reports that government funding for Dr. John Marks's addiction treatment clinic will be cut on April 1, 1995. Following television broadcasts such as this one from *60 Minutes*, Dr. Marks stated, "The British embassy in Washington got real heat from the Americans. They asked the English to *harmonize* their practice with the rest of the world." Despite the fact that a two-year investigation by the Chesire Drug Squad, tracking 112 addicts who had been through the program, "found a 96 percent reduction in crimes," political pressure has been brought to bear to terminate government support of the program. Dr. Marks hopes to continue his work with private funding. *(The Drug Policy Newsletter*, no. 25, Winter 1995: p. 21).

➤ **DISCUSSION QUESTION**

Would you be in favor of implementing a program such as the one described in this article in the United States? Consider in your answer potential crime rates, potential addiction rates, and the welfare of addicts.

Alone Among Its Peers: The United States' Refusal to Join the International Movement to Abolish Capital Punishment

■ *LAWRENCE D. WOOD*

INTRODUCTORY NOTES

The last article in this section addresses the issue of capital punishment. While there are certainly a few American criminologists who support the death penalty, it seems that most of them are firmly opposed. And perhaps it is with this issue that criminologists have been most ineffectual in swaying public opinion or public policy. The reason the advice of criminologists is so often disregarded lies in the fact that one's position on the death penalty (as with crime itself) is probably more a matter of values and emotions than of rationality and logic. Values and emotions seldom yield to facts and figures. The fact that most studies show that the death penalty does not deter crime, and that some show it may actually exacerbate crime by providing an example of brutality—these facts seem to be irrelevant in the face of the values and emotions of much of the American public.

The next article addresses that fact that the United States stands alone in the Western industrialized world in its exercise of the death penalty. While the death penalty has been and continues to be associated with repressive regimes, the U.S. is using it more and more. While other nations that are making the transition from military or communist governments to democratic societies often immediately abolish capital punishment, the U.S. legislatures devise more and more crimes to which it should be applied.

The way a society defines crime, and the way it deals with crime, and the kind of crime problem that it faces—all of these tell us very important things about the society itself. Think, for example, about the types of crimes "typifying" Salem, Massachusetts, in the seventeenth century (witchcraft), or Chicago in the

SOURCE: This is a revised version of a paper originally published as "Alone Among Its Peers: The United States' Refusal to Join the International Movement to Abolish Capital Punishment," by Lawrence D. Wood, Occasional Paper Series, no. 4. (Buffalo: Human Rights Center, State University of New York at Buffalo, 1991). This research was made possible by a grant from The Baldy Center for Law and Social Policy of the State University of New York at Buffalo. Reprinted with permission from the author and The Baldy Center.

1920s (bootlegging and gangland violence), or Alabama in the early 1960s (civil disturbance and police violence). Knowledge of these crimes and the way they were handled tells us very much of what we need to know about these societies (our society, historically). Since positions on the death penalty are so heavily reliant on values, our distinctive dependence on this extreme punishment must surely tell us something about our culture.

One of the most striking differences between the United States and other industrial countries is America's enthusiasm for execution.[1]

INTRODUCTION

On March 30, 1990—just four days before Robert Alton Harris was scheduled to become the first person to be executed in California in more than twenty-three years —200 members of Italy's parliament sent Governor George Deukmejian a signed petition in which they urged him to commute Harris's sentence and abolish capital punishment. "The death penalty is against the value of human life in every case," their petition declared. "Leave inactive your state's gas chamber to give the world an example of civility, to affirm the coherence of the choice of democracy [and] to respect the international treaties on human rights."[2]

Italy's petition exemplified the international effort to persuade our country to stop executing criminals. Every other Western industrialized nation has effectively abolished the death penalty for all offenses.[3] These countries, many of whom we consider to be our closest allies, have learned that the death penalty serves no legitimate interests and violates the most fundamental human rights. The purpose of this paper is to critically examine America's failure to learn this same lesson.

It begins by reviewing the recent history of capital punishment in this country. One of the most significant developments occurred in 1972, when the United States Supreme Court effectively abolished the death penalty after finding that it was being administered in an unconstitutionally arbitrary manner. Four years later, however, the same Court—citing the overwhelming popular support for capital punishment— upheld the constitutionality of newly drafted capital sentencing statutes. Unfortunately, the Court continues to place too much emphasis on public opinion. Last year, for instance, it found that the absence of a national consensus against executing juvenile and mentally retarded offenders meant that such executions were not cruel and unusual within the meaning of the Eighth Amendment.[4]

The second section of this paper explores the international movement to eliminate capital punishment. Forty-one countries have now completely abolished the death penalty,[5] seventeen more have abolished it for all but exceptional offenses such as military crimes,[6] and twenty-five may be considered abolitionist in practice.[7] The abolitionist movement continues to gain momentum at an astonishing rate,[8] but it has yet to sweep across the United States.

The third section of this paper examines international treaties that encourage the abolition of capital punishment. The United States has signed these agreements and therefore has a duty to refrain from acts which defeat their purpose. Nevertheless, it has taken no action to abolish the death penalty or restrict its application.

The paper's final section recounts how, in one remarkable case, the British government refused to extradite a murder suspect to this country until American prosecutors agreed not to seek the death penalty at his trial. While the significance of this incident should not be exaggerated, it underscores the international community's commitment to changing American policy on the death penalty.

CAPITAL PUNISHMENT IN THE UNITED STATES

In the 1972 case *Furman v. Georgia*,[9] the United States Supreme Court was presented with the following question: "Does the imposition . . . of the death penalty in [Georgia and Texas] constitute cruel and unusual punishment in violation of the Eighth and Fourteenth Amendments?"[10] The Court was under unusual pressure to resolve this issue because: (1) more than 100 death penalty appeals were pending before the Court; (2) no one had been executed in the United States since 1967; and (3) more than 600 prisoners were awaiting execution in thirty-two states.

In an extremely close decision, the Court found that Georgia and Texas imposed the death penalty in an unconstitutionally arbitrary manner and reversed the lower courts' decisions to let these states execute their prisoners. The Justices entered similar orders in 116 other death penalty appeals[11] and effectively prevented the execution of every death row prisoner in the country. "In striking down capital punishment," wrote Justice Marshall,

> this Court does not malign our system of government. It pays homage to it . . . . In recognizing the humanity of our fellow human beings, we pay ourselves the highest tribute. We achieve "a major milestone in the long road up from barbarism" and join the [other nations] of the world which celebrate their regard for civilization by shunning capital punishment.[12]

Furman was immediately hailed as a decisive victory in the war against capital punishment. Jack Greenberg, then director of the NAACP's Legal Defense and Education Fund, even issued a statement proclaiming "there will no longer be any more capital punishment in the United States."[13] Unfortunately, he was wrong.

Since *Furman* did not hold that capital punishment was unconstitutional *in and of itself* (only Justices Brennan[14] and Marshall[15] so held), it failed to settle the death penalty controversy. As Chief Justice Burger wrote in his dissenting opinion:

> [T]here is no majority of the Court on the ultimate issue presented in these cases [and] the future of capital punishment in this country has been left in an uncertain limbo. Rather than providing a final and unambiguous answer on the basic constitutional question, the collective impact of the majority's ruling is to demand an undetermined measure of change from the various state legislatures and Congress . . . . I am not altogether displeased that legislative bodies have been given the opportunity, and indeed unavoidable responsibility, to make a thorough re-evaluation of the entire subject of capital punishment.[16]

American lawmakers eagerly accepted this "unavoidable responsibility." Within a year, state legislatures across the country were considering bills to restore the death penalty. And by 1976, thirty-five states had enacted new capital statutes and more than 460 people had been sentenced to death.

In *Gregg v. Georgia*,[17] the Supreme Court upheld the constitutionality of Georgia's newly drafted capital sentencing statute. Writing for the majority in this 1976 decision, Justice Stewart, who in *Furman* had declared that the death penalty was "unique . . . in its absolute renunciation of all that is embodied in our concept of humanity,"[18] declared that it no longer offended our concept of decency:

> Four years ago, the petitioners in *Furman* [argued] that standards of decency had evolved to the point where capital punishment no longer could be tolerated . . . . [T]he petitioners in [*Gregg*] renew the "standards of decency" argument, but developments during the four years since *Furman* have undercut substantially the assumptions upon which their argument rested . . . . [I]t is now evident that a large proportion of American society continues to regard it as an appropriate and necessary criminal sanction. The most marked indication of society's endorsement of the death penalty for murder is the legislative response to *Furman* . . . . [A]ll of the post-*Furman* statutes make clear that capital punishment has not been rejected by the elected representatives of the people.[19]

Justice Stewart's argument implied that whatever a large proportion of American society *regards* as appropriate *is* appropriate, and thereby limited the Court's role to endorsing the views of the majority.[20]

Unfortunately, the majority of Americans still support capital punishment. A recent New York Times/CBS poll showed that public support for the death penalty remains close to the record highs reached at the end of the 1988 presidential campaign.[21] Public opinion on this issue, however, is often based on an incomplete understanding of the relevant facts.[22] Most people have never considered the evidence showing that the death penalty does not deter violent crime[23] and is applied in a racially discriminatory manner.[24] Nor are they aware that people in this country have been sentenced to death and sometimes executed for crimes they did not commit.[25] America's political leaders—with their ability to gather information and address large segments of the population—are uniquely qualified to educate the public on this issue, but most do nothing because they are loath to challenge popularly held views and risk losing an election.

Politicians in other countries have displayed more courage. In Canada, for instance, Prime Minister Pierre Trudeau led the successful campaign to abolish the death penalty despite the fact that most Canadians supported capital punishment. In a 1976 address, he asked:

> Are we, as a society, so lacking in respect for ourselves, so lacking in hope for human betterment, so socially bankrupt that we are ready to accept state vengeance as our penal philosophy? To retain [the death penalty] in the Criminal Code of Canada would be to abandon reason in favor of vengeance; to abandon hope and confidence in favor of a despairing acceptance of our inability to cope with violent crime except in violence.[26]

Few American politicians share Trudeau's courage. Recently, in a desperate attempt to win votes, candidates from across the country strived to demonstrate the depth of their commitment to capital punishment. In Florida, for instance, Governor Bob Martinez strengthened his re-election campaign with a commercial in which he bragged he had "signed some ninety death warrants" during his administration.[27]

In California, San Francisco's former mayor, Dianne Feinstein, revived her dying campaign for the Democratic nomination for governor with a commercial in which she proudly declared she was the only Democratic candidate who supported the death penalty.[28] Her opponent, Attorney General John Van de Kamp (who personally opposes capital punishment),[29] responded with a commercial that showed the door to a gas chamber opening as a voice intoned that Van de Kamp had, as a district attorney and then as attorney general, "put or kept 277 murderers on death row."[30]

In Texas, ex-Governor Mark White kicked off his campaign for the Democratic nomination for governor with a commercial in which he sauntered past the photographs of every criminal sent to the electric chair during his administration. One of his opponents, Attorney General Jim Mattox, responded with a commercial in which he bragged that he had personally attended thirty-two executions. And after suffering the political misfortune of receiving an endorsement from a newspaper published by the convicts on Texas's death row, Ann Richards fought her way back into the campaign by constantly reminding voters of her strong support for capital punishment.[31]

One candidate from Tennessee even promised that, if elected, he would "throw the switch" at every execution. During his campaign for the Republican nomination for governor, Scott Shepherd declared:

> This issue is very important to me. Some voters make comments such as "Yes, this candidate supports the death penalty, as long as he doesn't throw the switch himself." If I'm elected, not only will I assume the duties of governor, but I will also be the state's executioner . . . . I will not put that responsibility on someone else . . . . I will be pulling the switch on "Old Sparky" myself. This is how serious I am about capital punishment.[32]

Very few candidates argued against the death penalty. Even Andrew Young, the former mayor of Atlanta, reversed his stand on capital punishment as he campaigned for the Democratic nomination for governor of Georgia. While acknowledging that education, jobs and housing are the real solutions to crime, he declared that the state must have "the right to put mad dogs to death."[33]

Fortunately, a handful of courageous politicians have challenged the majority and called for an end to the death penalty. One such hero of the abolition movement was Toney Anaya. During his four-year term as New Mexico's governor, he stayed all executions in the state. Then, shortly before leaving office, he commuted the death sentences of all five prisoners on New Mexico's death row. While this infuriated many (including Governor-elect Garrey E. Carruthers),[34] Anaya never apologized for his decision. After noting, in one of his last speeches as governor, that "the United States stands alone among the so-called civilized and industrial nations . . . in applying capital punishment," he declared that "[t]he death penalty is inhumane, immoral . . . and incompatible with an enlightened society."[35] He also expressed his hope that "New Mexico can become the birthplace of an idea whose time has come—the elimination of the death penalty."[36]

THE INTERNATIONAL MOVEMENT TO ABOLISH CAPITAL PUNISHMENT

The international movement to abolish the death penalty has grown steadily and rapidly. Since 1976, the year capital punishment was reinstated in America, the following twenty-six countries have either completely abolished the death penalty or limited its application to military crimes: Portugal,[37] Canada,[38] Denmark,[39] Spain,[40] Luxembourg,[41] Nicaragua,[42] Norway,[43] Brazil,[44] Fiji,[45] Peru,[46] France,[47] Netherlands,[48] Cyprus,[49] El Salvador,[50] Argentina,[51] Australia,[52] Philippines,[53] Haiti,[54] Liechtenstein,[55] East Germany,[56] New Zealand,[57] Romania,[58] Namibia,[59] Ireland,[60] Belgium,[61] and Nepal.[62]

Some of these countries abolished the death penalty very quickly. Argentina, Brazil, Haiti, Namibia, Peru, the Philippines and Romania, for instance, all outlawed capital punishment immediately after emerging from periods of political repression. In other countries, abolition took more time and required strong political leadership —something that is noticeably absent in the United States.

INTERNATIONAL COVENANTS AND TREATIES

On December 10, 1948 the United Nations General Assembly adopted the Universal Declaration of Human Rights. Article 3 of this Declaration provides that "[e]veryone has the right to life, liberty, and the security of person . . . . No one shall be subjected to torture or to cruel, inhuman or degrading treatment or punishment."[63] Since that time, there has emerged a growing consensus that the death penalty violates these fundamental principles. On December 20, 1971 the General Assembly adopted Resolution 2857, which states:

> [I]n order to guarantee the right to life, as provided for in Article 3 of the Universal Declaration of Human Rights, the main objective to be pursued is that of progressively restricting the number of offenses for which capital punishment may be imposed, with a view to the desirability of abolishing this punishment in all countries.[64]

International human rights treaties also impose restrictions on the application of the death penalty and encourage its abolition. The American Convention on Human Rights, for instance, provides that the "application of [capital punishment] shall not be extended to crimes to which it does not presently apply,"[65] and that "the death penalty shall not be re-established in states that have abolished it."[66] And the International Covenant on Civil and Political Rights imposes restrictions on the use of the death penalty in countries that have not abolished it,[67] and asserts that "[n]othing in this article shall be invoked to delay or prevent the abolition of capital punishment by any State Party to the present Covenant."[68]

The American Convention and International Covenant also prohibit the execution of juvenile offenders.[69] The United States has signed the International Covenant and therefore has a clear obligation to "refrain from acts which would defeat the object and purpose" of this agreement.[70] Nevertheless, it continues to sanction the execution of offenders under the age of eighteen.[71] America's willingness to execute minors separates it from almost every other nation in the world, *including those that retain the death penalty*. Since 1979 Amnesty International has recorded only eight executions of juvenile offenders. Three of these took place in the United States.[72]

CAPITAL PUNISHMENT AND NON-EXTRADITION

Jens Soering was an honor student at the University of Virginia in March, 1985, when his girlfriend's parents, Derek and Nancy Haysom, were brutally stabbed to death.[73] Soering and his girlfriend fled the country after discovering that they had become prime suspects in the murder investigation, but they were arrested six months later in England on an unrelated charge.[74]

When news of Soering's arrest reached Virginia, an investigator from the Bedford County Sheriff's Department came to England and questioned Soering for three days.[75] During the course of this interrogation, Soering admitted he killed the Haysoms because they opposed his relationship with their daughter.[76] On the basis of this confession, a Bedford County grand jury indicted Soering for capital murder.[77]

When the United States requested Soering's extradition, the British Embassy responded with a request of its own:

Because the death penalty has been abolished in Great Britain, the Embassy has been instructed to seek an assurance . . . that, in the event of Mr. Soering being surrendered and being convicted of the crimes for which he has been indicted . . . the death penalty, if imposed, will not be carried out. Should it not be possible on constitutional grounds for the United States Government to give such an assurance, the United Kingdom authorities ask that the United States Government undertake to recommend to the appropriate authorities that the death penalty should not be imposed or, if imposed, should not be executed.[78]

On June 1, 1987 James Updike, the Bedford County prosecutor assigned to the case, assured the British Government that:

should Jens Soering be convicted of the offense of capital murder as charged . . . a representation will be made in the name of the United Kingdom to the judge at the time of sentencing that it is the wish of the United Kingdom that the death penalty should not be imposed or carried out.[79]

This very limited assurance satisfied the British Secretary of State, who, on August 3, 1988, agreed to extradite Soering to Virginia.[80]

By that time, however, Soering had filed an application with the European Commission of Human Rights[81] in which he argued that Britain's decision to extradite him to the United States would, if implemented, violate the European Convention's prohibition against "torture [and] inhuman or degrading treatment."[82] Specifically, Soering argued that if he was sent back to Virginia, he could be sentenced to death and forced to spend a prolonged period of time enduring both the conditions on death row and the "anguish and mounting tension of living in the ever-present shadow of death."[83]

Although the Commission ultimately rejected Soering's arguments, it referred his case to the European Court of Human Rights.[84] This Court upheld Soering's claim and issued an opinion stating that Britain's "decision to extradite Soering to the United States would, if implemented, give rise to a violation of [the European Convention's prohibition against torture or inhuman and degrading treatment]."[85]

The British Government was in no way bound by the Court's decision. Nevertheless, it declared it would not extradite Soering until it received adequate assurances that, if convicted, he would not be sentenced to death.[86] On August 1, 1989 the United States acceded to this demand and agreed not to seek the death penalty in Soering's case.[87]

Of course, one country's refusal to extradite a murder suspect to the United States will not, in the long run, greatly affect American policy on the death penalty. But the importance of Soering's case should not be dismissed, for it reveals the depth of another country's commitment to the principle of abolishing capital punishment, and to helping us understand, and eventually accept, this principle.

CONCLUSION

During a 1984 debate on capital punishment, a member of Western Australia's Legislative Council stated:

Many countries . . . have repealed the death penalty since 1900 [and] I think it is rather an indictment of this State that we still have on our statute book the sentence of death of a human being, and that in Western Australia we are still fighting a battle that was fought and won decades ago in other enlightened civilized societies.[88]

Western Australia eventually won this battle,[89] but here in the United States (where public support for the death penalty is very high) it rages on.

The fear of violent crime has certainly contributed to the public support for capital punishment, but so have the politicians who exploit this fear. In highly effective thirty-second television commercials, they affect great concern over the escalating crime rate, which they propose to counter through the use of the death penalty. Executing a few people a year, however, will do nothing to reduce the crime rate because only a tiny percentage of the more than 14 million "index crimes"[90] committed every year in this country are capital offenses (i.e., offenses that are punishable by death).

The simple truth is that the death penalty cannot answer our prayers for a safer society. It is a false god, and it diverts our attention away from the real solutions to crime, such as increased employment, suitable housing, and meaningful education. But because these issues are difficult to address in dramatic, thirty-second campaign ads, politicians desperate to convince the public that they are "tough on crime" will probably continue to embrace the death penalty.

That is a shame, because if America's political leaders would just follow the example set by their counterparts in countries such as Canada, Denmark, France, Norway, Australia, New Zealand, Ireland, and so many others, they could lead a successful campaign to abolish capital punishment.

➤ DISCUSSION QUESTIONS

In the introductory notes to this article, the point was made that the nature of a society's crime problem and the way a society deals with its crime problem tell us much about the society itself. What does our crime problem today and the way we handle it tell observers from other countries about American society? More specifically, what do you think our use of the death penalty tells observers from other industrialized countries about American society?

NOTES

1. Anthony Lewis, *A Rage To Kill,* N.Y. Times, May 18, 1990, at A31.

2. Stein and Morain, *San Quentin Diary; Warden Restricts Harris's Visitors After Marijuana Is Found In Cell,* L.A. Times, March 31, 1990, at A23.

3. See Appendices I and II.

4. Stanford v. Kentucky, 492 U.S. 361 (1989) (upholding the constitutionality of executing offenders under the age of eighteen); Penry v. Lynaugh, 492 U.S. 302 (1989) (upholding the constitutionality of executing mentally retarded offenders). See *infra* note 20.

5. See Appendix I.

6. See Appendix II.

7. These countries retain the death penalty for ordinary (non-military) offenses, but have not executed anyone for at least ten years. See Appendix III.

8. Within just the past seven months, Romania, Namibia, Ireland, Belgium, and Nepal all decided to completely abolish the death penalty. See *infra* notes 58–62.

9. 408 U.S. 238 (1972).

10. Id. at 239.

11. Stewart v. Massachusetts, 408 U.S. 845 (1972); Orders, 408 U.S. 933–40 (1972) (granting certiorari, and vacating and remanding the 116 cases).

12. Furman, 408 U.S. at 371 (Marshall, J., concurring) (citation omitted).

13. Zimring and Hawkins, *Capital Punishment And The American Agenda,* 37 (Cambridge University Press, 1986).

14. Furman, 408 U.S. at 305 (Brennan, J., concurring).

15. Id. at 370–71 (Marshall, J., concurring).

16. Id. at 403 (Burger, C.J., dissenting).

17. 428 U.S. 153 (1976).

18. Furman, 408 U.S. at 306.

19. Gregg, 428 U.S. at 179–81.

20. The Court still lets political majorities define the scope of Eighth Amendment protection in death penalty cases. In Penry v. Lynaugh, 492 U.S. 302 (1989), the Court held that "there is insufficient evidence of a national consensus against executing mentally retarded people . . . for us to conclude that it is categorically prohibited by the Eighth Amendment." Id. at 335. And in Stanford v. Kentucky, 492 U.S. 361 (1989), the Court held there was no national consensus against executing juvenile offenders who commit murder when they are only sixteen or seventeen years old. Writing for the majority, Justice Scalia stated:

> Of the 37 States whose laws permit capital punishment, 15 decline to impose it upon 16-year-old offenders and 12 decline to impose it upon 17-year-old offenders. This does not establish the degree of national consensus this Court has previously thought sufficient to label a particular punishment cruel and unusual.

Id. at 370–71. In a powerful dissenting opinion, Justice Brennan attacked Scalia's analysis, saying it would return the task of defining the contours of Eighth Amendment protection to political majorities and thereby undermine the very purpose of the Bill of Rights, which was "to withdraw certain subjects from the vicissitudes of political controversy [and] place them beyond the reach of majorities . . . . " Id. at 391 (Brennan, J., dissenting) (citation omitted). Brennan also noted that:

> Of the nations that retain capital punishment, a majority—65—prohibit the execution of juveniles. . . . Since 1979, Amnesty International has recorded only eight executions of offenders under 18 throughout the world, three of these in the United States. . . . In addition to national laws, three leading human rights treaties ratified or signed by the United States, explicitly prohibit juvenile death penalties. Within the world community, the imposition of the death penalty for juvenile crimes appears to be overwhelmingly disapproved.

Id. at 389–90 (citations omitted). For more detailed discussion of international covenants that prohibit juvenile executions, see *infra* notes 67–72 and accompanying text.

21. Oreskes, *The Political Stampede On Executions,* N.Y. Times, April 4, 1990, at A13 [hereafter *Political Stampede*].

22. In Furman v. Georgia, 408 U.S. 238 (1972), Justice Marshall declared that "American citizens know almost nothing about capital punishment." Id. at 362 (Marshall, J., concurring). More specifically, he said, they are unaware of the following:

> that the death penalty is no more effective a deterrent than life imprisonment; that convicted murderers are rarely executed, but are usually sentenced to a term in prison; that they almost always become law abiding citizens upon their release from prison; that the costs of executing a capital offender exceed the costs of imprisoning him for life; that while in prison, a convict under sentence of death performs none of the useful functions that life prisoners perform; that no attempt is made in the sentencing process to ferret out likely recidivists for execution; and that the death penalty may actually stimulate criminal activity.

Id. at 362–63. Marshall hypothesized that if the American public were better informed, "the great mass of citizens would conclude. . . that the death penalty is immoral and therefore unconstitutional." Id. at 363. In 1975 Austin Sarat and Neil Vidmar, both of whom held fellowships at Yale Law School, empirically tested Marshall's hypothesis and found it to be correct. Austin Sarat and Neil Vidmar, *Public Opinion, the Death Penalty, and the Eighth Amendment: Testing the Marshall Hypothesis,* Wisconsin Law Review, 1976, pp. 171–97.

23. For a thorough discussion of the death penalty's deterrent effect, or lack thereof, see Hugo Adam Bedau, *The Death Penalty In America,* 3d ed. (New York: Oxford University Press, 1982), pp. 93–185.

24. David C. Baldus, George G. Woodworth and Charles A. Pulaski, Jr. conducted an exhaustive statistical study to discover why, in the state of Georgia during the 1970's, defendants convicted of murdering white victims were sentenced to death approximately eleven times more often than those convicted of murdering black victims. After studying more than 2,000 murder cases, the researchers found that: (1) the race of the victim (and, to a lesser extent, the race of the defendant) was a significant factor in every stage of the judicial process, from indictment to sentencing; and (2) defendants convicted of killing whites were twenty percent more likely to receive the death penalty than those convicted of killing blacks. (These findings have now been published. See David C. Baldus, George G. Woodworth and Charles A. Pulaski, Jr., *Equal Justice and the Death Penalty: A Legal and Empirical Analysis* (Boston: Northeastern University Press, 1990).

Warren McClesky, a black man convicted of killing a white police officer in Georgia, used the Baldus study to: (1) support his contention that Georgia's capital sentencing system was administered in a racially discriminatory manner; and (2) challenge the constitutionality of his death sentence. Unfortunately, the United States Supreme Court rejected McClesky's claim and upheld the constitutionality of his sentence, stating that he had failed to provide sufficient evidence of *intentional* discrimination. McClesky v. Kemp, 481 U.S. 279, 292–97 (1987). While acknowledging that statistics are routinely accepted as proof of an intent to discriminate in housing and employment cases, the Court refused to accord the Baldus study the same evidentiary weight because, according to the Court, disparities in sentencing are an inevitable part of the criminal justice system. Id.

25. See Hugo Adam Bedau and Michael A. Radelet, *Miscarriages of Justice in Potentially Capital Cases,* Stanford Law Review, vol. 40, No. 1, November 1987, pp. 21-179. The authors present compelling evidence that 350 defendants convicted of capital crimes in this country between 1900 and 1985 were innocent. In most of these cases, the discovery of new exculpatory evidence led to an acquittal, pardon, or commutation of the defendant's sentence (often years after the sentence had been imposed). In twenty-three cases, however, the innocent prisoner was executed.

26. Amnesty International, *The Death Penalty Is Not The Answer* (1987).

27. *Political Stampede, supra* note 21.

28. Id.

29. Van de Kamp declared that, despite his personal beliefs, he is professionally committed to enforcing the death penalty. *Feinstein Gets Police Group Endorsement,* The San Francisco Chronicle, April 25, 1990, at A10.

30. *Political Stampede, supra* note 21.

31. Fletcher, *Death Penalty Wagon Rolls In U.S.,* Times Newspaper Limited, March 30, 1990 (NEXIS, Wire Service).

32. *Shepherd Promises To Pull Switch On Chair,* United Press International, April 9, 1990 (NEXIS, Wire Service).

33. Will, *A Passion For Pecans,* The Washington Post, May 3, 1990, at A25.

34. Carruthers is an extremely strong and vocal supporter of capital punishment. During his campaign, he said "The first thing I want to see on my desk after I'm elected Governor is the paperwork necessary to restart the death penalty." McCarthy, *Toney Anaya's Enlightened Use Of Power,* The Washington Post, December 14, 1986, at G2.

35. Anaya, *A Departing Governor Defies Death Sentences,* The Los Angeles Times, December 14, 1986, section 5, at 3.

36. Id.

37. Portugal's Constituent Assembly outlawed capital punishment on April 2, 1976. Article 25 of its Constitution now provides that human life is inviolable and that the death penalty may never be imposed. Amnesty International, *When The State Kills . . . The Death Penalty: A Human Rights Issue,* New York: Amnesty International (1989), 193 [hereafter *When The State Kills*].

38. Canada abolished the death penalty for all peacetime offenses in July, 1976. While it may still be imposed for certain military offenses, no one has been executed since December 11, 1962. *When The State Kills,* at 116–17.

39. Denmark completely abolished capital punishment in May, 1978 by repealing a 1952 statute that authorized the imposition of the death penalty for certain military offenses. *When The State Kills,* at 128.

40. Spain's Constitution (which established the country's first democratic government since the Spanish Civil War and was ratified by popular referendum on December 23, 1978) prohibits the imposition of the death penalty for all peacetime offenses. Spain retains the death penalty for certain military offenses, but no one has been executed since September 15, 1975. *When The State Kills,* at 207.

41. Luxembourg's Chamber of Deputies abolished the death penalty on May 17, 1979. *When The State Kills,* at 169–70.

42. Nicaragua abolished capital punishment on August 21, 1979, just one month after the fall of Anastasio Somoza Debayle's repressive regime. Article 5 of the Statute on Rights and Guarantees of Nicaraguan Citizens now provides that "[t]he right to life is inviolable and inherent in the human person. In Nicaragua there is no death penalty." *When The State Kills,* at 184.

43. Norway's government passed a bill to abolish the death penalty in 1979. A government spokesman said the decision to introduce this legislation was motivated by a desire to contribute to the international campaign against capital punishment. *When The State Kills,* at 187.

44. Brazil abolished capital punishment for all peacetime offenses in 1979. Its Constitution still provides that this penalty may be imposed for certain military offenses, but no one has been executed since 1855. *When The State Kills,* at 111.

45. Fiji abolished the death penalty for all peacetime offenses in 1979. It has been retained for certain military crimes, but no one has been executed since 1980. *When The State Kills,* at 134.

46. Peru abolished capital punishment for all peacetime offenses shortly after the civilian government resumed power in 1980. The death penalty may still be imposed upon military personnel who commit crimes against the state, but no one has been executed since 1979. *When The State Kills,* at 190–91.

47. After France's National Assembly approved a bill to abolish the death penalty, the much more conservative Senate was expected to delay the bill's passage. However, following two days of heated debate—during which Justice Minister Robert Badinter called on the Senate to abolish the death penalty and "bring France out of the dark ages"—it approved the legislation and rejected an amendment that would have required a national referendum on the issue. Reuters News Service, September 30, 1981 (NEXIS, Wire Service).

48. The Dutch Parliament abolished capital punishment on February 17, 1983. *When The State Kills*, at 183.

49. On December 15, 1984 Cyprus's Council of Ministers approved a bill to abolish the death penalty for all peacetime offenses. When the parliamentary committee introduced this legislation, it declared that "[l]aw and order are adequately protected by all other means offered and there is no sufficient reason for maintaining the death penalty in the case of premeditated murder." Cyprus retains the death penalty for certain military crimes, but no one has been executed since June 13, 1962. *When The State Kills*, at 127.

50. El Salvador abolished the death penalty for all peacetime offenses in 1983. *When The State Kills*, at 131–32.

51. Argentina abolished the death penalty for all peacetime offenses in August, 1984, just eight months after the civilian government returned to power. *When The State Kills*, at 102.

52. In 1922 Queensland became the first Australian state to abolish the death penalty. It was followed by Tasmania (1968); Victoria (1975); South Australia (1976); and Western Australia (1984). The Australian Commonwealth abolished the death penalty in 1973 by passing the Death Penalty Abolition Act, which outlawed capital punishment in the territories that were under the national government's direct jurisdiction. Australia's death penalty was not completely eliminated, however, until the State of New South Wales repealed its capital sentencing statute in 1985. *When The State Kills*, at 102–103.

53. The Philippine Constitution, which was ratified in a national referendum in February, 1987, abolished the death penalty for all offenses. *When The State Kills*, at 191–92.

54. Haiti's death penalty was abolished during a national referendum on March 29, 1987. *When The State Kills,* at 144.

55. Liechtenstein's parliament abolished the death penalty when it adopted a new penal code on June 24, 1987. In proposing the adoption of this code, the government declared that retaining the death penalty would be contrary to the international campaign against capital punishment. *When The State Kills*, at 169.

56. On July 17, 1987 East Germany became the first Soviet-bloc country to abolish the death penalty. The Council of State issued a decree declaring that abolition was "in accordance with the recommendations . . . of the United Nations for the gradual removal of the death penalty from the lives of nations." It also stated that by abolishing capital punishment, East Germany demonstrated its commitment to "the preservation of human rights as a whole." *When The State Kills*, at 136.

57. On November 22, 1989 New Zealand's parliament passed a bill to abolish the death penalty for treason, the country's only capital crime. The legislation's sponsor, Bill Dillon, said there was no evidence to support the contention that capital punishment was an effective deterrent against treason, and a government spokesman declared that the death penalty was "morally repugnant". *New Zealand Abolishes Death Penalty,* Xinhua General Overseas News Service, Nov. 23, 1989 (NEXIS, Wire Service). Dillon's legislation also empowered the minister of justice to refuse to extradite prisoners to countries where they could be sentenced to death for their crimes. See *infra* notes 73–86 and accompanying text for more information on the refusal to extradite.

58. After driving Nicolae Ceausescu from power, Romania's National Salvation front marked the arrival of a new decade of freedom by abolishing the death penalty on January 1, 1990. Harvey Morris, *Romania Abolishes Death Penalty In New Year Reforms,* The Independent, January 2, 1990, at 8.

59. Namibia became the world's newest independent nation on March 21, 1990. Its constitution, which legal experts regard as a possible model for South Africa (Hack, *Namibia Gets Its Independence*, Newsday, March 21, 1990, at 13), provides that:

> The right to life shall be respected and protected. No law may prescribe death as a competent sentence. No Court or Tribunal shall have the power to impose a sentence of death upon any person. No executions shall take place in Namibia.

Amnesty International, *Death Penalty News,* at 1 (March, 1989).

60. On April 5, 1990 the government announced it will soon introduce legislation to abolish the death penalty for Ireland's two remaining capital offenses: treason, and murder of a government official or police officer. *Irish Government Will Move To Abolish Death Penalty,* The Chicago Tribune, April 6, 1990, at M4.

61. After convicted murderer Willy DeCoene was sentenced to death in December, 1989, the King commuted his sentence to life imprisonment. (The Crown has, with only one exception, commuted every death sentence since 1863). Then, from his prison cell, DeCoene demanded his own execution. He proclaimed that his country should be condemned for "handing down penalties which it does not carry out," and said he would take his case to the European Court of Human Rights. DeCoene's case has embarrassed the Belgian government and motivated its Council of Ministers to draft legislation abolishing the death penalty. Dickson, *Death Wish Embarrasses Belgians,* Financial Times, January 10, 1990, at 2.

62. Nepal abolished the death penalty on July 29, 1990. A spokesman for Nepal's Law and Ministry Society declared that capital punishment is incompatible with the country's new democratic spirit. *Nepal Abolishes Death Penalty,* Press Laws, Kyodo News Service, July 30, 1990 (NEXIS, Wire Service).

63. G.A. Res. 217A (III), U.N. Doc. A/810 (1948).

64. G.A. Res. 2857 (XXVI) (1971).

65. The American Convention on Human Rights, (1979) 1144 U.N.T.S. 123, O.A.S.T.S. 36, art. 4(2).

66. The American Convention on Human Rights, (1979) 1144 U.N.T.S. 123, O.A.S.T.S. 36, art. 4(3).

67. The International Covenant on Civil and Political Rights, (1976) 999 U.N.T.S. 171, art. 6(2).

68. The International Covenant on Civil and Political Rights, (1976) 999 U.N.T.S. 171, art. 6(6).

69. Article 4(5) of the American Convention states "[c]apital punishment shall not be imposed upon persons who, at the time the crime was committed, were under eighteen years of age." And Article 6(5) of the International Covenant provides that a "sentence of death shall not be imposed for crimes committed by persons below eighteen years of age."

70. The Vienna Convention on the Laws of Treaties, (1979) 1155 U.N.T.S. 331, art. 18.

71. See *supra* note 20.

72. The other five took place in Bangladesh, Pakistan, Rwanda and Barbados. Barbados's parliament, however, recently passed a bill prohibiting the execution of juvenile offenders. Attorney General Maurice King, the legislation's sponsor, said the bill was essential if Barbados was to fulfill its obligations under the American Convention on Human Rights and the International Covenant on Civil and Political Rights. King also declared that his country's "long and distinguished record on human rights could only be enhanced by the measure." *Barbados: Death Penalty Abolished for Offenders Under Eighteen,* Inter Press Service, November 30, 1989 (NEXIS, Wire Service).

73. Soering v. United Kingdom, Series A, vol. 161, 11 E.H.R.R. 439, ¶ 12 (1989).

74. Id.

75. Id. at 13.

76. Id.

77. Id.

78. Id. at 15. The Embassy based its request on Article IV of the United Kingdom–United States Treaty, which provides that:

> If the offense for which extradition is requested is punishable by death under the relevant law of the requesting Party, but the relevant law of the requested Party does not provide for the death penalty in a similar case, extradition may be refused unless the requesting Party gives assurances satisfactory to the requested Party that the death penalty will not be carried out.

Id. at 36.

79. Id. at 20.

80. Id. at 24.

81. Id. at 24 and 76.

82. The Convention for the Protection of Human Rights and Fundamental Freedoms, (1955) 213 U.N.T.S. 221, E.T.S. 5, art. 3.

83. Soering v. United Kingdom, 11 E.H.R.R. 439, 106.

84. Id. at 78.

85. Id. at 111.

86. *Britain Willing To Return Soering To Face Trial,* United Press International, August 2, 1989 (NEXIS, Wire Service).

87. Id.

88. *When The State Kills,* at 71–72.

89. See *supra* note 51.

90. The F.B.I. uses eight "index crimes" to measure U.S. crime rates: murder, aggravated assault, rape, robbery, burglary, larceny, auto theft, and arson.

APPENDIX 1

Countries that have completely abolished the death penalty (as of August 7, 1990).

Australia	Iceland	Panama
Austria	Ireland**	Philippines
Belgium*	Kiribati	Portugal
Cape Verde	Liechtenstein	Romania
Columbia	Luxembourg	San Marino
Costa Rica	Marshall Islands	Solomon Islands
Denmark	Micronesia	Sweden
Dominican Republic	Monoco	Tuvalu
East Germany	Namibia	Uruguay
Ecuador	Nepal	Vanuatul
Finland	Netherlands	Vatican City State
France	New Zealand	Venezuela
Haiti	Nicaragua	West Germany
Honduras	Norway	

Total: Forty-one countries

*   Belgium is currently in the process of repealing its death penalty statute. *See supra* note 61.
**   Ireland's parliament is expected to abolish the death penalty later this year. *See supra* note 60.

APPENDIX 2

Countries that have abolished the death penalty for all ordinary (non-military) offenses (as of August 7, 1990).

COUNTRY	DATE OF ABOLITION FOR ORDINARY CRIMES	DATE OF LAST EXECUTION FOR A MILITARY OFFENSE
Argentina	1984	----
Brazil	1979	1855
Canada	1976	1962
Cyprus	1983	1962
El Salvador	1983	1973
Fiji	1979	1964
Israel	1954	1962
Italy	1947	1947
Malta	1971	1943
Mexico	----	1937
Papua New Guinea	1974	1950
Peru	1979	1979
Sao Tome and Principe	----	----
Seychelles	----	----
Spain	1978	1975
Switzerland	1942	1944
United Kingdom	1973	1964

Total: Seventeen countries

APPENDIX 3

Countries that are abolitionist *in practice* (as of August 7, 1990). These countries retain the death penalty for ordinary offenses but have not executed anyone for at least ten years.

COUNTRY	DATE OF LAST EXECUTION
Andorra	1943
Anguilla	1820
Bahrain	1977
Bermuda	1977
Bhutan	1964
Bolivia	1974
British Virgin Islands	- - - -
Brunei Darussalam	1957
Cayman Islands	1928
Comoros	**
Cote d' Ivoire	- - - -
Djibouti	**
Greece	1972
Hong Kong	1966
Madagascar	1958
Maldives	1952
Montserrat	1961
Nauru	**
Niger	1976
Paraguay	1928
Senegal	1967
Sri Lanka	1976
Togo	- - - -
Turks and Caicos Islands	- - - -
Western Samoa	**

Total: Twenty-five countries

** These countries have not executed anyone since gaining independence.

PART FOUR

Correctional Systems

Confronting Crime:
The Conservative Model

■ *ELLIOTT CURRIE*

INTRODUCTORY NOTES

Classical criminologists of the eighteenth and nineteenth centuries (such as Cesare Beccaria and Jeremy Bentham) and today's neoclassical criminologists (such as James Q. Wilson and Ernest van den Haag) both adhere to an economic model of crime. This model views the criminal as acting on the basis of a rational cost-benefit analysis: if the benefits of the crime outweigh the costs, then crime is the result. Interestingly, however, adherents of the economic model in past centuries tended to be liberals calling for more humane treatment of criminals, while today the economic model is favored by conservatives calling for more punitive measures. That is, for example, Beccaria argued that overly severe punishments made crime rational. (For example, if one faces the death penalty for a crime, she or he would be wise to kill off all witnesses.) Wilson, a major proponent of the conservative model of criminology, on the other hand, holds that crime in the U.S. is due to the leniency of our criminal justice system.

Both the classical and the neoclassical criminologists fall within the domain of deterrence theory. Accordingly, the "costs" of crime can be manipulated by changing any of three variables: swiftness, certainty, and the severity of punishment. The modern conservative economic model—which emphasizes severity—has a number of shortcomings. First, while great weight is given to increasing the costs of crime, discussion of manipulating the "benefits" of law-abiding behavior is conspicuously absent from their works. Second, the economic model arguably places too much emphasis on the role of rational decision-making in the commission of a crime, especially for violent crime which very often involves an act of passion. And third,—of swiftness, certainty, and severity—the latter has been tried the most in the last few decades, and it seems to have had little or no impact on crime. Currie focuses his critique of "the conservative model" on this last shortcoming.

SOURCE: From *Confronting Crime: An American Challenge* by Elliott Currie, pp. 22–50 (abridged). Copyright © 1985 by Elliott Currie. Reprinted by permission of Pantheon Books, a division of Random House, Inc.

To understand why we've arrived at our present impasse in dealing with crime, we must first reconsider the assumptions that have guided the dominant policies on crime in America throughout the past decade. This means taking a hard look at the conservative argument about the causes of crime.

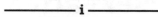

At first blush, that may seem a contradiction in terms: during the seventies, conservatives often ridiculed the very idea of searching for the causes of crime. James Q. Wilson took this stance to its most adamant extreme in his influential book, *Thinking About Crime.* To those who contended that crime could be dealt with only by attacking its root caus-es, Wilson said, he "was sometimes inclined, when in a testy mood, to rejoin: stupidity can only be dealt with by attacking its root causes. I have yet to see a root cause," he continued,

> or to encounter a government program that has successfully attacked it, at least with respect to those social problems that arise out of human volition rather than technolog-ical malfunction. But more importantly, the demand for causal solutions is, whether intended or not, a way of deferring any action and criticizing any policy. It is a cast of mind that inevitably detracts attention from those few things that government can do reasonably well and draws attention toward those many things it cannot do at all.

On closer inspection, however, it's clear that Wilson's statement confuses two quite different arguments. The first is that it makes no sense to talk about the social or "root" causes of crime at all, either because such causes do not exist or because no one knows what they are or how to find them. The second is an essentially political, rather than conceptual, argument—that government either cannot or should not intervene in the conditions that many criminologists had held to be root causes of crime. The first argument is difficult to take seriously (Professor Wilson, indeed, has recently abandoned it himself); after all, it is hardly possible to say anything very compelling about crime—or any other social problem—without working from some assumptions about why the problem exists. And, in fact, beneath their rhetoric about the futility of looking for the causes of crime, conservatives have offered at least the elements of a causal theory of their own.

That theory has never been carefully articulated, and it changes form with the writer. But it is always some variant of the idea that crime is caused by inadequate "control," that we have a great deal of crime because we have insufficient curbs on the appetites or impulses that naturally impel individuals toward criminal activity. Most conservative writers regard these lurking appetites as a fundamental part of "human nature." As Wilson put it in *Thinking About Crime,* a "sober" or "unflat-tering view of man" tells us that "wicked people exist" and that "nothing avails but to set them apart from innocent people." Several years later, President Ronald Rea-gan, in a similar vein, told a convention of police chiefs that "some men are prone to evil, and society has a right to be protected from them."

The difficulty with this as an explanation for crime is not that it is untrue—but that, at this sweepingly general level, it is unhelpful. No one would deny that wicked people exist or that human beings have destructive and predatory impulses against which others must be protected. But such generalizations cannot help us understand why crime is so much worse at some times or places than others. Why are people in

St. Louis so much more "prone to crime" than those in Stockholm or, for that matter, Milwaukee? Why are people in Houston not only far more likely to kill each other than people in London or Zurich, but also much more likely to do so today than they were twenty-five years ago?

Faced with these questions, the criminological Right has countered with a number of intellectual ploys. One is simply to ignore or deny the difference between our crime rates and those of other industrial societies. Thus, in *Thinking About Crime*, Wilson scorned the idea that crime was, as he put it, "an expression of the political rage of the dispossessed, rebelling under the iron heel of capitalist tyranny"; that this view was thoroughly misguided, he asserted, was proven in part by the fact that "virtually every nation in the world, capitalist, socialist, and communist, has experienced in recent years rapidly increasing crime rates."

One problem with this assertion is that, stated so flatly, it was simply untrue. Several capitalist countries, most notably Japan and Switzerland, did not experience rapidly rising crime rates in the sixties and seventies; and there was at least one socialist developing country, Cuba, whose rates of criminal violence fell rather dramatically. Moreover, although many other developed societies did suffer rising levels of crime in the sixties and seventies, the rises were primarily in property and drug offenses, not in violent crimes like homicide. In the midseventies—just as Wilson was portraying every country as racked by rapidly rising crime—it was still possible for two respected Scandinavian criminologists to conclude that the risks of victimization by criminal violence remained quite low in Denmark and Norway; indeed, the Danish and Norwegian homicide rates had been "fairly constant" for forty or fifty years.

An even more important difficulty with the Wilson argument is that the industrial countries whose rates of criminal violence did rise in the sixties and seventies usually began—and ended—at such low levels that to emphasize the similarities between those countries and the United States obscured the much more compelling and dramatic point—the scale of the differences. After what Wilson and others described as nearly two decades of unremitting increases in crime "throughout the world," by the late seventies (in per capita terms) about ten American men died by criminal violence for every Japanese, Austrian, West German, or Swedish man; about fifteen American men died for every Swiss or Englishman; and over twenty for every Dane. During the sixties and seventies, murder rates increased in some of those countries and didn't in others—but in none of them, when Wilson wrote, did they begin to approach those of the United States; nor do they today; nor are they likely to in the foreseeable future.

Obviously this stubborn reality causes tough problems for an argument that blames crime on a vaguely defined and immutable "human nature." Consider Wilson's remarks on the prospects for reducing robbery rates. "A sober view of man," he wrote in 1975, "requires a modest definition of progress. A 20 percent reduction in robbery would still leave us with the highest robbery rate of almost any Western nation but would prevent about sixty thousand robberies." The internal contradiction in Wilson's reasoning is painfully clear. The wide cross-national variations in crime to which he alludes completely undercut the explanatory power of a "sober view of man"—for "man" is presumably no worse in the United States than in Denmark or Switzerland. But the differences in robbery rates between these places are staggering.

In his more recent work, Wilson acknowledges that several factors—the effects of "real and imagined" racism, the "sharpening of consumer instincts through the mass media," the increased availability of handguns, and the abandonment of the inner city by "persons with a stake in impulse control," among others—may have a special impact on crime in America. Nevertheless, Wilson continues to insist on the curious argument that since the recent increase in crime "is not a peculiarly American phenomenon, but a feature of virtually every industrialized society," a "true understanding of crime depends on what these nations have in common, not what differentiates them." This remarkable conclusion allows Wilson to retain intact what turns out to be his central premise: that an "ethos of self-expression" common to most modern societies is the fundamental cause of the industrial world's crime problem. In the process, the uniqueness of the American situation simply drops out of sight.

The argument from human nature, then, is really too general to be of much help. A similarly unhelpful abstraction lies at the heart of the most systematic conservative theory of the causes of crime—what is called, I think misleadingly, the *economic model* of crime. There could, of course, be as many economic models of crime as there are economic theories, but in fact the conservative model is based on just one: the brand of neoclassical economics developed by the "Chicago School." In this model, whether a potential offender commits a crime or not is determined by calculated choice based on a rational weighing of the relative costs and benefits (or *utilities*) of committing the crime versus not doing so. In an early and often-quoted formulation, the University of Chicago economist Gary Becker argued that someone commits a crime

> if the expected utility to him exceeds the utility he could get by using his time and other resources at other activities. Some persons become "criminals," therefore, not because their basic motivation differs from that of other persons, but because their benefits and costs differ.

Similarly, the conservative economist Gordon Tullock wrote some years later, "If you increase the cost of committing a crime, there will be fewer crimes." Still more recently, the philosopher Ernest van den Haag put the same argument in terms of the "comparative net advantage" of crime over other activities. "The number of persons engaged in any activity, lawful or not," van den Haag writes, "depends on the comparative net advantage they expect."

> Thus, the number of practicing dentists, grocers, drug dealers, or burglars depends on the net advantage which these practitioners expect their occupations to yield compared to other occupations available to them.

Human behavior, criminal or otherwise, is assumed to be like any other exchange in the marketplace. Armed with this conveniently simplified view of human motivation, conservatives have generally blamed the crime rate on the lack of punishment—crime is common because it's "cheap"—although they could just as plausibly argue that where crime rates are especially high, the "comparative net advantage" of lawful behavior must be particularly low. In practice, conservative criminology has concentrated on increasing the "cost" of crime; increasing the relative "benefits" of lawful activity has taken a distinctly subordinate place. To van den Haag, for example,

> our only hope for reducing the burgeoning crime rate lies in decreasing the expected net advantage of committing crimes (compared to lawful activities) by increasing the cost through increasing the expected severity of punishments and the probability of suffering them.

Van den Haag's emphatic rejection of the other side of the "cost-benefit" equation is hardly unique. As a group of researchers from New York's Vera Institute of Justice have pointed out in a careful review of the economic literature on crime and punishment, "one important cost—deterrence through the application of formal criminal sanctions (arrest, conviction, and punishment)—is emphasized by economists to the virtual exclusion of the role of other factors, such as incentives derived from improved employment opportunity." Given the practical difficulty of increasing arrest and conviction rates, partisans of the economic model have in effect placed most of their bets on increasing punishment—especially through longer and more frequent prison sentences.

On the most abstract level, it certainly isn't unreasonable to believe that perceptions of "cost" have some weight in determining the course of individuals' behavior. But to make the basic argument stick as an explanation of *variations* in crime rates —why a particular country or period has more crime than others—it is necessary to go further: to show that the "costs" of crime are, in those instances, actually lower than in other times or places with less crime. To the extent that the criminological Right offers an explanation of American crime patterns *vis-à-vis* those of other countries (or other periods in our own history), it is that the costs of crime are peculiarly low here and, at least by implication, lower than in the past.

A recent *Wall Street Journal* editorial, for example, explained the rising crime rates of the late 1970s and early 1980s this way:

> The sharp increase of crime in many states has undoubtedly resulted from the absence of punishment. . . . As the certainty of punishment rises, prison populations will rise. But so will the cost of crime. If states stay on their present course, it is reasonable to expect that the present surge in prison populations will cease. There will be less crime and fewer people going to jail. If so, it will be worth the cost of correcting those years of neglect.

This view of the roots of America's crime problem would doubtless bring ready assent from most conservatives. But how well does the claim of an "absence of punishment" in recent years—and of a penal system crippled by "years of neglect"—fit the reality?

ii

There is a fundamental difficulty for the conservative argument: It is hard to maintain that our high rates of crime are caused by insufficient punishment when our penal system is one of the most punitive in the developed world. We lock up offenders at a far greater rate than any other advanced society (except the Soviet Union and South Africa—where the comparison is not wholly appropriate, since many prisoners are political offenders, not "street" criminals). At the beginning of the eighties, the incarceration rate in the United States was about 217 per 100,000. At the opposite extreme, the Dutch rate was about 21 per 100,000. In between lay most of the rest of the world's industrial societies, many clustered toward the lower end of the scale: Japan's rate was 44 per 100,000, Norway's 45, Sweden's 55, West Germany's 60, Denmark's 63, France's 67, Great Britain's a relatively high 80 per 100,000.

In part, these low rates reflect some countries' use of prison as only a last resort, for the most dangerous offenders; in part they reflect a common practice of incarcerating criminals for relatively short periods. The latter is especially true in Holland, where the average time served in the late 1970s was an astonishing 1.3 months, versus about 5 months in Britain and about 16 in the United States. The shorter sentences are not simply a reflection of the less serious range of offenses in Holland; average sentences handed down for a given *class* of offenses also differ greatly. Thus the average maximum sentence for robbery was 150 months in the U.S. federal prisons and 68 months in the state prisons; in the Dutch prisons, it was 19 months.

Moreover, many Western European countries deliberately decreased their use of imprisonment during the sixties and seventies, while beginning in the seventies we moved relentlessly in the other direction. The average Dutch robbery sentence fell to 19 months in 1981 from 32 months in 1950; between 1951 and 1975, the Dutch prison population as a whole dropped by *half*.

Given these huge and growing disparities between our rates of imprisonment and those of otherwise comparable societies, how can anyone argue that our crime rate (as the *Wall Street Journal's* editors put it) "has undoubtedly resulted from the absence of punishment"? One attempt to maintain the argument is to turn it on its head, and claim that given the severity of the American crime problem, we make relatively limited use of incarceration—so that the likelihood of punishment for convicted offenders is actually smaller here. Wilson, for example, draws an analogy with medical care; to claim that we "overimprison" people in the United States, he writes, "is like disproving the need for hospitals by saying that the United States already hospitalizes a larger fraction of its population than any other nation," for it "implies that we are sending people to prison without any regard to the number of crimes committed (or sending them to hospitals without regard to whether they are sick)." The "proper question," Wilson insists, is "whether we imprison a higher fraction of those arrested, prosecuted, and convicted than do other nations." His answer is that we do not.

There are two things wrong with Wilson's argument. To begin with, it is not at all clear why this is the "proper question." For if it is offered as an explanation of high crime rates in America, the argument is perilously close to circular, since it does not tell us why so many crimes are committed here in the first place. A closer look at the medical analogy reveals the logical problem. If one country already possesses more hospitals per capita than any other, but still produces more sickness, it is implausible to blame its comparative ill health on the relative lack of hospitals. To be sure, a country with a lot of illness will "need" many hospitals, just as a country with a lot of crime will "need" many prisons. But if we want to understand either why so many people are ill to begin with or how we could prevent these excessive levels of illness in the future, we will need to look at other aspects of the country—sanitation, nutrition, environmental hazards, perhaps even cultural values—or we will be fruitlessly building hospitals forever to accommodate the ever-increasing flow of the sick. The same logic ought to apply in the case of criminal justice. If we already imprison people at a higher rate than other countries, we cannot blame our own uniquely high crime rate on the underuse of imprisonment, without reasoning in a circle. If we want to understand why so many people here have become criminals, we will need to look at other factors that distinguish us from more fortunate countries.

But there is an even more immediate difficulty with Wilson's argument—its facts are wrong. Wilson's only source of evidence for his contention that the United States is relatively sparing in its use of prison is a 1978 study by the Yale economist Kenneth I. Wolpin. This analysis showed that in the 1960s—when American incarceration rates were much lower than they are today—the chance of imprisonment for convicted robbers was higher in England than in the United States (although the

American sentences were more severe): between 1961 and 1967, a convicted robber's chance of going behind bars was 48 percent in England and 31 percent in the United States (for an average sentence of 2.9 years in England, 3.5 years in America).

On the surface, these figures lent some credence to the notion that the British might be "tougher" on robbers, if only in the sense of greater consistency, not severity, of punishment. The trouble is that Wolpin's analysis—as he pointed out himself in a later study—neglected to include in its estimates of incarceration rates the great numbers of convicted offenders sent to local *jails* in the United States—a crucial omission indeed, since including them in the calculations completely reversed the outcome.

Wolpin's later, more inclusive, study compared robbery in the United States (specifically California), England, and Japan. This time he found that convicted robbers were considerably more likely to go to prison or jail in the United States than in either England or Japan. Wolpin's study covered the years from 1955 to 1971—well before the prison "boom" of the seventies that doubled the American incarceration rate. But even then, a convicted robber had a 63 percent chance of going behind bars in California, versus 48 percent in England and 46 percent in Japan. English robbers, furthermore, spent only about half as much time behind bars as either Japanese or Californians. Meanwhile, according to official statistics, California's robbery rate averaged over seventeen times the British rate and over twenty-eight times the Japanese. Developments over time are also revealing. In all three countries, as Wolpin's later study showed, convicted robbers were *less* likely to go to prison at the end of the period than at the beginning. But this consistent decline in the "costs" of robbery had completely contradictory effects on robbery rates in the different countries: robbery increased in California and still more in England, but declined rather dramatically in Japan.

In short, contrary to Wilson's claims, we do indeed incarcerate more of those arrested and convicted than the British and Japanese—who, in turn, use incarceration more readily than, for example, the Swiss or the Dutch. Wolpin's studies do bring up an important distinction: the Japanese and the British *catch* criminals more often than we do, and generally convict them more frequently once caught. Why this should be so is a difficult and unresolved question. Suffice it to say here that the difficulty in apprehending criminals has little to do with the *leniency* of American justice; and while the difficulty in convicting them once caught may have some relation to American court practices, the evidence indicates that any effects of this on the crime rate are quite small. The fundamental point at issue here remains: the United States is indeed the most punitive of advanced Western industrial societies toward those offenders brought to the stage of sentencing.

➤ DISCUSSION QUESTIONS

Of the three variables considered in deterrence theory—swiftness, certainty, and severity of punishment—this article focuses on the failure of severity to impact on the crime problem. What changes could be made in the American criminal justice system that might increase the swiftness and severity of punishment? And what would be the objections to these changes?

NOTES

Page(s)

216 Wilson quotation: James Q. Wilson, *Thinking About Crime* (New York: Random House, 1975), p. xv.

216 "Wicked people exist": Wilson, *Thinking About Crime,* p. 235.

217 Wilson quotation: *Thinking About Crime,* p. xiii.

217 "Several countries": see Marshall B. Clinard, *Cities with Little Crime,* Cambridge: Cambridge University Press, 1978); David Downes, "The Origins and Consequences of Dutch Penal Policy Since 1945," *British Journal of Criminology* 22, no. 4 (October 1982); Robert J. Smith, *Japanese Society: Tradition, Self, and the Social Order* (Cambridge: Cambridge University Press, 1983); and Luis Salas, *Social Control and Deviance in Cuba* (New York: Praeger, 1979).

217 Denmark and Norway: Hauge and Wolf, "Criminal Victimization in Three Scandinavian Countries." A more recent Swedish study similarly found little change in criminality among cohorts of Swedish youth who entered the most crime-prone age groups between the late sixties and the late seventies. "The most striking aspect" of this study, the researchers conclude, "is the *stability* of criminal activity among the cohorts." Hans von Hofer, Leif Lenke, and Ulf Thorsson, "Criminality Among Thirteen Swedish Birth Cohorts," *British Journal of Criminology* 23, no. 3 (July 1983).

217 "Twenty for every Dane": calculated from *Statistical Abstract,* 1980, p. 187.

217 "Sober view of man": Wilson, *Thinking About Crime,* p. 223.

217 Wilson quotation: *Public Interest,* Winter 1983, pp. 38–39.

218 Becker quotation: cited in James Thompson *et al., Employment and Crime: A Review of Theories and Research* (Washington, D.C.: National Institute of Justice, 1981), pp. 31–32.

218 Tullock quotation: Gordon Tullock, "Does Punishment Deter Crime?" *Public Interest,* Summer 1974, p. 105.

218 Van den Haag quotations: Ernst Van den Haag, "Could Successful Rehabilitation Reduce the Crime Rate?" *Journal of Criminal Law and Criminology* 73, no. 3 (Fall 1982): 1025, 1035.

219 Vera quotation: Thompson *et al., Employment and Crime,* p. 37.

219 *Wall Street Journal:* quoted in Bureau of Justice Statistics Newsletter, February 1983, p. 14.

219 International incarceration rates: Eugene Doleschal and Anne Newton, *International Rates of Imprisonment* (Hackensack, N.J.: National Council on Crime and Delinquency, 1981.

219 Dutch sentences: Downes, "Dutch Penal Policy," pp. 330–334; see also D.W. Steenhuis *et al.,* "The Penal Climate in the Netherlands: Sunny or Cloudy?" *British Journal of Criminology* 23, no. 1 (January 1983). American sentences: U.S. Bureau of Justice Statistics, *Prison Admissions and Releases, 1981* (Washington, D.C.: Department of Justice, 1984). Average time served for robbery in the early eighties was 61.5 months in Maryland, 40.8 in North Carolina, and 33.5 in Pennsylvania; these figures, moreover, do not include the time prisoners spent in local jails before sentencing—which, for robbers, averaged nearly 8 months in Illinois. Herbert Koppel, *Time Served in Prison* (Washington, D.C.: U.S. Bureau of Justice Statistics, 1984).

220 Wilson quotation: James Q. Wilson, "Dealing with the High-Rate Offender," *Public Interest,* Fall 1982, p. 68.

220 Wolpin study: Kenneth I. Wolpin, "An Economic Analysis of Crime and Punishment in England and Wales, 1894–1967," *Journal of Political Economy* 86, no. 5 (October 1975).

221 Second Wolpin study: Kenneth I. Wolpin, "A Time-Series Cross-Sectional Analysis of International Variations in Crime and Punishment," *Review of Economics and Statistics* 62, no. 3 (August 1980).

ARTICLE 23

Global Report on Prisons

■ *HUMAN RIGHTS WATCH*

INTRODUCTORY NOTES

The modern prison—as a place to warehouse convicted felons—is largely an American invention. Before the modern day prison, there were places (often dungeons) used for housing prisoners before trials, but once convicted, punishments usually consisted of exile, fines, pillories, floggings, brandings, or executions.

The first penitentiary was credited to the Quakers who were seeking more humane means of dealing with offenders. Their prison model—the foundation for what criminologists call the "Pennsylvania system"—held prisoners in solitary confinement, allowing them to ponder the error of their ways. Though it was meant to be a humanitarian reform, its humaneness came to be seriously questioned when the deleterious effects of isolation became obvious.

Soon after the Pennsylvania system came the "Auburn system," containing tiered cells and requiring regimented discipline—this came to be the model for subsequent prisons in the U.S. and around much of the world. Strong beliefs in Christian reform also backed the operation of the Auburn system. However, this system also came quickly under attack for its brutal treatment of prisoners. Paradoxically, the prison movement and the prison reform movement began almost simultaneously.

Though prisoners tend to receive very little sympathy from the public, it should be noted that they are in a particularly vulnerable position. While branding, flogging, and stocks may seem cruel by modern standards, they did, at least, have the advantage of being public punishments; and public scrutiny can serve as a means of controlling abuses. However, in prisons, there is often little or no public oversight. Without the presence of independent human rights organizations such as Amnesty International or Human Rights Watch many prison personnel around the world would feel little compunction to curtail the abusive treatment of their inmates.

Conservative American critics often criticize the correctional system for mollycoddling its inmates. Indeed, as you read this next selection, you may find that the American penal system compares rather favorably to many of the other countries mentioned in this report. But keep in mind that most of these other countries are "Third World" and/or repressive societies that do not have very distinguished records when it comes to human rights. When compared to modern democratic societies, the American penal system does not fare quite so well.

SOURCE: The Human Rights Watch, "The Human Rights Watch Global Report on Prisons," (New York: Human Rights Watch, 1993): 65–92. Reprinted with permission.

RULES

A standard step in any prison investigation is to examine the rules setting forth prisoners' rights and obligations and the sanctions for violating those rules. Such rules do exist in most countries and in most—though there are several notable exceptions —they generally conform to international standards. Also, on paper, most countries have a mechanism for prison oversight and a system of remedies to address inmates' grievances. The questions to ask, however, are whether prisoners are informed of the rules; whether they are made aware of the remedies; how are they supposed to learn about them; and whether there is a functioning mechanism to enforce compliance.

The provision of written rules to inmates is an absolute necessity for the observance of human rights in prisons. Unless they are informed of the rules, even those inmates who desire to conform are likely to commit acts that will be considered infractions warranting punishment. Moreover, prisoners may be readily deprived of privileges that should be available to them under the law and not know about it. When there is no general access to the rules governing day-to-day living conditions, prisoners feel (and are) dependent on the good will of the staff if they seek a specific improvement in their situation.[1] The lack of consistently applied rules engenders confusion and insecurity and gives leeway to staff arbitrariness. Finally, a grievance procedure that is unknown to prisoners is obviously a sham.

In Spain, a country with progressive prison legislation and an admirable set of prison rules, prisoners had no access to those rules at the time of a Human Rights Watch delegation visit, according to numerous interviews with inmates. The authorities assured us that every prisoner was issued a brochure outlining the rules, but when we asked to see a copy, nobody in the office of the director of the prison system could find one. (The rules were later sent by messenger to our hotel.) The Spanish prison administration banned distribution of a book prepared by a nongovernmental organization that provided information about the rules, rights and remedies available to prisoners under the law.

In Egypt many prisoners were astonished to learn from our representatives that they were supposed to be visited once a month by a special inspector charged with investigating prisoners' complaints and addressing grievances.

In some countries, prisoners who inform their fellow inmates about their rights get into trouble. In the United States all prisons by law must provide inmates with access to legal services or legal libraries.[2] Prisons are equipped with law libraries and prisoners may challenge various aspects of their imprisonment in court. Some prisoners acquire substantial legal expertise in the course of their incarceration; the term "jailhouse lawyer" has been coined to describe a prisoner who becomes a legal expert and lends his or her help to other inmates. But we have received numerous testimonies and letters complaining that jailhouse lawyers are often singled out for harassment by the staff.

In Indonesia Human Rights Watch documented a case of a security prisoner who eventually died in a prison hospital from tuberculosis. According to one source, during his incarceration he had frequently been beaten and put in an isolation cell, sometimes for months at a time. He was regarded as a troublemaker by the guards for informing other prisoners about their rights, demanding that those rights be observed, and sending letters of complaint to the head of the prison and the Director General of Corrections.

In communist Poland prison rules setting out the rights and duties of prisoners were routinely kept secret. In the aftermath of the imposition of martial law in 1981, there were also reports of prisoners who were punished for asking to consult copies of the principal international document outlining prison conditions, the U.N. Standard Minimum Rules for the Treatment of Prisoners.[3] This situation changed dramatically with the advent of democracy in Poland in 1989. When we inspected Polish prisons in 1990, prisoners showed us copies of the prison rules that were available to them in their cells. In China, prisoners are never provided with a copy of a written set of rules but, instead, are required to memorize them. Guards check on this knowledge; not remembering all the words is a punishable infraction. Meanwhile, detailed regulations on various aspects of imprisonment are secret in China. The "Detailed Rules for the Disciplinary Work of Prisons and Labor Reform Detachments," issued in 1982, are available only in special, "internal-use-only" publications that may only be seen by officials.

It is not only important that inmates should be informed of the rules but, of course, that the rules should be observed. Unless they are enforced, their existence on paper is meaningless in assessing human rights conditions, a fact that some governments fail to appreciate. On some occasions during our prison investigations, when Human Rights Watch criticized specific aspects of prison conditions, governments would simply cite the law. In Spain many provisions of the admittedly progressive laws are seldom or never enforced by the government in practice, including the requirements that all prisoners should be housed in individual cells; that no prison should hold more than 350 inmates; and the very stipulation that prisoners should be informed about the rules and their rights under those rules.

RECOMMENDATIONS

As is obvious, the availability of the rules and access to legal documents by all prisoners are crucial in safeguarding human rights in prisons. In order to assure this, Human Rights Watch recommends that:

- every prisoner should be issued a copy of the rules upon his or her arrival in the prison; if for technical reasons it is impossible to provide each prisoner with a personal copy, regulations should be posted in a place accessible at all times by all prisoners;

- a system should be established for illiterate prisoners to be thoroughly informed about the regulations;

- prisoners should never be required to memorize the regulations;

- prison libraries accessible to all prisoners should have copies of the country's prison-related laws and of the U.N. Standard Minimum Rules for the Treatment of Prisoners;

- each prison should be required to report annually on its compliance with the country's prison rules and reports should be available publicly;

- a grievance procedure should be established to permit complaints—without fear of reprisals—about violations of the rules and for enforcement of compliance.

DISCIPLINE

Disciplinary measures are punishment on top of punishment. In total institutions such as prisons, where every aspect of an inmate's life is controlled, many measures affecting the everyday life of a prisoner can be punishments and the list of punishments used in prisons all over the world is almost endless. Disturbingly, Human Rights Watch discovered that in country after country, punishments meted out within the prisons are cruel, humiliating, and frequently applied in an arbitrary fashion without the slightest vestige of due process.

Punishments may range from a verbal reprimand, or a written notation in a prisoner's record, to the denial of certain privileges—such as access to television, being allowed to smoke, the opportunity to participate in social events or purchase goods from a commissary—to forfeiture of good time (a way of gaining earlier release), transfer to a higher security institution, confinement in segregation or punishment cells, or restraint in fetters or shackles.

As Human Rights Watch investigated disciplinary measures in prisons, we examined the country's prison regulations to see what measures were legally authorized. Often, we found that there were two sets of punishments: authorized and unauthorized. Both were used. The latter usually involved physical violence.

We also studied the range of offenses—it is often revealing to discover what constitutes an infraction in a particular prison system—and the corresponding penalties. In addition, we examined the degree of due process in determining penalties, and whether prisoners were afforded any possibility of appeal.

Types of Offenses

Disciplinary measures are necessary because inmates often violate the rules and sometimes commit serious offenses. Though penalties should be imposed when an inmate attempts to escape, destroys property, inflicts violence on his fellow prisoners or staff, smuggles drugs into the prison, or otherwise disrupts order in the institution in a serious way, the offenses for which some prison systems in fact impose penalties go far beyond such matters.

In communist Czechoslovakia it was against the rules, and thus punishable, to listen to the radio; to own a book or writing pad; to receive more than one letter from one's family; not to take off one's cap when talking to a guard; to call someone "comrade" in an ironical fashion; to finish work early; or to lie on the bed during the day; study; or write letters for illiterate fellow prisoners. At the time of our 1990 visit, following the democratic transformation in Czechoslovakia, pretrial detainees in Slovakia were still forbidden to exercise in their cells or to wear watches, or to sit or lie on the beds during the daytime.

In China inmates may be punished for not remembering all the words of the regulations; not admitting guilt; standing by the window; speaking loudly; or not arranging one's bedroll properly.

In Romania prisoners may be punished, usually by beatings on the palms of their hands, for lying on the bed during the day or taking too long while using the bathroom. Inmates are required to stand with their faces toward the wall, usually in the cell corner or at the end of a hallway, whenever a stranger enters the area.

In Turkey prisoners are prohibited to write, draw, or put up a picture on a cell wall. It can also be an offense to fail to prevent crimes or disciplinary infractions by other prisoners or else to fail to notify the administration of such matters.

Corporal Punishment

The following discusses the use of physical violence as a punishment in retaliation for infractions, real or perceived. The use of random violence is discussed in the "Beatings and Restraints" section.

Among the countries where we investigated prison conditions, only two authorized corporal punishment in their prison-related laws. South Africa's Correctional Services Act 8 of 1959 authorizes the use of corporal punishment "not exceeding six strokes, if the prisoner is a convicted prisoner apparently under the age of forty years." During our 1992 visit, a Human Rights Watch delegation was told that such punishment was being used less and less often. The Minister of Correctional Services told Parliament that corporal punishment was used 120 times in 1989, 102 times in 1990 and just 44 times in 1991.[4]

Egyptian Law No. 396 of 1956 authorizes the beating of juveniles and the whipping of adult prisoners as a disciplinary penalty, in specific violation of Egypt's Constitution, which prohibits inflicting physical or mental harm on prisoners. Prisoners under seventeen years of age may be beaten ten times with a thin stick, and adults may receive up to thirty-six lashes with a specially designed whip. According to prison officials, whipping is used to punish major offenses such as striking a guard or attempting to escape.

But various forms of physical violence are used in retaliatory fashion in almost all the prison systems we investigated; moreover, violence is employed in Egypt and South Africa far in excess of what is envisioned by the law. A prisoner in Egypt was whipped for writing a letter of complaint to the country's president. Another prisoner, who had written to the president denouncing that whipping, told our delegation that a few days later he was also beaten on sensitive parts of his body by security officers and then placed in a punishment cell.

A Palestinian prisoner told us that he and some eight other prisoners went on a hunger strike in July 1991 to protest their continuing detention without charge in Egypt's Abu Za'bal prison. "We were taken out separately and beaten with sticks and with hands," he told the Human Rights Watch delegation.[5]

A Somali citizen, Mohammed Mahmud Shak, died on November 29, 1991 in an Egyptian prison after he was severely beaten following an attempted escape the previous July. About a hundred guards had taken turns beating him.

In November 1992 two prisoners in the Boniato prison in Cuba were beaten for conducting a hunger strike. The previous February another Cuban prisoner, Francisco Diaz Mesa, died from a beating he had sustained for banging on the bars of his cell to protest the denial of medical attention he needed, reportedly for pneumonia.

In China, according to one recently released political prisoner, inmates were beaten if they refused to work. Beatings in Chinese prisons have been frequent, by all accounts. Another recently released prisoner reported that guards sometimes beat inmates simply because they did not like their physical appearance.

In Czechoslovakia in June 1990—after the Velvet Revolution—a female prisoner was beaten by some six guards for looking out the window and calling out to her boyfriend.

In Kenya, a prisoner released from a maximum security prison in 1989, offered the following testimony: "Take, for example, a case when the prisoner is found with half a cigarette; when he is taken to the duty officer all the prison guards in the office will be hitting the prisoner with their batons. The most horrifying aspect of this beating is that the guards normally have as their target some of the most sensitive parts of the body, mainly the knee and hand joints, and at the end of this the prisoner can hardly walk."[6]

In a lockup in Romania we encountered a young man whose hands were swollen from beatings with a rubber truncheon for offenses such as taking too much time while in the bathroom and sleeping during the day. Many inmates reported being beaten on the palms of their hands, and several more reported witnessing such incidents.

In Puerto Rico we interviewed an inmate who described an incident in which guards kicked an inmate in his genitals in retaliation for making a complaint.

PUNITIVE SEGREGATION

Solitary Confinement

> I hold this slow and daily tampering with the mysteries of the brain to be immeasurably worse than any torture of the body; and because its ghastly signs and tokens are not so palpable to the eye and sense of touch as scars upon the flesh; because its wounds are not upon the surface, and it extorts few cries that human ears can hear; therefore I the more denounce it, as a secret punishment which slumbering humanity is not roused up to stay.[7]

Thus wrote Charles Dickens after visiting the Eastern Penitentiary in Philadelphia in 1842. At the time, solitary confinement lasted for the duration of the sentence in this prison. The cell walls were thick; each had a small yard; and each cell had a double door—one of solid oak, the other of iron grating. Hence, prisoners never saw each other and their only human contact was with the guards. Typically, they had looms in their cells, or a workbench with tools, so even work was solitary.

But Dickens could have written that passage today referring to China. Xu Wenli, an editor of a *samizdat* magazine, was arrested in April 1981. He was placed in a solitary cell, and was put to work there, attaching ornamental buckles to shoes. In 1985, in a document he managed to smuggle out, he recorded:

> I have always had a north-facing cell and have been kept in solitary confinement throughout. Since I have been able to exchange a few words each day with the prison orderlies, however, along the lines of "Lovely weather, isn't it," I have not yet been reduced to losing my ability to speak.

That smuggled document, several hundred pages long and detailing conditions of his imprisonment, earned Xu a transfer to a "special regime cell" where he spent the next several years under yet worse conditions (see below).

The duration of solitary confinement applied as punishment is usually limited by a country's law. But law and practice are all too often two entirely separate matters. In China, Article 62 of the *secret* "Detailed Rules for the Disciplinary Work of Prisons and Labor Reform Detachments" of 1982 stipulates: "Except in the case of condemned prisoners for whom final approval of execution is still pending and also the case of prisoners currently undergoing trial, the period of solitary confinement is in general not to exceed a period of seven to ten days. The maximum permissible period is fifteen days."

In Cuba a 1988 delegation that included a representative of Human Rights Watch was told that prisoners could not be kept in a punishment cell for more than twenty-one days. But one prisoner, serving twenty years for espionage, told the delegation that he had been held in solitary confinement from 1981 to 1985.

In South Africa solitary confinement may last for up to forty-two days if authorized by a magistrate.[8] Yet Breyten Breytenbach, one of the country's foremost writers, arrested for returning to the country illegally from exile in Paris and trying to set up a mixed-race democratic organization, was held in solitary confinement for two of the seven years of his imprisonment.[9]

In Poland an inmate interviewed in a punishment cell during our 1989 visit talked to us of his fears about "losing his mind." Another said, "I get depressed very easily, and stupid thoughts come to mind, like suicide."[10] The maximum time in isolation was then six months. It was subsequently reduced to one month.

In addition to concerns over the length of time inmates spend in solitary confinement, we were also distressed by how easily this supposedly most serious of sanctions is meted out to prisoners.

In Russia almost any violation of the rules—including cursing at or showing disrespect for the guards, refusing to work, arguing with other inmates, or not meeting a production quota—can result in a term in a punishment cell.

In Cuba an inmate was punished with forty-five days in solitary confinement for writing a letter to the Nicaraguan leader, Violeta Chamorro, congratulating her on winning the presidential election.

Vaclav Havel, now the President of the Czech Republic, was put in solitary confinement once for drafting letters for an illiterate gypsy.

Isolation in Conjunction with Other Measures

Even though isolation is usually considered the most severe disciplinary measure, in several countries Human Rights Watch found that it was applied in combination with additional sanctions.

An inmate in Poland told us, "I'm beginning to feel crazy; I get no mail, no cigarettes, no visits."[11]

In South Africa inmates in disciplinary segregation are often further punished through reduced diet. Similarly, in Cuba, prisoners in punishment cells are fed only twice a day and one of those "meals" barely qualifies as such.

In Romania inmates in isolation are required to get up at 5 A.M. and to stand in their cells until 10 P.M. During that time, beds are folded up against the wall. The light is kept on day and night.

In the United States, inmates in segregation in the women's jail in Los Angeles may be additionally punished with a special diet, consisting of fully nutritional but utterly tasteless balls of a specially-prepared blend of nutritive substances.

In Russia during solitary confinement prisoners are forbidden to have possessions with them and are denied almost all other rights, including the right to exercise.

In several countries, physical restraints are used as an additional punishment in isolation cells.

Punishment Cells

Punishment cells, in addition to separating some inmates from the rest of the prison population, are frequently designed specifically to inflict physical hardships on their occupants.

In Indonesia, a former prisoner held in Besi prison in Java, described the punishment cell there as one meter square—too small to lie down.

In Russia, punishment cells—where up to three prisoners at a time may be segregated from the rest of the population—are very small (about eleven feet by ten feet), have stucco walls (which are painful to lean against), often have no windows, and have very dirty toilets. Beds in punishment cells have no mattresses.

In South Africa punishment cells are bare except for a mat on the floor for a prisoner to sleep on and a sink and a toilet. We were also told of the use of so-called "dark cells," with no windows and barely enough space to lie down.

In Cuba, punishment cells in the notorious "rectangle of death" in the Combinado del Este prison in Havana, where many of the most prominent political prisoners served their sentences, were about ten feet long and four feet wide. Up to two people were held in each, although there were triple concrete bunks—with no bedding—indicating that three could be housed there as well. The toilet was a hole in the floor that often becomes clogged, spilling into the cell. Every cell was separated from the hallway by two doors: a barred one, partially covered by sheet metal, and a wooden one that completely shuts out ventilation and light from the hallway and was arbitrarily opened or closed by prison guards. Just inside the wooden door was a very dim light bulb, by which one could not even see one's hands. Similar cells are used in punishment wings of three other men's prisons that we saw.

In Zaire punishment cells have no windows and no ventilation; prisoners may be held in them for up to forty-five days.

In the U.S. cells in the punishment Q-wing at the Florida State Prison had no windows and very poor ventilation.

In China, the "strict regime" cell to which Xu Wenli was transferred after publicizing the conditions of his earlier imprisonment (see above), was a windowless, damp vault in which a light bulb shone relentlessly day and night. The cell was too small to stand up straight. It crawled with insects. There was a strip of matting on the concrete floor to sleep on and a bucket placed in a corner served as a toilet. Xu spent no less than three-and-a-half years in this cell.

In a Romanian lockup, our delegation saw two windowless cells measuring two-and-a-half by two feet, approximately half the size of a telephone booth. There was no source of light and no possibility to sit comfortably. In several interviews with inmates, we were told that these cells were used frequently, often for a few hours at a time. Such cells are known as *chiquitas* in Nicaragua where they were used in pre-trial detention facilities during the Sandanista period, also for a few hours at a time.

In Brazil we documented a particularly horrific example of the use of a punishment cell. In February 1989, Military Police called to São Paulo's Police Precinct 42 in response to a disturbance that erupted in the lockup, forced fifty-one men into a cell measuring less than fifty square feet, with a heavy metal door and no windows, and held them there for more than an hour. When the door was opened, eighteen prisoners were found to have suffocated to death.

THE USE OF PHYSICAL RESTRAINTS

Chains, leg irons, fetters, and shackles are prison-related artifacts one might associate with medieval times rather than the end of the twentieth century. Yet, in several countries, Human Rights Watch found various types of physical restraints are used today to punish prisoners. We want to stress a clear distinction between the legitimate use of physical restraints employed temporarily to subdue a frenzied prisoner, or as a security precaution for particularly violent or dangerous prisoners during transfers or on similar occasions, and the punitive use of physical restraints.

Leg irons and handcuffs are commonly used as a means of punishment in Romania. During our delegation's 1991 visit, we observed numerous prisoners who were shackled in leg chains and/or handcuffs for extended periods. One prisoner told us he had spent eight months in chains in Section Two of the Poarta Alba prison. At Gehrla prison, eight prisoners who had participated in the August 1990 revolt at this prison were still in leg irons and handcuffs when our delegation visited in October of the following year. We spoke to one prisoner who had been sentenced to an extra three years in prison for participation in that revolt. In addition he had been kept in restraints for fourteen months. He was unable to lift his arms above his chest and had callusses where the handcuffs rubbed his wrists.

Nor had things changed much in Romania the following year (1992) when our next delegation received repeated reports of the use of chains, handcuffs (including handcuffing an inmate to the wall in one case) and leg irons as punishment in the lockups.

In China prison rules, which all cadres and inmates are supposed to learn by heart, authorize the use of chains and fetters for those who violate the regulations "in more serious cases."[12] A wide variety of implements are in use, including handcuffs, ankle fetters, and chains. Under the law, the time limit for the use of physical restraints (with the exception of prisoners condemned to death) is fifteen days; in practice, however, such time limits are ignored.

In South Africa restraints are used as an additional means to punish those in isolation. During a 1993 visit by a Human Rights Watch delegation, we saw one inmate in an isolation cell with a chain about a foot-and-a-half long around his ankles.

In India physical restraints—fetters, shackles and handcuffs—are employed more commonly than punishment cells to deal with those who commit infractions. The use of these restraints is prescribed by the Jail Manuals, which spell out in great detail the specific manner in which prisoners should be treated. The Punjab Jail Manual, for example, provides for three kinds of handcuffs. An iron bar variety may not weigh more than twenty-one pounds. As for the leg fetters, one variety that is specified and whose use in practice was reported to us in interviews, has a bar that holds the legs apart. Though the manual says that the bar may be no more than sixteen inches in length, a former inmate gave us a description of a much longer bar that holds the legs apart in such a manner as to cause great pain after the legs have been kept in this position for an extended period. The manual allows the sixteen-inch bar to be used for up to ten days at a time, and other leg fetters may be used for up to three months at a time.

In Zaire, leg chains and metal spans are used in many prisons, mostly in the interior of the country. The restraints often cause severe burns to the skin and require a hacksaw to be removed.

PUNISHMENTS RELATED TO CONTACTS WITH RELATIVES

Reduced contacts with relatives are often used as a disciplinary measure and are a matter of serious concern. Any such measure to penalize a prisoner for some infraction also penalizes his or her family.

In some countries inmates who commit infractions are transferred to a different institution as a punishment. This often makes family visits more difficult or impossible. It is a particularly serious problem in countries that span great distances.

In Puerto Rico inmates "who cause trouble" are sometimes transferred to a prison in the continental United States. This usually ends visits because air travel is both time-consuming and expensive.

In Spain inmates are sometimes transferred from one end of the country to another as punishment. This measure is used particularly against riot leaders, real or suspected.

In the United Kingdom we were told of a practice nicknamed "ghosting," for particularly disruptive prisoners. This consists of moving such an inmate frequently throughout the prison system, presumably to make it impossible to establish ties within any prison population. It also makes it difficult for relatives to visit such a prisoner. One prisoner reported he had been held in more than thirty institutions during a four-year period.

In addition, a ban on correspondence and visits is frequently used in conjunction with punitive segregation.

UNUSUAL FORMS OF PUNISHMENT

Prison administrations are inventive not only in defining offenses but in designing punishments. In addition to the sanctions described above which are used in many prison systems, Human Rights Watch encountered a few that are peculiar to a single system.

In China prisoners reported that guards would sometimes make an inmate stand naked in the middle of his cell for such offenses as talking to a neighbor during the night.[13] Also in China, inmates are sometimes made to sit motionless for hours every day, staring at a wall, so that they "repent their sins."[14]

In Egypt an inmate's clothes may be shredded as a punishment in addition to placement in a punishment cell.

In the U.S., 1990 court records describe a punishment called "strip status."[15] An inmate was stripped of all clothing, bedding and personal possessions. He was then expected to "earn" back items piece-by-piece through good behavior. The Oregon correctional authorities, under whose jurisdiction this practice was applied, claim this punishment is no longer in use.

A prisoner in Indonesia was punished for playing music by a requirement to walk stooped for two hours. Another form of punishment in Indonesia was to force an inmate to kick rocks with his feet. And a particularly cruel form of punishment for political prisoners in Cuba has been the denial of medical attention.

The Punitive Use of a "Privilege" System

In South African prisons, almost everything that is not prohibited is declared to be a "privilege": possessions, letters, visits, access to reading material, permission to write literary pieces, authorization to have a TV set in one's cell and more. Inmates are divided into "privilege" groups A, B, C, and D, regardless of their security classification and the type of institution they are in. All prisoners start in group C; their classification is reviewed at half-year intervals, by an "Institutional Committee" (composed of prison staff members), which upgrades or downgrades prisoners according to their behavior. Under this system a prisoner has to gain the most basic rights—such as contact visits with relatives—through a spotless disciplinary record. Even then, it takes at least one year to move from the entry, or C level, to A group, the only one permitted contact visits.

COLLECTIVE PUNISHMENT

In several countries, we heard complaints that prisoners are often punished as a group without respect to whether they were individually involved in committing an infraction. Collective punishment is, of course, a serious violation of due process; it also adds to a prisoner's feeling that he or she has lost individuality and become a pawn in a large system.

When we visited the Barbetron maximum security prison in South Africa, we found that one whole section was then deprived of access to sports and recreation as punishment for a gang fight several weeks earlier.

In the U.S., at the time of our visit to the Immigration and Naturalization Service (INS) detention center at Krome, Florida (where illegal aliens were held), we were told that all the women in the institution were being punished for a protest by some of them that consisted of messing up the bathroom.

Collective punishment is most frequent in the aftermath of prison protests and disturbances.

DUE PROCESS IN DISCIPLINARY PROCEDURE

Every prison should have a disciplinary procedure and prisoners should be informed of the offenses for which they are punished and the extent of that punishment. They should also be given an opportunity to defend themselves and to appeal. Even though such a procedure usually exists on the books in most countries Human Rights Watch visited, more often than not it was violated in practice.

In particular, we are concerned that in most countries, punishments are meted out arbitrarily by prison officials without external oversight and that there is no effective mechanism for appeal. This often leads to the application of sanctions that are disproportionately harsh for the offenses committed, and affords the staff opportunities to exercise undue pressure or to avenge personal grievances.

UNDECLARED PUNISHMENTS

In countries where law is respected and where disciplinary sanctions in prisons require due process, a problem nevertheless arises when measures are taken that are declared not to be punishment but, in fact, are punitive. Such measures may be imposed arbitrarily by the prison staff, without the possibility of an appeal, and with no time limit on their duration.

In England and Wales, under Prison Rule 43, the prison director may decide to separate some prisoners from the general population for the maintenance of the "good order and discipline" of the institution. Prisoners in England and Wales are generally entitled to a disciplinary hearing if they are charged with a disciplinary offense, but the invocation of Rule 43 circumvents this right. No specific offense is needed to mark a prisoner for segregation and Rule 43 does not specify duration.[16]

In the United States, many prison systems— including the federal, more than thirty state systems and some local jails—have recently designated separate institutions or parts of institutions for the confinement of prisoners under particularly harsh conditions and exceptionally strict security. Such assignment often amounts to solitary confinement for years on end. In the Florida State Prison at Starke, some inmates are held in windowless cells from which they are allowed out only three times a week, for ten minutes, to shower. Otherwise, they are alone in the cell. Such confinement may last for extended periods; some of the inmates Human Rights Watch interviewed in that prison had not been outdoors for several years. In the Maximum Control Complex in Westville, Indiana, inmates are locked in their cells for between twenty-two-and-a-half and twenty-four hours a day, never see anyone except their guards, and are often punished through the loss of access to reading materials, among other measures.

In Marion, Illinois, the harshest prison within the U.S. federal system and the model for these particularly punitive prisons, where an average stay lasts three years, prisoners are locked in their cells around the clock, except for recreation (between seven and eleven hours a week, depending on classification). Yet placement there is technically not considered a disciplinary measure; it is administrative, and as such is not preceded by a hearing. As a result an inmate is afforded no possibility of appeal, and this sanction is open-ended. The decision to confine an inmate in such an institution is made by prison administrators alone and is often based on the mere prediction that an inmate will be dangerous or predatory rather than on any actual infraction.

In Israel conditions in the modern ultra-maximum security wing of Nitzan prison are the strictest in the system and are the cause of grave concern. According to officials, prisoners are assigned to the wing on the grounds that they pose a physical danger to guards or other prisoners. However, assignment to Nitzan is clearly used as a means of punishment, particularly against Islamists whose original crimes are considered exceptionally heinous or whom the authorities wish to punish for other reasons. Inmates, all of them Palestinians from Israel or the occupied territories, are confined to their one-man cells twenty-three hours a day, and may never go out unless handcuffed. They must wear legcuffs during visits by relatives and lawyers. Conditions at Nitzan's Ward Eight are harsher than at other facilities in ways that have little to do with protecting others. The cells are partly below street level and have poor ventilation and little natural light; access to reading materials is more restricted than at other prisons; and beatings by guards are reported to be more common than at other facilities of the Israeli Prison Service.

RECOMMENDATIONS

Sanctions for violating the rules are necessary in prisons, as they are in any society or community if it is to function properly. But, as the examples cited in this chapter demonstrate, a fundamental right—freedom from cruel and unusual punishment—is often ignored when it comes to punishing prisoners. To eradicate cruelty inflicted on prisoners by prison staff is not a matter of huge investments. What is needed most of all is a policy decision at the central level of the country's prison administration and the will to enforce this policy. Human Rights Watch believes that disciplinary measures, whether authorized or not, should be closely scrutinized by all those monitoring prison conditions: official prison inspectors, judges, nongovernmental organizations, and international bodies. In addition Human Rights Watch specifically recommends that:

- disciplinary measures should be standardized countrywide and set at the central administration level;

- prisons should keep a log of all punishments meted out;

- every prison system should have a means of monitoring the use of disciplinary measures in prisons, independent of the penal administration; the results of such monitoring should be a matter of public record;

- prison officials who employ extralegal disciplinary measures should themselves be disciplined;

- a disciplinary sanction may only be applied when the offense for which it is meted out has been specified in advance and the prisoner has been informed that such conduct is prohibited;

- upon their arrival in an institution, prisoners must be informed what constitutes an offense and the corresponding penalty;

- prisoners must be given an opportunity to appeal a disciplinary sanction to an independent decision-maker;

- no disciplinary sanction may be imposed indefinitely (i.e., "pending review");

- corporal punishment may never be imposed;

- denial of medical care may never be imposed as punishment;

- deprivation of food or deliberately distasteful food should never be used as punishment;

- deprivation of bedding and clothing should never be used as punishment;

- physical restraints may never be used for disciplinary purposes. When used to restrain a distraught or violent prisoner, they may only be used temporarily, and care must be taken not to cause physical injuries;

- prisoners should not be required to "gain" their basic rights with good behavior; punishments consisting of loss of privileges should be clearly defined and limited in time;

- collective punishment may never be imposed;

- disciplinary measures restricting contacts with relatives should be used as punishment solely for infractions related to those contacts (smuggling contraband, for example). Punitive transfer to distant institutions should never be imposed;

- solitary confinement should be used sparingly and never for longer than a few days;

- punishment cells, whether solitary or collective, should have toilet facilities and such basic furniture as a bed with bedding as well as proper light and ventilation. Cells that are intended to cause physical hardship (because they are too small, very stuffy or dark, for example) should never be used.

BEATINGS AND RESTRAINTS

Many of the human rights abuses that occur in prisons involve the violation of perhaps the most fundamental right of all: the right to physical integrity. Frequently, prisoners are deliberately subjected to a high degree of violence and physical abuse intended either as retaliation or summary punishment or to achieve a particular goal, such as obtaining a confession, breaking a prisoner's morale, extorting a bribe or simply intimidating the inmate. In some cases, the goal may also be sexual.

The most frequent reports of torture, beatings and other physical abuses come from police stations and take place during the investigatory stages of imprisonment. In some countries, torture is routinely used to extract a confession or information, in political and criminal cases alike. In a few instances, torture and other forms of police brutality function as a form of summary punishment, usually with tacit official sanction and explicit—especially in the cases of criminal rather than political suspects—public approval.[17] By and large, Human Rights Watch has considered torture separately from the general problem of prison conditions. We have published numerous reports on torture including some devoted almost exclusively to this question. Here, we focus on physical abuses against prisoners that, for the most part, are not related to the investigation as such.

Sentenced prisoners or prisoners in whose cases investigation has been completed are far from being free from official physical abuse. New arrivals to a prison are frequently beaten by guards to intimidate them. At some prisons, random bursts of violence, or violent searches, are reported to take place without apparent provocation by prisoners, and are presumably intended to maintain a constant level of fear. There are also reports of sexual abuse by the staff, usually with respect to women.

TORTURE TO EXTORT BRIBES

In India and in Indonesia police routinely beat virtually all criminal suspects. In both countries bribes—by the detainee or by the family—are reportedly paid to avoid torture. This system can only work if those who cannot pay are indeed tortured and the reputation of the police is such that those who can pay will not hesitate to do so quickly. Though the extortion of bribes appears to be the main purpose for the physical abuse of detainees in India, an important contributing factor is widespread public endorsement of summary punishment against those believed to have engaged in crime.

BEATINGS AND HUMILIATION OF NEW ARRIVALS

In several countries newly arriving prisoners are subjected to particularly brutal and demeaning treatment, meant, apparently, to intimidate them. In country after country, we received testimonies about "Let's get acquainted" beatings.

One former prisoner provided this detailed testimony describing a gruesome rite of initiation in Kenya:

> When we first got in there, we were told to take all our clothes off. They make you jump up and down to prove that nothing is being carried in your body. Then you are made to bend over naked and they search your anus with a cane. They do it like torture. Then

they make you sit squatting—still naked—for long hours at a time, and tell you they will "initiate" you. They told us "you people are going to see." You are left squatting naked in the cell, in the dark, and suddenly they burst in and beat you thoroughly with sticks and batons. They attack you particularly on the joints, on your shoulders, head, knees, and elbows. You will be beaten like that for some time—over a period of days. After three days, our names were then read out for what kind of work we would be doing and our "initiation" ceremony would be finished.[18]

Accounts from Egypt echo this one from Kenya. A former security detainee described to us his treatment when he arrived at the Tora Istikbal prison in March 1991, after eighteen days of detention and torture. Upon his arrival in the prison, his head was shaved, after which he was brought to a holding area where there was a line of security force soldiers. He and the other detainees were forced to walk down the line, past the soldiers. "Each one takes a punch at you," he told us. A trade unionist, imprisoned in 1989 in the same institution, also got a special "reception." He and the other detainees who arrived with him were made to cross a gauntlet of security forces soldiers. Another prisoner, a U.S. citizen, witnessed similar beatings of newly arrived prisoners in the al–Khalifa prison in Cairo. He said that he saw a "long bull whip, black or brown," on the booking table. Though he was not beaten, the other new arrivals at the same time were whipped and beaten with sticks.[19] In Turkey, similarly, according to interviews we conducted with former political prisoners, nonpolitical newcomers are often beaten.

In the Agua Santa prison in Rio de Janeiro we also received reports about "initiation" torture sessions. An official report by the Ministry of Justice revealed the existence of a room the inmates called the "maracana," where inmates were allegedly beaten and asphyxiated with smoke from burning paper.

RANDOM BURSTS OF VIOLENCE

Violence Against the Physical Integrity of Inmates

Violence in prisons is often completely random; prisoners are not able to anticipate the moment or guess the occasion for these sudden eruptions. In some countries, prisoners insisted to us that the guards must derive some perverse pleasure from such abuse. Whether or not tormenting prisoners does serve some such needs of their keepers, it serves another purpose well. It sows terror and maintains anxiety among inmates. And this, as one former prisoner in China put it, "simply makes it easier for the staff to 'maintain order.'" Violence in Chinese prisons is indeed frequent and comes in many different forms, including beatings; whipping a prisoner who has been ordered to drop his pants; assaults with electric batons; and more.[20]

In Jamaica we received numerous reports of violence from death row inmates. Guards frequently beat the condemned and took away whatever private possessions they might have accumulated. This is particularly cruel because death row inmates, even without such random bursts of violence, live in constant anxiety. The general prison population is also not free from such abuse. Former prisoners interviewed by the Jamaican Council on Human Rights reported random beatings, usually with sticks, sometimes with boards or straps. Frequently three or four warders would beat one prisoner; in fact it was rare for just one guard to beat a prisoner.

In Kenya, according to former prisoners, strip searches, anal searches, beatings, psychological humiliation and grueling physical exercises are an integral part of the prison system.

In Romania, in the course of our 1991 visit, we were told that: "On occasion the guards take the prisoners out of their cells and make them lie on the floor in the halls. Then they walk on them and polish their shoes with their clothes. This happened to us about four months ago."[21]

We also heard testimonies of unprovoked, random violence against prisoners in Brazil and Egypt.

Violent Cell Searches

A cell is the only place where a prisoner can create some private space for himself, the place where he or she stores such private belongings—usually very few—may be permitted. Violent cell searches, which we discovered in many prison systems, are usually marked by the destruction of these few possessions. Prisoners told us that the resulting pain is not simply a consequence of that loss, but involves a sense of physical violation as well. Indeed, violent, random cell searches seem intended less to capture prohibited objects or substances, but rather to instill precisely this sense of physical violation and the concomitant increase in the sense of insecurity.

In Brazil, we heard of frequent "blitzes," assaults during which guards usually did not beat prisoners but broke everything in the cell. "The guards burst in without notice, with dogs," one inmate told us in a typical account, "and get us out of the cell. Those who won't go, get hit. They then break all our possessions, step on and smash the little furniture and other things we make [inmates often make miniature objects of matches or other pieces of wood], and break the radios and TVs we get from our families."[22]

In Czechoslovakia, we were told that, a few weeks prior to our 1990 visit to the Pizen-Bory prison, guards had entered a cell block and smashed everything.[23]

In China's Hunan province, the raids are ostensibly carried out to inspect cells and ascertain that no forbidden goods are concealed. They have gained the metaphorical name, "Saochai descending from the mountain top." *Saochai*, meaning "those who sweep the firewood," is prison slang for officers of the People's Armed Police, who patrol the prison perimeter. The phrase "descending from the mountain top" refers to the occasions on which the officers are ordered down from their watch towers to conduct the raids on the cells.[24]

In Turkey we also compiled reports of guards bursting into cells and tearing up everything in sight—books, bedding, or clothing. In Jamaica death row cells are the frequent target of such raids. In Egypt violent searches are sometimes accompanied by violence against the prisoners. In one prison, for example, prisoners had a chemical sprayed into their eyes during a cell search.

SEXUAL ABUSE

Sexual abuse, usually against women, is frequently used during investigation as a means of intimidation or torture. Human Rights Watch has documented such practices in several of its reports, including *Double Jeopardy: Police Abuse of Women in Pakistan.* At times, rape is evidently used merely as a means of domination.

In the Spanish Town lockup in Jamaica, several women whispered to one member of our mission that the guards took them out of the cell at night and forced them to have sexual relations. In India we received numerous reports of rapes in police custody that seemed to serve one purpose only: the pleasure of the constables. A former inmate interviewed in Puerto Rico said that on her third day at the Vega Alta women's prison, she heard another inmate screaming in her cell. At the time there was a general lock down. The screaming inmate subsequently told her that she had been raped by male guards. In the late 1980s there was a wave of reported sexual assaults by male guards at the California Institution for Women.

Men are not entirely spared sexual abuse by guards. In Kenya former prisoners reported a practice dubbed "terror" in the prison slang. Every morning, prisoners were required to take off their clothes, come out of their wards and squat. This was ostensibly done as part of a search but, as one former prisoner insisted, "The guards carrying out the search are more interested in the nakedness of the prisoners than in the search."[25]

In more than one country, we have also received reports of prison guards deliberately placing vulnerable prisoners in cells in which they would be raped by their fellow inmates.

VIOLENCE AGAINST PARTICULARLY VULNERABLE INMATES

Violence Against Women

Women are especially vulnerable to violence while in custody and in some countries we encountered instances of particular cruelty against them. In Kenyan prisons beatings are the most common form of physical abuse against women.

The Bombay Lawyers Committee reported after interviewing all the women held in the Bombay Central Jail in 1987 that more than 50 percent complained about violence and abuse. (It is worth noting that Indian law makes extrajudicial confessions inadmissible at trial, so obtaining a confession could not have been the goal.) Women in Bombay complained of being whipped with belts, especially on the thigh and upper leg, or of being hung with a pole around the back of the neck and arms, or of having their hair yanked by two policemen from either side—all this, usually, with threats of worse to come.

Violence in Punishment Cells

In South Africa we received reports of beatings of prisoners confined to punishment cells and thus *defacto* held incommunicado. We heard similar reports in Egypt. In Cuba prisoners told us they were beaten as they were taken to punishment cells.

RECOMMENDATIONS

Violence by those charged with law enforcement—that is police and prison staff—is a serious and troubling phenomenon and reflects a low regard for the rule of law. But in contrast to some other aspects of prison conditions, violence and cruelty perpetrated by the prison staff can be decreased by changes in policy and attitude. Simple policy changes do not necessarily require huge investments. Our observations in Poland and Czechoslovakia, in whose prisons physical abuses had been rampant under communism and where they have been largely eliminated since the democratic transformation of 1989, prove that improvements are possible. Governments must make it a priority to eradicate violence from their places of confinement. In particular Human Rights Watch recommends that:

- prison guards guilty of physical abuses should be disciplined and, in serious cases, prosecuted for assault, rape or other criminal offenses;

- prisoners should have access to legal information so they can be aware which practices by the staff are illegal under the country's laws, and they should be afforded a way to file confidential complaints;

- so as to allow identification of assailants and thus decrease the possibility of assault, prison staff should always wear identification badges. The failure to wear such a badge should be considered a disciplinary infraction;

- in countries where practices of physical abuse are reported by the press or by domestic or international human rights monitors, independent investigative commissions should be established to examine these accusations, identify those responsible for such abuses and to take the disciplinary measures required to eliminate such behavior and provide the information to law enforcement agencies required to initiate prosecutions.

➤ DISCUSSION QUESTIONS

Recommendations are made at several points throughout this report. Do any of these recommendations seem unreasonable? Are there any that you would add?

NOTES

1. See Dunkel & van Zyl Smit, *Imprisonment Today and Tomorrow: International Perspectives on Prisoners' Rights and Prison Conditions* (Boston: Kluwer, 1991), p. 726.

2. *Bounds v. Smith* 430 U.S. 817, 97 S.Ct., 1491, 52 L.Ed.2d (1977).

3. Paul R. Williams, *Treatment of Detainees: Examination of Issues Relevant to Detention by the United Nations Human Rights Committee* (Geneva: Henry Dunant Institute, 1990), and *U.N. Human Rights Committee Report,* 1987 (A/42/40), p. 17.

4. *S.A. Barometer,* vol. 6, no. 19 (September 25, 1992).

5. Middle East Watch, *Prison Conditions in Egypt* (New York: Human Rights Watch, 1993), p. 91.

6. Africa Watch, *Kenya: Taking Liberties* (New York: Human Rights Watch, 1991), p. 167.

7. Charles Dickens, *American Notes.*

8. Dirk van Zyl Smit, *South African Prison Law and Practice* (Durban: Butterworth, 1992).

9. Breytenbach describes his prison experience in *The True Confessions of an Albino Terrorist* (New York: Farrar, Straus & Giroux, 1985).

10. Helsinki Watch, *Prison Conditions in Poland* (New York: Human Rights Watch, 1991), p. 30.

11. Helsinki Watch, *Prison Conditions in Poland: An Update* (New York: Human Rights Watch, 1991), p. 30.

12. Asia Watch, *Anthems of Defeat: Crackdown Hunan Province* 1989–1992 (New York: Human Rights Watch, 1992), p. 77.

13. Human Rights Watch interview, December 1992.

14. Asia Watch, *Anthems of Defeat*, p. 94.

15. *Honed v. Maass*, 745 F. Supp. 623 (D.Or. 1990), cited in Human Rights Watch, *Prison Conditions in the United States* (New York: 1991), p. 47.

16. Prison Rule 43 states: "Where it appears desirable, for the maintenance of the good order and discipline or in his own interests, that a prisoner should not associate with other prisoners, either generally or for particular purposes, the prison director may arrange for the prisoner's removal from association accordingly." Helsinki Watch, *Prison Conditions in the United Kingdom* (New York: Human Rights Watch, 1992), p. 17.

17. See Americas Watch, *Police Abuse in Brazil: Summary Executions and Torture in São Paulo and Rio de Janeiro* (New York: Human Rights Watch, 1987).

18. Africa Watch, *Kenya: Taking Liberties* (New York: Human Rights Watch, 1991), p. 167.

19. Middle East Watch, *Prison Conditions in Egypt* (New York: Human Rights Watch, 1993), pp. 92, 96.

20. For detailed descriptions of various forms of physical abuse see Asia Watch, *Anthems of Defeat: Crackdoun in Hunan Province* 1989–1992 (New York: Human Rights Watch, 1992), pp. 74–75, 80.

21. Helsinki Watch, *Prison Conditions in Romania* (New York: Human Rights Watch, 1992), p. 20.

22. Americas Watch *Prison Conditions in Brazil* (New York: Human Rights Watch, 1989), pp. 25–26.

23. Helsinki Watch, *Prison Conditions in Czechoslovakia: An Update* (New York: Human Rights Watch, 1991), p. 14.

24. Asia Watch, *Anthems of Defeat*, pp. 81–82.

25. Africa Watch, *Kenya*, p. 168.

The Case for Going Dutch: The Lessons of Post-War Penal Policy

■ *DAVID DOWNES*

INTRODUCTORY NOTES

The substance of this article might seem alien to most Americans. The writer, an Englishman writing in favor of the liberal policies in the Dutch prison system, never questions the motives or authenticity of the prisoners that he has interviewed, nor does he discuss the issue of retribution. Indeed the Dutch public does not seem nearly as retributive as the American public. Americans reading about the correctional system in The Netherlands are likely to think that Dutch prisoners do not suffer enough.

Furthermore, the author does not consider how such liberalized policies might impact recidivism or deterrence. The fact that this author can write and publish this article without mention of recidivism or deterrence suggests a philosophy or attitude towards crime that is completely foreign to most Americans. Apparently, Dutch and American correctional priorities are quite different: high on our list of priorities are crime control and retribution, whereas the Dutch seem to place a much higher priority on the humane treatment of the offender—and their crime rates remain quite low.

Many Americans reading this article may wonder how the Dutch can manage to be so lenient toward their criminals; such leniency seems unnatural. The American may think that it is human nature to despise the criminal. But the sociologist is very leery of the concept of human nature. Traits attributed to human nature are almost always learned instead. Brief mention is made in this article of an "active fostering of community tolerance and media support for broadly rehabilitative rather than punitive policies," suggesting that Dutch attitudes toward crime are acquired through a process of learning. Surely, other aspects of the Dutch culture foster such an attitude in a less active fashion.

Likewise, our punitive attitudes toward crime, rather than reflecting some inborn trait, are also learned in the culture. For example, while the Dutch media are fostering tolerance, our media are constantly hammering us with exaggerated stories of skyrocketing crime rates, blood and gore, random acts of sadism, abused legal loopholes, and cushy prisons. It's no wonder that we think that it's human nature to despise the criminal.

SOURCE: David Downes, "The Case for Going Dutch: The Lessons of Post-War Penal Policy," *The Political Quarterly,* vol. 63, no. 1 (1992): 12–24. Reprinted with permission from Blackwell Publishers.

The 1980s proved a better decade for comparative criminology, at least for the study of penal policy and practice, than most periods since the 1780s, when John Howard's third, revised edition of *The State of the Prisons in England and Wales* was greatly extended to include 'preliminary observations and an account of some foreign prisons and hospitals'. Howard had few notable successors, though two were de Beaumont and de Tocqueville, out of whose mission to report *On the Penitentiary System in the United States and Its Application to France* (1833) sprang *Democracy in America*. The next peak, over a century away, was Rusche and Kirchheimer's *Punishment and Social Structure* (1939), though Kropotkin's remarkable *In Russian and French Prisons* (1887) and Durkheim's theory of penal evolution (1902) are related endeavors. Explaining this abeyance in comparative inquiry would take an essay in itself, but the rise of positivism—which placed an almost exclusive focus on the individual properties of the offender—and the faith in progress and prosperity as solvents of criminality which would supersede imprisonment, are likely causes. Perhaps it was only by the late 1970s that such forms of optimism declined to the point where the comparative method was restored to salience.

In Britain, more immediately compelling reasons existed that encouraged a revival of comparative inquiry in differing criminal justice and penal systems. The impasse in penal policy borne of the rising crime rate, the failure of measures to reduce or even stem the rising prison population, the loss of faith in rehabilitation and the degrading character of the prison estate culminated in industrial conflict between prison staff and the Home Office. The Committee of Inquiry under Mr. Justice May (1979),[1] despite winning a wider policy brief, disappointed by its tepid reformism, though it yielded a crucial step forward by its recommendation of an inspectorate independent of the Prison Department. Policy was locked into a separation of powers that forbade any coordination of objectives by the executive and the judiciary; into an acceptance of the equation between rising crime rates and prison populations; and into an inability to translate soaring costs into anything but declining standards. That things did not have to be so was signified by a small but significant number of societies whose penal policies and practices contrasted sharply with our own.

Of these, The Netherlands provided the major instance of achieving durable reforms on the basis of substantial reductions in the prison population until the mid-1970s and phased increases in line with capacity during the 1980s until now. Far from being irrelevant to our predicament, their achievement embodies options we have so far largely ignored, although—with publication of the Woolf Report—we now have the basis for comparable action. Indeed, Woolf and his team of assessors visited and interviewed prisoners in Canada, The Netherlands and Spain as part of their inquiry for the second, more policy-oriented section of the report (1991).[2]

THE COMPARATIVE BACKGROUND

The essential facts about trends in the prison populations of the two countries since 1945 are well known and attested. They are that the daily average populations stood in 1950 at much the same level in terms of prisoners per 100,000 of the population as a whole. By 1975, the Dutch prison population had fallen to less than half that of 1950, whereas that of England and Wales had doubled, leading to a difference in the ratio of prison:general population of 1:4 in contrast to the 1:1 ratio of 25 years earlier. Since 1975, the gap has narrowed to 1:2 following greater proportionate rise in the Dutch than the English prison population over the past 10 years. On August 30, 1991, Dutch prisoners numbered 6,970, those in England and Wales 46,701 (including 1,534 in police cells), 47 and 96 per 100,000 respectively.[*] Though the gap is closing, the difference remains striking. It should be noted that crime rates in both countries were much the same in 1950 and 1990, despite growing at different rates in the interim.[3]

It should also be noted that, historically, over much of the century before 1990, until the mid-1950s, the Dutch prison population stood at a higher level, on this basis, than the English; that the Dutch prison system until the post-1945 period was in many respects as harsh, in the respect of solitary confinement harsher, than the English;[4] and that measures of the tolerance of Dutch public opinion in relation to crime (most recently in the 1988 cross-national victim survey) do not reveal any markedly greater leniency towards or acceptance of crime than in this country. These facts rule out any recourse to historical inevitability of innate population characteristics as explanations for the sharp divergence in post-war penal trends between the two countries. Nor can they be explained away as the product of differences in the crime and clear-up rates; the masking of imprisonment; or the use of alternative institutional measures. In 1980, differences in sentence lengths accounted for 38 percent, and the use of custodial sentences for 23 percent, of the gap between Dutch and English prison population levels; i.e., almost two-thirds of the variation was accounted for by sentencing variables.[5]

While the course of the variation can be clearly laid out, its causes remain more contentious. It is arguably easier to account for the trend in England than in The Netherlands, since in this country the twin criteria of consistency and seriousness of offense, insofar as these have been identified as key predictors of sentence, broadly fit the trends. As the crime rate has risen, so has the prison population: though, it should be noted, by no means in parallel fashion, for a seven-fold rise in the crime rate since 1950 has been accompanied by a smaller rise of 150 percent in the prison population—logically, attempts to reduce the resort to imprisonment have met with some success. However, comparatively speaking, in relation to other European countries, not only The Netherlands, this relative decarceration has been too limited to provide breathing space for fundamental penal reconstruction. The causes for the far more striking decarceration in The Netherlands are plausibly to be found in the extent to which the Dutch judiciary embraced rehabilitative measures as an alternative to custody in the 1950s, a development upheld in policy terms by the public prosecutors even when after the mid-1960s, rehabilitative measures receded in judicial popularity. The quiet revolution in judicial sentencing of the 1950s and 1960s persisted even when, in the late 1970s, the steeper rise in the crime rate led to an end to actual falls in the prison population, and enables the Dutch prison population, despite the expansion of the past decade, to remain virtually the lowest in Europe. While lack of opposition to such trends is not in itself a cause, the active fostering of community tolerance and media support for broadly rehabilitative rather than punitive policies was crucial to their development.

The substantial falls in the prison population presented penal policy-makers and practitioners with an opportunity for reconstruction which they built on systematically and steadily from the Fick Committee Report of 1947 onwards. Dutch prisons

---

[*]Editor's Note: Compare these figures to the rate of incarceration per 100,000 population in the United States of 455 (*The Sentencing Project*, Americans Behind Bars: One Year Later, 1992).

had been noted for their severe austerity and commitment to virtual solitary confinement—the historical basis for their one-to-a-cell policy maintained until present. The Fick Committee introduced far more freedom of association into regimes, the precondition for liberalization of conditions that has become the hallmark of their system. The combination of the one-to-a-cell rule and liberal modes of regulation has been accompanied in the 1970s and 1980s by the extension of prisoners' rights to take much fuller account of the basic premise that the situation in prison should include no unnecessary restraints.[6] It is notable that staff, as well as prisoners, strongly assent to the wide array of changes that embrace greatly extended home leave, longer visits, unlimited correspondence, more use of the telephone, TV and radio provision in cells, prisoners wearing their own clothes and retaining some personal possessions, a juridically-based complaints commission and other forms of contact with the outside world.[7] Organizationally, the creation of staff teams was the main breakthrough in putting such reforms into practice.

DUTCH REFORMS IN PRACTICE

That prisoners found Dutch prisons to be far more humane and less damaging and embittering than those in England was the clear outcome of a series of interviews with 27 prisoners in 1985, 13 of whom had experienced both Dutch and English jails. (13 were British prisoners in Dutch prisons, 14 Dutch prisoners in English jails, at the time of interview.) In terms of staff-prisoner relations, relations between prisoners, rights, privileges, conditions and the quality of life, there was near-unanimity on the superiority of the Dutch system. Two themes that recurred throughout the prisoner's accounts were first, the ways in which the experience of imprisonment is shaped by its *depth* as well as its length; and secondly, the extent to which the English prison experience was deformed not so much by any direct infliction of brutal or cruel forms of physical control but rather by the oppressiveness of the often trivial rules and regulations that govern life within the walls. By depth of imprisonment is meant the openness of the prison to life in the outside world, both in terms of actual opportunities for contact with family and friends by visits, home leave, letters and the telephone, and also by the permeation of the institution by outside world agencies, whether recreational (visiting pop groups, etc.), informational (access to the media, newspapers, etc.) or social (visits by students, politicians, academics, etcetera are more feasible in The Netherlands than in England).[8]

Visits and home leave clearly emerged as crucial ways of keeping relationships alive and reducing the inhumanity of confinement. Visits are more liberally available than in Britain, for example two hours a week as distinct from one hour a fortnight in prisons, though less in the remand houses. Home leave is far more generously available, every weekend from open, every fourth weekend from semi-open and bi-monthly in the last year from closed prisons. Where home leave is not possible, and especially for foreign prisoners (for whom it is not allowed), private (or conjugal) visits have since 1980 been allowed in closed prisons once a month for prisoners serving sentences of six months or more. Such visits were not necessarily for sex, but allowed an intimacy and self-expression not possible on a routine visit. As one prisoner put it: "Sometimes we just cuddle each other and weep." Another prisoner linked the significance of reducing both the length and the depth of imprisonment: "They don't put people away here for 12, 15, 18 years, when your marriage breaks down, you come out, you've got nothing. Here, you can have private visits, you can have sex, you can plan a family, you've got something to come out to." Both staff and prisoners alike argued that the results were less dependence on drugs, less homosexuality and less violence. Research by Grapendaal[9] has confirmed that inmate attitudes are far less oppositional where outside world contacts are most frequent: reducing the depth of imprisonment is thus crucial for lessening potential for disruptive conflicts, from which the Dutch system is far freer than that in Britain.[10]

Since the mid-1980s, the gross differences between the two systems with regard to sanitation, access to phones and the right to unlimited and uncensored correspondence have been lessened, though much remains to be done on even these counts. One area of glaring disparity remains the types and levels of work and pay. In Holland, for example, pay levels of 12 to 15 pounds a week contrast sharply with those in England and Wales of 3 to 4 pounds. Tobacco is half the price in Dutch jails. Since letters and phone calls are charged, in general, smokers may have to choose between the next phone call and the next cigarette. The effect of this extremely low rate of pay was seen by Dutch prisoners in English jails as much needless friction: "You get at most three packets of cigarettes a week. So if they buy (extra) letters, something happens in the family, then they can't buy the tobacco. So they feel bad, they get things out of proportion, then trouble breaks out without reasons." "Two stabbings over a quarter-ounce of tobacco—I can't believe it." Long hours of work for so demeaning a pittance fuel anger and resentment. Another right to suffer as a result is education, since time off for classes reduces wages even further. By contrast in The Netherlands, the higher wages mean prisoners can afford the extra food and toiletries that mean "you can live decently". Such instances show that high minimum standards and an increasing frequency of openness as the prisoner's career progresses provide the best incentives for good order. Even with the prison population at its current level, much could be done *now* to extend visiting, home leave, pay levels and to introduce private visits for those long-term prisoners ineligible for home leave, as the Woolf Inquiry has strongly recommended.

The interviews with Dutch prisoners in English jails were conducted at Blundeston (2), Camp Hill (3), Northeye (5) and Styal (4) in July 1985. That none of the four prisons selected by the Prison Department for interviews with Dutch prisoners was a local prison, where problems of under-staffing and over-crowding are at their most severe, serves to give added weight to the generally strong adverse views expressed by the prisoners. Indeed, Northeye was to be the site of considerable damage caused by the prisoners in the wake of the prison officers' action in 1986, damage so extensive that its closure has since been announced. As a category C prison,* Northeye should have been one of the easiest in the system in which to do time. And, indeed, it was favorably compared with Canterbury, where the prisoners, all of whom were in custody for drug smuggling (4 for cannabis, 1 for methadone and a single ounce of cocaine), had been held on remand. Yet their experience of Northeye was one of near-suffocating boredom interlaced with high levels of irritation and frustration stemming from the mesh of petty rules that permeated life in the institution:

Over-crowding was resented: "Here you share billets with five others in a (nissen) hut meant for four." "Well over capacity." "Here not a minute not a second, privacy—never. . . Here it is terrible. First, I was in a billet with five other people, two or three

---

*Editor's Note: Much like our system of maximum, medium, and minimum security prisons, the British grade their prisons from "A" to "D", with "A" being the most secure, and "D" the least secure.

radios, the noise is terrible. If I wanted to listen to Dutch news, other radios go louder. I saw doctor about aggressive feelings. I wanted a double room and doctor recommended it. Screws said nothing to do with doctors . . ." In this case, he persisted and was later moved to a double room (i.e., sharing with only one prisoner). For this prisoner, the overwhelming difference between the Dutch and English prison experience lay in the guarantee of privacy of one-to-a-cell. Other prisoners echoed his feelings at a lower intensity.

Rules within rules proved mystifying and unaccountable: "Some screws treat you like shit, trip you up on little rules" was one prisoner's summary of his main grievance. Examples included loss of seven days remission for going to the dining room at the wrong time, an instance of unfair punishment since others lost only three days remission for the same offense. Another example was the loss of 14 days remission for "having a joint", the same penalty as another prisoner received for possessing a "huge chunk of cannabis". The Governor was seen as imposing "silly rules" about purchasing toiletries; for example, only powdered toothpaste was permitted. On hot days, lying in the grass was sometimes allowed instead of gym, sometimes not—reasons were *never* given. Trivial as many of these complaints sound, their cumulative impact—echoed in interviews in the other English prisons—was to produce an almost impalpable atmosphere of pent-up grievances that weakened the credibility of the system for the prisoners.

Rights were generally found wanting by comparison with the Dutch system. For example, wages in 1985 were only 2.70 pounds a week maximum against 12 pounds or so in Holland. Because tobacco was cheaper in Dutch jails, prisoners there were even better off by comparison than wage differences alone indicate. As the staple commodity on which most prisoners spent their wages as a priority, tobacco purchasing would often exhaust the wages of a prisoner in England but take only a small fraction of his counterpart's in Holland. The tensions flowing from such artificial scarcity are notorious: "A lot go down over Rule 43 due to debt over dope and tobacco!" Letters and visits were also far less generously obligatory or permitted, and phone calls rarely granted, in the English system. The lack of democracy in the prisons was also remarked upon: "Every prison officer is like God. No complaints are possible. In Holland, if the Governor says no, and you think you have a right, you can appeal to a Commission, one of whom has to be a jurist, and you might get your right."

Such statements afforded only an oblique view of the state of the prisons in general, but they stem from a group who were usually keen to avoid trouble in the less pressurized part of the system. Interestingly, physical conditions that are usually singled out for particular censure in the English system, were not the main substance of their criticisms, perhaps because in the training prisons conditions are better than average, and also because the older Dutch prisons are by no means so superior to the English in these respects as is often assumed. As an Australian penal administrator stated, following a more focused study of Dutch prison management than my own:

> . . . if the physical environment in some of the older prisons was sometimes disappointing, the social environment was strikingly different to that to which I am accustomed . . . In the wings, the workshops and recreational and communal areas, there was a notable lack of tension. A number of social and physical factors contributed to this impression; the fact that prisoners and detainees wore ordinary clothing and subdued styling of the officers' "uniform", the use of standard fittings and furnishings in buildings that in Australia would bristle with locks, bars, and hardened glass, the intermingling of staff and inmates were some of the factors involved. Even more telling was the naturalness of the interactions

observed between members of the staff as well as between staff and inmates. To say that the prisoners appeared "natural" in their relations with staff is not to imply that their interactions were always cordial. Prisoners expressed annoyance in our presence but their feelings were focused on specific grievances and the response they received from staff conveyed not a hint of questioning their right to be angry. It should, however, be said that the social environment was generally friendly, robust and, as far as I could judge, devoid of the point-scoring that tends to characterize staff/inmate relations in Australian prisons.[11]

None of this should be taken to imply that imprisonment in The Netherlands is devoid of the experience of grief, pain, and sense of loss and desperation endemic in the situation of total confinement. Against the near-overwhelming acclaim of the Dutch prisons by comparison with the English should be set the reversal of that picture at the pre-charge stage of remand in custody; the fact that the perimeter guards in closed prisons are armed; and that in the early 1980s the suicide rate among Dutch prisoners, formerly far lower than in England, rose for a time to surpass it.

Important as they are, these factors should not be allowed to detract too greatly from the comprehensive character of the humane relations in Dutch prisons relative to both our own and those of virtually every other society. As Vinson concluded: "The patient and continual reform of the Dutch prison system is a story of remarkable achievement",[12] an achievement that has so far absorbed the strains imposed by its recent expansion, though the trend in suicide rates may reflect the need for greater understanding of the needs of foreign prisoners at the remand stage in particular.[13]

Not least, Dutch prisons, though not without a history of disturbances and protests, have been spared the damage and injury inflicted by prolonged and extensive rioting and occupations. In his response to my letter requesting information on this topic, Mr. van der Goodbergh, head of the Directorate of the Care of Delinquents and Juvenile Institutions, writes as follows:[14]

> After World War II there has been a number of serious disturbances with more or less damage at Dutch prisons, but in our opinion all of them are far less serious than the one at Strangeways prison.

The only remotely comparable cases both occurred at Groningen remand center in 1971 and 1974. In neither case were the staff members or the inmates killed or injured, though the first event involved hostage-taking and the second arson. Both riots lasted less than 24 hours. Those events helped spur the Report of the Van Hattum Committee, whose recommendations for substantial improvements in prisoners' rights and conditions have been progressively introduced from 1977 onwards, making the Dutch procedure for grievance resolution arguably the best in Europe.[15] The key element here is the prisoner's access to a specially constituted Grievance Committee separate from but overlapping in membership with the Visiting Committees, chaired by a jurist and able to consider any complaint about disciplinary measures or the withholding of rights.

Recent developments in The Netherlands have seen a doubling of the prison population since 1981 and its projected growth to 8,095 in growth to '93, phased to match expanded capacity but nevertheless amounting to a rate of 55 per 100,000, roughly the point at which Italy and Belgium now stand. While there are many who would not mourn the passing of the era in which The Netherlands could claim the lowest penal population in the world, and there has been a distinct thinning of the anti-penal ozone layer formed by a tolerant mass media and a public readily assuaged by expert anti-custodial opinion, there are a few signs that suggest such remorseless growth, from an admittedly small base, may come to be resisted. Prevalence rates for hard drug use are declining from a peak in 1988, and as the fear of a crime-related drug explosion—drug dealers account for a good fifth of the prison population—blew Dutch penal policy off-course, its abatement may bring a rethinking of the wisdom of penal expansion. The Netherlands remains, however, the major European entrepot nation, and the Schipol factor—non-Dutch and especially Third World drug couriers arriving with their kilos of heroin—could block such changes. Secondly, new non-custodial alternatives may begin to work in Holland, though their uneven record elsewhere can only breed skepticism. And thirdly, the crime rate has stabilized since the mid-1980s to lend reassurance to the judiciary that the length of custodial sentences should once more be reined in.

On the issue of standards, however, it can be said that they have remained high and that the reforms have not been eroded. They are more than ever necessary now that the Dutch prison population is serving longer sentences, is increasingly composed of foreign prisoners and those of Dutch nationality but from non-Dutch ethnic minority backgrounds: some 40 and 30 percent respectively. There is a growing mismatch between the location of the new prisons and the communities they serve. However, Dutch prisons remain small, holding an average of 80–120 prisoners; staff/prisoner ratios are twice as favorable as in Britain; and the one-to-a-cell principle has so far been upheld, though not without threats of industrial action. As a result, and despite signs of a return to bureaucratic managerialism in penal administration, conditions and rights far superior to those in this and most other countries mean that signs of real discontent are very uncommon, even in the less well-structured remand prisons.

DISCUSSION

The riot at Strangeways is hardly explicable as an isolated event. Neither the postwar record in Britain nor the stark nature of the contrasts between our penal system and those of such countries as The Netherlands allows so comfortable a conclusion. The build-up of tensions in the prison system since the early 1960s has been subjected to many analyses of their source in the defects of the system as a whole, rather than in errors of judgment by individuals or groups within particular institutions. These pressure-cooker establishments cannot always rely on "scenting the wind" and talented administrators. If the system is badly conceived, the pressure will blow in time.[16] Such conclusions had become commonplace by the 1980s. This country hardly lacked for well informed analyses of impending crises. Particularly prescient were the studies by Richard Sparks, whose *Local Prisons in Crisis* appeared as long ago as 1972,[17] and *The Future of the Prison System* by King and Morgan (1980).[18] The question that logically arises is: why has so little attention been paid to such well-attested and indeed well-worn warnings?

At least in part, the answer must be that the warnings *were* heeded, but policymakers failed to transform an awareness of the problem into the fashioning of appropriate solutions, or were prevented from doing so by the nature of the system. After all, successive Home Secretaries, most notably Roy Jenkins in the mid-1970s, who cited the figure of 42,000 prisoners as the maximum the prisons could hold without risk of serious disturbances, have urged the courts to make more sparing use of custody. If their words were not heeded, it is arguably the absence of a framework for translating their policies into practice to which we should look for an explanation.

The most salient difference between the English and the Dutch penal system is that in The Netherlands no prison governor is allowed to accept any admission for whom there is no cell, whereas in England (as in Britain as a whole) prisons must accept all those who are sent there by the courts. It is not by any means an idle defense of the prison system for its functionaries to disclaim, as a consequence, full responsibility for the condition of the penal estate. But the situation in The Netherlands does not rest on relative leniency at the point of sentence alone. As Rutherford has stressed,[19] the Dutch prisons are protected from undue pressures of numbers and over-crowding, by a variety of "shields" which operate to equate numbers and capacity. Flexible administration can create the space for those the courts regard as too serious offenders for non-custodial sentence, by granting home leave, interruptions to sentences and the earlier release of less serious remand prisoners. The queuing system for the taking up of a prison place for less serious offenders provides another safety valve. The system of public prosecution enables certain cases to be dealt with by waiving prosecution. In short, an array of devices has been evolved to protect the prisons from over-use. Prison administrators and staff, as well as prisoners, are thus protected from the near intolerable pressures that afflict their English counterparts.

This entire set of processes could still, however, be wrecked if the judiciary were to adopt far more punitive levels of custodial sentencing. The relatively marked reluctance of sentencers in The Netherlands to resort to long prison sentences remains the pre-condition for the humanity of its penal system. The shift from an unusually mild to a relatively punitive penal climate since the 1970s, signalled to the Government's *Society and Crime* policy plan of 1985,[20] and consolidated in the recent *Law in Motion* proposals of 1990,[21] is reflected in sentencing trends. Between 1982 and 1988, the average length of sentence rose by 76 percent, though the number of unconditional prison sentences fell by 4 percent. Rises in the use of custody and sentence length were especially evident in cases of hard drug–dealing (46 percent and 53 percent); rape (18 percent and 70 percent); and robbery (55 percent and 22 percent), but *all* offenses were dealt with by longer terms of imprisonment. It was tempered, however, by a clear determination to resort to custody less frequently in notionally less serious offenses, so that numbers sentenced to custody for soft drug–dealing fell by 50 percent, assaults by 7 percent, and in traffic cases, mostly drunken driving—where blood alcohol tests showed a real decline anyway—by 58 percent. After 1992, closer European integration could spell further increases if a pattern emerges whereby fears of the spread of organized crime lead to international sentencing norms. The activation of measures to ease the transfer of prisoners to their country of origin may also further pressurize the Dutch system, if their prisoners elect to return while those from other countries choose to stay. On present trends, by the end of the century, the Dutch prison population rate would be verging on current levels in Britain. Almost inevitably, their high standards of rights, ethos and conditions would be eroded in the process.

CONCLUSIONS

For these reasons, and despite the fact that better overall use of resources and patterns of decision-making could improve things in the strictly penal context, sentencing remains the key to lasting penal reform. Our prisons sorely need the kind of breathing space enjoyed in The Netherlands in the 1960s and 1970s to equip themselves for the practice of genuinely humane containment and the pursuit of resocialization in the broadest sense. A pre-condition for such a transformation is a substantial reduction in the prison population. Such a reduction is unlikely to be achieved by measures which have been tried and found wanting in the past, such as the creation of yet further alternatives to custody. A coherent criminal justice policy is the necessary foundation for a penal policy which alone can prevent the repetition of disturbances such as those at Strangeways.[22] An essential component of such a policy would be a more effective framework for the guidance of sentencers, such as a Sentencing Council, whose agenda would include "reductionist" objectives and whose guidelines would be grounds for appeal against sentence. Such a framework would not erode the independence of the judiciary in its most basic sense, anymore than judicial independence in The Netherlands has been undermined by their judges' respect for the recommendations of public prosecutors. That judges should be independent is as cardinal a principle of the rule of law in The Netherlands as in England. What stands in need of challenge is the interpretation of judicial independence in England, which goes far beyond independence in the realm of cases to oppose any policy framework other than that flowing from the Court of Appeal, whose unavoidably piecemeal character allows gross inequitability to arise from major variations in sentencing between courts.

Three main conclusions can be drawn from the comparative study of the two systems. First, certain fashionable remedies can be rejected, e.g. the privatization of prisons, since their alleged benefits can be shown to have been more surely achieved by other means. Secondly, the humane social relations and procedural rights in Dutch prisons have proved an effective antidote to riots and disturbances of the scale and character suffered in British prisons. Thirdly, the achievement of comparable standards in British prisons seems unattainable without their being shielded from adverse pressure of numbers that produces the "high cost of squalor"[23] of imprisonment in this country. Taken together, these conclusions lead to the view that substantial reductions in current levels of custodial sentencing are an essential accompaniment to, if not a precondition for, resolving the main problems of penal conditions and relations. Changes in the framework of judicial sentencing policy seem essential to that end.

➤ DISCUSSION QUESTIONS

Many Americans believe that our criminal justice system mollycoddles criminals and that our prisons are just too cushy to act as a deterrent. Suppose this is true in the United States, then why don't the Dutch have higher crime rates? What do you think the differences in attitudes say about our respective societies?

NOTES

1. Mr. Justice May (Chairman), *Report of the Committee of Inquiry into the United Kingdom Prison Services,* Cmnd. 7673, HMSO, London, 1979.

2. Lord Justice Woolf and Judge Stephen Tumin, *Report of an Inquiry into Prison Disturbances, April 1990.* Part II, Cm. 1456, HMSO, London, 1991.

3. The exception to the picture of rough parity in crime rates between the two countries, or even a somewhat lower rate in The Netherlands, that emerges from comparing annual official criminal statistics and regular victim survey data, is to be found in Jan van Dijk, Pat Mayhew and M. Killias, *Experiences of Crime Across the World: Core Findings of the 1989 International Crime Survey,* Kluwer, Deventer, 1990. The relatively high victimization rate in Holland compared with the low rate for England and Wales must, however, be seen in the context of the telephone survey method employed, which arguably involved larger underestimates for the worst-hit housing estates in this country.

4. Herman Franke, "Dutch Tolerance: Facts and Fables", *British Journal of Criminology,* vol. 30, 1990, pp. 81–93.

5. David Downes, *Contrasts in Tolerance: Post-War Penal Policy in The Netherlands and England and Wales,* Clarendon Press, Oxford, 1988, Chap. 2.

6. C. Kelk, "The Weal and Woe of Deprivation and Liberty", *Symposium on the Centenary of the Deprivation of Liberty in The Netherlands,* Ministry of Justice, The Hague, 1987.

7. Tony Vinson, *Impressions of the Dutch Prison System,* Ministry of Justice, The Hague, 1985.

8. David Downes, *op. cit.,* Chap. 6.

9. M. Grapendaal, "The Inmate Subculture in Dutch Prisons", *British Journal of Criminology,* vol. 30, 1990, pp. 341–57.

10. Though a more extensive study in Swedish and American prisons by Ulla Bondenson found that regime differences made little impact on the pace and character of "prisonisation": see her *Prisoners in Prison Society.*

11. Tony Vinson, *op. cit.,* p. 7.

12. *Ibid.,* p. 43.

13. W. Bernasco, A.J.F.M. Kerkhof, and B. van der Linden, "Suicidal gedrag van gedetineerden in Nederland", *Tijdschrift voor Criminologie,* 1988, pp. 61–76.

14. Personal communication.

15. Jan A. Nijboer and Gerhard J. Ploeg, "Grievance Procedure in The Netherlands", Chap. 16 in Mike Maguire, Jon Vagg and Rod Morgan (eds), *Accountability and Prisons: Opening Up a Closed World,* Tavistock, London, 1985, pp. 229–44.

16. David Downes, *Law and Order: Theft of an Issue,* Fabian Society, London, 1983, p. 23.

17. Richard Sparks, *Local Prisons in Crisis,* Heinemann, London, 1972.

18. Roy King and Rod Morgan, *The Future of the Prison System,* Gower, Farnborough, 1980.

19. Andrew Rutherford, *Prisons and the Process of Justice: The Reductionist Challenge,* Heinemann, London, 1984.

20. Ministry of Justice, The Netherlands, *Society and Crime: A Policy Plan for the Netherlands,* State Publications, The Hague, 1985.

21. Ministry of Justice, The Netherlands, *Law in Motion: A Policy Plan for Justice in the Years Ahead,* The Hague, 1990.

22. This is not to say that crime prevention and public order are the sole preserve of the criminal justice system. Far from it: social and economic measures should be given much higher priority in confronting crime. See, in particular, Elliot Currie, *Confronting Crime: An American Challenge,* Pantheon, New York, 1985.

23. Andrew Rutherford, *op. cit.*

ARTICLE 25

The Mutter-Kind-Heim at Frankfurt am Main: "Come Together— Go Together," An Observation

■ MARIE C. DOUGLAS

INTRODUCTORY NOTES

Here, again, another European penal practice will strike many Americans as being very foreign. Americans are often heard to complain that U.S. prisoners are pampered, prisons are more like hotels, and it's no wonder that they do not deter. Below, Douglas describes the Mutter-Kind-Heim, a prison in Germany that allows female prisoners to keep their young children with them at the prison. Many of the women leave the prison during the day to work while their children, for example, are being taken to the zoo by prison "educators"; when the woman returns to the prison, she cooks dinner for her and her child. Douglas reports a zero percent recidivism rate for inmates of this prison (however, without more sophisticated evaluation research, this recidivism rate cannot be attributed to the program itself), and that the program is for the sake of the children more than the mothers. It's not difficult to imagine that the child of a mother in prison in the U.S. often faces a difficult life—one which may in fact lead to the child eventually getting into trouble with law. Thus, a program such as the Mutter-Kind-Heim could lead to a reduction of crime in future generations.

It is difficult to ascertain the ultimate goal of criminal justice. Is it to protect society, or is it to punish the criminal? These goals do not necessarily go hand in hand as many Americans have come to believe in recent decades.

The guns had fallen silent, the rubble was gradually becoming orderly, two German states had arisen out of one, the occupying Americans were regulating life in Frankfurt am Main, and Frau Doctor Helga Einsele was returning home through Austria from a wartime exile in Kaliningrad. This diminutive woman would become an active reformer and a true visionary in women's corrections.

SOURCE: Marie C. Douglas, "The Mutter-Kind-Heim at Frankfurt am Main: 'Come Together—Go Together,' An Observation," from the *International Journal of Comparative and Applied Criminal Justice*, vol. 17, no. 1: 181–187. Copyright 1993. Dr. Dae H. Chang, editor, Wichita, Kansas. Reprinted by permission.

Einsele began work with the Americans as the warden in the Frauen-vollzugsanstalt Frankfurt-Preungesheim in 1947, and finally took over complete control from the U.S. in 1953. The practice in Germany, prior to the Nazi regime, had been to house women prisoners with their infant children. The American administration continued the separation inaugurated by the Nazis, but Einsele intended that the mother and child should once again remain together.

The Department of Justice in the mid-fifties adamantly refused Einsele's request for a childbirth facility in a proposed new building, but Einsele did gain access to a doctor and a mid-wife. The sympathetic doctor moved Einsele one step closer to her in-house nursery when he began delivering babies at the prison and refusing to separate mothers from nursing infants.

The move to the new prison in 1955 provided space for a maximum of six babies, and a prison congress held in 1956 under Attorney General Fritz Bauer recognized the existence of the babies in-house. At this time, the prison detained pretrial offenders and juvenile women, ages 14–18, as well as adult sentenced offenders. In 1959, Einsele pioneered a work-release program for juvenile women and created an "apartment" inside the walls for these girls. The rudiments of a formal nursery program were also put in place in 1959. Six places were provided for six mothers and children. Five out of six eligible mothers elected to keep their children with them.

The early sixties saw the abolishment of the German Haft or workhouse. Those women sentenced to a Haft had traditionally kept their children with them. Women now sentenced to prison took their workhouse experience inside the walls with them, and began to demand the same rights they had enjoyed in the Haft. As a result, space was provided for six to eight mothers for five years, but the children were housed in a separate department and the mothers in a traditional cell house.

Fritz Bauer, who had championed Einsele's work, was dead by this time. However, he had founded the Humanistiche Union (Humanistic Union) and had established an annual prize. The first recipient of the prize, awarded in 1969 during a prison reception, was Helga Einsele.

The sixties was a time of political reform in West Germany. Civil rights movements and a reactive bourgeoisie were joined by vocal prisoners' rights groups, resulting in the formation of the still active Kinderheim Preungesheim Verein (Association). Between 1966 and 1967, women's groups in Parliament pressured the Department of Justice and the Department of Finance, and successfully committed 600,000 DM to build the now famous Mutter-Kind-Heim.

The Verein, duly registered with the government, initially paid for the supervision of the Mutter-Kind-Heim, and used donations to support studies for development of the program. Prisoners' fines could also be directed to the Verein. Initially, a commission upon which Einsele served allowed the mother to keep her child with her for up to five years in this new facility.

In the years 1966–1967, the entire women's prison had a recidivism rate of 45%. In 1973, Einsele had had fifty mothers move through her Mutter-Kind-Heim. The recidivism rate was 0%. Additionally, no children appeared back in the criminal justice system at the Hesse juvenile unit.

Einsele enjoyed continued success with her program through 1975, when she retired. She credits not only the Mutter-Kind-Heim itself but the pre-release and post-release support systems which were in place.

Six months prior to release, a five member panel from the Beratungesstelle fur Frauen went to the prison to begin the process of acclimatizing the inmate to the world she and her child would re-enter. Einsele supervised this endeavor for three years, and engineered the creation of a halfway house, funded by both city and state welfare departments. The newly released mother and child could remain there for two months or longer, if necessary. Einsele continually contacted in person ex-prisoners as a gesture of support.

First and foremost in Dr. Einsele's pioneering correctional philosophy is the Kindeswohl, "the welfare of the child". She believes the Mutter-Kind-Helm, while "okay" for the mother, is absolutely "good", the "best thing for the children". She believes in "individualized and just" treatment for the women and hopes to see the women gain self-respect and confidence through their newly realized nurturing skills. Einsele says that this ". . . individualized treatment is a small grade to walk".

Einsele has built upon the concept that mother and child should not be separated; they must "come together" and "go together". In 1988, the present Mutter-Kind-Heim opened its doors to achieve that goal.

Situated in the suburbs of Frankfurt, the burgeoning financial capital of the new Germany, is the four prison complex of the Justizvollzugsanstalt. The complex is comprised of a men's geschlossen or "closed" prison, a women's "closed" prison, and two Mutter-Kind-Heim prisons, one offenen or "open" and one "closed".

The closed unit accommodates five mothers and their children. These mothers work in the prison complex during the day, three in the women's closed prison and two in the Mutter-Kind-Heim itself. These two work directly under the supervision of a housekeeper who teaches domestic skills to the women. The children from the closed unit are picked-up each weekday morning at 7:30 A.M. to be transferred to the open Mutter-Kind-Heim where they spend the day in the company of the children housed in the open unit. They are returned at 3 P.M. for each mother to individually prepare dinner for her child.

The closed Mutter-Kind-Heim provides individual units of two rooms for each mother, one for her and an adjoining room for her child. There are laundry facilities and bathrooms in abundance, including bathinettes for the babies. A main kitchen is located on the ground level, and an auxiliary kitchen is located upstairs to provide for the inmates after the 10:00 P.M. evening lock-down. The facility includes day rooms or living rooms, play rooms for various ages, and a dining room. The facility is as non-institutional as possible. The Mutter-Kind-Heim has its own play yard and its own kitchen and flower gardens. Everything imaginable is provided for the children, from toys to playpens to books to carriages.

The open house accommodates eighteen inmates and their children. Here, the mother works outside of the prison community. She leaves at 7:00 A.M. and must return by 5:00 P.M. to prepare her child's evening meal. She may then go back out with the child, but must return the child by 8:00 P.M. The mother may again leave, if she has arranged for her child's care, but must return by the 10:00 P.M. lock-down. The physical plant in the open house is similar to that of the closed house, but is four floors instead of the two floors of the closed house. The emphasis is still on creating a non-institutional environment for the children, and a learning environment for the mothers.

The children, who can number more than the twenty-three inmates if one mother has two or more children, are in the care of what the administration calls "educators". There are four to five of these women, who have been in specialized training for three years. From 7:30 A.M. to 3:00 P.M., these women are chauffeurs, nurses, mothers, teachers, and playmates. The children's meals are individually prepared and served family-style. The cafeteria concept does not exist. The day is spent in the city, in the countryside, at the zoo, at a farm, at a movie, or in a park. The educators are *required* to be creative and to develop challenging ways for the children to spend their days. They normally return the children to the prison for lunch at 11:30 A.M., followed by a nap.

These children do not realize they are housed in a prison. The two Mutter-Kind-Heim units are constructed in such a way that the children don't see gates, bars, and razor-wired walls. They come and go through gardens and city streets. It is interesting though, that the children use some words not normally part of the two year old vocabulary. Rapid-fire children's conversations are peppered with words such as "guard", "gate", "lock-down", and "keys". Those "keys" become particularly significant to the children. People with keys can get children where they want to go and keys can obtain treats, toys, and food. They are keenly aware that their mothers do not have keys and cannot always get a child what he or she wants. This, at times, causes some consternation on the part of the mothers who can be confronted with a child who wants to remain with the educator or social worker at the end of the day rather than return to a mother with no keys! The prison team, composed of social workers, educators, directors, psychologists, and pediatricians attempted to confront the "key" problem in 1990. They purchased sets of toy keys, but much to their chagrin, found the effort totally wasted. The children immediately tried to use the keys, found them useless, and discarded them at once.

The population of the two Mutter-Kind-Heim units is primarily West German. The second largest faction is Colombian, followed by inmates from Ghana, Zaire, and American military personnel. The Colombian women are usually very poor prostitutes paid by Colombian drug dealers to carry the drugs into Germany. The hapless women, sometimes using their children as "mules", are arrested at the Frankfurt airport. Their situation is compounded by the language barrier. Their children rapidly learn German, however, hampering communication with their Spanish-speaking mothers. The sentences of the Colombian women are short, usually one year, and upon release they are put on a plane back to Colombia.

The women from Ghana and Zaire present a different problem. They were brought to Germany for the labor force and cannot be expediently dispatched home after release, but, like their German sisters, must be reabsorbed into the community at large.

Violent offense convictions are few in this system. Most women are convicted of drug-related crimes, theft and burglary, and fraud and deceitful practices. Neither drug addicts nor women in terrorist groups are considered for admission to the Mutter-Kind-Heim. One exception to political prisoners was made when a well-educated Neo-Nazi mother was admitted. She "did her time" and did not espouse her politics. Inmates range in age from 23–42, and have an average sentence of one year.

When the inmate enters the system, she lives her first six months in the closed unit. During that time, she may see the child's father, her boyfrierd or husband, for two hours every fourteen days. If her behavior and development warrant, she moves to the open house at the end of the six months.

The Mutter-Kind-Heim program has as its principal goal the release of a woman who has a bankable skill and a knowledge of child-care. Emphasis is placed on housekeeping skills, sewing skills, and routine nursing skills. Gymnasium and university educational programs are available, but the vast majority of these inmates cannot be trained in such programs. At the present time, two inmates out of twenty-three are in conventional education programs.

Every thirty days, mother and child, both closed and open units, are taken into the city to shop. Regardless of where the mother works, in or out of the prison walls, she must save one-third of her salary for the time of her discharge. Therefore, she must learn to balance the remaining two-thirds for shopping for herself and her child. This shopping trip is, by the way, the only meaningful vehicle that can be used as punishment for rule infractions, as anything else would interfere with the well-being of the child. Earlier in the program, the prison or the state paid for the shopping trip purchases. This, however, negated the lessons to be learned by the mother on how to budget. Consequently, she now spends her own money, and learns how to shop for baby lotion, clothing, and other needs.

The medical care of the children is provided by the state. Two pediatricians see each child each Thursday. The state also provides psychological counseling for any mother experiencing difficulty with her role as a parent. The mothers are attended by an obstetrician-gynecologist. Those inmates arriving in prison pregnant are housed in the regular women's closed prison until the beginning of the eighth month when they are moved to the Mutter-Kind-Heim. Delivery is in a city hospital.

Although German law allows the child to remain with the mother until the age of six, recent studies conclude that the child should leave by the age of three. A 1981 study by the Institut fur Sozialarbeit und Sozialpedagogic am Stockborn has strongly recommended that the child be out of the Mutter-Kind-Heim with the mother by age three.

How then to implement the "Come Together—Go Together" theme of the program? The program today will not accept an inmate from whom they would have to separate a child. The sentence length must be commensurate with release by the child's third birthday. Recently, a pregnant inmate convicted of manslaughter applied to the Mutter-Kind-Heim. The Director agreed to accept her if her sentence was seven years or less. Allowing for good time, she could be released by her child's third birthday.

Upon release today, the inmate-mother faces a truly critical situation. She will leave prison with her savings of one-third of her salary, all her child's belongings, state money for one night's lodging in the city, and a sewing machine. This gift of a sewing machine is still in the testing stages. The theory is that the previously unemployable woman can do piece work at home with her newly learned skills. (The proverbial jury is still out on this one.) The released inmate is eligible for state aid in the amount of 420 DM per month, 225 DM per child, and receives her rent free. This woman now faces a dire housing shortage all over Germany, must seek employment, and must find day-care for her child. (The Frankfurt prison complex houses guards on the top floors of two buildings in an attempt to overcome the critical German housing shortage. This practice was initiated two years ago.) According to the Social Work Director of the Mutter-Kind-Heim, the mother also faces extreme loneliness. Few of her male relationships survive prison, and she leaves behind her prison friends.

The staff is prohibited from communicating with the inmates when they are released, but the women may contact staff members. It is surmised that the well-adjusted women never call and that one only hears from "those who suffer". Still, in the four years that the present director has been in his position, he has never had a mother return to prison. He states that the overall recidivism rate since the program's inception in 1975 is almost nil.

The program has, of course, always had its critics. The Green Party in particular has been most vociferous. They have, for example, focused on the previously addressed "key" issue in an attempt to prove the frustration and resulting punishment of innocent children living in prison with recalcitrant mothers. Dr. Einsele was incensed with this approach, stating that ". . . all children play with keys! I've raised four and I know!"

Critics further contend that the children are punished, not the mothers. Additionally, other inmates feel abused in comparison to the Mutter-Kind-Heim prisoners. The nay-sayers lose, however, when faced with the irrefutable lack of recidivism from these mothers.

And the children? Of course they are not the prisoners or the wrong-doers. Alternatives to the Mutter-Kind-Heim such as foster care or institutional care or adoption are unacceptable when the children can reside with their mothers in a clean, healthy, loving environment. The alternative care options would be punishment of innocents!

The three most difficult issues facing the Mutter-Kind-Heim program today are totally diverse. The first problem is the complete interdependence between the mother and child and the resulting transfer of the mother's emotions to the child. An enlightened administration is tackling this issue head-on. The second problem defies a ready solution. That problem is AIDS. In the main women's prison in Frankfurt alone, 30% of the women are HIV positive, 260 inmates in the closed prison, and 45 in the open prison. The ramifications of this problem can seriously affect the Mutter-Kind-Heim program.

The third problem confronting the administration is the mother's absolute right to deliver her child to whomever she chooses outside the prison. She may decide on an unqualified individual, much to the detriment of the child's well-being. Recently, a baby in the overnight care of an inmate's boyfriend was returned to the prison in an alcoholic stupor. The inmate demanded that the baby return to the same individual the next weekend. The Direcktor personally appeared at the man's residence, examined the baby, suspected alcohol had again been ingested, and simply bundled up the baby and returned him to the Mutter-Kind-Heim!

As a result the administration is faced with a triple-edged sword: the child is not a prisoner, the mother may choose her child-care custodian/provider, and the Direcktor must protect the child. Inmate-mothers are presently vehemently espousing their rights, while the administration is seeking reasonable solutions to this dilemma.

However, in a world replete with bureaucratic failures, the creative and imaginative light of Frau Helga Einsele shines brightly and persistently. Nor has her energy and determination flagged with her advanced years. In January of 1992, she said, "It is time to go on the barricades again!" This time, she is addressing the issue of excessive sentences for women convicted of murder.

A unique experiment that has worked, Dr. Einsele's units now flourish throughout the German penal systm. The Frankfurt units are explored by press and media and examined by scholars. The program has proven that the mother and child may come together, go together and not return. Would that some measure of this humanity permeate the thinking of the rest of the world's systems of criminal justice.

➤ DISCUSSION QUESTIONS

What are your initial impressions of the Mutter-Kind-Heim? Would you favor such a policy in the U.S.? Why or why not?

REFERENCES

Institut fur Sozialarbeit und Sozialpadagogic Am Stockborn, 1991.

Kinder brauchen ihre Mutter. Mutter-Kinder-Heim, Frauenvollzugsanstalt Frankfurt-Preungesheim, 1990.

Interviews

Einsele, Helga. Founder and former Director, Mutter-Kind-Heim, Frauenvollzugsanstalt Frankfurt-Preungesheim, Frankfurt am Main (January, 1992).

Hermes, Claus. Social Work Director, Mutter-Kind-Heim, Justizvollzergsanstalt Frankfurt am Main III (August, 1991).

Some Effects of Extreme Overcrowding in Peruvian Prisons

■ *FRED ZAMPA*

INTRODUCTORY NOTES

As mentioned earlier, deterrence theory emphasizes the swiftness, certainty, and severity of punishment. Of these three, certainty is likely the most problematic in the United States. A great number of offenders are not caught; those who are caught are often not prosecuted; those who are prosecuted may plea bargain to a lesser charge; and those who are convicted may receive probation.

The system is far from ideal, but it might be the best we can achieve given that criminal justice resources are finite. If, as stated in the following article, approximately 90 percent of cases are plea bargained, a 10 percent reduction in plea bargaining would result in nearly a 100 percent increase in cases going to trial—in a court system that is already overloaded. A drastic reduction in plea bargaining could result in people waiting for years to go to trial, as they do in Peru.

Prison overcrowding is a serious problem in corrections today. Besides humanitarian objections, overcrowding certainly interferes with what little chances there are of rehabilitating the prisoner; and it has been implicated in inmate violence as well as prison riots. Prison overcrowding is already a problem in the U.S.; states are routinely put under court order to reduce their overcrowding; and some states have already had to reassess their mandatory sentencing laws because of prison overcrowding. But if all those who pled guilty or who were found guilty were actually sent to prison, we would be facing an overcrowding problem of enormous magnitude—much as they face in Peru.

As it currently operates, the prison system in Peru offers an interesting opportunity for comparison in that some prisons are extremely overcrowded while others stand well below capacity. Based primarily on tours and extensive interviews conducted as part of a Fulbright-Hays grant during the summer of 1989, this paper will attempt to delineate some of the effects of prison hypercrowding as they have materialized in Peru.

SOURCE: Fred Zampa, "Some Effects of Extreme Overcrowding in Peruvian Prisons," *Criminal Justice Policy Review*, vol. 5, no. 1 (1991): 133–141. Published by Imprint Series, Indiana University of Pennsylvania. Reprinted by permission.

STRUCTURE OF THE PRISON SYSTEM

In direct contrast to the prison system in the United States, the Peruvian system is not at all "fragmented." The structure consists of a classic bureaucratic pyramid known as the National Institute of Penology (I.N.P.E.), which terminates at the top in one Chief, responsible for all correctional institutions, personnel, inmates, and budget for the entire country. Directly below the Chief there are a Technical Director, who is in charge of all operations, and a Director of Personnel. A simple, hand-carried letter from the Technical Director was sufficient to admit me and a colleague into any prison and, in fact, proved quite impressive to local wardens. Regional Directors report to the Central Office. Prison Directors (wardens) report to Regional Directors. While there are some local lock-ups, they seem to be used only for the very short holding period before the prosecutor files a complaint. No distinction is made between "prison" and "jail." While most of the top level administrators are lawyers, I.N.P.E. also operates its own college which offers a three year program and is the source of regional personnel.

The system includes 110 prisons which are able to operate at an average yearly cost of only $180 per inmate.[1] These include five prisons for women, one for terrorists, and one jungle penal colony. Of the 17,000 inmates, only 25 percent have been convicted while the rest await trial. Although forms of parole and "good time" exist, they do not apply to the unconvicted.

The constitution of Peru specifies that the goals of the corrections system shall be rehabilitation and reintegration. This was echoed by Edwardo Fritz Calmet (personal communication, June, 1989), the prison system Technical Director, who said, "The Peruvian philosophy is re-education, rehabilitation, re-incorporation, and re-adaptation." It is easy to find manifestations of this philosophy. Prisoners are classified by the danger they represent. There is a combined system of parole and "2 for 1" good time (up to 50 percent sentence reduction). Judges of Penal Execution report monthly on parolees. Further, prisoners can go into their own businesses and deal independently with free-world suppliers and purchasers. They can keep personal items such as clothing, radios, and cooking utensils. Women prisoners can keep their younger (to age 5) children with them. As a result, Peruvian prisons sometimes take on a non-sterile, village atmosphere. The warden of the Chorrillos women's prison contends that "partly the difference in atmosphere results from the Catholic tradition of forgiveness versus the American Protestant tradition of vengeance" (Pilar Godos Gutieriez, personal communication, June, 1989). Indeed, virtually all of the wardens, guards, social workers, judges, instructors, medical personnel and psychologists seemed to take the goal of rehabilitation quite seriously and were most anxious to exchange ideas.

CROWDING AND MALDISTRIBUTION

Peru's prisoner population is quite unevenly distributed even though the system is centrally organized. Some prisons are well past their designed capacity while others are under-utilized. For example, the Chorrillos prison for women in Lima was originally constructed in 1957 to hold 250 inmates but has housed 900 and currently holds 540 (216 percent of designed capacity). Lurigancho prison was built in 1968 for 1,200 inmates but currently holds about 6,000 (500 percent of designed capacity). Here, three new inmates enter for every one who leaves. Meanwhile, Socabaya prison in Arequipa houses only 540, even though it was designed for 800 (68 percent of designed capacity). Some upcountry prisons are virtually empty. This intensive maldistribution is largely due to laws which require accused persons to await trial in the department (state) where they were arrested. Since much of Peru's population clusters around Lima, so do its criminal arrests and prison population.

Prisons are crowded for other reasons as well. First, the Peruvian justice system, which is based on the Napoleonic Code, imprisons accused persons until their trials —which frequently take as long as the sentence length to occur. The result of this lack of bail is that 75 percent of the prison population is comprised of unconvicted prisoners. Further, there is no plea bargaining because the trial system is essentially non-adversarial. With no jury and with the prosecutor and defense functioning largely as information providers, a "judge of instruction" gathers data on both guilt and innocence for presentation to a panel of judges. There is no right to a jury trial to be bargained away. Indeed, with this collaborative approach there is no one to plea bargain with.

Exceptionally long sentences in Peru also contribute greatly to prison overcrowding. The mean time of seventeen months served in the United States can be roughly compared to the average sentence length of ten years in Peru—with a maximum reduction down to five years for parole/good time (Bureau Of Justice Statistics, 1990:83). This becomes even more severe for drug-related cases. The average drug case sentence is fifteen years with no parole or good time available, even for minor offenders.[2] Currently, drug offenders constitute 40 percent of the prison population —including one senile, ninety year old drug courier who can not be released, pardoned, or paroled despite everybody's wish to do so. According to the former director of the Ministry of Justice, "prison history here is before and after the coca leaf, and this is due to pressure from the United States" (Albierto Varillas, personal communication, July, 1989).

Other than police discretion and parole, the only mechanism for holding down prison populations in Peru is the presidential pardon. Fortunately for the system, pardons appear to generate good will for the president and have been issued by the thousands on such special occasions as Fathers' Day.

EFFECTS OF CROWDING—CONDITIONS

After two decades of massive population increases in the United States, our jails are at an average of 98 percent of capacity and our prisons are at 109 percent–125 percent (Bureau Of Justice Statistics, 1990:80). Given that Chorrillos is frequently over 200 percent of capacity and Lurigancho is at 600 percent and rising, it seems reasonable to say that these (and other) prisons are hypercrowded. The effects are equally severe.

As one might well expect, living conditions are the first casualty of heavy population pressures. At Lurigancho, inmates are everywhere: housed in service buildings, sleeping in doorways and under toilets, and living outdoors in whatever shelter they can find. It is crowded, dirty, dark, smelly, gloomy, and hopeless. Toilets are usually clogged, and there is frequently an inch of standing water in common bathrooms. Violence is endemic, with one or two deaths and many stabbings every month.

Although the prison at Chorrillos has managed to stretch to twice its capacity, resulting population pressures clearly take their tolls. All inmates have a bed, but only the chapel remains well maintained and unused as dormitory space. Since even the kitchen has succumbed, inmates do their own cooking on multiple outdoor campfires. Similarly, individual laundry hangs everywhere. A positive result is that the courtyards have the character of a village on a busy market day. Human interactions appear to resemble more closely relationships in the outside world than might be the case if the facility were run in a more "institutional" manner. Nevertheless, anything mechanical is likely to be broken. Buildings seem to be disassembling themselves. Repair is non-existent. The warden noted with frustration that "our deteriorating infrastructure is due to the fact that all of our budget must now go to routine operations" (Pilar Godos Gutieriez, personal communication, June, 1989).

Lest we believe that such conditions are merely the Peruvian way, it should be noted that Socabaya prison (68 percent of capacity) is quite a tolerable place. Rooms are neat and clean. In dorms all the beds are made and organized into straight lines. The atmosphere is comparatively light and airy. Kitchens, workshops, and recreation areas are used as kitchens, workshops and recreation areas.

EFFECTS OF CROWDING—INMATES' RIGHTS

Despite the fact that Peru's constitution and penal code have impressive listings of "rights of the person," inmates' rights have been largely obliterated in the face of hypercrowding. Over and over, virtually all officials interviewed had some version of a statement which said that "of course, inmates have a constitutional right to _____, but due to the current crisis we have been unable to. . . ." For example, at Lurigancho the warden noted that inmates awaiting trial are supposed to be treated quite differently from those who have been convicted—"but funds keep that from happening" (Pedro Cadenas, personal communication, June, 1989). Asked about conjugal visits, the warden at Chorrillos said that "while the law grants that right, we just do not have the facilities" (Pilar Godos Gutieriez, personal communications, June, 1989). According to the wife of one inmate, her husband had been due for release three months before. But because of the work load and because of strikes at the I.N.P.E. central office, his papers had not yet been processed. Not only do the prisons frequently keep people beyond their release date, they sometimes lose track of inmates to the point that they must be searched out when their papers do arrive.

The slow processing of criminal cases by the courts in Peru has yet another effect on prisoners' rights. Frequently, the maximum sentence length and the time to trial are the same. At this confluence of events there is great pressure on the courts to prevent embarrassment for the system by finding the defendant guilty—with a sentence of time served. Thus, guilty or innocent, defendants are frequently released at trial. While this situation should make it clear why we value our own right to speedy justice, it is not really a violation of civil rights in Peru. However, it is a violation of inmates' rights. Whenever the time before trial exceeds 50 percent of the maximum sentence length, inmates' rights to good time and opportunity for parole are effectively taken away without cause. Indeed, it is better to be found guilty sooner than innocent later.

EFFECTS OF CROWDING—GOALS

The philosophical goals of the Peruvian corrections system (rehabilitation) have been the third casualty of hypercrowding. The underpopulated Socabaya prison is an industrial and industrious place. To interview a prisoner is to take him away from work on which he is intent. Professionals such as the doctor, dentist, and psychologist work as a team and are generally pleasant and hopeful about their efforts. Social workers counsel inmates and administer standardized tests. The nurse gives family planning lectures. The warden believes that most of his inmates are well accepted back into the community and he intends to expand the sports field and increase the prison's agricultural output (Alberto Caytaino, personal communication, July, 1989).

By contrast, the warden at Chorrillos notes that "there is no money for rehabilitation. We have no formal programs now" (Pilar Godos Gutieriez, personal communication, June, 1989). At Lurigancho the school, auditorium, crafts area, and industrial pavilions are all used for housing. "So there is no job training and inmates cannot support their families. Inmates spend most of their time inside the pavilions,.. and the psychologists and social workers are figureheads due to the population;.. they only work at release" (Pedro Cadenas, personal communication, 1989). It quickly becomes clear that the real goal for everyone at Lurigancho is to get through the day.

EFFECTS OF CROWDING—STAFF

This leads us directly to yet another effect of hypercrowding: demoralized staff workers. Work in such an environment is simply not very satisfying. In 1986, over 700 employees of I.N.P.E. resigned *en masse*. Currently, all perimeter security has been taken over by the Civil Guard (a police unit). There is some apparent bureaucratic tension between the Guard and I.N.P.E. personnel. At Chorrillos, there are only eight perimeter guards and 18 inside guards for 540 prisoners. Guards at Lurigancho are rotated out monthly. ". . . and," stated Warden Cadenas (personal communication, 1989), "they don't want to come here because it is well known that a prison assignment is not a way to get ahead in the Civil Guard." The warden, who is frustrated for both his personnel and his inmates, wants out himself and laments the fact that he is the only permanent employee. He has been there five months on an assignment that could last as long as another six.

EFFECTS OF CROWDING—SECURITY

You can not lock a cell door if there are two inmates sleeping in the doorway, or if the toilet in the cell also must serve the people sleeping on the catwalk. Security is not only a lost goal, but a practical impossibility under conditions of hypercrowding.

At Socabaya, prisoners are locked into their cells or dorms at night and locked out of them during the day. There is classification by danger. There are restrictions concerning which prisoners are allowed into various areas. Prisoners are counted daily. Though they are seldom needed, television cameras and electronic vibration sensors are available to monitor buffer areas where inmates are not allowed.

At Lurigancho there is effective perimeter security complete with fortress walls, a "no-man's land," and well armed tower guards, but little else. There is no electricity in the electric fence. Individual cells are never locked and main pavilion (cell block) entrances click shut but require only a screwdriver to open from either side. Asked whether there are many escapes, Warden Cadenas (personal communication, June,

1989) replied, "As far as I know, there have been no escapes since I arrived—but we do not count the prisoners except in pavilions three and eleven." It is widely believed at Lurigancho that escapes can be purchased for about $3,000. On some occasions such as Fathers' Day it is common to process and admit well over 7,000 visitors. It simply is not possible to restrict them to visiting areas. Asked whether they had conjugal visits, one guard simply shrugged and said, "How would we know?" Indeed, visitors have been lost. In one extreme instance, two women were kidnapped and hidden for two weeks. Guards found them only after they had been raped and were near death.

The search was hampered by the fact that there are places in Lurigancho where guards simply refuse to enter. After walking through the "Pampas" with guards literally beating back a milling tide of inmates, the warden congratulated us with apparent amazement. His last visitors, a group of Canadian prison wardens, had refused to enter any of the pavilions—let alone THAT one. I saw no particular need to tell him that what appeared to be bravery may actually have been ignorance. Asked whether the Pampas held particularly violent offenders, the warden merely replied that there was no system of classification left.

One can hardly assert the usual controls over such a place. Inmates do not view solitary confinement as punishment, but as welcome privacy and a chance for an individual bathroom. Rather than trying to restrict contraband, guards are quite happy that prisoners have ready access to their "basic paste" (cocaine). Indeed, it is inmates who control day to day life in Lurigancho. Pachecho, a most personable gentleman, is an elected inmate delegate who has his own bodyguards, behaves like an official, and "can get things done" with inmates in exchange for favors and direct access to the warden. There is also a "director general" who controls all of the delegates. He has his own staff and an office near the warden's. While it is hardly new, the control system is clearly one of accommodation between inmates and staff.

LESSONS FROM PERU

There are lessons to be learned from all of the foregoing. First, there is great support here for the long held sociological notion that informal structures are an essential part of any social organization. In the United States, many informal mechanisms within the overall system work to keep prison overcrowding below Peruvian extremes. At the police level, we have arrest discretion, arbitration of interpersonal (but criminal) disputes, encouragement of out-of-court settlements, arrest/detention-as-punishment and other such means of exerting control while avoiding the official procedures which would otherwise increase the number of cases placed formally into the system.

In our courts, formal and informal devices such as bail-as-preventive detention, costs-as-fines, or due process–as–punishment perform a similar function. However, these pale in the face of plea bargaining. If 80 percent–95 percent of our cases are plea bargained, then this extra-legal, informal mechanism has virtually become the real system (Blumberg, 1979:168). To the extent that plea bargaining in fact reduces the number or length of prison sentences, it also reduces prison crowding. Indeed, the bargaining strength of the prosecutor weakens as prisons fill to the point that they lack space for new inmates.

In our prison system itself, "good time" and parole, formally intended as control and rehabilitation measures, have informally been used to reduce population and to effectively level out sentence disparities. Inmate-initiated lawsuits and consequent court orders regarding living conditions, once despised, are now sometimes welcomed by prison officials for use as leverage in wresting operating funds from legislatures (Duffee, 1989).

In Peru the problem of rigid formality seems to lie primarily with the courts. Although the subject is beyond our scope here, we can safely conclude from Amnesty International (1989) that Peruvian police are not overly constrained by formal controls. Additionally, this paper has documented that the prisons' very survival mechanism is to operate well outside their own goals, roles, and rules.

The courts, however, send virtually all who are arrested on to prison, fully investigate all cases, and put all cases through a trial. Judges of Penal Execution calculate parole release dates mathematically and with little leeway. I.N.P.E. would remedy its population maldistribution except that the courts require inmates to await trial where they were arrested. Lurigancho would like to release its senile 90 year old inmate except that, despite a personal plea from Peru's president, the courts have been unable to find an appropriate loophole—just as they were unable to mitigate his sentence in the first place.

There are apparently fewer opportunities for "stretch" in the Peruvian courts. With no bail, no equivalent of plea bargaining, no equity law, no law of precedents and a general tendency to follow the letter of the law, the courts have thoroughly overwhelmed themselves and done the same to the prisons.

A second lesson may well be that the frequent absence of certain civil rights in Peru has had no apparent value in speeding the criminal justice process. Both in its overall character and in its specific policies and practices, much of the Peruvian system presents functional equivalents of the reforms often proposed for the United States by advocates of a "get tough" approach to crime control. This vocal school of thought contends that our sentences should be more swiftly imposed, more certain, and more severe; that criminals ought not to have various rights; that police ought to have fewer restrictions; that prisoners ought not to be coddled; and more. In this classic dilemma, civil rights are seen as expendable in expectation of greater efficiency and crime control (Packer, 1964; Blumberg, 1979: 67–70).

In the case of Peru, the police have immense power. Since an arrest, in combination with a nod from the prosecutor, automatically means that the defendant will spend years incarcerated to await trail, the policeman's word is effectively a prison sentence. Therefore, once a criminal is caught, the punishment is indeed swift, certain and severe (long). Furthermore, the court system provides no bail to "put criminals back on the street," no jury to "sway," no speedy trial requirement, no pesky presumption of innocence or guilt, no adversarial defense to "delay justice" and no plea bargaining to give criminals a chance of "getting off easy." And, given their living conditions, no one would be likely to refer to the crowded Peruvian prisons as "country clubs that coddle criminals."

Clearly, any desired payoff in efficiency has not materialized in Peru. Prisons are packed with minor offenders and courts routinely take six years to get serious cases to trial and, although this aspect is outside the scope of this paper, it is likely that "untying" the police has led to brutal police rather than to a decrease in crime (Amnesty International, 1989). Indeed the lack of crime control has reached such legendary levels that women are routinely warned not to wear earrings lest they be snatched along with bits of earlobe.

In the United States, however, civil rights requirements force selectivity upon our otherwise production-oriented criminal justice bureaucracy (see Blumberg, 1979:154, for a discussion of the displacement of justice goals by production goals). Arrest and arraignment rights keep police from offenses which are not worth the bother. Trial rights give defendants some negotiating power, which has led to plea bargaining, which forces prosecutors to select charges and cases. Prisoners' rights, particularly those regarding living conditions, prevent "deteriorating infrastructure" and force the courts and prisons to decide which inmates they truly want to detain. Whether it tends to select the serious, best, easy or emotional cases, our criminal justice system is reluctantly, and only to a degree, kept from overwhelming itself. Perhaps the very civil rights so often criticized in the United States do not really hamper "efficiency" but instead have the effect of allowing the system to function at all.

But what of overcrowding itself? Clearly, the most direct lesson is that prison crowding has effects which go beyond those, such as living conditions and convicts' rights, which "merely" hurt inmates. Those who contend that a person who has committed a crime should be "hung from the walls" will need also to consider the eventual effects of overcrowding on prison staff and on security. At present rates, and despite the relief offered by our informal mechanisms, a Lurigancho may be in our future.

➤ DISCUSSION QUESTIONS

If we interpret this article as a warning to "get tough" proponents in the U.S., how realistic is this warning? Referring to this article, what negative consequences might we realistically expect if we continue getting tougher on crime and criminals in the U.S.?

NOTES

1. Monetary amounts in this paper have been converted to American dollars.

2. More directly comparable figures for actual time served in Peru and the United States are not available.

REFERENCES

Amnesty International 1989 Peru: A human rights emergency. *Focus*, (December):3–6.

Blumberg, A. S. 1979 *Criminal Justice Issues and Ironies*. New York: New Viewpoints.

Bureau of Justice Statistics 1990 *BJS Data Report, 1989*. Washington, D.C.: U.S. Department of Justice.

Duffee, D. E. 1989 *Corrections Practice and Policy*. New York: Random House.

Packer, H. L. 1964 *"Two models of criminal process."* University of Pennsylvania Law Review, 113:1–68.

Community Corrections and the NIMBY Syndrome

CANADA

■ *SHEREEN BENZVY-MILLER*

INTRODUCTORY NOTES

It seems proper to conclude this section on corrections with a selection pertaining to community corrections. While institutional corrections (i.e., facilities that operate as "total institutions"—confining inmates 24 hours per day—such as prisons, jails, and reformatories) may receive the bulk of public attention, the majority of offenders are placed in non-institutional or "community-based" corrections (including probation, parole, community service, restitution, electronic monitoring, halfway houses, and various combinations of the above).

Unless a prisoner is going to spend the rest of his or her life in prison, he or she, of course, will have to be let back into the community. The prison experience often does little to prepare the ex-offender for reimmersion.

The philosophy behind halfway houses, the subject of this article, is that of reintegration. Halfway houses provide ex-offenders with the opportunity to reestablish ties with their families and with social service agencies that may be able to help them with their transition to "normal" life. While in the halfway house, the ex-offender also has the opportunity to find and start a new job.

In order to have these opportunities, prisoners are sometimes allowed to spend the latter part of their prison sentences in a halfway house. Much of the public finds this objectionable, seeing it as another form of "mollycoddling" convicted criminals. However, advocates of reintegration theory argue that such a policy is designed for the good of the community, not for the welfare of the ex-offender, per se. If the ex-offender is successfully prepared for reimmersion into the community, then he or she will be less likely to re-offend.

Though there have certainly been some innovations, American corrections have been remarkably resistant to change. While evaluation research often shows community-based programs to be less costly and as or more effective (in terms of recidivism) than institutional corrections (especially with certain types of offenders), the community-based programs are extremely vulnerable politically. If an offender in a community-based program commits a serious crime, he or she will likely get enormous public/media attention, and there will be political pressure to

SOURCE: Shereen Benzvy-Miller, "Community Corrections and the NIMBY Syndrome," *Forum on Corrections Research*, vol. 2, no. 2 (1989): 18–22. Reprinted with permission.

close the program down. In evaluating the effectiveness of community-based corrections vis-á-vis institutional corrections, it seems there are at least two equally or more important hidden variables, in addition to the variables of cost-effectiveness and recidivism: fear and retribution—neither of them particularly rational. Even if the two types of programs are equally effective in protecting the public (which should dispel the fear), many Americans will opt for institutional corrections because they want to see the offender suffer (retribution). For this reason it is likely that community corrections (namely, halfway houses) face even greater obstacles in the U.S. than in Canada, as described below.

In 1975, in St. John's, Newfoundland, the John Howard Society had an option to purchase a house on Leslie Street to operate as a half-way house for "non-violent" offenders subject to City Council's approval. On December 30, City Council issued a permit to the agency to run the house; but a week later it began looking for a way to rescind the permit after residents of the street presented a 231-name petition against it. A briefing session was held in January 1976 with both the residents of the street and the sponsors of the house and City Council. The sponsors tried to assure the residents that only "non-violent" offenders would be admitted to the house. The residents of the street remained unmoved and expressed grave concern about having ex-inmates in their neighborhood. Clearly several people were truly terrified at the prospect. While the counselors admitted that they had been consulted by the sponsors, they claimed that they had not understood what was at stake. One month later, the permit was rescinded and the John Howard Society had to cancel the proposed project and look for a different site.[1]

This story could have been told yesterday as easily as 13 years ago, and it could have been set in almost any city in North America. It demonstrates what has come to be known as the NIMBY (Not In My Back Yard) syndrome. Where does this syndrome come from? What does it mean for community corrections? How do we overcome it? These are the leading questions to be dealt with in any discussion of how to enhance the role and contribution of corrections.

WHAT IS COMMUNITY CORRECTIONS?

The notion of community-based corrections encompasses a wide variety of programs, including diversion, probation, parole, community service and fine option programs. Most of these programs have a relatively low profile and therefore are not likely to give rise to public concern of the "NIMBY" variety. For example, few members of the general public are likely to be aware of the presence of a probationer or a person doing community service work in their midst.

Parolees, on the other hand, stand apart. It is usually the more serious offenders that require gradual release to halfway houses. The unavoidable fact is that supervised release to a halfway house is necessarily associated with a very visible physical structure—a house—that is often located in a residential neighborhood. This puts offenders, literally, in somebody's backyard. For this reason, from the public's point of view, halfway houses are the most worrying and troublesome aspect of community corrections.

The reintegration of offenders is not a modern innovation. Keeping offenders in the community dates back to ancient Greece and Rome, and Renaissance Europe, where criminals were punished by the community alone.[2] Nor are halfway houses a recent development in corrections. In the United States, the first such houses were an outgrowth of religious and moral idealism and were established by groups like the Salvation Army and the Volunteers of America in the mid-1800s.[3]

Today the movement toward increased use of community corrections comes from the disillusionment with incarceration as the primary focus for criminal justice systems. The search for alternatives to imprisonment is international in scope.[4] Clearly, if community corrections is the wave of the future, correctional authorities will have to become very creative in developing intermediate sanctions that provide a viable range of options to sentencing judges. If the halfway house is to play an important role, as a "half-in" option, the NIMBY syndrome must be overcome.

Prisons are costly to build and to operate, frequently overcrowded and in many ways inhumane. Most importantly, they do not seem to be particularly effective at rehabilitating offenders and curbing increasing crime rates. Community-based support and treatment services are intended to fulfil some of the rehabilitation functions that institutions do not provide.

For non-violent offenders, community residential facilities can provide a cost-effective alternative to imprisonment. For violent offenders, by promoting the gradual integration of the individual into the social and economic life of the community after part of the sentence has been served in prison, facilities such as group homes respond to the long-term needs of society. These houses have been among the alternatives of choice because they provide some degree of supervision while mitigating the harm of isolation from the community.

Although the research on public attitudes toward community corrections is spotty, there is evidence that the humanitarian aims of the halfway house are strongly supported in principle by the public.[5] Problems seem to arise mainly when communities are called upon to put their well-meaning principles into practice. It is particularly difficult to promote the idea of halfway houses for violent offenders.

IN CANADA

Both federal and provincial correctional authorities fund halfway houses. There are 56 provincially funded facilities in Ontario alone. Provincial halfway houses usually house offenders under their jurisdiction, that is, young offenders and offenders sentenced to two years less a day.

Federally funded halfway houses provide community facilities to offenders serving sentences of two years or more. Approximately $25 million each year is spent to house 1,200 federal prisoners in 170 halfway houses across Canada.[6] Most of these facilities are run by private-sector agencies, whose operations are regulated by standards established by the Correctional Service of Canada.

The Correctional Service of Canada (CSC) and provincial government correctional agencies attempt to work in partnership to support the effective operation and expansion of a wide range of halfway houses or Correctional Residential Facilities (CRC).[7] These CRCs (and halfway houses generally) are essential in that they provide:

a) an effective alternative to conventional forms of incarceration;

b) a bridge between institutional care and the community;

c) a catalyst for innovation and change in corrections;

d) a vehicle for community and citizen involvement.[8]

In order for community corrections to be effective and for these functions to be fulfilled, offenders must not be simply located in the community but integrated into it. If offenders are isolated, they will not develop the meaningful social ties that are the *raison d'etre* of community corrections.

The importance of the location of the halfway house in a community setting has been clearly established. It is also a matter of common sense. If halfway houses were located in distant rural settings, far from employment opportunities and treatment programs, they would cease to be viable alternatives to incarceration.

WHAT ARE PUBLIC ATTITUDES TOWARD HALFWAY HOUSES?

The key question, in the context of the NIMBY syndrome, is whether these facilities have an adverse effect on the communities in which they are located. There is a significant amount of research to indicate that group homes for the mentally disordered, the physically disabled and the elderly do not have any adverse effects on residential neighborhoods.[9] There is considerably less material on the impact of halfway houses or correctional group homes.

What is clear, however, is that when faced with the prospect of having a CRC in a residential neighborhood, the community can be expected to manifest the NIMBY syndrome.[10] There are three reasons for this: 1) people have attitudes toward and perceptions of offenders that have little to do with reality; 2) people fear crime and expect that close physical proximity to offenders will expose them to greater risk; 3) people are afraid that a group home will somehow taint the neighborhood and cause property values to plummet.

What little research there is in Canada, however, indicates that the presence of a correctional halfway house does not have any impact on the crime rate in the neighborhood in which the home is located.[11] Furthermore, property values in all neighborhoods fluctuate and no research has shown that these fluctuations are affected one way or another by the presence of a halfway house. Adverse public opinion regarding these issues may well be due to lack of knowledge. It is interesting to note that people who are aware of a group home in their neighborhood are less likely than people who are unaware of the presence of a group home to feel that property values are threatened or that the crime rate is increasing.[12]

More interesting still is the finding that most residents of neighborhoods where a halfway house is located are unaware of its existence.[13] This is not surprising, as most halfway houses keep an intentionally low profile in the community.[14] The reasons are simple: residents of the home are usually struggling to adjust to life in the community and it would be counterproductive to have them singled out. It is in the long-term best interests of the correctional community for halfway houses to be as inconspicuous as possible so that there will be no public relations problems.[15] Because people are usually unaware of the existence of a halfway house in their area, adverse public opinion tends to be a direct consequence of isolated and notorious incidents involving group home inmates, which arouse fear and indignation. This is true of neighborhoods that have a group home as well as those that do not. In fact, some community members who are strong opponents of halfway houses prior to having one next door come to realize that their fears are for the most part unfounded, and become welcoming neighbors.[16] When a tragedy such as a murder or an assault takes place in any community, people's attention will be focused by the media on the locale and circumstances surrounding the incident. Naturally, if the incident involves a parolee or ex-offender, the entire criminal justice process to which this individual was previously subjected may be called into question. Similarly, when the tragedy takes place in a halfway house or is perpetrated by a resident of such a facility, the public may have questions concerning the circumstances that led up to the incident. This does not mean, however, that neighbors will immediately call for the abolition of halfway houses.

In fact, after the murder of Celia Ruygrok, a night supervisor at Kirkpatrick House, a halfway house for men in Ottawa, the John Howard Society held several open house discussion sessions, which were attended by neighbors and concerned citizens. Several helpful suggestions for improving procedures at the house were made by those in attendance. Two of the neighbors who took an interest in how to prevent similar tragedies from recurring subsequently joined the Board of Directors of the Society. Gerald Ruygrok, Celia's father, has since become a tireless advocate for maintenance of high standards of professionalism and staff training in community corrections.

IMPACTS OF THE NIMBY SYNDROME

There is no research that details the harmful effects of the public's negative views on community corrections. It is difficult to measure the influence of the public on community corrections policy. Some areas that might be interesting to explore in this regard are:

In Sentencing

- Are judges loath to use community corrections options in sentencing in very high profile cases or for certain types of offenses regardless of the appropriateness of such penalties for certain specific offenders?

- Are judges affected by the prospect of attracting criticism as the result of incomplete or exaggerated media accounts of sentencing decisions involving the use of less severe community sanctions?

- A question in a public opinion survey done for the Canadian Sentencing Commission proposed two solutions to the problem of prison overcrowding: 1) build more prisons, or 2) sentence more offenders to alternatives to imprisonment. When asked how they would prefer government money spent, 70% of respondents favored the latter alternative.[17] This is an indication that, in principle at least, Canadians support the concept of community corrections. There have also been some indications that the Canadian public support the use of halfway houses specifically.[18] This support was found to exist by several focus group studies done by two different polling companies in the last two years. Are these sentiments getting through to the judiciary? Should it be relevant to the sentencing process?

In Parole

- Parole boards are often criticized for keeping the release decision-making process secret. If the process were to be opened up, would pressure from the public give these decision-makers less latitude to give marginal cases a chance at release for fear that any risk is too much risk?

- If halfway houses are now being used primarily to house non-violent offenders because the community has made it clear that violent offenders are not welcome and that release decision-makers should not take any risks, what are we doing with violent offenders? Clearly, prisoners sentenced to life imprisonment can be detained forever only if they constitute a risk. All other prisoners must be released at some time. If the NIMBY syndrome or the public's fear prevent gradual release, society will surely suffer greater harm for not providing transitional programs to offenders.

WHAT CAN BE DONE?

Future policies must be built on facts and the identification of effective measures, so that the positive aspects of correctional group homes in the community are increased and the potentially negative aspects are avoided.[19] Development of these measures is the responsibility of those who operate halfway houses and those who fund them, as well as those in the criminal justice system who control the process through which offenders pass before becoming residents of community correctional centers.

One of the essential ingredients to bolstering public confidence in the halfway house system is a strong, visible commitment to it by correctional authorities. This means providing offenders with the treatment and support necessary for reintegration into the community, which requires resources. Social services are essential, but it is even more important for halfway houses to have enough qualified staff to provide support and assistance in all areas from life skills to counselling and, where appropriate, security.[20] If Canadians, as the research suggests, are sympathetic to the concept of community corrections, then we must be prepared to pay for adequate staffing and staff training for halfway houses and other community residential facilities. This means that the correctional authorities who fund halfway houses must ensure that salaries are at high enough levels to attract and retain professionals. High staff turnover is detrimental to the quality of service that is provided and to the security of the public, and is therefore potentially harmful to the community in the long run.

Beyond the actual measures that control the risk to the community, it is important to educate members of the community to the realities and importance of community corrections. Because the public is not likely to take an interest in the plight of offenders except when personal safety (or property) is perceived to be threatened, it is up to correctional professionals to assume the lead role in recruiting community support and involvement in community corrections. This said, it becomes a question of deciding what elements of corrections should be emphasized in any public education campaign.

Undoubtedly, the first issue that must be tackled is public concern over safety. Myths must be dispelled about the nature of the offender population in Canada and the percentage of offenders who have committed serious crimes against the person and are eventually released to CRCs. Another important point has to do with the average length of stay of most residents in CRCs or policies related to length of stay. It may be very difficult to prevent a NIMBY reaction to release programs for violent/sex offenders, who make up a substantial proportion of our penitentiary population. It is of course extremely important that the public be made to understand that it is precisely this group that needs supervised release the most.

Second, open and honest discussions of the process undertaken to determine the fitness of an offender for release into the community must take place in order for the public to begin to understand and trust that the selection process, although not infallible, does involve judicious choice and extensive research. (Of course, it may be difficult to explain that some of the offenders who are the worst risks are released automatically on Mandatory Supervision.)

Third, research on the extent to which prisons can and should be used for rehabilitation of offenders, and on the cost and effectiveness of incarceration for these purposes relative to community facilities should be shared with the public. Most public opinion experts agree that the public is very pragmatic on most issues and is usually interested in practical, cost-effective solutions to problems.

Fourth, the purpose of community corrections as a well-established and effective form of treatment, rather than an act of clemency, must be brought to the public's attention. Before this can happen, however, research on the effectiveness of treatment in the community must be undertaken.

Fifth, correctional experts should explain the potentially negative effects of incarceration for certain individuals and for the community at large: incarceration is an expensive correctional tool for non-violent offenders that is likely to increase an individual's dependence on the system by decreasing the individual's ability to manage life in the community. Emphasis should be placed on the advantages of community corrections and halfway houses, which do not require the maintenance of costly institutions with large staff and do not remove offenders from employment and other opportunities to maintain productive lives.[21]

CONCLUSION

NIMBY is a syndrome that arises in relation to many issues from low-cost housing[22] to special-needs housing for mentally disordered individuals and the elderly, to halfway houses for criminal offenders. It is almost always a symptom of fear. For the most part, this fear seems to spring from ignorance. If more information were provided, the symptoms would, in many cases, disappear. An informed public may be a more accommodating public.

Over twenty years ago the American Correctional Association suggested that halfway houses "should be in as good a neighborhood as community attitudes will permit."[23] In other words, community attitudes set limits on where CRCs can be set up. It is difficult to say how far we have progressed since the mid-sixties.

Increasing public awareness and promoting changes in attitude is a slow process. Research is needed to produce accurate and honest information. Both qualitative and quantitative research must be continuously conducted to ensure that people do not have unrealistic expectations of corrections generally and community corrections specifically, and that misconceptions and misinformation do not contaminate the people's sentiments. The process will require a long-term commitment, but it must first be seen as a priority and it must be supported by sufficient funding.

➤ DISCUSSION QUESTIONS

By way of concluding this article and the book, what changes do you foresee in the future of criminal justice in the United States, and how do you feel about the changes you foresee?

NOTES

1. Zeitoun, L. (1976). "The Development of Community-based Residential Centres in Canada." Extracted from a speech given at the First International Conference on Community Residential Care for the Disadvantaged or Socially Stigmatized, July 1976, University of Surrey, Guildford, Surrey, U.K.

2. Smykla, J.O. (1981). *Community-based Corrections: Principles and Practices.* New York: MacMillan, 7.

3. Smykla (1981), 12.

4. In fact, the theme for the Eighth United Nations Congress on the Prevention of Crime and Treatment of Delinquency in Havana in 1990 is the search for "credible non-custodial sanctions."

5. Environics (1989). "Qualitative Investigation of Public Opinion on Sentencing, Corrections and Parole," *Focus Canada,* September 1989; and Decima Focus Group Study, Toronto, April 27, 1988. See also Doeren, S., & Hageman, M. (1982). *Community Corrections,* Cincinnati: Anderson Publishing Co., 16.

6. Crawford, T. (1988). "Halfway Houses: Pleading a Case with Society," *The Toronto Star,* February 20, 1988.

7. For the purpose of this discussion, no distinction will be made between CRCs and Community Correctional Centres (CCC), which are run by CSC itself.

8. National Parole Board and Correctional Service of Canada (1989). *Community Correctional Centres and Community Residential Centres: A Study of their Comparative Utilization.*

9. Kappel, B. (1986). *Community Impact Study: The Effect of Locating Correctional Group Homes in Residential Neighborhoods.* Toronto: Canadian Training Institute. See also material presented to the Ottawa Task Force on Special Needs Housing, 1987 to present.

10. This is supported by findings in Environics, *Focus Canada,* September 1989.

11. Kappel, B. (1986). *Community Impact Study,* 45.

12. Kappel, B. (1986). *Community Impact Study,* 45. See also Metropolitan Toronto Branch of the Canadian Mental Health Association (1986). Re: Action, Fall, 1986; and Goodale, T., & Wichware, S. (1979). "Group Homes and Property Values in Residential areas," *Plan Canada* 19/2, 162.

13. Kappel found that only 11% of the residents of a neighborhood where there was a halfway house were aware of its existence.

14. The staff of Fergusson House, a group home for adult women in conflict with the law, described the interaction of the home with the community as minimal. Beyond the immediate neighbors who have asked permission for their son to use the basketball hoop, the only members of the public who come to the house are volunteers or people who are sympathetic to the plight of the residents and want to make donations of clothing or housewares. Beyond these

contacts, the residents make use of social services and other community facilities much as most families do.

15. In an informal discussion with the staff of McPhail House, an "open custody" group home for female young offenders, it was explained to this writer that efforts are taken to keep the music at a respectable decibel level during barbecues in the yard and to keep the property neat to prevent disturbing neighbors. As any parent can attest, this is not always easy when the residents are 15- and 16-year-old girls who, but for some problems, are average teenagers who "could be anyone's kids."

16. English, K. (1986). "Neighbors Happy with Group Homes: Once Bitter Opposition Dissolves as Homes Run Without Problem," *The Sunday Star,* October 26, 1986.

17. Doob, A.N., & Roberts, J.V. (1987). "Public Attitudes Toward Sentencing in Canada" in Walker, N., & Hough, M. *Sentencing and the Public.* London: Gower.

18. Environics (1989). "Qualitative Investigation of Public Opinion and Sentencing, Corrections and Parole," *Focus Canada,* September 1989; and Decima Focus Group Study, Toronto, April 27, 1988.

19. MacNeil, J., & Kappel, B. (1986). *Executive Summary, Community Impact Study: The Effects of Locating Correctional Group Homes in Residential Neighborhoods,* 18.

20. These observations came from discussions with the staff at McPhail House and Fergusson House, two facilities for women in conflict with the law that are run by the Elizabeth Fry Society of Ottawa.

21. Smykla (1981), 49.

22. Glannone, F. (1989). "Ignorance, Meanness Typify NIMBY," *The Toronto Star,* May 31, 1989.

23. American Correctional Association (1966). *Manual of Correctional Standards.* College Park, Maryland: The Association, 137.